D1478211

The Anxieties of Idleness

The Bucknell Studies in Eighteenth-Century Literature and Culture

General Editor: Greg Clingham, *Bucknell University*

Advisory Board: Paul K. Alkon, *University of Southern California*
Chloe Chard, *Independent Scholar*
Clement Hawes, *The Pennsylvania State University*
Robert Markley, *West Virginia University*
Jessica Munns, *University of Denver*
Cedric D. Reverand II, *University of Wyoming*
Janet Todd, *University of Glasgow*

The Bucknell Studies in Eighteenth-Century Literature and Culture aims to publish challenging, new eighteenth-century scholarship. Of particular interest is critical, historical, and interdisciplinary work that is interestingly and intelligently theorized, and that broadens and refines the conception of the field. At the same time, the series remains open to all theoretical perspectives and different kinds of scholarship. While the focus of the series is the literature, history, arts, and culture (including art, architecture, music, travel, and history of science, medicine, and law) of the long eighteenth century in Britain and Europe, the series is also interested in scholarship that establishes relationships with other geographies, literatures, and cultures of the period 1660–1830.

Titles in This Series

Tanya Caldwell, *Time to Begin Anew: Dryden's* Georgics *and* Aeneis

Mita Choudhury, *Interculturalism and Resistance in the London Theatre, 1660–1800: Identity, Performance, Empire*

James Cruise, *Governing Consumption: Needs and Wants, Suspended Characters, and the "Origins" of Eighteenth-Century English Novels*

Edward Jacobs, *Accidental Migrations: An Archaeology of Gothic Discourse*

Regina Hewitt and Pat Rogers, ed., *Orthodoxy and Heresy in Eighteenth-Century Society*

Sarah Jordan, *The Anxieties of Idleness: Idleness in Eighteenth-Century British Literature and Culture*

Deborah Kennedy, *Helen Maria Williams and the Age of Revolution*

Chris Mounsey, *Christopher Smart: Clown of God*

Chris Mounsey, ed., *Presenting Gender: Changing Sex in Early Modern Culture*

Roland Racesvkis, *Time and Ways of Knowing Under Louis XIV: Molière, Sevigne, Lafayette*

Laura Rosenthal and Mita Choudhury, eds., *Monstrous Dreams of Reason*

Katherine West Scheil, *The Taste of the Town: Shakespearean Comedy and the Early Eighteenth-Century Theater*

Philip Smallwood, ed., *Johnson Re-Visioned: Looking Before and After*

Peter Walmsley, *Locke's* Essay *and the Rhetoric of Science*

Lisa Wood, *Modes of Discipline: Women, Conservation, and the Novel after the French Revolution*

http://www.departments.bucknell.edu/univ._press

The Anxieties of Idleness

Idleness in Eighteenth-Century British Literature and Culture

Sarah Jordan

Lewisburg
Bucknell University Press
London: Associated University Presses

Associated University Presses
2010 Eastpark Boulevard
Cranbury, NJ 08512

Associated University Presses
16 Barter Street
London WC1A 2AH, England

Associated University Presses
P.O. Box 338, Port Credit
Mississauga, Ontario
Canada L5G 4L8

The paper used in this publication meets the requirements of the American
National Standard for Permanence of Paper for Printed Library Materials
Z39.48-1984.

Library of Congress Cataloging-in-Publication Data

Jordan, Sarah, 1958–
    The anxieties of idleness : idleness in eighteenth-century British literature and
culture / Sarah Jordan.
        p. cm. — (Bucknell studies in eighteenth-century literature and culture)
    Includes bibliographical references and index.
    ISBN 0-8387-5523-2 (alk. paper)
    1. English literature—18th century—History and criticism.   2.
Unemployment in literature.   3. Working class—Great Britain—History—18th
century.   4. Unemployment—Great Britain—History—18th century.   5.
Unemployed—Great Britain—History—18th century.   6. Leisure—Great
Britain—History—18th century.   7. Working class in literature.   8.
Unemployed in literature.   9. Leisure in literature.   10. Anxiety in literature.
I. Title.   II. Series.
    PR448.U54 J67   2003
    820.9′355—dc21   2002026056

PRINTED IN THE UNITED STATES OF AMERICA

For my mother, who taught me to love books,
and for my father, who taught me how to write about them.

Contents

Acknowledgments

This book has taken me a long time to write, and so I have many people to thank. It began as a dissertation supervised by Susan Staves, whose love of and knowledge about all things eighteenth-century first convinced me that there was no more fascinating period of literature. Her keen sense of humor and joyful erudition continually delighted and inspired me, even as her rigorous scholarship awed (and occasionally terrified) me. Carol Houlihan Flynn and Anne Janowitz read all or part of the dissertation at various stages, and they provided invaluable suggestions, insight, and encouragement. Louise Gossett, from whom I took many undergraduate classes long ago, taught me lessons about good reading and writing that continue to stand me in good stead. Inzer Byers, another of my inspiring undergraduate teachers, first showed me the power of uncovering histories, especially those written in the margins.

I also want to thank the friends who have discussed parts of the book with me, providing advice, inspiration, and information from areas outside my ken: Rebecca Baggett, Bonnie Burns, Ian MacInnes, Lynn Parker, and Elizabeth Sagaser, especially. In their different ways, all have helped this project take form. Members of my writing group, Bille Wickre and Judith Lockyer, have given me intelligent readership, sanity, sisterhood, and laughter; these have helped keep me going, even in some difficult times. I am very grateful to them. The English department at Albion College has given me kind and smart colleagues from whom I've learned a lot, and I appreciate Charles Crupi and, again, Judith Lockyer for being such wise and generous department chairs.

Albion's wonderful librarians have been extremely helpful with interlibrary loans. I am also am grateful to Kay Pierce for undertaking the loathsome task of converting the book's citations to the Chicago style, and to a grant from the Hewlett-Mellon Fund for Faculty Development at Albion College for the money with which to pay her. Portions of this book have appeared as articles in *The Age of Johnson* and *Eighteenth-Century Life;* I am grateful to editors for permission to reprint them.

I want to thank Greg Clingham and the other editors at Bucknell University Press and the Associated University Presses for their com-

9

petence, courtesy, and good advice. Working with them has been an astonishingly pleasant experience.

Patti Lutsky, my partner and the least idle person I know, has provided a great deal of support, both emotional and financial. I thank her for her generosity, for her patience with a project that seemed at times unlikely ever to end (and that threatened to cover every surface in the house with books), and for her perspective. This book would never have come to be without her belief in it and in me.

As the daughter of a librarian mother and an English-professor father, my becoming an academic was perhaps overdetermined. Nancy Jordan, my mother, filled my ravenous appetite for books throughout my youth. I will always be grateful to her for that and for her faith that I could be a scholar. Finally, I would like to thank James Jordan, my father and teacher, whose influence on me and my work has been profound. Much of this book, especially the chapters on Johnson and Cowper, is deeply indebted to discussions with him. Ever since I learned to read and write, his astute and patient guidance has shaped my prose style and my ways of reading. His love of literature, his encyclopedic knowledge of it, and his wisdom have inspired me to follow in his footsteps, although I know that I can't fill his shoes.

The Anxieties of Idleness

1

Introduction

THE FIRST SENTENCE OF ADAM SMITH'S *THE WEALTH OF NATIONS*
(1776) proclaims that "The greatest improvement in the productive
powers of labour, and the greater part of the skill, dexterity, and judgment with which it is any where directed, or applied, seem to have been
the effects of the division of labour."[1] A few pages later, Smith proffers
a remarkable sentence discussing the profusion of material goods this
division makes available to even the humblest laborer and listing the
huge number of workers and trades necessary to provide these goods:

> Were we to examine, in the same manner, all the different parts of his dress
> and household furniture, the coarse linen shirt which he wears next his skin,
> the shoes which cover his feet, the bed which he lies on, and all the different
> parts which compose it, the kitchen-grate at which he prepares his victuals,
> the coals which he makes use of for that purpose, dug from the bowels of the
> earth, and brought to him perhaps by a long sea and a long land carriage, all
> the other utensils of his kitchen, all the furniture of his table, the knives and
> forks, the earthen or pewter plates upon which he serves up and divides his
> victuals, the different hands employed in preparing his bread and his beer,
> the glass window which lets in the heat and the light, and keeps out the
> wind and the rain, with all the knowledge and art requisite for preparing
> that beautiful and happy invention, without which these northern parts of
> the world could scarce have afforded a very comfortable habitation, to-
> gether with the tools of all the different workmen employed in producing
> those different conveniencies; if we examine, I say, all these things, and con-
> sider what a variety of labour is employed about each of them, we shall be
> sensible that without the assistance and cooperation of many thousands, the
> very meanest person in a civilized country could not be provided, even ac-
> cording to, what we falsely imagine, the easy and simple manner in which
> he is commonly accommodated.[2]

This compendious sentence conveys a sense of the variety and proliferation of objects and occupations in the eighteenth century. Although
Smith is praising this multifariousness, the very length and complexity
of his sentence also seems to betray some anxiety, some attempt not

only to represent but to contain this profusion. While the division of labor and increase of trades and professions were essential to the growing wealth and power of Britain, they also contributed to a sense of society as increasingly divided and confusing. How were all the different workers employed in all the different occupations to come together in a unified nation? Who or what could comprehend this society and hold it together?

Traditionally, as John Barrell explains in *English Literature in History, 1730–80: An Equal, Wide Survey*,[3] this cohesive and comprehending force was the landed, leisured gentleman. He alone, free from the need to earn a living, was "disinterested"—uninvolved with the competing claims of occupations and the desire to profit from them. Elevated by his hereditary estate above the sordid fray, he alone could see and understand the whole and, thereby, keep it in order. His privileged leisure gave him the opportunity to grow wise. Thus he was entitled to rule the nation; the right to vote was based on the qualification of owning land. Edmund Burke, writing (perhaps somewhat nostalgically) in 1791, described a "true natural aristocracy" with a legitimate right to rule. His description (comprising another remarkable eighteenth-century sentence filling a full page of small type) claims that this natural aristocrat, this governing gentleman, must be "bred in a place of estimation . . . [and] see nothing low and sordid from [his] infancy," must "stand upon such elevated ground as to be enabled to take a large view of the widespread and infinitely diversified combinations of men and affairs in a large society," and must "have leisure to read, to reflect, to converse."[4]

At the same time, however, the authority of this gentleman was being called into question. To draw again from Barrell's work, this time from *The Birth of Pandora and the Division of Knowledge*, the eighteenth century saw "the invention of a new account of what it is to be human—to be human is now to be an *economic*, rather than a political animal." This new account, he argues, involves

> a challenge to the claim of the independent gentleman that he (and he alone) enjoyed that comprehensive view of society which enabled him to see the interests of everyone, of the public. Either no one has such a view, it was now argued, or someone else has it, but it could by no means be the exclusive property of the aristocratic man of virtue. Might it not be necessary to have mixed more in the world of work—and in the modern world of commerce—to know what was in the interests of a commercial society?[5]

In other words, in this increasingly economic and work-oriented society, the knowledge and moral authority of the leisured gentleman was no longer a given for everyone.

It was necessary, then, to find something besides the gentleman's comprehension which could hold society together. I want to argue that this societal cement was work itself or, more specifically, the virtue of industriousness. Although Barrell does not explicitly make this argument, he seems to imply it when he says in *An Equal, Wide Survey* that "as the pride in and preoccupation with the growing wealth of Britain increased, so did a sense of the virtues necessary to support and continue that power, of which the most important was industriousness," and that "industriousness was . . . understood as a stable virtue, which by stabilizing the volatility of the interested passions could offer, to a society defined in economic terms, a stability similar to that which the virtue of disinterestedness had offered to a society where self-interest had seemed primarily a force for political dissolution."[6] If industriousness was seen, then, as not only central to the wealth and power of the nation, but as the very glue that held society together, then idleness had to be a terrible danger, a threat to the social order.

I

Linda Colley's important and influential *Britons* has established that during the eighteenth and the first third of the nineteenth century "a sense of British national identity was forged, and . . . that the manner in which it was forged has shaped the quality of this particular sense of nationhood and belonging ever since."[7] She goes on to argue that the British defined themselves as a nation against various outsiders, notably the French ("They defined themselves against the French as they imagined them to be, superstitious, militarist, decadent and unfree")[8] and that

> imagining the French as their vile opposites, as Hyde to their Jeckyll, became a way for Britons—particularly the poorer and less privileged—to contrive for themselves a converse and flattering identity. The French wallowed in superstition; therefore, the British, by contrast, must enjoy true religion. The French were oppressed by a bloated army and by absolute monarchy: consequently, the British were manifestly free. The French tramped through life in wooden shoes, whereas the British—as Adam Smith pointed out—were shod in supple leather and, therefore, clearly more prosperous.[9]

One supposed attribute of the French against which the English defined themselves that Colley does *not* list, however, is found in *The Contrast/ 1792/ Which Is Best*, a print designed by Lord George Murray that was etched by Thomas Rowlandson and widely distributed

throughout England by the Association for Preservation of Liberty and
Property against Republicans and Levellers. Obviously an anxious response to the Revolution, the print shows two circles, within which are
depicted emblems of "British Liberty" and the contrasting "French Liberty." The British circle portrays a statuesque Britannia holding the
Magna Charta in one hand and the scales of justice in the other. The
British lion sleeps peacefully by her side, and a British man-of-war ship
floats in the ocean behind her. The French circle, on the other hand,
depicts a snarling, witchlike figure with snakelike hair. Thin and mus-
cular, she brandishes a sword with one hand and with the other holds
a pitchfork on which is impaled the head of the decapitated gentleman
on whose body she is standing. Behind her is another gentleman hang-
ing from a lamppost.[10] The figures are striking, but what interests me
even more are the words printed under each circle. Clearly intended to
be opposites, most of the words refer to the oppositions Colley mentions— Religion vs. Atheism, Morality vs. Perjury, Personal Security
vs. Cruelty, Justice vs. Injustice, Property vs. Famine, and National
Prosperity vs. National and Private Ruin, for instance. But another pair
of words is "Industry" and "Idleness," with the former going to the
British and the latter to the French, even though the French Marianne

Thomas Rowlandson, British 1756–1827. *The Contrast, 1792—Which is Best?*
Etching with watercolor, 1792. Fine Arts Museums of San Francisco, Achenbach
Foundation for Graphic Arts, 1963.30.2221.

might seem far more industrious than Britannia: after all, Marianne is busily cutting off heads and trampling corpses, while Britannia sits quietly beside her dozing lion, merely holding up a scale. This print seems to me to represent some of the moral and national importance attached to the idea of industriousness in eighteenth-century Britain, and I want to argue that industriousness needs to be seen as an important aspect of British national identity.

Colley mentions that the other people, besides the French, against whom the British defined themselves included "the colonial peoples they conquered, peoples who were manifestly unlike them in terms of culture, religion, and colour."[11] I agree with her point, as I discuss later, but I want to disagree somewhat with her assertion that the British "came to define themselves as a single people not because of any political or cultural consensus at home, but rather in reaction to the Other beyond their shores."[12] I think that some Britons defined themselves as the *true* British, even against other British people. In *The Sense of the People: Politics, Culture and Imperialism in England, 1715–1785*, Kathleen Wilson builds on Colley's argument that, in Wilson's words, "empire was an instrument of national consolidation, unifying the British against the French, the nation's primary 'other.'" Wilson contends, "The 'others' identified or subdued through the imperial project were internal as well as external, domestic as well as foreign, within as well as without."[13] It is my argument that the discourse of idleness played a large part in defining these "others," both foreign and domestic, and thus in defining "true" Britishness.

II

One reason that idleness became, in the eighteenth century, an important quality against which to define Britishness is that people were beginning to be defined less by birth and more by occupation and money. In *A Polite and Commercial People: England, 1727–1783*, Paul Langford speaks of the difficulty of assessing rank at this time: "Social standing depended on numerous considerations: family (by birth or marriage), property (real and personal), profession or employment, and less definably 'connections', 'politeness', and 'breeding' (which did not necessarily imply good birth or upbringing)."[14] He speculates that an annual income of between forty and fifty pounds would be enough to "aspire to membership of the middling rank,"[15] a calculation which indicates how essential income was to social standing; and in theory, at least, earned income was closely related to one's industriousness. Once the middling rank was achieved, many, it seemed, longed to move up the social ladder to the class of gentlemen and ladies; and here again money, thought to be available to the truly industrious, seemed to provide the means. "It was a common observation," Langford says,

> that in England the appearance of a gentleman was seemingly sufficient to make him one, at least in the sense of his acceptance as such by others. The Swiss traveller De Saussure, at the end of George I's reign, noted that any well-dressed person wearing a sword was treated as a gentleman. By the end of the next reign, the novelist Richard Graves could claim that 'Sir' and 'Your Honour' were accorded anyone 'that appears in a clean shirt and powdered wig'.[16]

Money, then, was coming to challenge, or at least to complicate, birth as the foundation of gentility, as the arbiter of social standing and social definition; and earned money was considered the reward of industriousness. For the middling sorts, industriousness had become a value that could entitle them to social prestige and respect. Thus idleness posed a threat to one's status and self-definition, as well as a threat to the larger society. Of course, a profound contradiction becomes apparent here: the middle classes, in aspiring to join the gentry, were using their industriousness to leave a class known for its industry and join a class which by definition was idle. Idleness, therefore, was somehow the desired reward for hard work, the ultimate attainment in social status, while it was also viewed as deeply threatening, to the self and to the nation.

With this sort of tension and contradiction involved in it, idleness took on an especially anxiety-provoking significance in the eighteenth century, one different from what it had held earlier. In the Middle Ages and Renaissance, "idleness" was just one of the elements encompassed by the capital sin sloth.[17] In *The Seven Deadly Sins: Society and Evil*, Stanford M. Lyman explains that "*Sloth* is but one medieval translation of the Latin term *acedia* . . . and means 'without care'."[18] Acedia or "spiritual dryness," as Lyman goes on to say, "finds expression in a lack of any feeling for the world, for the people in it, or for the self. *Acedia* takes form as an alienation of the sentient self first from the world and then from itself."[19] Aldous Huxley's essay "Accidie" tells us that accidie was called by the early desert-dwelling Christians "the *demon meridianus*; for his favourite hour of visitation was in the heat of the day. He would lie in wait for monks grown weary with working in the oppressive heat, seizing a moment of weakness to force an entrance into their hearts." The demon inspired in the monks "disgust and lassitude," which pulled them into "the black depths of despair and hopeless unbelief."[20] The eighteenth-century view of the sin deemphasized despair and spiritual aridity, seeing these problems (which now fell into the categories "melancholy" or "spleen") as results of the primary failing, idleness. Lyman argues that "the sinfulness of sloth is dependent upon the perception of the endowed nature of man. Belief in man's freedom and control makes of sloth a sin . . . . "[21] In a society like eighteenth-century England, then, where change and movement, for some, seemed possible, idleness came into prominence as a central transgression, both a spiritual and a secular danger.

III

In this book I concentrate on the significance of idleness to ideas about class, gender, and race and colonialism. I also examine how the preoccupation with idleness affected the eighteenth-century writer. The poles of industry and idleness were important to the self-construction of the middle classes, whose famous "rise," of course, began during the eighteenth century.[22] While genteel idleness was still attractive to many of the middling ranks, it was also, as we have seen, being questioned. As Leonore Davidoff and Catherine Hall explain in *Family Fortunes: Men and Women of the English Middle Class, 1780–1850*, the middle-class challenge to upper-class authority was based both on the economic success of the middle classes and on their claim to moral superiority:

> Middle-class farmers, manufacturers, merchants and professionals in this period, critical of many aspects of aristocratic privilege and power, sought to translate their increasing economic weight into a moral and cultural authority. Their claim to moral superiority was at the heart of their challenge to an earlier aristocratic hegemony. They sought to exercise this moral authority not only within their own communities and boundaries, but in relation to other classes.[23]

This moral authority, this middle-class respectability which became so important in this century and the next, was, I want to argue, based to a large degree on the class's claim to possess industriousness. Thus the assumption of laboring-class idleness (which I discuss in my second chapter), oxymoronic as that sounds, was an essential part of middle-class ideology. If not only the aristocratic, but the laboring, classes were constituted as idle, the middle classes could see themselves as the industrious members of the nation, responsible for its strength and riches. As writers like Hannah More insisted over and over, only those members of the working classes who displayed impeccable industriousness could aspire to share in the respectability of the middling ranks.

Gender identity, in this period, was also increasingly constructed by idleness and work. For the middle classes—and their ideology began, by the end of the century, to permeate the classes above and below them—work and leisure grew to define maleness and femaleness. Work began to shift from that which a gentleman did not do, indeed *could* not do if he were to retain his gentle status, to an activity defining responsible masculinity. This industrious middle-class man embodied a change from the older, aristocratic notion of masculinity. As Davidoff and Hall explain, the traditional upper-class idea of masculinity was "based on sport and codes of honour derived from military prowess, finding expression in hunting, riding, drinking and 'wenching'"[24] —leisured activities. Middle-class masculine identity, in contrast, "was equated with an emerging concept of 'occupation'."[25] Competence as adult men depended on competence in money-earning employment.[26] To work industriously and successfully, to acquire material goods and support dependents, were increasingly seen as the acts that defined manhood. The older notion of upper-class masculinity still lingered, though, and to cling to it was for some men a way to resist the demands of bourgeois manliness. William Cowper, for instance, as I discuss in my sixth chapter, although conspicuously opposed to hunting, riding, drinking, and wenching, liked to consider himself a "mere gentleman," refusing to feel responsible for earning a living. He did not even support himself, much less anyone else, and he invoked the older aristocratic ideals to justify his idleness.

Femininity, on the other hand, became ever more identified with leisure during the eighteenth century. As I discuss in my third chapter, the idleness of middle-class women was increasingly enforced in this period, both by practical and by ideological means. As several feminist writers complained, traditionally female paid employments were being usurped by men, leaving non-laboring-class women little work to do outside the home, and the growing separation of home from workplace and the increase in numbers of servants employed meant that ladies had less work to do within the home as well. This restriction of ladies to the private, domestic sphere meant that they were often viewed as leisure personified, as ornamental companions of man's leisure, and this view then worked back to reinforce the "separate spheres" restrictions.[27] While it was becoming possible, at this time, for a man to work for a living and still be considered a gentleman, a woman who worked could seldom be considered a lady. It was as though the older notion of aristocratic ease for both sexes was now being projected onto women: a hard-working man could still be a gentleman, as long as his wife and daughters were leisured.

The discourse of idleness was also central, I argue in my fourth chapter, to another important concern of Britain in this period: its command over many nonwhite peoples through slavery and imperialism. The long eighteenth century saw Great Britain expand from a small group of countries in the Northern Atlantic into an empire on which the sun could never set. It also saw an increasing desire for the systematizing of nature. Both these projects, the expansion of empire and the creation of taxonomies, led to accounts of and theories about nonwhite peoples. In *The Reinvention of the World: English Writing, 1650–1750*, Douglas Chambers speaks of this period's growing awareness of the vast variety to be found on the planet and the resulting "desire for a system that would contain an increasingly diverse world."²⁸ As in the sentence from Adam Smith with which I began this chapter, the British attitude toward the abundance and chaos to be found in other lands is a mixture of exultation and anxiety. The people and natural resources there could be exploited to bring great riches into the nation, and of course they often were. The new information and specimens brought back by travelers could also add greatly to the nation's store of scientific knowledge. And yet this sense of a wild profusion of things as yet unknown was not altogether comfortable. Once again, the discourse of idleness and industry helped to order and control. Theories about climate and race soon invested the white race with the virtue of industriousness while assigning idleness to the darker nations. This categorizing of the races worked perfectly in accord with Britain's related project of control—the physical and political control of nonwhite peoples through slavery and imperialism.

For eighteenth-century writers, I want also to argue, idleness was a particular source of anxiety. It was during this period that writing moved from being seen as an activity for leisured gentlemen (or at least those patronized by gentlemen) to being a professional activity at which many made their livings. Clifford Siskin's interesting recent book *The Work of Writing: Literature and Social Change in Britain, 1700–1830* tells us that it was in the eighteenth century that "writing first classified itself within the everyday world of work—Defoe actually described it as a 'very considerable branch of English commerce'."²⁹ As the reality of the impoverished hack writer in Grub Street, scratching out a living with his pen, collided with the still-important image of the writer as courtly gentleman, taking up his pen to fill some empty moments, the writer struggled with the problem of idleness. The newly professional writers of the period were beginning to assert their independence from patrons, but frequently could not altogether break away from the system of patronage. Alexander Pope, for instance, was enormously proud of the financial

independence he had earned with his writing, and he certainly disdained sycophants; but he liked to think that Twickenham, his villa, was
"like the house of Patriarch of old,"[30] and he was, as his biographer
Maynard Mack admits, eminently capable of "hold[ing] his witty own"
in the realm of potential-patron-pleasing flattery.[31] Samuel Johnson's
famous reply to Lord Chesterfield could stand as the professional writer's declaration of independence from patrons, yet Johnson's eventual
acceptance of a pension (despite his jokes about pensioners in the *Dictionary*) shows that he was not wholly wedded to his independence. The
nature of professional writing, often on deadline, additionally plunges
the writer into wrestlings with idleness — [32] who can forget Johnson's
essay on the evils of procrastination, written as the printer's boy waited
at the door? For all these reasons, idleness was especially fraught with
problems for writers of this period. In my fifth and sixth chapters I examine some of the ways these problems with idleness affected the work
and lives of Johnson and Cowper.

I want to make one final important point about the anxiety over idleness
in this period: much of it is played out in writing. This point might seem
almost too obvious to mention, but, as Siskin reminds us in his important new book, printed writing was, in the early years of the long eighteenth century, still a "newly disturbing technology." Siskin argues that
"the proliferation of writing—through print and through silent reading—worked to induce and shape substantial change. . . ."[33] Further on,
he asserts that this period saw "a sweeping reorganization and recon-
struction of the human according to the criterion of productivity, including—and, in many ways, transpiring through—the increasingly
important behavior of writing."[34] I agree entirely with this point, but
what Siskin (and others writing about time-discipline and productivity
in this period)[35] does not fully discuss is that in order to have a model
of productivity, a culture also must have a model of nonproductivity. In
order to enforce productivity, a culture must also disparage and punish
nonproductivity. My argument is that the eighteenth century named
this lack of productivity "idleness," and the project of this book is to
examine how this discourse of idleness was shaped by, and in turn
helped shape, the literature and culture of eighteenth-century Britain.

IV

I will end this introduction with a discussion of James Thomson's
The Castle of Indolence (1748),[36] in part because Thomson was, as Lisa
M. Steinman puts it, "one of the most widely read poets of the eigh-

teenth century, the period when Britain entered what historians call the modern age,"[37] and partly because the cultural conflicts I discuss in this project take fascinating form in this poem. Perhaps it is fitting that *The Castle of Indolence* is the last poem James Thomson completed, for many of its often-remarked-upon ambiguities mirror the conflicting feelings and opinions about industry and idleness with which Thomson—and, as I have argued, his century—had to contend. The poem presents in a concentrated form contradictions that appear more diffusely in some of Thomson's other writing and that also seem apparent between the public poet and the private man. That the Whiggish panegyrist of progress, public service, imperialism, and industry, the praiser of the spread of civilization and the rise of cities, was a famously indolent man who preferred to live in semirural retirement, indicates a conflict within Thomson that *The Castle of Indolence* displays splendidly. The poem also indicates, I believe, the more widespread conflict that I have argued existed in the eighteenth century: a cultural ambivalence about idleness, and an attendant uncertainty about the roles of the gentleman and the writer.

Many critics have commented on the ambiguities of *The Castle of Indolence*, particularly on the sense that the poem undermines its ostensible purpose, to praise industry and decry indolence: The first canto, which tells of the enchanted castle of the Wizard of Indolence and its inhabitants, is generally felt to be superior to the second, in which the Knight of Arts and Industry, retired after his labors of civilizing the world and raising Britain to the heights of glory, is called back into active service to vanquish the Wizard.[38] Certainly much of the first canto convincingly presents idleness and indolence as delicious and desirable. Stanza iii, for instance, charms the reader with soothing visual images and sound effects, particularly repeated l's, r's, and m's:

> Was nought around but Images of Rest:
> Sleep-soothing Groves, and quiet Lawns Between;
> And flowery Beds that slumbrous Influence kest,
> From Poppies breath'd; and Beds of pleasant Green,
> Where never yet was creeping Creature seen.
> Mean time unnumber'd glittering Streamlets play'd,
> And hurled every-where their Waters sheen;
> That as they bicker'd through the sunny Glade,
> Though restless still themselves, a lulling Murmur made.

Several stanzas captivate with lush fantasies of physical comfort and pleasure. In stanza xxvi, the Master-Porter takes off the guests' restricting clothes and arrays them in caps, slippers, and gowns that are

> Loose, as the Breeze that plays along the Downs,
> And waves the Summer-Woods when Evening frowns.
> O fair Undress, best Dress! it checks no Vein,
> But every flowing Limb in Pleasure drowns,
> And heightens Ease with Grace.

Stanza xxxiii describes the halls of the castle, where

> Soft Quilts on Quilts, on Carpet Carpets spread,
> And Couches stretch around in seemly Band;
> And endless Pillows rise to prop the Head;
> So that each spacious Room was one full-swelling Bed.

Stanza xxiii compares the "melting" and "unknitting" effects of indolence to surrendering to sexual pleasure:

> So when a Maiden fair, of modest Grace,
> In all her buxom blooming May of Charms,
> Is seized in some Losel's hot Embrace,
> She waxeth very weakly as she warms,
> Then sighing yields Her up to Love's delicious Harms.

Other sections of the first canto evoke a delicate, lovely fairy-world or dream-landscape. Stanza xx compares the crowds pouring in through the gates of the castle to a moonlit vision of fairies:

> as when beneath the Beam
> Of Summer-Moons, the distant Woods among,
> Or by some Flood all silver'd with the Gleam,
> The soft-embodied Fays through airy Portal stream.

A similar vision is conjured up in stanza xxx; as the castle's inhabitants wander off to pursue their own pleasures, they are compared to what a shepherd in the Hebrides might see in the sunset:

> on the naked Hill, or Valley low,
> The whilst in Ocean *Phoebus* dips his Wain,
> A vast Assembly moving to and fro:
> Then all at once in Air dissolves the wondrous show.

As strong as these enchanting images of idleness, though, are the pictures of its pains. In this sense, Thomson resembles Samuel Johnson, who, as I will discuss, also portrays idleness as both voluptuously inviting and intensely horrifying. Both Thomson and Johnson figure the dark side of idleness as stagnation, dissolution, and living death. When the Knight of Arts and Industry's companion Bard is attempting to convince the inhabitants of the Wizard's castle that industry is superior to idleness, he employs images of stagnation, asking: "Is not the Field, with lively Culture green, / A Sight more joyous than the dead Morass?" and "Does not the Mountain-Stream, as clear as Glass, / Gay-dancing on, the putrid Pool disgrace?"[39] A few stanzas on, he uses the ideas of idleness both as stagnation and living death: "Who does not act is dead; absorpt intire / In miry Sloth, no Pride, no Joy he hath: / O Leaden-hearted Men, to be in Love with Death!" (II liv). Still later in the same speech, he uses images of dissolution and, again, death, saying that for those whose "every Power [is] dissolved in Luxury" to escape "from the powerful Arms of Sloth" is "rising from the Dead" (II lxi). The most disturbing pictures, though, occur after the Knight has waved his antimagic wand and the landscape around the castle is transformed:

> Sudden, the Landskip sinks on every Hand;
> The pure quick Streams are marshy Puddles found;
> On baleful Heaths the Groves all blacken'd stand;
> And, o'er the weedy foul abhorred Ground,
> Snakes, Adders, Toads, each loathly Creature crawls around.
>
> (II lxvii)

This, presumably, is what the land would look like without cultivation, without work. The next stanza presents a nightmare vision of society without the civilizing force of industry:

> And here and there, on Trees by Lightning scath'd,
> Unhappy Wights who loathed Life yhung;
> Or, in fresh Gore and recent murder bath'd,
> They weltering lay . . . .
>
> (II lxviii)

Near the end of the poem come two other sketches, opposite extremes of uncultivated bleakness. First the unfortunate folk see "a Desart wild" which is "bare, comfortless, and vast; / With Gibbets, Bones, and Carcases defil'd." None of the rewards of work are present—"There nor trim Field, nor lively Culture smil'd; / Nor waving Shade was seen, nor Fountain fair"—only, in a neat reversal of the luscious "Quilts on Quilts" image of Canto I, "Sands abrupt on Sands lay loosely pil'd" (II lxxvii). Next, a landscape of horrible wetness and cold appears: "Then, varying to a joyless Land of Bogs, / The sadden'd Country a grey Waste appear'd," full of "putrid Streams and noisome Fogs," its ground "jagg'd with Frost, or heap'd with glazed Snow." Those who did not heed the Knight's call to industry are hounded forever through these lands: "Through these Extremes a ceaseless Round they steer'd, / By cruel Fiends still hurry'd to and fro, / Gaunt *Beggary*, and *Scorn*, with many Hell-Hounds moe" (II lxxviii).

That Thomson is able so convincingly to describe both the pleasures and pains of idleness is not surprising, since he, like Johnson, was personally acquainted with "that most fatal Syren Indolence," as he phrased it in a letter to Elizabeth Young.[40] In his 1847 memoir of Thomson, Sir Harris Nicolas says that "the besetting sin of Thomson's character was indolence."[41] Thomson's biographer Douglas Grant says that "His indolence was notorious" and that his "usual hour of rising was . . . noon,"[42] and he recounts the story of Dr. Charles Burney paying him a visit at two in the afternoon. Burney found him in bed, "with the curtains closed and the windows shut" and, "on asking the poet why he stayed so long in bed, received the answer, 'Why, Mon, I had not motive to rise'."[43] Thomson's more recent biographer, James Sambrook, also indicates that Thomson's indolence was well known among his friends, frequently getting in the way of his duties in correspondence,[44] and, more seriously, keeping him from making money. After the loss of his sinecure in 1737, another post, "it was said," was kept open for him, "but the poet, according to Murdoch, 'was so dispirited, and so listless to every concern of that kind, that he never took one step in the affair: a neglect which his best friends greatly blamed in him'"; this neglect was attributed to "unaccountable indolence."[45] Sambrook quotes one of Thomson's friends who complained about his failure to do anything to ensure the success of the author's benefit night of one of his plays: "There is but one Man in England more Indolent than myself and that is Thompson [*sic*]. Would you believe it, he has never sent me a single Tickett to dispose of."[46] In his *Life* of Thomson, Johnson alludes to the financial trouble Thomson's idleness caused: "The affairs of others . . . were not more neglected than his own. He had often felt the inconveniences of idleness, but he never cured it; and was so conscious of his own character, that he talked of writing an Eastern Tale of *The Man who Loved to be in Distress*."[47] Perhaps the most outrageous story of Thomson's indolence comes from the *Letters and Literary Remains* of Mrs. Thrale: "Thomson, the author of the 'Castle of Indolence,' was once seen lounging round Lord Burlington's garden, with his hands in his waistcoat pockets, biting off the sunny sides of the peaches."[48]

Surely Thomson's personal preference for idleness must have often sat uneasily with his public stance as a poet who celebrated activity and progress, who presented industry as responsible for raising men from a brutish state of nature to glorious civilization, and for Britannia's rule

of the waves. And, particularly since *The Castle of Indolence* began as a
personal joke (Thomson's friend Patrick Murdoch says it "was, at first,
little more than a few detached stanzas, in the way of raillery on himself,
and on some of his friends, who would reproach him with indolence"),[49]
and since it took him fourteen or fifteen years to complete the poem,
leading to jokes that he, like his self-portrait in the poem, the bard
"more fat than Bard beseems" who "loathed much to write" "his ditty
sweet" (I lxviii), was too indolent to finish it,[50] it is easy to read its ambiguities as expressing this conflict, as many have.[51] Sambrook, for instance, says, "The characters of the Wizard and the Bard, the castle and
its destroyer, articulate very clearly and bring into head-on collision the
two poets inside Thomson . . .: they are the retired dreamer whose object is pleasure and the active teacher whose object is moral instruction."[52] This reading is sound, but, as I mentioned earlier, I think the
ambiguities of the poem go beyond Thomson's personality to a more
general cultural ambivalence about idleness. Should the virtuous gentleman stay in the public realm, devoting himself to public service?
Thomson implies he should in his "To the Memory of the Right Honourable the Lord Talbot," when he ringingly praises him for his refusal
to leave the public fray:

> Nor could he brook in studious shade to lie
> In soft retirement indolently pleased
> With selfish peace. The Syren of the wise
> (Who steals the Aonian song, and in the shape
> Of Virtue woos them from a worthless world)
> Though deep he felt her charms, could never melt
> His strenuous spirit, recollected, calm
> As silent night, yet active as the day.
> . . . .
> Vain is the virtue that amid the shade
> Lamenting lies, with future schemes amused,
> While wickedness and folly, kindred powers,
> Confound the world. A Talbot's, different far,
> Sprung into action—action, that disdained
> To lose in living death one pulse of life,
> That might be saved; disdained, for coward ease
> And her insipid pleasures, to resign
> The prize of glory, the keen sweets of toil,
> And those high joys that teach the truly great
> To live for others, and for others die.[53]

Certainly the age revered its statemen and felt that the nation's glory
depended on men's willingness to act in the world. And yet there was

also a venerable tradition that said the path to virtue lay in retirement, in withdrawing from a fallen world. In his "Hymn on Solitude," Thomson writes in this tradition:

> Hail, mildly pleasing Solitude,
> Companion of the wise and good;
> But from whose holy piercing eye
> The herd of fools and villains fly.
> Oh! How I love with thee to walk,
> And listen to thy whispered talk,
> Which innocence and truth imparts,
> And melts the most obdurate hearts.[54]

Later on in the poem, Thomson invokes Liberty, that most British of virtues, perhaps trying to hint that virtuous retirement may be good for the nation:

> Descending angels bless thy train,
> The virtues of the sage, and swain —
> Plain Innocence in white arrayed
> Before thee lifts her fearless head;
> Religion's beams around thee shine
> And cheer thy glooms with light divine;
> About thee sports sweet liberty;
> And wrapt Urania sings to thee.[55]

One could argue, perhaps, that these different attitudes represent a change in the poet's mind between the 1725 "Hymn" and the 1737 "To Talbot," but an examination of "Autumn" from *The Seasons* will show that Thomson can express both views within the same poem. In the beginning of "Autumn" is the long paean to a personified Industry, the "rough power! / Whom labour still attends, and sweat, and pain," but who is also "the kind source of every gentle art / And all the soft civility of life: / Raiser of human kind!"[56] Thomson describes the wretched life of early man, how "the sad barbarian roving mixed / With beasts of prey; or for his acorn meal / Fought the fierce tusky boar — a shivering wretch!" (ll. 57–59), until "Industry approached, / And roused him from his miserable sloth" (ll. 72–73). In one of his splendid prospect passages, Thomson describes Industry's showing man how to use the earth's resources, tearing "from his limbs the blood-polluted fur," wrapping him "in the wooly vestment warm, / Or bright in glossy silk, and flowing lawn," filling his table with "wholesome viands" and pouring the "generous glass around" (ll. 84–88). Industry leads him on "To pomp, to pleasure, elegance, and grace," sets "science, wisdom, glory in his view" and bids him "be the lord of all below" (ll. 92–95), then teaches him about government and public service:

> Then gathering men their natural powers combined,
> And formed a public; to the general good
> Submitting, aiming, and conducting all.
> For this the patriot-council met, the full,
> The free, and fairly represented whole;
> For this they planned the holy guardian laws,
> Distinguished orders, animated arts,
> And, with joint force Oppression chaining, set
> Imperial Justice at the helm, yet still
> To them accountable . . .
>
> (ll. 96–105)

The passage goes on for another fifty lines, describing the glorious rise of cities, the growth of commerce and the British navy, and the progress of art: "All is the gift of industry, — whate'er / Exalts, embellishes, and renders life / Delightful" (ll. 141–43).

This vision of industry, progress, and public service is stirring indeed, but an equally stirring vision occurs at the end of "Autumn," this time a picture of the sweets and virtues of retirement. The passage begins by proclaiming that "The happiest he" is the man "who far from public rage / Deep in the vale, with a choice few retired, / Drinks the pure pleasures of the rural life" (ll. 1336–38). "Sure peace is his," Thomson goes on to say, and a life "Rich in content, in Nature's bounty rich" (ll. 1257–59). In retirement can be found virtues like "simple truth" and "plain innocence," and blessings such as "Health ever-blooming." Although the phrase "unambitious toil" suggests work, it seems more a boon than a requirement, and the phrase is balanced in the next line by "Calm contemplation, and poetic ease" (ll. 1273–77). The public, active life is painted in unflattering colors; the commerce so admired in the earlier passage becomes cruel luxury, from which the retired man's life is fortunately free:

> What though, from utmost land and sea purveyed,
> For him each rarer tributary life
> Bleeds not, and his insatiate table heaps
> With luxury and death?
>
> (ll. 1246–49)

What in the earlier passage are the glories of imperialism is here mere lust for blood or gold:

Let others brave the flood in quest of gain,
And beat for joyless months the gloomy wave.
Let such as deem it glory to destroy
Rush into blood, the sack of cities seek —
Unpierced, exulting in the widow's wail,
The virgin's shriek, and infant's trembling cry.

(ll. 1278–83)

The noble giving of law and governing of society become oppression, deception, and hypocrisy:

Let these
Ensnare the wretched in the toils of law,
Fomenting discord, and perplexing right,
An iron race! and those of fairer front,
But equal in humanity, in courts,
Delusive pomp, and dark cabals delight;
Wreathe the deep bow, diffuse the lying smile,
And tread the weary labyrinth of state.

(ll. 1291–98)

The life of man before the onset of civilization is seen not, as it was in the earlier passage, as barbarous and brutish, but as Edenic: "the life / Led by primeval ages uncorrupt / When angels dwelt, and God himself, with man!" (ll. 1349–51). The retired man, rather than learning to exploit nature, learns from nature: "O Nature! all-sufficient! over all / Enrich me with the knowledge of thy works" (ll. 1352–53), the poet cries.

These two strong and opposing arguments for the merits of a public and active or retired and contemplative life are also prominent, of course, in *The Castle of Indolence*. The arguments the Wizard of Indolence makes for retirement should be discredited by what the Knight of Arts and Industry and his Bard later say, but they remain plausible, especially when one remembers that the Knight himself had to be called out of retirement to fight the Wizard.[57] Certainly the Knight has led, prior to his retirement, a strenuous life, learning "every Science, and . . . every Art / By which Mankind the thoughtless Brutes excell" (II ix), striving "a barbarous World to civilize" (II xiv), and crowning his toils by raising Britain to perfection and world rule. But if retiring from the scene of action is altogether evil, how can the blameless Knight seek "from the toilsome Scene to part, / And let Life's vacant Eve breathe Quiet through the Heart" (II xxiv)?[58] The description of his life in retirement sounds similar to the "primeval ages uncorrupt" passage at the end of "Autumn": "His Days, the Days of unstain'd Nature, roll'd, / Replete with Peace and Joy, like Patriarch's of old" (II xxv). Although from the Knight's "deep Retirement" "Th' amusing Cares of Rural Industry," which consist here of beautifying and cultivating his estate, are not "banish'd" (II xxvii), something interesting happens in the description of his accomplishments. The subject of the many verbs in the passage is not the Knight, who is presumably the person acting to cause the changes being described, but rather the objects being acted upon themselves:

> Still, as with grateful Change the Seasons pass,
> New Scenes arise, new Landskips strike the Eye,
> And all th' enlivened Country beautify:
> Gay Plains Extend where Marshes slept before;
> O'er recent Meads th' exulting Streamlets fly;
> Dark frowning Heaths grow bright with *Ceres'* Store,
> And Woods imbrown the Steep, or wave along the Shore.
>
> (II xxvii)

Active agency has been given to the plains, streams, heaths, and woods, rather than to the Knight. This removal of human agency occurs elsewhere in the poem, as I will discuss later; its effect here, I think, is in a sense to give the Knight credit for doing work without—now that he is a gentleman—showing him actually working. When the Knight was young and poor, knowing no beverage but "the flowing Stream" and no food but what he killed or gathered for himself (II vii), he could be shown to catch "in hand the Spade or Plough," to ply "the strong mechanic Tool" (II xii) in addition to his more knightly pursuits, but now that he is the retired owner of an estate, such hands-on toil is unseemly and risks a loss of status. So although the Knight's retirement may be said not to be indolent since he is still actively improving his estate, when we look closely we see that the estate is really transforming itself.

Another reason, besides the Knight's own retirement, why it is hard for the poem entirely to discredit the Wizard's arguments in favor of withdrawing from the active world is that these arguments had a valued classical tradition and were seriously used by other eighteenth-century writers. That the pious William Cowper could in 1782 publish "Retirement," a poem making many of the same arguments the Wizard puts forth, indicates in what esteem these ideas could still be held, even as they were being questioned. In stanza xvii of Canto I, the Wizard invokes this classical tradition; "The Best of Men have ever lov'd Repose," he begins, and ends with a specific example: "So SCIPIO, to the soft *Cumaean* Shore / Retiring, tasted Joy he never knew before." The Wizard also, in another standard move, implies that people stay in the

active world only from avarice, the "savage Thirst of Gain" (I xi); here
in the castle they do not engage in the "grievous Folly" of "heap[ing] up
Estate" (I xix). He characterizes the political and commercial activities
which will be praised in Canto II unflatteringly, telling his guests they
will not "on upstart Fortune fawn," "sell fair Honour for some paltry
Pounds," "proul in Courts of Law for human Prey," or "In venal Senate
thieve"; all this is equivalent to "rob[bing] on broad High-way" (I xiii).
He assumes that ambition is sinful; his guests will be "Above the Reach
of wild Ambition's Wind" and will enjoy the "Repose of Mind" of
which virtue consists (I xvi).[59] The Wizard's arguments are strength-
ened even more by the "of vanity the mirror" passage, in which the narrator describes in several comic sketches the useless activities of "Idly-
Busy Men" who "Upon this Ant-Hill Earth" "Run bustling to and fro
with foolish Haste" (I xlix). That the narrator, not the Wizard, provides
these sketches increases their credibility, and the sketches themselves
follow a long-lived satirical custom; years later, as we will see in my
sixth chapter, Cowper would invent similar ones for "Retirement" and
The Task.

The opposing rhetoric of Canto II, of course, also claims for its side
virtues valued by the eighteenth century. When the Knight of Arts and
Industry has arrived at the castle in Canto II, his Bard makes a long
speech attempting to persuade the castle's denizens to leave it. He tells
them that it was not "by Vile Loitering in Ease" that Greece and Rome
achieved their glory (II l); and that "Had unambitious Mortals minded
Nought / But in loose Joy their Time to wear away" mankind would
still be in a rude state of nature, grazing "With Brother-Brutes," lacking
the "towery Fronts" of cities and the arts that "made us opulent and
gay" (II li). He assumes (as the Wizard assumes the opposite, without
arguing the point), that ambition and the desire for fame are goods,
warning his listeners that "For Sluggard's Brow the Laurel never
Grows; / Renown is not the Child of indolent Repose" (I l), and saying
if all had "alone the Lap of Dalliance sought," "None e'er had soar'd to
Fame, None honour'd been, None prais'd" (II li). As the Wizard invokes the name of Scipio, the Bard invokes Maro, Milton, Shakespeare,
and Spenser as examples of those whose work we would lack if they
had sought repose. The nationalistic warfare the Wizard decries becomes in the Bard's words magnanimous, scorning one's "Ease for others' Good," toiling "rapacious Men to tame," standing devoted "in the
Public Breach," and for one's country being "prodigal of Blood" (II
liii). The "venal senate" of the Wizard's speech becomes a place
"Where, by the solemn Gleam of Midnight-Lamps, / The World is
pois'd, and manag'd mighty States" (II lx). These opposing presentations of worldly activity given by the Wizard and the Bard—as greedy,

trivial, sinful, and destructive, or noble, civilizing, virtuous, and constructive—resemble those at the end and beginning of "Autumn," and,
like those presentations, they offer the reader alternatives that appear
almost equally plausible.

Another aspect of *The Castle of Indolence* which contributes to its ambiguity, and which also has to do with an anxiety in eighteenth-century
society, is its confusion about (or obfuscation of) questions of class. As
John Barrell argues, the poem tries to "justify . . . the fruits of social
division, while at the same time denying that any serious social divisions
exist."[60] Some of the rewards of industry the Bard describes, renown
and wealth, are, as Barrell notes, unavailable to the working classes,[61]
while others of the rewards of industry, the physical health and moral
virtue brought about by a simple, vigorous life of labor are, again as
Barrell notes, "unavailable and inappropriate to those who do not perform" physical labor.[62] The Bard may, like so many comfortable-class
writers in the eighteenth century, assert that "Perhaps the happiest of
the Sons of Men" is the "toiling Swain," because he is saved from sloth,
vanity, and avarice; as the Bard confidently—or defensively?—says,
"rich in Nature's Wealth, he thinks not of Increase." But clearly the
upper classes are not going to join this swain in his plowing, hoeing,
and digging (II lv). And if they did, their status as members of the gentry would be threatened. Yet the Bard and the Knight appear to be of-
fering all these rewards to all members of society, leading to a tension
in the poem. An attempt to resolve this tension is made in stanza lx of
the second canto, where the Bard explains what will be the fate of those
who choose to leave the castle and follow the Knight:

> Some he will lead to Courts, and Some to Camps;
> To Senates Some, and public sage Debates,
> . . . .
> To high Discovery Some, that new-creates
> The Face of Earth; Some to the thriving Mart;
> Some to the Rural Reign, and softer Fates;
> To the sweet Muses Some, who raise the Heart. . . .

This list attempts to draw together the upper and the lower classes, the
lord and the toiling swain. It argues that although their rewards may
be different—and that difference, perhaps, threatens to undermine the
poem's refusal to recognize idleness and industry as class-related
states—they all have a place in society, and all are workers. In fact, the
fate of the toiling swain is said to be "softer." This line, however, intro-
duces another hint of ambiguity; it may, to quote Barrell again,

> apply to those engaged in the activities of agriculture, so often seen through
> the glass of Pastoral as more indolent than those of the town. . . . But [it is]

equally plausible that it is the rich who are here being offered a life of rural retirement and repose—a promise smuggled into this list of social duties as if it was truly one of them. The line can be read either way: it can reassure the poor that they work no harder than the rich; and it can hint to the rich that they need not work at all.[63]

Thus in attempting to resolve a tension, the passage opens up a new ambiguity.

Another of the poem's tensions lies in that an idle existence, obviously, is far more available to members of the upper than the laboring classes, and if, in the real world, some people are going to lie about doing nothing, others have to work hard to provide the necessities of life. But if Thomson does not want to portray indolence—which he is, at least on the most official level of his poem, presenting as sinful—as the province of the gentry, he must have no servants in his castle, no one virtuously working while others doze on the couch of sloth. He gets around this problem, as he did the problem of presenting the retired Knight as working but not working, by avoiding human agency. The delectable description of the castle's cuisine lacks a person cooking or serving the food and wine; instead, "some hand unseen" provides them. A line or two farther, even an invisible, disembodied hand is unnecessary: the guest "need but wish" and the comestibles themselves provide the action: "Fair-rang'd the Dishes rose, and thick the Glasses play'd" (I xxxiv). Another disembodied hand has done the decorating of the castle: in its tapestries, "by a cunning Hand, / Depeinten was the Patriarchal Age . . ." (I xxxvii). In the following stanza, the hand disappears and the pencil acts of its own accord: "Sometimes the Pencil, in cool airy Halls, / Bade the gay Bloom of Vernal Landskips rise . . ." (I xxxviii). Thus Thomson can present the comforts of a gentleman's country estate without the uncomfortable spectacle of some people working to provide the pleasures that the others enjoy.

The third way in which the lack of human agency in *The Castle of Indolence* is used both to assert and deny can be found in stanza xlviii of the first canto when, after a digression, the narrator says, "But, fondly wandering wide, / My Muse, resume the Task that yet doth thee abide." The notion that an inhabitant of the castle would have a task to perform contradicts the wizard's assertion that no tasks exist here, that all may do as they please—but then, it is the poet's *muse*, rather than the poet himself, who is said to have the task. In fact, whenever the narrator uses the first person and brings himself into the story, he soon brings in his muse, also, and it is his muse who has the agency, who is actually acting. When the narrator makes his first appearance, he is doubting his ability to "attempt such arduous String" since he has "spent [his]

Nights, and nightly Days" in the castle, "this Soul-Deadening Place" (I xxi). In the next stanza, though, he tells his muse not to "stoop to low Despair," since she (not he himself) will "yet sing of War, and Actions fair, / Which the bold Sons of BRITAIN will inspire . . ." (I xxxii). When the narrator declares his inability to describe the dreams of the castle's guests, it is his muse who fails: "My Muse will not attempt your Fairy-Land: / She has no Colours that like you can glow;/ To catch your vivid Scenes too gross her Hand" (I xlv). In the second canto, although the narrator has escaped from the Castle of indolence and begins by saying that *he* "now must sing of Pleasure turn'd to Pain" (II i), soon he is chiding his muse, not himself, for sloth: "Come then, my Muse, and raise a bolder Song; / Come, lig no more upon the bed of Sloth . . ." (II iv). The idea that the muse inspires the poet is, of course, a poetical commonplace, but the coupling of a muse with the idea of a task and with anxiety about how well that task may be completed, indicates, I think, a conflict about the role of the writer. Is he a professional with a job to do, or a muse-inspired gentleman? Is he the Bard, employed by the Knight to play "His *British* Harp" (II xlvi) for a particular purpose, or is he "The Harp of Aeolus" whose music is "Full easily obtain'd," with the "God of Winds" doing the work (I xl)?

The several, and contradictory, outbursts in the poem about the failures of patrons and copyright laws also testify to this uncertainty about the writer's role. This uncertainty, I would argue, was held not just by Thomson, the patron-seeking, sinecure-holding praiser of liberty and industry, but by many in the eighteenth century, as the idea of the courtly poet was replaced by that of the Grub-Street hack. A stanza which begins, "Is there no Patron to protect the Muse" goes on to complain of "the Laws [that do] not guard that noblest Toil" (II ii); thus what starts by being a lament that no one provides writers with the unearned support that is their due ends by being a complaint that booksellers withhold from them the "Bread" that all others who "swink and moil" are sure of.[64] Another stanza that begins with a lament that "Our Patrons now even grudge that little Claim, / Except to such as sleek the soothing Rhyme" ends by declaring Liberty as "Th' *Eternal Patron*" and that "The best, and sweetest far, are Toil-created Gains" (II xxiii). Like many in his century, Thomson was unsure whether to place the writer on Mount Parnassus or in the marketplace.[65]

In her review of Sambrook's biography, Margaret Anne Doody, like many readers, describes the ambiguities of *The Castle of Indolence* as revealing Thomson's personal tragedy:

In 'The Castle of Indolence' he had given away his mental state and his wishes: but in order to succeed in utterance he had felt compelled to go through the motions of destroying his own inclinations, his dreams and emotional refuge. Perhaps the destruction that the moral Thomson wrought upon his lovely castle was a desecration of himself. . . . He himself was imaginatively invaded in 'The Castle' by the intrusive Whig colonising force represented in the Knight of Industry, his estate plundered, taken over by superior and worthy energetic Englishmen who flattened his little shelter. There is a tragedy here. . . ."[66]

There is truth to this view, but one also could see the poem as a triumph, a masterwork of its ambivalent age. In it, Thomson manages to present idleness as delightful and horrifying, virtuous and sinful, the privilege and sign of the gentleman, and a vice no gentleman would stoop to. This is what his age, as much as his personality, needed him to say.

2

Six Days Shalt They Labor:
Idleness and the Laboring Classes

WHEN, IN 1704, DANIEL DEFOE WROTE IN *GIVING ALMS NO CHARITY*
that "there is a general Taint of Slothfulness upon our Poor, [so that]
there's nothing more frequent, than for an *Englishman* to Work till he
has got his Pocket full of Money, and then go and be idle, *or perhaps
drunk*, till 'tis all gone, and perhaps himself in Debt . . . ,"[1] he was voic-
ing a belief that would continue to be firmly and generally held by the
middle and upper classes throughout the eighteenth century. Again and
again, throughout this period, comes the chorus of assertions that the
poor are essentially idle, that they must be kept constantly laboring or
they will be constantly idle. Only the ever-present threat of starvation
will force them to work. Most discussions of the poor and many discussions of trade and economics contain restatements of this notion. In his
Fable of the Bees (1714, 1723), for instance, Bernard de Mandeville says,

> Every Body knows that there is a vast number of Journey-Men Weavers,
> Tailors, Clothworkers, and twenty other Handicrafts; who, if by four Days
> Labour in a Week they can maintain themselves, will hardly be persuaded
> to work the fifth; and that there are Thousands of labouring Men of all sorts,
> who will, tho' they can hardly subsist, put themselves to fifty Inconve-
> niences, disoblige their Masters, pinch their Bellies, and run in Debt, to
> make Holidays. When Men shew such an extraordinary proclivity to Idle-
> ness and Pleasure, what reason have we to think that they would ever work,
> unless they were oblig'd to it by immediate Necessity?[2]

In 1759, John Clayton's disingenuously named *Friendly Advice to the Poor*
said of the sufferings of the poor, "But it is a melancholy Truth, which
cannot be concealed, and must not be dissembled, that much of the
Poor's Misery is owing to themselves; and may with great Justice be
imputed to that Idleness, Extravagence, and Mismanagement, which
are as notorious, as the Poverty that proceeds from them."[3] Joseph
Townsend's 1786 *Dissertation on the Poor Laws. By a Well-Wisher to Man-*

kind announces that "The poor know little of the motives which stimulate the higher ranks to action—pride, honour, and ambition. In general
it is only hunger which can spur and goad them on to labour . . . ,"[4] and
it goes on to say that they resemble "the animal described by travellers
under the name of Nimble Peter; a creature so inactive, that, when he
has cleared one tree, he will be reduced to skin and bones before he
climbs another, and so slow in all his motions, that even stripes will not
make him mend his pace."[5]

In this chapter I want to examine this comfortable-class[6] belief in the
essential idleness of the poor, to investigate what was behind the tremendous cultural attention paid to laboring-class idleness. As I will discuss in the second and third sections of this chapter, some of the factors
prompting the preoccupation with idleness stemmed from eighteenth-
century ideas and feelings about money. The belief in the idleness of the
poor worked to the financial advantage of those who employed them;
and laboring-class idleness was fiercely felt to be a threat to the wealth
both of the nation and of the middle- or upper-class individual. By constructing the laboring classes as naturally idle and by enforcing laboring-class industriousness, then, the comfortable classes were protecting
their own economic interests. And since the middle and upper classes
worried that the idle poor might have time and energy to plot revenge
or revolution, policing laboring-class idleness was another way the comfortable classes tried to remain comfortable. In the fourth section, I look
at some of the methods the middle and upper classes employed in this
policing, at the ways they attempted to persuade and coerce the poor
into constant labor. In the fifth section, I explore another, less prag-
matic reason for the comfortable-class insistence on laboring-class industriousness: that industriousness turned idle—useless and potentially
threatening—people into hardworking "hands." Thus the bodies of the
poor, which, I also argue, were seen as unbearably grotesque, could be
rhetorically reduced to the parts which benefited the middle and upper
classes. Finally, in my sixth section, I examine ways some laboring-class
writers of the period tried to resist the consumption of their bodies'
labor—and, in a sense, of their bodies themselves—by the leisured.

I

Before proceeding further, perhaps it would be useful to define exactly what is meant by laboring-class "idleness." While what is considered idleness in the middle and upper classes is complicated and hard
to pin down, the definition of laboring-class idleness is fairly straightforward. It seems to be based on three ideas. First, the poor are not

entitled to leisure time: as Charles Hall said in 1805, "leisure in a poor man is thought quite a different thing from what it is to a rich man, and goes by a different name. In the poor it is called idleness, the cause of all mischief."[7] Therefore, any pause in work other than what is absolutely required for sleep, meals, and devotion is idleness. Second, the poor have an obligation to do work that will profit the middle and upper classes. A laboring-class person may be very busily engaged in activity, but if that activity brings rewards only to himself, it is idleness. For instance, Douglas Hay's essay "Poaching and the Game Laws on Cannock Chase" tells us that the main argument given for forbidding "persons of inferior rank" from hunting — although it seems likely that most laboring-class hunters felt the need for meat more than for sport — was that they should not squander "that time, which their station in life requireth to be more profitably employed." Therefore the antihunting laws were to prevent the poor from "idleness."[8] A turn-of-the-century writer said a poacher is "an idle, worthless fellow, who takes infinitely more pains to secure a scanty pittance, than half such labour properly directed would do to procure him a comfortable subsistence."[9] Even "infinite pains," if not directed to approved, "useful" ends, constitute idleness. A 1743 *Gentleman's Magazine* article declares that "in a trading Country, the Time of the meanest Man ought to be of some Worth to himself, *and to the Community*" (emphasis mine).[10] A laboring-class person, this idea insists, has no right to spend time in ways that do not benefit his betters.

The third idea which I think is behind the definition of laboring-class idleness is that the poor must work with their *bodies*; mental labor, when engaged in by the poor, is not labor at all, but idleness. Many of the arguments against the establishment of charity-schools were based on this notion. Although this idea was not universally held — some people of the period *were* in favor of teaching the poor to read and write — it was often and strongly put forth. Bernard de Mandeville, for instance, in "An Essay on Charity, and Charity-Schools" in *The Fable of the Bees*, says, "The Welfare and Felicity . . . of every State and Kingdom, require that the Knowledge of the Working Poor should be confin'd within the Verge of their Occupations . . . ." He adds that while "Reading, Writing and Arithmetick, are very necessary to those, whose Business require such Qualifications," they are "very pernicious to the Poor, who are forc'd to get their Daily Bread by their Daily Labour." Furthermore, since most children at school could be "employ'd in some Business or other," "every Hour those of poor People spend at their Book is so much time lost to the Society," and, since "Going to School in comparison to Working is Idleness," doing so will unfit poor children for "downright Labour."[11] Mandeville first published these statements in

1714, but the same ideas were being asserted much later in the century. Historian Henry Home wrote in 1788, "Charity-schools at present are more hurtful than beneficial: young persons who continue there so long as to read and write fluently, become too delicate for hard labour, and too proud for ordinary labour. Knowledge is a dangerous acquisition to the labouring poor. . . ."[12]

Even some of the reformers who themselves established charity-schools were quite concerned that the poor not stop laboring with their bodies and restricted what was taught accordingly. Hannah and Martha More, who industriously founded schools for the "savages" (the word occurs frequently in the *Mendip Annals*, Martha More's record of their "charitable labours" in this realm) of Cheddar and its environs, wanted the poor to be able to read the Bible, but not to know how to write. As Hannah More[13] explains it in a letter, "my plan for instructing the poor is very limited and strict. They learn of week-days such coarse works as may fit them for servants. I allow of no writing. My object has not been to teach dogmas and opinions, but to form the lower class to habits of industry and virtue." On Sundays the students read tracts, the catechism, spelling-books, the prayer-book, and the Bible; the younger students were treated to "Watts' Hymns for Children."[14] In Hannah More's story "A Cure for Melancholy," the good Mrs. Jones, who seems to be a thinly disguised More, contrasts other charity-schools to the one she is establishing:

> Girls who come out of charity-schools, where they have been employed in knitting, sewing, and reading, are not sufficiently prepared for hard and laborious employments. I do not in general approve of teaching charity children to write for the same reason. I confine within very strict limits my plan for educating the poor. A thorough knowledge of religion, and of some of those coarser arts of life by which the community may be best benefitted, includes the whole stock of instruction, which, unless in very extraordinary cases, I would wish to bestow.[15]

Even when More did find a "very extraordinary case," the "milkwoman poet" Ann Yearsley, she seemed to worry about this "case's" giving up the work of her body for the work of her mind: More wrote in a 1784 letter to Elizabeth Montagu, who joined with her in patronizing Yearsley, "You judge with your usual wisdom in saying that she shou'd not be corrupted by being made *idle* or *useless* . . . "[16] (emphasis hers). As Donna Landry says in *The Muses of Resistance: Laboring-Class Women's Poetry in Britain, 1739–1796*: "There is something too near idleness about the life of writing for More to countenance Yearsley's taking it up. . . ." She adds, "For Yearsley to work seriously at her writing would be for her not to 'work' at all."[17] More speaks of some of her own writing, the Cheap Repository Tracts, as a "laborious undertaking,"[18] but Yearsley's writing is not labor enough.[19]

Other laboring-class writers had, like Yearsley, to fight against this notion that their writing was idleness. Linda Zionkowski's essay "Strategies of Containment: Stephen Duck, Ann Yearsley, and the Problem of Polite Culture" discusses the dismay with which several nonlaboring-class authors viewed the publication of poetry by laborers, quoting an essay in the *Grubstreet Journal* which worried, "To have the fields neglected, and the loom forsaken, is a melancholy prospect; and looks as if we should in time have neither bread to eat, nor cloths to put on." For laboring-class poets to work at writing, authors like Pope, Swift, and Johnson feared, was "to neglect the work suited to their station": to be, in other words, idle.[20] The poet Elizabeth Hands, for many years a domestic servant,[21] impishly confronts this idea in "A Poem, On the Supposition of an Advertisement appearing in a Morning Paper, of the Publication of a Volume of Poems, by a Servant Maid" (1789). The ladies chatting over their tea in this poem wonder what such poems could have as their subjects—"A servant write verses! says Madam Du Bloom; / Pray what is the subject?—a Mop, or a Broom?"[22]—and declare that a servant's time should be better spent:

> For my part I think, says old lady Marr-joy,
> A servant might find herself other employ:
> Was she mine I'd employ her as long as 'twas light,
> And send her to bed without candle at night.[23]

Poetry is not the sort of writing in which a servant should be engaged:

> I once had a servant myself, says Miss Pines,
> That wrote on a Wedding, some very good lines:
> Says Mrs. Domestic, and when they were done,
> I can't see for my part, what use they were *on*;
> Had she wrote a receipt, to've instructed you how
> To warm a cold breast of veal, like a ragou,
> Or to make cowslip wine, that would pass for Champaign;
> It might have been useful, again and again.[24]

What is important in laboring-class activity is that it is useful to the comfortable classes.

Mary Leapor, another poet who probably worked as a domestic servant, also had to cope with this idea that writing is, for the laboring class, idleness. Many of the poems in her book of poetry (volume 1 published in 1748, volume 2 in 1751) contain references to poetry writing as idleness, dreaming, sinning; and over and over she is pleading to be allowed to continue her writing despite the reproaches of friends, relatives, and employers.[25] Her poem *An Epistle to Artemisia. On Fame* shows Mira receiving a scolding for spending time writing:

> Then comes *Sophronia*, like a barb'rous *Turk*:
> "You thoughtless Baggage, when d'ye mind your Work?
> "Still o'er a table leans your bending Neck:
> "Your Head will grow prepost'rous, like a Peck."
> "Go, ply your Needle: You might earn your Bread;
> "Or who must feed you when your Father's dead?"
> She sobbing answers, "Sure I need not come
> "To you for Lectures; I have store at home.
> "What can I do?"
>   "—Not scribble."
>   "—But I will."
> "Then get thee packing—and be aukward still."[26]

This passage, as Landry says, "vividly summarizes the objections to writing as an employment for members of the laboring classes expressed so frequently in the eighteenth-century discourse on patronage." Landry also speculates that this poem might indicate that Leapor was dismissed from service for her "willful scribbling."[27] Certainly, at least, the line indicating that Mira had plenty of lectures against her writing at home is factual. Leapor's friend and patron Bridget Freemantle tells us in her account of Leapor, published in the second volume of Leapor's one book, that Leapor's parents tried to discourage her writing:

> He [Leapor's father] informs me she was always fond of reading every thing that came in her way, as soon as she was capable of it; and that when she had learnt to write tolerably, which, as he remembers, was at about ten or eleven Years old, She would always be scribbling, and sometimes in Rhyme; which her Mother was at first pleas'd with: But finding this Humour increase upon her as she grew up, when she thought her capable of more profitable Employment, she endeavour'd to break her of it; and that he likewise, having no Taste for Poetry, and not imagining it could ever be any Advantage to her, join'd in the same Design: But finding it impossible to alter her natural Inclination, he had of late desisted, and left her more at Liberty.[28]

Leapor's parents, like the meddling "friends" in her poems, wanted her to engage in "more profitable Employment," but Leapor struggled to be allowed to write.[29] Landry argues that for Leapor "the scene of writing itself is a site of resistance to a culture organized around productive labor, defined as 'not writing' . . ."[30]; I would say the same is true for many, if not all, laboring-class writers of the period. To engage in the mental labor of writing was also to labor against the cultural idea that the poor should work only with their bodies.

II

The bodily labor in which the poor must engage should, the comfortable classes insisted, start early and continue constantly: the belief in the basically idle nature of the poor led to an urgent desire to set them to work as early as possible and to keep them at work nearly all their waking hours. If laboring-class children were just caught early enough and kept laboring constantly enough, they would be "inured" to the hardships that are to be their lot. As John Barrell says in *The Dark Side of the Landscape,*

> The truly benevolent attitude in the period, expressed everywhere in the writings on the poor, is that their children should, in their own best interests, be so brought up as to be 'inured'—the word occurs over and over again—'inured' to hard labour; they must experience the pain of overwork so early, that it becomes not a pain at all, but an ever present absence of feeling. . . .[31]

Mandeville argues against educating poor children, since those "who are to remain and end their Days in a Laborious, Tiresome and Painful Station of Life, the sooner they are put upon it at first, the more patiently they'll submit to it for ever after."[32] "By bringing them up in Ignorance," he says farther on, "you may inure them to real Hardships without being ever sensible themselves that they are such."[33] Cunningham says that "at four years of age, there are sundry employments at which children can earn a living," but that, besides monetary considerations, "there is a very considerable use in their being, somehow or other, constantly employed, at least, twelve hours in a day," since "by these means, we hope, that the rising generation will be so habituated to constant employment" that it will, he ends perhaps rather optimistically, "at length, prove agreeable and entertaining to them. . . ."[34] Being "early initiated in the habits of industry," as a *Gentleman's Magazine* article puts it,[35] was seen as the key to social usefulness, moral goodness, and worldly success—or survival, frequently the only success the laboring classes could boast. In "The Shepherd of Salisbury Plain," one of Hannah More's Cheap Repository Tracts (which were written between 1795 and 1798), the excruciatingly poor but equally virtuous hero of the piece explains to the benevolent gentleman who stops to talk with him that he is careful to set all members of his numerous family to work as early as possible. The children have been bred

> to such habits of industry, that our little maids, before they are six years old, can first get a half-penny, and then a penny a day by knitting. The boys, who are too little to do hard work, get a trifle by keeping the birds off the corn. . . . When the season of crow-keeping is over, then they glean or pick stones; any thing is better than idleness, sir, and if they did not get a farthing by it, I would make them do it just the same, for the sake of giving them early habits of industry.[36]

A constellation of ideas about labor and the poor seems to be behind these recommendations of early and unceasing work. One idea is that if the poor have never tasted ease, they will not miss it and will therefore be content with constant work. Another idea, closely related to this, is the one Barrell puts forth in the passage I quoted earlier: that the pain of overwork will, by overwork itself, be converted to numbness. A third idea is that, just as idleness begets more idleness, so industriousness leads to more industriousness. The rule in physics that a body in motion tends to remain in motion holds true also, in this view, for the bodies of the poor. Temple, writing anonymously in *A Vindication of Commerce and the Arts; Proving that They Are the Source of the Greatness, Riches and Populousness of a State* (1758), expresses this notion: "Nothing can preserve a disposition for labour, but the daily and constant practice of it. The more a man labours, the less irksome it becomes; the less he works, the more burdensome the task."[37] It is not surprising, then, to find writers of the day insisting on the six days of labor prescribed in the fourth commandment. Henry Fielding speaks for many[38] when he says sternly in *An Enquiry into the Late Increase of Robbers* (1751), "*Six Days shalt thou labour*, was the positive Command of God in his own Republic."[39]

From this notion that the poor would be as idle as they could be and that they should be prevented from even an hour's idleness, evolved the doctrine of the utility of poverty.[40] Briefly, this doctrine holds that employers should be careful to pay workers just enough to allow them to live, if they worked constantly (or, in a variation on the idea, that the prices of provisions should be kept so high as to require the poor to work constantly in order to purchase the necessities of life). This practice would ensure that the workers would have neither the time nor money to waste carousing at the alehouse or in other "unproductive" activities. This idea is repeated constantly in eighteenth-century writings about the poor. Mandeville, for instance, says with his usual acerbity that the poor "have nothing to stir them up to be serviceable but their Wants, which it is Prudence to relieve, but Folly to cure."[41] Temple agrees, proclaiming in *A Vindication of Commerce and the Arts* that "The only way to make [the poor] temperate and industrious, is to lay them under a necessity of labouring all the time they can spare from meals and sleep, in order to procure the common necessaries of life."[42] Arthur Young, another firm believer in the utility of poverty, expands on the doctrine in his *Six Months Tour through the North of England* (1771): "In general, all these branches [of manufacture] find, that their best friend is an high price of provisions. . . . The manufacturers themselves, as well as their families, are in such times better cloathed, better fed, and in easier circumstances, than when prices are low; for at such times they never worked six days in a week; numbers not five, or even four. . . ."[43] In his *Farmer's Tour through the East of England* (1771), Young makes this oft-quoted assertion: "If you talk of the interests of trade and manufactures, everyone but an idiot knows that the lower classes must be kept poor or they will never be industrious."[44]

Clearly, the utility of poverty doctrine provided employers with a splendid excuse for paying low salaries. Not only was getting as much labor for as little money as possible good for business, but low wages, by this doctrine, also benefited the workers. If they had to work every waking moment to earn enough to keep themselves alive, they would be prevented from the sin of idleness, as well as from the bad behavior in which they were likely to engage in their idle time; thus they would benefit, morally and spiritually. They would even benefit financially, according to the doctrine's logic, because they would have no time to waste money on drink and inappropriate luxuries. Thus poverty led to prosperity. The nation benefited too from the workers' low pay. Low labor costs allowed Britain to compete in foreign markets, the constant employment of the laboring classes gave them no time for criminal activity (including, as I will discuss later, revolutionary activity), and the prosperity low wages led to would reduce the poor rates. Paying one's workers barely enough to survive on, then, was an act of benevolence and patriotism—no wonder belief in the doctrine was so widespread and firmly held. Possibly there was another reason, too: perhaps the utility of poverty doctrine served to prevent the guilt that some of the comfortable might otherwise have felt from the knowledge that they owed their comforts to the work of those who enjoyed far fewer luxuries and far less ease.

Many eighteenth-century writers who were not by any means in favor of class equality were astonishingly willing to acknowledge that the poor worked so the rich did not have to, that the poor had not only to provide for their own needs, but also to provide surplus to meet the needs and wants of their betters. John Bellers's 1714 *Essay for Imploying the Able Poor* asserts that "without Labourers there can be no Lords; and if the poor Labourers did not raise much more Food and Manufacture than what did subsist themselves, every Gentleman must be a Labourer, and every idle Man must starve."[45] Even such conservative writers as Hannah More and Edmund Burke assert that the rich derive their ease from the labor of the poor. More writes in *Coelebs in Search of a Wife* (1808) that "to assist their own labouring poor is a kind of natural debt, which persons who possess great landed property owe to those from the sweat of whose brow they derive their comforts, and even their riches."[46] In *Thoughts and Details on Scarcity* (1795), Burke says that the rich "are the pensioners of the poor, and are maintained by their superfluity. They are under an absolute, hereditary, and indefeasible dependance on those who labour. . . ."[47] In a way, these writers seem to be anticipating Marx's remark in *Capital* that "leisure time for a privileged class is produced by converting the whole lifetime of the masses into labour time."

These admissions that the rich owe their wealth and leisure to the labor of the poor may have provoked in some of the comfortable a degree of guilt, or at least an anxiety that the utility of poverty doctrine might not prove universally acceptable. This guilt or anxiety seems to be a motivation for the protestations one finds in writing about the poor that the poor are really as happy as, or even happier than, the rich.[48] For instance, an odd moment occurs in Mandeville's *Fable of the Bees* when, in the midst of hundreds of pages of frank admission that the poor have to do hard and unpleasant work and live frugally so that the rich may do only what suits them and live sumptuously, he suddenly declares that the poor are as well-off as the rich. "Abundance of hard and dirty Labour is to be done," he says, "and coarse Living is to be complied with: Where shall we find a better Nursery for these Necessities than the Children of the Poor? none certainly are nearer to it or fitter for it." So far he is his usual harshly realistic self. But then he adds, "Besides that the things I called Hardships, neither seem nor are such to those who have been brought up to 'em, and know no better. There is not a more contented People among us, than those who work the hardest and are the least acquainted with the Pomp and Delicacies of the World."[49] Joseph Townsend makes a similar move in his *Dissertation on the Poor Laws*. After saying that it is necessary for some members of society to be poor "that there may always be some to fulfill the most servile, the most sordid, and the most ignoble offices in the community," he says that these useful folk do not really mind doing the dirty work: "By custom they are reconciled to the meanest occupations, to the most laborious works, and to the most hazardous pursuits; whilst the hope of their reward makes them chearful in the midst of all their dangers and their toils."[50]

These assertions of the superior circumstances of the poor are more common, though, in writings directed to the poor themselves, and in these texts the motive behind the assertions seems to be fear that the poor might wrest from the comfortable some of their privileges—or at least take some revenge against them. The authors of conduct books for servants, perhaps realizing that servants have a daily and close-up view of the luxury and leisure others enjoy and that a servant's awareness of this inequality might have negative consequences for his or her employer, assure their servant readers that their situation is a happy one. In the "Duties of Servants" section of his book *The Relative Duties of Parents and Children, Husbands and Wives, Masters and Servants* (1705), William Fleetwood declares, "Servants may have more of the *Labours* of Life, but then they have less of the *Cares*, than other People; their *Bodies* are more fatigu'd and exercis'd, but their *Minds* are less perplex'd: They are only concern'd in *one* matter, to do the work that lies before them, whilst others have a *world* of things to think on, and look after."[51] The anonymous author of *A Present for Servants, from their Ministers, Masters, or Other Friends* (tenth edition, 1787) makes a similar comparison between the labors of servants' bodies versus those of masters' minds:

> how free is the Servant's Life, and void of those Troubles to which even your own Masters and others that live round you are frequently exposed? They have great rents to pay, and the Money hardly got to pay them with; they have Meat and Drink to provide for you, and Wages at the Years End; one trespasses on their Fields, and another defrauds them of their Debts. . . . And you see all this, but feel it not. You have no Care (next to the pleasing God) but to do your Work in the Day, and sleep quietly in the Night. Are not these Burdens on their Minds, greater than any you bear on your Shoulders?[52]

Near the end of the century, when fears of laboring-class revolution deepened,[53] texts directed at the poor became more insistent about the pleasures of poverty. As William Cobbett, who, the subtitle of his autobiography tells us, progressed from his beginnings as a plowboy "to a seat in parliament," says in his autobiography, the "millions of 'Tracts, Moral and Religious'" were being disseminated "for the purpose of keeping the poor from cutting the throats of the rich." He adds, "The gist of the whole of the 'Tracts' was to inculcate content in a state of misery! To teach people to starve without making a noise! What did all of this show? Why, a consciousness on the part of the rich, that the poor had not fair play; and that the former wished to obtain security

against the latter by coaxing."[54] In More's tract "The Shepherd of Salisbury Plain," the praiseworthy shepherd discusses for several para-
graphs the reasons the poor should be content. When his interlocutor
says, "Your's is a troublesome life, honest friend," the shepherd replies,
"To be sure, sir, . . . 'tis not a very lazy life; but 'tis not near so toilsome
as that which my GREAT MASTER led for my sake. . . ." He emphasizes that "God is pleased to contrive to make things more equal than
we poor, ignorant, short-sighted creatures, are apt to think." "You
think, then," sums up the gentleman talking to him, "that a laborious
life is a happy one." "I do, sir," says the shepherd, "and more so especially, as it exposes a man to fewer sins."[55]

Jonas Hanway's *Virtue in Humble Life* (1774), which is structured as
a dialogue between a father and his daughter, who is preparing to go
out into service, is full of assertions that, as the father puts it, "the gra-
cious design of Providence" has put "the *rich* and *poor* more upon an
equality, than either of them generally imagine."[56] The father repeatedly
tells the daughter that "The rich, who devote themselves most to amusement, more frequently grow sick of life, than us who are poor, and labour for our bread."[57] The "poor *rich people*,"[58] as the daughter is moved
to call them, must, the father says, "work for *amusement*."[59] A couple of
pages later, he adds, "Persons who have all their time on their hands,
have a much harder task than you seem to be aware of. You and I spend
the greatest part of our time in labour and rest; and consequently, so
much the less amusement serves us: and we have a quicker and more
sincere relish of it, than the wealthy, who are *hackneyed* in the road of
amusement."[60] Like many writers on this topic, Hanway presents the
rich as forced to play in the same way that the poor are forced to work.[61]

One of the most notable attempts to convince the poor that they have
no need to resent the rich is William Paley's tract "Reasons for Contentment: Addressed to the Labouring Part of the British Public" (1792).
In the first place, Paley implies, it is only those members of the laboring
class who are guilty of idleness who worry about the inequalities of society:

> So long as a man is intent upon the duties and concerns of his own condi-
> tion, he never thinks of comparing it with any other; he is never troubled
> with reflections upon the different classes and orders of mankind, the ad-
> vantages and disadvantages of each, the necessity or non-necessity of civil
> distinctions, much less does he feel within himself a disposition to covet or
> envy any of them.[62]

Then he goes on to assert what a blessing constant employment is, and
that "the want of it composes one of the greatest plagues of the human

soul: a plague by which the rich, especially those who inherit riches, are exceedingly oppressed."[63] He argues that, although an "article which the poor are apt to envy in the rich, is their *ease*,"[64] actually they are mistaken:

> Now here they mistake the matter totally. They call inaction ease, whereas nothing is farther from it. Rest is ease. That is true; but no man can rest who has not worked. Rest is the cessation of labour. It cannot therefore be enjoyed, or even tasted, except by those who have known fatigue. The rich see, and not without envy, the refreshment and pleasure which rest affords to the poor, and choose to wonder that they cannot find the same enjoyment in being free from the necessity of working at all.[65]

Having proved, then, that laborers enjoy an ease which the "exceedingly oppressed" rich can only envy—here again, the rich are portrayed as having no choice in the matter—Paley paints a pretty pastoral picture:

> I have heard it said, that if the face of happiness can anywhere be seen, it is in the summer evening of a country village; where, after the labours of the day, each man at his door, with his children, amongst his neighbours, feels his frame and his heart at rest, every thing about him pleased and pleasing, and a delight and complacency in his sensations far beyond what either luxury or diversion can afford. The rich want this; and they want what they must never have.[66]

He sketches a similar scene a little later: "I have no propensity to envy anyone, least of all the rich and great; but if I were disposed to this weakness, the subject of my envy would be, a healthy young man, in full possession of his strength and faculties, going forth in a morning to work for his wife and children, or bringing them home his wages at night."[67] One might note, however, that for all Paley's talk of the enviableness of labor, the laborer in these pictures has finished, or not yet started, his work. Paley does not show him sweating in the fields at noon. Paley's pictures display another strategy upper- and middle-class writers employ to disarm the threat of laboring-class resentment: the move toward domesticity. Increasingly, throughout the century, reformers tried to persuade laboring-class people that the pleasures of home and hearth exceeded those of the alehouse and other public amusements.[68] Concern for the families and morals of those who spent too much time and money drinking with cronies was probably one motivation of the reformers, but I think another motivation was the fear that alehouse talk might turn toward revolution. If workers spent their evenings separately, each by his own fireside, they were far less likely to

combine into bodies that might threaten the bodies of the rich. As early
as the late 1740s, when riots were occurring in the southern counties,
Arthur Young worried about workers having time and money enough
"for the ale-house and disorderly meetings."[69] Hannah More taught laboring-class women to brew their own beer, so their men would have
no excuse for going to the pub. In her story "A Cure for Melancholy:
Showing the Way to Do Much Good with Little Money," the charitable
Mrs. Jones encourages the village squire to shut down the local ale-
houses. "You would not believe," says the narrator,

> how many poor families were able to brew a little cask, when the temptation
> of those ale-houses was taken out of the way. Mrs. Jones, in her evening
> walks, had the pleasure to see many an honest man drinking his wholesome
> cup of beer by his own fire-side, his rosy children playing about his knees,
> his clean cheerful wife singing her youngest baby to sleep, rocking the cra-
> dle with her foot, while with her hands she was making a dumpling for her
> kind husband's supper.[70]

This sort of pleasant domestic scene appears in other texts written for
and about the poor of the period. *Virtue in Humble Life* depicts "the husbandman and laborer happy at their own fire-side, whilst prattling
babes rest fondly on their knees. . . ."[71] In "Sorrowful Sam; or, The Two
Blacksmiths," a Cheap Repository Tract, the benevolent gentleman Mr.
Stephens makes a laborer who is too fond of the alehouse feel guilty
and reform by saying, "What a pleasure it must be to you of an evening
when your work is done, to sit here in your great chair, with your little
prattlers on your knees, to hear them read their pretty books, and say
their prayers before they go to bed."[72] The rosy children may well benefit from their fathers' being there to tuck them in bed, but the comfortable classes also may sleep more soundly for knowing the poor are at
home listening to childish prattle, not in the alehouse discussing class
resentment.

III

Still another reason for the comfortable-class insistence on laboring-
class industriousness is that industrious workers were seen not only to
provide, but actually to *be*, the nation's wealth (a wealth in which they
were supposed to have no share, according to the utility of poverty doctrine). A 1736 *Gentleman's Magazine* article says that "it is an undoubted
Maxim, that the Wealth of a Nation consists in the Numbers of People
well employed;"[73] and indeed it was a maxim.[74] John Bellers's *Proposal*

for Raising a College of Industry (1696), for instance, states that "the Labour of the Poor" is "the Mines of the Rich;"[75] Mandeville's *Fable of the
Bees* asserts that "in a free Nation where Slaves are not allow'd of, the
surest Wealth consists in a Multitude of laborious Poor."[76] Many writers tried to compute the exact value of the industrious laborer. Lawrence Braddon, for instance, calculated that *"every poor Briton*, which
shall be born alive, will be . . . more worth, to *Great Britain, than Twenty
Pounds in broad Gold* . . . ."[77] Other writers based their arguments for
lowering the laboring-class mortality rate on the financial loss these
deaths occasioned. John Bellers, in his essay arguing for "the Improvement of Physick" (1714), asserts that "Every Able Industrious Labourer, that is capable to have Children, who so Untimely Dies, may
be accounted Two Hundred Pound Loss to the *Kingdom*."[78] Ruth K.
McClure's *Coram's Children* tells us that in 1759, Jonas Hanway wrote
a text defending the London Foundling Hospital, in which he argued
that the hospital was preferable to the workhouse, the alternate destina-
tion for abandoned children, since the hospital was "saving some of its
infants, and, Hanway calculated, every life saved represented by the
age of fifty a net gain to the public of £176 10s."[79] This sort of "political
arithmetick," as William Petty titled his 1690 book, allowed the arithmeticians to transform the labor, or even the very lives, of the poor into
so much wealth to be added to the general stock of the nation. As Peter
Linebaugh says in *The London Hanged*, "Petty's technique of computa-
tional abstraction allowed the mind to concentrate on instruments of
measurement that appeared to possess their own objectivity, so that social relations among people would appear as reified relations among
things."[80]

As one might expect, the idle poor appeared to the political arithmeticians as untapped wealth.[81] "The Poor without Imployment," wrote
Bellers in 1714, "are like rough Diamonds, their Worth is unknown."[82]
In *Giving Alms No Charity*, Defoe expresses a commonly held view: that
"all the Labour of a Person who was Idle before, is so much clear Gain
to the General Stock."[83] Many writers attempted to calculate the exact
value of this potential gain—which, while the idle remain that way, is
seen of course as loss. Bellers, in proposing one of the innumerable
workhouse schemes put forth in the eighteenth century, works out the
following word-problem:

> Supposing that there are Seven Millions of People in the Nation, and that
> one in Fourteen, either will not work, or that wants it; that is, Five Hundred
> Thousand Men, Women, and Children. And reckoning that they might
> Earn, one with another, Six-pence a Day, a Head, it comes to Twelve Thou-
> sand Five Hundred Pounds a Day; which is Seventy Five Thousand Pounds

a Week. That makes Three Millions, Nine Hundred Thousand Pounds a Year, which the Nation loseth.

To which add but Twelve-pence a Head, a Week, the Nation may be at Parish Rates, and other Gifts to the Poor, and it comes to One Million, Three Hundred Thousand Pounds a Year: Which Account in the whole, makes the Loss and Charge to the Nation to be FIVE MILLIONS, TWO HUNDRED THOUSAND POUNDS A YEAR.[84]

Gentleman's Magazine published several calculations of potential riches. For instance, a 1734 article urging an increase in the fishing industry says, "Now, if the extending the fishing Trade would employ but 100,000 People, of those who are at present at least Useless, and if we compute the Labour of each at an Average to yield 6 *д.* a-Day, the Nation would thereby annually gain 900,000 *l.* a Sum well worth our Attention."[85] A more modest calculation was included in a newsletter of the Society for Promoting Christian Knowledge:

Suppose England and Wales to contain Ten Thousand Parishes and that but Ten persons in every Parish, one with another, were by some method employed, who were perfectly idle before, then the whole number of Persons so set to work would be One Hundred Thousand, and if they would work but 300 days in the year and, one with another, earned but a half-Penny a day the produce of their labour at the year's end would amount to £62,500.[86]

The transformative power that would turn the idle into all these vast riches was, of course, industry. Industry, like a sort of alchemy, would turn the poor from "burdens"—the word is used frequently[87]—to wealth. "If the education of the youth of paupers, were duly attended to" asserted a writer in *Gentleman's Magazine* in 1790, "and they were brought up to habits of industry, the generality of them, instead of becoming a burden, would be an increase in wealth . . . ."[88] Cunningham declares, "Any method, therefore, that will enforce labour and industry . . . will convert what would otherwise be a burthen, into the riches and strength of the state."[89] He goes on to pen a paean to his favorite virtue:

What a variety of blessing follow in thy train, O Industry! By thee our poor would be made happy, our riches would increase, more employment would be created for our shipping, our naval power would be extended, and our riches and power would secure to us the quiet possession of our properties. . . . By thy auspicious influence! we should be able to carry on a glorious war, or to make a safe and honourable peace.[90]

Josiah Wedgwood composed a similar tribute to industry in his 1783 pamphlet *An Address to the Young Inhabitants of the Pottery*. After pointing out the improvements that (he argues) had taken place in England over the last generation, he says, "Industry has been the parent of this happy change—A well directed and long continued series of industrious exertions," and he goes on to claim that the nation now "attract[s] the notice and admiration of countries which had scarcely heard of us before; and how far these improvements may still be carried by the same laudable means which have brought us thus far, has been one of the most pleasing contemplations of my life."[91] Industry had the power to make magical changes in Britain—in its landscape, in the conditions under which its citizens lived, and in its wealth, security, and status as a world power.

The political arithmeticians, then, were convinced of the evils of laboring-class idleness. An industrious laborer was the nation's wealth; an idle one was not only a burden—swelling the poor rates, begging in the streets, possibly committing crimes—but was robbing the nation of the wealth his labor could potentially bring it. Wasting his time was wasting Britain's money; and the time-is-money equation was becoming increasingly important in the eighteenth century. As E. P. Thompson explains in his essay "Time, Work-Discipline, and Industrial Capitalism," the labor of people working for themselves tends to be task-oriented, while employed labor tends to shift toward time-orientation. "This measurement," he says, "embodies a simple relationship. Those who are employed experience a distinction between their employer's time and their 'own' time. And the employer must *use* the time of his labour, and see it is not wasted: not the task but the value of time when reduced to money is dominant. Time is now currency: it is not passed but spent."[92] Thompson says that before the coming of widespread industrialization, workers set their own pace, perhaps working more slowly at the beginning of the week than at the end: "The work pattern was one of alternate bouts of intense labour and of idleness, wherever men were in control of their own working lives."[93] (He speculates that this may be "a 'natural' human rhythm.")[94] This rhythm of course was forced to change: as Robert W. Malcolmson says in *Popular Recreations in English Society, 1700–1850*, the "irregularity of the pre-industrial employment of time" was "found to be inconsistent with the necessity of making full use of the substantial investments in fixed capital (large buildings, new machinery, and the like). . . ."[95] Thus the factory bell and the supervisor's watch came to replace the laborer's will.[96]

The time-is-money equation provided another weapon in the attack on laboring-class idleness: the idea that idleness is a sort of theft. Servants and apprentices were especially liable to be told that idleness is stealing, since all their time was thought to belong to their masters. Richardson's *Apprentice's Vade Mecum* (1734) makes this point that "an Apprentice has no Time that he can properly call his own, but is accountable to his Master for every Hour"[97] at least eight times in its eighty-four pages, warning its young reader repeatedly against misspending "his Master's Time," as this is robbery: "to a *Handicrafts-Man*, Time is the same thing as Money, and to squander away that, is consequently the same as to rob him of so much Money."[98] In its "Advice to Apprentices," the *London Tradesman* (1734) says that time-wasting is "a Crime against moral Honesty,"[99] and it exhorts young men to "avoid idle Company and Ale-Houses," for "the Time [an apprentice] spends there must be stolen from his Master. . . ."[100] Conduct books for servants also frequently remind their readers that their time belongs to their employers. *A Present for Servants, from their Ministers, Masters, or Other Friends* makes this typical assertion: "When you hired yourselves, you sold your Time and Labour to your Masters, all but what God and Nature more immediately required to be reserved: And, besides the Sin against God in Idleness, you defraud your Master, if you idle away an hour that should be employed in his Business."[101] Even Eliza Haywood's relatively reasonable *Present for a Servant-Maid* (1743) says, "while you are in the Condition of a Servant, your Time belongs to those who pay you for it; and all you waste from the Employment they set you about, is a Robbery from them."[102]

These texts for servants and apprentices also often mention the evils of "eye-service," quoting Colossians 3:22: "Servants, obey, in all things, your masters according to the flesh; not with eye-service, as menpleasers, but in singleness of heart fearing God." *The Relative Duties* uses this text as the epigraph for its "Duty of Servants to Masters" section; Thomas Seaton's *Conduct of Servants in Great Families* (1720) also uses the verse as an epigraph. *A Present for Servants* cautions against "the Eye-Service which the Apostle condemns, . . . when hypocritically you seem earnest in his Work when his Eye is upon you, but loiter away your Time when he has turned his Back."[103] These frequent reminders about the sinfulness of eye-service insist that surveillance is ceaseless—even if the master is not watching at the moment, God is. As the good mother of "The Good Mother's Legacy," a Cheap Repository Tract, tells her daughter, "do thy work diligently; for though the eye of thy mistress be not over thee, the eye of God is upon thee."[104] In *The Making of the English Working Class*, E. P. Thompson says of Methodism that "there was a constant inner goading to 'sober and industrious' behaviour—the visible sign of grace—every hour of the day and every day of the year. Not only 'the sack' but also the flames of hell might be the consequence of indiscipline at work. God was the most vigilant overseer of all."[105] Certainly Methodism did stress diligence and work-discipline,[106] but as the non-Methodist texts quoted above seem to show, the desire to instill in laboring-class people an internalized watcher-out for idleness is not exclusive to Wesleyans.

IV

Another way eighteenth-century culture tried to instill an inner work-compulsion in the poor was to promise success for industry and dire punishment for idleness. Of course, success above a mere survival level was rarely available to members of the laboring classes, since they were seldom paid enough to allow them to rise in the world.[107] The industrious apprentice is the figure most often presented in texts as able to achieve worldly success through diligent work, but in general, as Sean Shesgreen says in his essay "Hogarth's *Industry and Idleness*: A Reading," "apprenticeship offered little hope of future reward; most masters took a son or near relation as one of their charges, and it was to this person alone that the fruits of the trade went."[108] William Hogarth's famous series *Industry and Idleness* (1747) may acknowledge this fact. On one level, of course, the twelve engravings illustrate what the mas-

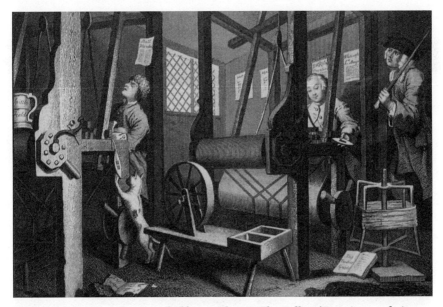

William Hogarth's *Industry and Idleness*, plate 1: The Fellow 'Prentices at their Looms. All photos from this series reproduced courtesy of Albion College Archives.

Industry and Idleness, plate 2: The Industrious 'Prentice Performing the Duty of a Christian.

Industry and Idleness, plate 3: The Idle 'Prentice at Play in the Church Yard, during Divine Service.

Industry and Idleness, plate 4: The Industrious 'Prentice a Favourite, and Entrusted by his Master.

Industry and Idleness, plate 5: The Idle 'Prentice Turn'd Away, and Sent to Sea.

Industry and Idleness, plate 6: The Industrious 'Prentice Out of his Time, and Married to his Master's Daughter.

Industry and Idleness, plate 7: The Idle 'Prentice Return'd from Sea, and in a Garret with a Common Prostitute.

Industry and Idleness, plate 8: The Industrious 'Prentice Grown Rich, and Sheriff of London.

ters were always telling their apprentices: work hard and you can end up as lord mayor of London; be idle and you will end on Tyburn's triple tree.[109] And certainly most masters read the series this way, since it was they who, as Ronald Paulson tells us in *Hogarth: High Art and Low, 1732–1750,* "bought the prints and displayed them for [their] apprentices' enlightenment."[110] But as both Shesgreen and Paulson point out in their interesting readings of the series, the didactic surface meaning of the prints is not the only one that can be found there.[111] Both critics focus on Plates 1 and 4 to achieve readings which argue that the success of Goodchild, the industrious apprentice, comes at least partly from his having been advantaged from the first, while Idle's untimely end might have as much to do with a lower-class status as with his bad behavior. In Plate 1, "The Fellow 'Prentices at their Looms," we notice first, of course, that Goodchild, with his *Prentice's Guide* lying carefully preserved before him and the ballads of Dick Whittington and the London Prentice tacked up behind him, is working diligently, while Idle, with his *Prentice's Guide* torn and dirty and the ballad of Moll Flanders pinned up at his loom, is dozing, unaware that a cat is playing with his shuttle. But a closer look might show us, as Paulson says, that Idle's loom is placed away from the window and supporting wall Goodchild enjoys, and that Idle's tattered clothes and plebeian features contrast sharply with Goodchild's neat clothes and aristocratic face:

Industry and Idleness, plate 9: The Idle 'Prentice Betray'd by his Whore, and Taken in a Night Cellar with his Accomplice.

a more literal-minded audience, identifying with apprentice against master, might see it as an effect of some initial deviance. If you are a poor ugly boy who lacks the favor of his master, the ability to please him, the energy of industry, and you have a dark spot for your loom, then you are doomed never to rise—indeed to descend lower.[112]

Shesgreen reads Plate 1 as revealing the harsh conditions with which most eighteenth-century apprentices had to contend: "Apprenticeship in the early eighteenth century amounted to virtual slavery. . . . Even highly respectable masters demanded an intolerable amount of work that was often monotonous, exhausting, and unhealthy."[113] The workroom in Plate 1, Shesgreen says,

might not inaccurately be described as having a number of prison-like characteristics. The setting is an isolated dungeon with a single leaded window which gives the impression of being barred. This confined space is crowded with complicated machines which must have appeared even more alien to contemporary viewers; it is worth observing that the looms distantly resemble the gallows in the penultimate scene.[114]

Shesgreen also notes that the tankard on Idle's loom suggests not only his shirking of work for drink, but "that there may be a relationship of

Industry and Idleness, plate 10: The Industrious 'Prentice Alderman of London, the Idle one Brought before him and Impeach'd by his Accomplice.

Industry and Idleness, plate 11: The Idle 'Prentice Executed at Tyburn.

Industry and Idleness, plate 12: **The Industrious 'Prentice Lord Mayor of London.**

causation between the monotonous, tyrannical machine and the apprentice's need to find refuge in alcohol."[115]

Plate 4, "The Industrious 'Prentice a Favourite," depicts on its didactic level Goodchild's being rewarded for his industry and good behavior. When we remember, though, that in Plate 2, Goodchild has been
shown courting the master's daughter, and when we notice the suggestions of class conflict in the foreground of the plate, the master's cat
hissing angrily at the dog belonging to the scowling porter, we begin to
question whether Goodchild's position as the master's favorite is due
solely to his virtues. Paulson argues that the laboring-class viewer of
the plate would read beyond the didactic message:

> When the apprentice—by which we mean the *idle,* not the industrious, that
> is, the basic ethos of the apprentice *until* he became a master—looked at
> Goodchild in Plate 4, joining his master in his countinghouse, emblematized
> by the print of Opportunity taking Time by the forelock, he saw at once a
> young man who in an earlier plate had courted his master's daughter and
> here clutches his keys and moneybag as if they were his own.[116]

Shesgreen points out that the antagonism between the cat and dog,
"each clearly identified with a different class of people in the action,
makes explicit the underlying economic and social conflict represented
in the scene."[117] He also attends to the background of the plate, noting

that "Between Plate 1 and Plate 4, a transformation is depicted as having taken place in West's business. His manufacture has expanded considerably. Labor is now divided and specialized. . . ."[118] Shesgreen also
notes that West is now employing women and children—cheap
labor—in his workroom, and that these changes between Plates 1 and
4 mirror actual changes in the weaving industry occurring at the time.
This move toward a factory system and its "resulting separation of labor
and capital," Shesgreen says, "is dramatically represented in the physical elevation and the distinctiveness of depiction accorded the leisured
master and his apprentice in contrast to the numerous laborers who are
presented so sketchily and so apart from their employers."[119] Shesgreen
suggests that Idle's dismissal and his consequent, and brutalizing, being
sent to sea, can be read as resulting from this "revolution in [his] trade,"
rather from than his idleness alone.[120] In *Industry and Idleness*, then,
Shesgreen sums up, Hogarth undermines his "narrowly propagandistic
and didactic" surface message to present

> a record of apprentice life in eighteenth-century England which is histori-
> cally accurate, psychologically insightful, and, on at least one level, dismay-
> ingly unpromising. This record represents the conditions of labor as
> oppressive, discouraging, and sometimes leading to compensatory conduct
> of disastrous consequences. It further suggests that success of a meteoric
> and spectacular nature is rare and not achieved on the basis of individual
> merit alone.[121]

Success and failure in the world, Hogarth seems to tell those of his
readers willing to receive the message, has more to do with class than
with industry and idleness.[122]

Hannah More's story "The Two Shoemakers," one of her Cheap Repository Tracts, reverses this situation of class advantage. More's Jack
Brown, the idle apprentice, is the "eldest son of a farmer in good circumstances, who gave the usual apprentice fee with him," while James
Stock, the industrious one, is only "the son of an honest labourer," and
has to be "bound out by the parish in consideration of his father having
so numerous a family, that he was not able to put him out himself."[123]
James is like a 'prentice guide in human form: the narrator tells us that
shiftless Jack is constantly pursuing entertainment, at which

> what was still worse even than spending his money, he spent his time too,
> or rather his master's time. Of this he was continually reminded by James,
> to whom he always answered, 'what have you to complain about? It is noth-
> ing to you or anyone else; I spend nobody's money but my own.' 'That may
> be,' replied the other, 'but you cannot say it is your own time that you
> spend.' He insisted upon it that it was; but James fetched down their inden-

tures, and there showed him that he had solemnly bound himself by that instrument, not to waste his master's property. 'Now,' quoth James, 'thy own time is a very valuable part of thy master's property.'[124]

As one might expect, James, though he is only a "parish 'prentice,"[125] as Jack says scornfully, prospers, showing himself to be so trustworthy and diligent that, when his drunken master dies, a group of business-men propose that he take over the shop and even lend him money to do so, as they "had not the least fear of being repaid, if it should please God to spare his life. . . ." The narrator ends this section of the story by saying that

> other apprentices will do well to follow so praiseworthy an example, and to remember, that the respectable master of a large shop, and of a profitable business, was raised to that credible situation, without money, friends, or connexions, from the low beginning of a parish apprentice, by sobriety, in-dustry, the fear of God, and, an obedience to the divine principles of the Christian religion.[126]

Members of the laboring classes who are not apprentices do not get to rise so high as this in the tracts and stories directed to them, but it is made clear that industry will be rewarded—or, at least, that idleness will not be. Whenever a charitable gentleman has a coin to dispense, he is sure to give it to someone whose hard work merits it. The tract "Sor-rowful Sam; Or, The Two Blacksmiths" can serve as representative for many tales of this type. It opens with Mr. Stephens, "a very worthy gentleman," moving to Devonshire and wondering "how he might prove useful to his industrious neighbors." He goes to visit Mary Par-ker, the wife of a blacksmith, and immediately she proves herself de-serving:

> he found Mary Parker in the best situation in which a good mother can be found, that is to say, taking care of her family; an infant lay asleep across her lap, while at the same time, she was putting a patch on her husband's waistcoat; her eldest girl was spinning; the second was learning to knit; a third was getting by heart her catechism; whilst a fine boy was unbinding a faggot to heat the oven: a lord's house could not be neater; the tables were rubbed as bright as a looking glass; and the pewter dishes on the shelf shone like silver.[127]

To reward this virtue, Mr. Stephens gives each of the children a shilling and convinces Mary's husband to stop tippling at the alehouse. The story ends as it begins, emphasizing the importance of industrious be-havior in determining who should receive charity from the wealthy:

In the course of a few years, the whole parish had reason to bless God, for sending so good a gentleman as Mr. Stephens among them, whose hand and heart were ever open to succour the distressed, and to help forward the industrious; but he would never waste his substance to pamper laziness, or to succour vice; he looked upon the industrious poor, as his children and friends, but from the drunkard, the liar, the swearer, and the thief, his bounty was withheld.[128]

Maria Edgeworth's surprisingly engaging tale *Idleness and Industry Exemplified, in the History of James Preston and Lazy Lawrence* (1804) also illustrates this moral that the industrious poor will be aided by benevolent gentlefolk. Little Jem, the only child of his widowed mother, loves their horse Lightfoot very much, but, as a consequence of the widow's serious illness the winter before, the horse will have to be sold to pay the rent. Jem is heartbroken, but soon sets out to earn what he can towards the two guineas needed to keep the animal:

> he knew that crying would do no good, so he presently wiped his eyes, and lay awake, considering what he could possibly do to save the horse — 'If I could get ever so little,' he still said to himself, 'it will be something; and who knows but landlord might then wait a bit longer? and we might make it all up in time; for a penny a day might come to two guineas in time.[129]

Bravely he sets about earning what he can, and he comes under the notice of a lady in the neighborhood by industriously performing, unasked, a small task for her. She employs him to work in her garden, where he performs twice as much work as another lad might do in the same time (beginning at six o'clock in the morning). Hearing her wish for a mat for people to wipe their feet on, he spends his few play hours trying to devise one, and "what toil! what time! what pains did it cost him, before he could make any thing like a mat!"[130] Finally he succeeds and proudly carries the mat to his mistress. When she asks how much money he expects for it, "Expect! — Nothing, ma'am," he says, "I meant to give it to you if you'd have it; I did not mean to sell it. I made it at my play hours, and I was very happy making it. . . ."[131] Impressed by his love of industry for its own sake, the lady arranges for him to make more mats, which she sells to her friends, thus enabling him to earn the much-desired two guineas and, after some suspenseful setbacks, to save his horse Lightfoot from being sold. The wealthy, like the Lord, help those who help themselves.

Far more common than examples of laboring-class people's rising or being aided because of their industry, though, are instances of idleness causing their destruction. Idleness sets one on a slippery slope that frequently ends in death, most often at the gallows. Hogarth's *Industry and*

Idleness, of course, shows idle Tom meeting his doom at Tyburn. On the didactic level of the progress, the sleeping on the job of Plate 1 leads to the gaming, Sabbath-breaking, and keeping of bad company in Plate 3, the whoring in Plate 7, and finally to the thievery in Plate 9 for which Tom must die in the great Tyburn scene of Plate 11. The whips, fetters, and ropes which decorate the borders of the first ten plates indicate that Tom's fate is being decided by his early indolent behavior, as do the nooses which hang on the side of the boat[132] and the gallows tree the sailor is pointing at in Plate 5. One sin inevitably leads to another, and idleness is often the first step on the road to Tyburn.[133] The plot of *Industry and Idleness* is, as Paulson points out, extremely conventional[134] and can be met with in a great number of eighteenth-century texts. The most famous such text, after Hogarth's, is probably George Lillo's bourgeois tragedy *The London Merchant* (1731).[135] This text also was one with which masters wanted their apprentices to be familiar. As William H. McBurney tells us in the introduction to his edition of the play, it was performed 179 times between 1731 and 1776, and had by midcentury become

> the traditional offering for Christmas and Easter holidays, since it was [quoting from Theophilus Cibber's *Lives of the Poets*] "judged a proper entertainment for the apprentices, &c. as being a more instructive, moral and cautionary drama, than many pieces that had usually been exhibited on those days with little but farce and ribaldry to recommend them."[136]

In an article on the play, David Wallace says that "well into the nineteenth century merchants subsidized performances of the play, making attendance mandatory for their apprentices."[137] Sean Shesgreen tells us that during the "uneasy year preceeding the 1736 [weavers'] riots, [the play] played no less than ten times, its longest run between 1733 and 1745."[138] The play tells the story of George Barnwell, a merchant's apprentice who is led by the evil prostitute Millwood to steal from his master and eventually to kill his uncle. Generally the first sin George commits, which sets him on the slippery slope to patricide and the gallows, is seen as being his fornication with Millwood. But before this event occurs, he commits the crime of idleness, staying at Millwood's house for supper rather than leaving to perform his duty to his master. At first he demurs, saying, "I am sorry I must refuse the honor that you designed me, but my duty to my master calls me hence. I have never yet neglected his service."[139] When Millwood plies him with tears, though, he gives in; and this first trangression is marked by Lucy, Millwood's servant and henchwoman, as pivotal: "So! She has wheedled him out of his virtue of obedience already and will strip him of all the rest, one after another, till she has left him as few as her ladyship or myself."[140] Although Lucy says it is obedience George is being robbed of, I would argue that it is industriousness as well.[141]

After this first of George's transgressions, Millwood does indeed strip him of all his virtues, leading him on from sin to sin until he has, in his own words, committed the worst crime possible:

> Murder the worst of crimes, and parricide the worst of murders, and this the worst of parricides. . . . I, with my own hand, have murdered a brother, mother, father, and a friend most loving and beloved. This execrable act of mine's without a parallel. Oh, may it ever stand alone—the last of murders, as it is the worst.[142]

Thus ends a chain of sin that began with neglect of work. Truly idleness has been, as the industrious apprentice Trueman says it is, the "worst of snares" for him.[143]

The tracts and tales for the poor that, as I mentioned above, tell of the good things which befall the industrious are even more emphatic about the punishments that are due the idle. Edgeworth's Lazy Lawrence is brought to realize the truth of what his neighbors have often told him, "that idleness was the root of all evil."[144] His idleness leads him to playing pitch-farthing with improper companions, as it is a "relief from the insupportable fatigue of doing nothing. . . . Gaming, cheating, and lying, soon became familiar to him; and, to complete his ruin, he formed a sudden and close intimacy, with . . . a very bad boy."[145] Eventually he is talked into stealing poor Jem's money, is found out and sent to Bridewell for a month. Jem tries to intervene for him, but is told that "it's better he should go to Bridewell now, than to the gallows by and by."[146] In More's "The Two Shoemakers," idle Jack Brown, from an early age, shirks profitable employment. When he becomes an apprentice, he neglects his work and his diversions take a darker turn: he begins frequenting the alehouse, and "the idle pastimes of the boy soon le[a]d to the destructive vices of the man."[147] His doting mother sets him up in a shop, but his lack of diligence leads to its failure, and he ends up imprisoned for debt, which tells us, as the narrator points out, that "idleness, vanity, and the love of *pleasure*, as it is called, will bring a man to a morsel of bread, as surely as those things which are reckoned much greater sins, and . . . they undermine his principles as certainly, though not quite so fast."[148] More does not finish Jack on the gallows; having contracted a fever in jail, he is allowed to repent and just live as "a poor, weakly cripple the rest of his life."[149] In fact, several idle characters in the Cheap Repository Tracts escape the gallows, but they never escape some form of punishment. In "Black Giles the Poacher: Containing Some Account of a Family Who Had Rather Live by Their Wits than Their Work," for instance, the title character is crushed under a brick wall that falls down as he attempts to steal a net lying on it; he "languishe[s] a few days and die[s] in great misery. . . ."[150] Sorrowful Sam of the story of the same name, a drunken idler who guzzles and sleeps his days away, is run over by a wagon and has to have both his legs amputated. In "The Good Mother's Legacy," Betty Andrews, despite her virtuous upbringing, goes out to service and goes astray, beginning with time-wasting. Eventually she is seduced by the butler, left "in sickness and poverty to bewail [her] unhappy fate,"[151] and ends up lying in her mother's barn, her bastard babe in her withered arms. Both she and the baby die.[152]

Some characters in the Cheap Repository Tracts do find that the "road to destruction which the hand of idleness will be forever pointing out to them" (as Cunningham puts it in his *Essay*) leads to the gallows, or at least to Botany Bay. Sorrowful Sam's wife, the slatternly Susan Waters, who "sits with her hands idling before her," fails to heed the warning of Mr. Stephens that "many a poor fellow, Susan, has been brought to the gallows by his mother's folly,"[153] and brings her children up in idleness. When her favorite son is eighteen, he is transported to Botany Bay, and the last words he says to her when, "loaded with chains, [he is] put on board the ship," are, "Mother, the sight of you is hateful to my eyes; for had you kept me to my school, when I was a child, I should not have spent my days in idleness, learning all manner of wickedness, which has brought me, so early in life, to this miserable pass."[154] The poem "Wild Robert" also depicts a criminal's blaming his bad mother for his fate. Robert, his neck already in the noose, hears his mother's voice begging for one last kiss. "Hence, cruel mother, hence," he says,

> Oh! deaf to nature's cry;
> Yours is the fault I liv'd abhorr'd,
> And unlamented die.

He goes on to explain:

> My hands no honest trade were taught,
> My tongue no pious pray'r;
> Uncheck'd I learnt to break the laws,
> To pilfer, lie, and swear.[155]

If he had only been taught habits of industry as a child, he would never have met with such a fate.[156]

V

We have seen, then, that a great deal of cultural energy was devoted to decrying and anticipating and preventing laboring-class idleness, and that several factors motivated the intense attention paid to this idleness. Another deeply felt notion that seems to be behind this concern with laboring-class idleness has to do with the way comfortable-class people tended to view the laboring-class body. When that body was engaged in work that would benefit "society"—by which was generally meant the middle and upper classes—it was, as we have seen earlier, viewed as valuable and useful. I would also argue, though, that laboring-class industriousness, on a less practical level, was deeply important to the middle and upper classes because it allowed them to reduce the bodies of the poor to their useful parts and thereby to render these bodies nonthreatening. When the laboring-class body was not working industriously, it could not be erased in this way. Seen as appetitive, dirty, uncontainable, and infectious, it became grotesque, an object of fear and revulsion.[157] These grotesque qualities were thought to be attributes of the idle; and frequently, also, the reverse is true—bodily attributes considered grotesque were seen as signs of idleness, and therefore of undeservingness. When the poor *were* working industriously, however, their bodies could be rhetorically reduced to their useful parts, and thereby they were rendered nonthreatening. The craving mouths and empty bellies of the poor could be erased, as all attention turned to the useful hands that were diligently building an empire.

One of the most often-discussed attributes and signs of the grotesque, idle laboring-class body is drunkenness. Drunkenness and idleness are constantly paired with each other, and, in a sort of circular logic, each is condemned as leading to the other: the poor should not be idle because they will then be drunk, and they should not be drunk because they will then be idle. Drink threatened to render the bodies of the poor incapable of working for the rich. As a 1743 essay in *Gentleman's Magazine* arguing against allowing "Spiritous Liquors" to be sold with less restraint says,

> all practices should be suppressed by which the lower Orders of the People are enfeebled and enervated; for if they should be no longer able to bear Fatigues, or Hardships, if an epidemical Weakness of Body should be diffused among them, our Power must be at an End, our Mines should be a useless Treasure, and would no longer afford us either the Weapons of War, or the Ornaments of domestic Elegance, we should no longer give Law to Mankind by our naval Power, nor send out Armies to fight for the Liberty of distant Nations.[158]

Henry Fielding's *An Enquiry into the Causes of the Late Increase in Robbers*
paints a similar picture of incapacitated laboring-class bodies, asking,
"What must become of the Infant who is conceived in *Gin*?" and worrying that "these wretched Infants" will not be able "to become our future
Sailors, and our future Grenadiers" and that they will not procure the
nation "all the Emoluments of Peace" nor to avert "the Dangers of
War." He goes on to envision a grotesque scene right out of Hogarth:
"Doth not this polluted Source, instead of producing Servants for the
Husbandman, or Artificer; instead of providing Recruits for the Sea or
the Field, promise only to fill Alms-houses and Hospitals, and to infect
the Streets with Stench and Diseases?"[159] Drunken idleness is not only
productive of grotesque stench and disease, but also evidence of laboring-class appetite. In his *Dissertation on the Poor Laws*, Joseph Townsend
says that "Drunkenness is the common vice of poverty. . . . [I]t is notorious, that with the common people the appetite for strong drink is their
prevailing appetite."[160]

It is not just the appetite for drink that is grotesque in the poor and
therefore a sign of idleness, but appetite in general. Although economic
logic would indicate that increasing workers' desires is likely to increase
the amount of work they do, the denunciation of both appetite and idleness in the laboring classes does not depend, as Peter Mathias says in
The Transformation of England, on any such logic, but on "a joint moral
condemnation."[161] William Temple writes of "the *ungovernable Appetites*
of the manufacturing Populace."[162] In *A Vindication of Commerce and the
Arts*, Temple expands on the grotesque consequences of these ungovernable appetites, when the poor are allowed to indulge them:

> If a labourer can procure by his high wages or plenty, all the necessaries of
> life; and have afterwards a *residuum*, he would expend the same, either in
> gin, rum, brandy, or strong beer; luxurize on great heaps of fat beef or
> bacon, and eat perhaps till he spewed; and having gorged and gotten dead
> drunk, lie down like a pig, and snore till he was fresh.[163]

He goes on to distinguish between the appetites of the rich and the
poor, making it clear that those of the poor are always grotesque: "A
porter may be viciously luxurious on fat bacon, tobacco, red herrings,
gin, malt-spirits, and with a nasty bunter, or stinking dirty fish drab;
whilst a nobleman may be innocently luxurious on ortelans, pine-
apples, Tokay and the richest wines, and foods accompanied with a fine
lady flaunting in jewels and brocade. . . ."[164] Temple's inclusion of female companions in these lists of foods and drinks underlines the point
that one grotesque bodily appetite slides into another in this rhetoric;
any laboring-class appetite signals an incontinent, immoral, idle body.

Even when the items desired are apparently more innocent and polite than gin or fat bacon, the laboring-class appetite for them is seen as grotesque. Tea might seem an unobjectionable beverage for the poor — "the cups / That cheer but not inebriate"[165] — but many people regarded the laboring-class consumption of it with censure. As Edgar S. Furniss says in *The Position of the Laborer in a System of Nationalism*, "The solicitude of the social observers of the eighteenth century over the increased consumption of tea and sugar," which, he adds truly, "appears almost ludicrous to the modern mind," comes partly from the beverage's expense and partly from the fear that it would injure the health, but largely from "the conviction that the habit of tea-drinking was wasteful of time and destructive of industry among a class of people whose duty was to labor continuously."[166] Arthur Young's "Tour" volumes are full of exclamations about the tea-drinking of the common people, which is always linked with idleness and high poor-rates; for instance: "Poor rates 1s.6d. in the pound. Idleness the chief employment of the women and children: all drink tea, and fly to the parishes for relief . . . . I apprehend the rates are burthened for the spreading laziness, drunkenness, tea-drinking, and debauchery. . . ."[167] One of Hannah More's Cheap Repository Tracts stories, "The Two Shoemakers," presents the shameful results of laboring-class appetites, including the desire for tea. Little Tommy Williams, "a poor dirty boy, without stockings and shoes," has been brought to this condition by the grotesque appetites and idleness of his mother. Tommy tells his interlocutor, from whom he has just begged a bit of bread and cheese, that their relatives "are grown tired of maintaining us, because they said that mammy spent all the money which should have gone to buy victuals for us, on snuff and drams." When asked if his mother does anything to help maintain them, he answers, "No, sir, for mammy says she was not brought up to work like poor folks, and she would rather starve than spin or knit; so she lies a-bed all the morning, and sends us about to pick up what we can, a bit of victuals or a few half-pence." Tommy then reveals that he has not spent the money he has begged today on food for himself, even though he is very hungry, because he has to buy tea for his mother: "Indeed mammy says she *will* have her tea twice a-day if we beg or starve for it."[168] Dirt, nakedness, appetite, and idleness are all merged into an image of morally reprehensible grotesqueness.

The virtuous, industrious poor have no appetites; they are content with and grateful for whatever their industry or the benevolence of their betters can procure for them. In "The Shepherd of Salisbury Plain," the exemplary shepherd contents himself and his large and hungry family with "a large dish of potatoes, a brown pitcher [of water], and a piece of a coarse loaf."[169] His little daughter Molly exclaims happily, "Father I wish I was big enough to say grace, I am sure I would say it very heartily to-day, for I was thinking what must *poor* people do who have no salt to their potatoes; and do but look, our dish is quite full."[170] The shepherd has been given a coin with which he might have bought "a morsel of bacon to relish his potatoes,"[171] but he has used it instead to pay a doctor's bill.[172] The *Mendip Annals*, a narrative Hannah More's sister Martha wrote of their "charitable labours," presents a far different meal, a scene of laboring-class appetite that horrifies the Mores. Going to visit the workers in a glasshouse, they find

> Both sexes and all ages herding together; voluptuous beyond belief. . . . The wages high, the eating and drinking luxurious—the body scarcely covered, but fed with dainties of a shameful description. The high buildings of the glass-houses ranged before the doors of these cottages—the great furnaces roaring—the swearing, eating, and drinking of these half-dressed, black-looking beings, gave it a most infernal and horrible appearance. One, if not two, joints of the finest meat were roasting in each of these little hot kitchens, pots of ale standing about, and plenty of early, delicate-looking vegetables.[173]

These joints of fine meat and delicate vegetables are far from the great heaps of fat bacon and red herrings of William Temple's visions, but they are still grotesque, shameful. Poor bodies have no right to such appetites.[174]

The above description displays other elements that are generally associated with the grotesque, idle, laboring-class body: filth and nakedness. Dirt and rags are signs, not of an extreme poverty that warrants relief, but of a shameful idleness that affords proof of undeservingness. Only the strictest cleanliness and the most unruptured covering of the body are badges of virtuous industry, as many of the Cheap Repository Tracts insist. "The Hubbub" contains contrasting portaits of two women who live in a poorhouse. Amy Talbot, who lives there because "as she had no turn for industry in her youth, she soon eat and drank up the little property left her by her parents," presents a grotesque spectacle: her skin, "which was quite tawny, was never washed"; her clothes are mere rags which she has to clutch together with the hand not holding a pipe.[175] Dame Apsley, on the other hand, who is in the poorhouse through no fault of her own, and who is given to utterances such as "Time, Sir, is the gift of God, and I must account to him for it,"[176] is "the picture of cleanliness, and good housewifery." She is mending her apron, "which, though very coarse, was as white as the driven snow."[177] The gentleman who engages these women in conversation gives Dame Apsley half a crown and "only a few halfpence to Amy, which he thought was more than such a dirty woman deserved."[178] The same message that the dirty and ragged deserve no aid occurs in "Black Giles the Poacher," where More tells her readers that, while some thought that "a beggarly looking cottage, and filthy ragged children, raised most compassion, and of course drew most charity," the opposite is true: "it is neatness, housewifery, and a decent appearance, which draw the kindness of the rich and charitable, while they turn away disgusted from filth and laziness. . . ."[179] The cottage of the aforementioned shepherd of Salisbury Plain proves that he and his family are worthy objects of charity; it is shabby, small, and scarcely furnished, but spotless: "notwithstanding the number and smallness of the children, there was not the least appearance of dirt or litter." The few sticks of furniture are rubbed "bright as a looking-glass," and the walls and trenchers are clean and white.[180] The shepherd's clothes are extremely worn but also flawlessly clean and intact: his coat has been "so often patched with different sorts of cloth, that it was now become hard to say which had been the original colour." The same is true of his stockings and shirt. This patching and darning, the narrator tells us, "while it gave a plain proof of the shepherd's poverty, equally proved the exceeding neatness, industry, and good management of his wife." The narrator goes on to assert that if she meets with a laborer whose stockings and shirt are "tight and whole," she knows she will find his cottage to be clean and his wife "notable, and worthy of encouragement."[181]

This concern with the "tightness" of workers' clothes is not peculiar to Hannah More. In *Virtue in Humble Life*, for instance, Jonas Hanway tells of a benevolent gentleman who "clothes a number of poor boys and poor girls every second year; on condition that they always appear tight and clean. . . ."[182] John Clayton, the author of *Friendly Advice to the Poor*, says that "if poor People would but keep themselves tight and whole, however mean their Garments were, they would at least bespeak the Neatness and Diligence of the Wearer, and might recommend them to the Notice of Such Friends as would possibly furnish them with better Cloaths. . . ."[183] In other words, if the poor would appear less in need of charity, they would receive more of it. In *The Dark Side of the Landscape*, John Barrell writes that what justifies this paradox, "of course, is that the good poor work, and take a decent pride in their appearance; while the undeserving, who do not work, feel no shame at the abject appearance they exhibit."[184] This is clearly the "logical" reason for the paradox, but perhaps a deeper reason behind it is that "tight and whole" clothes serve to separate the laboring-class bodies they cover from the sight and proximity of the comfortable. Torn and worn-through garments cannot perform this reassuring function. The grotesque bodies of the poor both peek out through, and are partly constituted by, the gaps and fissures in their ragged clothes, which fail to contain the threat of their needing bodies.

The appetitive, dirty, ragged, grotesque poor who are not deserving objects of charity seem to become, in the discourse of their middle- and upper-class observers, "objects" of another kind. Townsend, arguing for voluntary private charity rather than parish aid to the poor, says, "Nothing in nature can be more disgusting than a parish pay-table, attendant upon which, in the same objects of misery, are too often found combined, snuff, gin, rags, vermin, insolence, and abusive language. . . ."[185] Clayton speaks in the beginning of his pamphlet of the "distressed Objects" with which "our streets still swarm;"[186] near the end, he says again that the streets swarm "with idle Vagrants, sturdy Beggars, and such wretched Objects as provoke Resentment rather than kindle Compassion."[187] These objects "are so familiarized to Filth and Rags, as renders them in a Manner natural;"[188] their idle neglect of good housekeeping "bespeaks a Love of Filth, a beastly Delight in wallowing in the Mire, an abject Mind that is altogether unworthy of Encouragement."[189] At another point, Clayton complains that "We cannot walk the Streets without being annoyed with such Filth as is a publick Nuisance; as well as seeing such Objects as provoke Resentment and Aversion."[190] The language here is so similar to that in the other complaints that it is a shock to realize a few sentences later *these* "Objects" are not the idle poor, but feces. The poor have slipped, in Clayton's rhetoric, from a metonymic association, to a literal identification, with excrement.

As we have seen, then, much writing about or addressed to the laboring classes represents the bodies of the idle poor as abhorrently dirty, inappropriately appetitive, and insufficiently contained, while representing those of the industrious poor as clean, free from appetite, and fully contained within "tight and whole" clothing. Another way of portraying industrious laboring-class bodies goes even farther in editing out potentially repellent, inconvenient, or threatening aspects of the body. This writing figuratively dismembers laboring-class bodies, discarding the alimentary canal that craves and pollutes, the skin that grows dirty and shows through the rags. The industrious worker's body is reduced to the hands or feet that perform the labor the comfortable classes require. This aspect differs from the others, of course, in that the poor are not literally dismembered, as they are believed to be literally appetitive, dirty, and ragged. Rather, the dismemberment occurs metaphorically and metonymically in discussions of the laboring classes. This rhetorical reduction of laboring-class bodies to their parts is occasionally imposed upon idle bodies, which metonymically become "useless mouths,"[191] or metaphorically become "the Spittle and Filth,"[192] the

"Warts and Wens, and other filthy Excrescencies"[193] of the body politic. But usually it is the industrious bodies of the poor which are so reduced to their parts. In the "body politic" metaphor, a familiar Renaissance notion, laborers are almost always positioned as the hands (or hands and feet), while the rich are the head which guides and directs the hands. The conduct book *A Present for Servants, From Their Ministers, Masters, or Other Friends*, for instance, tells its servant readers that "as it is in the natural, . . . so it is in the political Body. . . . As the Hands need the Head for Guidance and Direction, so does the Head need the Hands for Work and Service."[194] In his *Proposals for Raising a College of Industry*, John Bellers backs up his argument that "a multitude of Scholars is not so useful to the Publick as some think" by saying that "the Body requir[es] more Hands and Legs to provide for, and support it, than Heads to direct it; and if the Head grows too big for the Body, the whole will fall into the Rickets. It's Labour sustains, maintains, and upholds. . . ."[195] Laurence Braddon's *To Pay Old Debts without New Taxes by Charitably Relieving, Politically Reforming and Judiciously Employing the Poor* (1723) says, "The poorer sort . . . are the hands and feet, the wealth and strength of the nation."[196]

Far more common than this metaphor, however, is the metonymic reduction of the laboring body to its useful parts (which, again, are generally the hands). The author of a 1751 article in *Gentleman's Magazine*, for instance, says his village has "upwards of 100 hands, weavers and combers."[197] All four volumes of Arthur Young's *Six Months Tour Through the North of England* contain references to "hands," the most telling of which declares that "In a word, idle people are converted by degrees into industrious hands."[198] Josiah Wedgwood wrote similarly in a 1775 letter that his workmen had become "a very good sett of hands."[199] Through the alchemy of industry, it seems, people can become hands. Calling laborers "hands" is, of course, a common figure of speech, but I would argue that on one level these rhetorical reductions of laboring-class bodies to their useful parts, these metaphorical and metonymic dismemberments, work to erase the threatening or disturbing aspects of the bodies. By using these tropes, a writer can focus on the parts of a worker that are of use to the middle and upper classes and ignore the rest of him.

Another sort of rhetorical dismemberment occurs in schemes for employing the poor. Authors of these schemes were frequently interested in employing everyone, no matter how disabled he or she might be. The infirmities of age or the weakness of childhood were no excuse for not working; as Clayton says, "there are many Branches of Business that require so little Skill or Labour, as that neither Children nor old People need to be totally excluded from their share of them."[200] Loss of sight or mobility was also no excuse; a *Gentleman's Magazine* article advocates establishing a fishery to help quell idleness, in part because "Young and old, lame and blind, might be useful" there.[201] The virtuous poor in the Cheap Repository Tracts never allow the loss of ability in one body part to prevent another part from working diligently; as good Dame Apsley of "The Hubbub" says, sewing away all the while, "if I am lame in my feet, that is no cause for my fingers being idle. . . ."[202] The shepherd of Salisbury Plain tells us that though his wife had "for several weeks lost the use of all her limbs except her hands," God had mercifully spared these, "so that when she could not turn in her bed, she could contrive to patch a rag or two for her family. She was always saying, had it not been for the great goodness of God, she might have had her hands lame as well as her feet, or the palsy instead of the rheumatism, and then she could have done nothing — but, nobody had so many mercies as she had."[203]

One of the more extreme examples of this desire to employ any poor person who has even one body part that can be put to use is found in Laurence Braddon's scheme *A Corporation Humbly Propos'd, For Relieving, Reforming, and Employing the Poor* (1720). Braddon claims that he can "propose a way how any Person, past [*sic*] Twelve Years of Age, that had neither Eye, nor Hand, and but one Foot, by the motion of that Foot, twelve hours in a Day, and without much force, should get, six Pence per Day. . . ."[204] In *The Body in Swift and Defoe*, Carol Houlihan Flynn cites Jonathan Swift's scheme to badge beggars, in which Swift declares that a beggar, "If he be not quite maimed," could "get half [his] Support by doing some Kind of Work in [his] Power." Flynn asks, "What is it to be 'not quite maimed'? Does one lack half an eye, part of a limb?" The "terrible mutilation"[205] that she finds suggested here in Swift is also visible in many of these sorts of schemes, as Braddon's fantasy of the eyeless, handless, one-footed worker diligently moving that foot twelve hours a day, to earn six pence and be of use to his country, vividly attests.

I noted earlier that the bodies of the poor were not literally dismembered, but in a way that is not true. The terrible working conditions of many eighteenth-century trades had mutilating effects on the bodies of laborers. One observer wrote of workers in the Cornish copper industry, who worked in intense heat and arsenic fumes, that "those who have been employed at [these places] but a few months become most emaciated figures, and in the course of a few years are generally laid in their graves. Some of the poor wretches who were ladling the liquid metal from the furnaces to the moulds looked more like walking corpses than living beings."[206] In 1700 an Italian physician described the effects

of lead poisoning on pottery workers: "For first of all their Hands begin
to shake and tremble, soon after they become Paralytick, Lethargick,
Splenetick, Cathetick and Toothless; and in fine, you'll scarce see a Pot-
ter that has not a Leaden Death-like Complexion."[207] A surgeon ministering to miners wrote that, "besides the ordinary accidents of burns,
wounds, contusions, luxations, or simple and compound fractures," he
often had to cope with "the blasting [of] one or both eyes, and the two
last fingers of the left hand, by gunpowder."[208] Lead miners were described as looking "pale and yellow," "lean as a skeleton," and "pale as
a dead corpse"; and an observer said of coal miners that "The murder-
ers' cell is a palace in comparison with the black spot to which they
repair; the vagrants' posture in the stocks is preferable to that in which
they labour."[209] It would seem that the punishments the idle poor were
thought to deserve were sometimes meted out also to the industrious.[210]

The most literal dismembering of all, however, was inflicted on those
whose lives ended on the gallows. The "Murder Act" of 1752 (25 Geo.
II, c. 37), looking for a way to add, as its preamble states, "some further
Terror and peculiar Mark of Infamy" to capital punishment, made it
part of a murderer's sentence that his body would, after execution, be
delivered over for dissection.[211] Peter Linebaugh's essay "The Tyburn
Riot Against the Surgeons" tells us with what horror the condemned
and their loved ones viewed this sentence, and to what lengths they
would go to try to prevent it.[212] Since idleness, as many eighteenth-century texts—most famously, Hogarth's series—insisted, was the first
step on the road to Tyburn, this dissection of executed bodies forms a
sort of macabre circle of cultural logic. The idle laboring-class body,
lacking useful parts to which it could be rhetorically reduced, was finally put to use, and literally reduced to parts, by the surgeons.

VI

Some laboring-class writers, not surprisingly, resisted the notion that
their bodies were grotesque unless they were working unceasingly for
the profit of their betters, and that their "useful" body parts could be
separated from the parts that needed, thought, and felt. These writers
told a different story about their laboring bodies, and I would like to
conclude by looking at a few of these writers and these differences. The
radical Parliamentarian William Cobbett discusses one of these differences, the notion of labor as property. A common statement about the
poor in middle- and upper-class discussions of them is that, as Jonas
Hanway's *Virtue in Humble Life* puts it, their "only property is their ability for labor."[213] For instance, Sir Frederick Morton's *State of the Poor;*

Or, An History of the Labouring Classes in England, From the Conquest to the Present Period (1797) describes the poor as those "whose capital is their labour," and says that the "stock [the poor person] possesses" is "his personal industry."[214] In *A Proposal for Making an Effectual Provision for the Poor* (1753), Henry Fielding argues that the very fact that the poor have "nothing but their Labour to bestow upon the Society" means "the Public hath a Right to insist" on this labor, "since this is the only Service which the Poor can do that Society, which in some way or other hath a Right to the Service of all its Members; and as this is the only Means by which they can avoid laying that Burthen on the Public which in case of absolute Incapacity alone it is obliged to support."[215]

The labor these writers refer to is, of course, always *bodily* labor: as Eden says, the "only patrimony" of the poor is "their bodily strength."[216] Cobbett agrees that physical labor is property, but carries the idea a step farther, achieving a radical conclusion. Rather than implying, as some of the comfortable-class writers seem to be doing, that labor is the only property to which the poor are entitled, Cobbett declares it the foundation of all other property. In his book *A Legacy to Labourers* (1834), he says,

> BLACKSTONE, who is the teacher and expounder of the laws of England, says (Book II. chap 1), 'that *bodily labour* bestowed upon any thing which before laid in common to all men, is universally allowed to give the fairest and most reasonable title to an exclusive property therein.' He says, that there is no foundation in nature, or in natural law, why a *set of words on parchment* should give to any one the dominion of land.
>
> Thus, then, we see that LABOUR must have been the foundation of all property.[217]

Cobbett makes the same point in his sermon "The Punishment of Oppressors" (1821): "All property has its origin in labour. Labour itself is property; the root of all other property; and unhappy is the community, where labourer and poor man are synonimous [*sic*] terms."[218] In this sermon Cobbett also addresses the closely related idea that labor is a commodity. Disagreeing with writers like the author of *An Essay on Trade and Commerce*, who says that labour is "a kind of commodity,"[219] and Edmund Burke, who says in "Thoughts and Details on Scarcity" that "Labour is a commodity like every other, and rises or falls according to demand,"[220] Cobbett asserts that "labour is not merchandise, except, indeed, it be the labour of a slave." The reason labor is not merchandise, he goes on to say, is that it "is altogether personal. It is inseparable from the body of the labourer. . . ."[221] For Cobbett, then, the bodily nature of the work laborers perform—and, as we have seen, the comfortable classes insist that the laboring classes perform *physical* labor—means that work is not alienable from the worker. It cannot be viewed as a commodity, to be bought with as little money as possible, regardless of the consequences to the bodies performing the work.

In *A Legacy to Labourers*, Cobbett puts an interesting twist on the tendency that I discussed earlier of middle- and upper-class writers rhetorically to reduce workers to their body parts. In an indignant reply to Malthus's recommendation that the destitute be refused "even the smallest portion of food," Cobbett cries,

> "Throw them back on *their own resources*," indeed! Their own resources are *their time* for their own use; their *untaxed* earnings; their *eyes*, to see where the things are that they want; their *legs*, to carry them within reach of those things; their *hands*, to take them; their *teeth*, to eat them; their *heads* and *backs* and *feet*, to wear them; and their *hearts* and *arms* to punish those who would hinder them in the free use of these their "*own resources*." These are the "*own resources*" of poor persons, if the laws of the community cast them off, and refer them back to that *law of nature*, which the stupid as well as hard-hearted MALTHUS says, has "*doomed them to starve*."[222]

Whereas some middle- and upper-class writers attempt to render laboring-class bodies nonthreatening by reducing them to the parts that are useful to the comfortable, Cobbett, in this passage, presents these body parts as useful to the workers and threatening to their betters.

Cobbett and other laboring-class writers produce another sort of twist on comfortable-class rhetoric of the laboring-class body. While, as we have seen, many middle- and upper-class writers present this body, especially when it is idle, as grotesquely and ungovernably appetitive, some laboring-class writers present comfortable-class consumption as also grotesque, because it is essentially cannibalistic. What the rich are consuming, in one way or another, are the bodies of the poor. In *The Body in Swift and Defoe*, Carol Houlihan Flynn argues that Swift and Defoe use "the figure of the cannibal to represent the failures of a society that 'devours' its poor to maintain its consumptive growth."[223] "Addison might crow that 'the Muff and the Fan come together from the different Ends of the Earth,'" Flynn says in another chapter, "but Swift saw more clearly that the muffs and fans came from rents 'squeezed out of [the] very Blood and Vitals' not only of Indostan, but of Ireland and the Irish natives. Swift employs the cannibal to call attention to a need that his contemporaries preferred not to own."[224] Cobbett also uses images of cannibalism to characterize middle- and upper-class exploitation of the poor, and he does so even more directly. In "The Punishment of Oppressors," he writes of the oppressive employer who hypocritically professes Christian virtue: "But what are we to say of the pretended friend of religion . . . who, with brotherly love on his lips, sweats down to a skeleton, and sends nightly home to his starving children, the labourer out of whose bones he extracts even the means of his ostentatious display of piety?"[225] Moving to a more explicit image of cannibalism, he asks what the man can be who can enjoy a feast "while he knows that the limbs which have created the feast are perishing with cold: while he knows the feast to be the fruit of unrequited toil, and that that which fills his body and makes his heart glad, is, if traced home, the flesh, blood and bones of the labourer?" "Give him the thing in kind," he adds, "cut up the carcase and serve it him in a charger"; and he finishes the sermon by saying the employer "has fattened on the gain of oppressions; he has 'eaten the flesh and drunk the blood of his poorer brother;' 'his feasting shall be turned into mourning, saith the Lord God, and his songs into lamentation'."[226]

The other two laboring-class writers I want to discuss here, the "thresher poet" Stephen Duck and the "washerwoman poet" Mary Collier, do not so explicitly use the figure of the cannibal to characterize middle- and upper-class exploitation of the poor, but they repeatedly present images of laboring-class sweat and blood being shed in the service of the rich.[227] This comfortable-class consumption of the bodily products of the poor forms a metaphor of cannibalism. Duck's poem *The Thresher's Labour* (1730) presents the bodily exertion and pain that go into the production of food for the tables of the more fortunate. As he says near the end of the poem:

> LET those who feast at Ease on dainty Fare,
> Pity the Reapers, who their Feasts prepare:
> For Toils scarce ever ceasing press us now;
> Rest never does, but on the Sabbath, show;
> And barely that our Masters will allow.
> Think what a painful Life we daily lead;
> Each Morning early rise, go late to Bed:
> Nor, when asleep, are we secure from Pain;
> We then perform our Labours o'er again:
> Our mimic fancy ever restless seems;
> And what we act awake, she acts in Dreams.
> Hard Fate! Our Labours ev'n in Sleep don't cease;
> Scarce HERCULES e'er felt such Toils as these![228]

The body's requirement for rest is not assuaged, and neither is its hunger and thirst:

> WITH Heat and Labour tir'd, our Scythes we quit,
> Search out a shady Tree, and down we sit:

> From Scrip and Bottle hope new Strength to gain;
> But Scrip and Bottle too are try'd in vain.
> Down our parch'd Throats we scarce the Bread can get;
> And, quite o'erspent with Toil, but faintly eat.
> Nor can the Bottle only answer all;
> The Bottle and the Beer are both too small.
>
> (ll. 134–41)

The pain and exertion that the worker's body undergoes materialize as sweat: "In briny Streams our Sweat descends apace, / Drops from our Locks, or trickles down our Face" (ll. 42–43).
And again,

> BUT when the scorching Sun is mounted high,
> And no kind Barns with friendly Shade are nigh;
> Our weary Scythes entangle in the Grass,
> While Streams of Sweat run trickling down apace.
>
> (ll. 120–23)

And yet again: "THE Morning past, we sweat beneath the Sun; / And but uneasily our Work goes on" (ll. 238–39).[229] Even all this exertion, while it may consume the workers—they are "*spent* so much with toil (l. 150, emphasis mine)—does not satisfy the employer:

> The Threshal yields but to the Master's Curse.
> He counts the Bushels, counts how much a Day;
> Then swears we've idled half our Time away:
> "Why, look ye, Rogues, d'ye think that this will do?
> "Your Neighbours thresh as much again as you."
>
> (ll. 71–75)

Though the worker may exhaust his body, expend its sweat, to profit and feed his betters, he is still called idle.

Mary Collier's *The Woman's Labour* (1739; expanded version, 1762) is, as its subtitle says, *An Epistle to Mr. Stephen Duck; in Answer to his late Poem, called The Thresher's Labour*. In her poem, Collier takes on Duck's essential erasure of the laboring-class woman's lot in life, her suffering, her exhaustion and bodily expenditure.[230] She argues convincingly that poor women must often work harder than their men. Not only must they "toil and sweat / To earn *their* Bread,"[231] but they also have to bear and tend the children, cook the food, and take care of the house:

> WHEN Ev'ning does approach, we homeward hie,
> And our domestic Toils incessant ply;
> Against your coming Home prepare to get

Our Work all done, our House in order set;
Bacon and *Dumpling* in the Pot we boil,
Our Beds we make, our Swine we feed the while;
Then wait at Door to see you coming Home,
And set the Table out against you come:
Early next Morning we on you attend;
Our Children dress and feed, their Cloaths we mend;
And in the Field our daily Task renew,
Soon as the rising Sun has dry'd the Dew.

(ll. 75–86)

The end of the working day in the fields means the beginning of the working night at home:

When Night comes on, unto our Home we go,
Our Corn we carry, and our Infant too;
Weary, alas! but 'tis not worth our while
Once to complain, or *rest at ev'ry Stile*;
We must make haste, for when we Home are come,
Alas! we find our Work but just begun;
So many Things for our Attendance call,
Had we ten Hands, we could employ them all.

(ll. 101–8)

When the agricultural harvest was over, poor women often had to turn to other sorts of paid work. Collier's powerful description of the hardships a washerwoman undergoes indicates that the bodies of laboring-class women, as well as those of men, were expended for the benefit of the comfortable classes. The laundress's day begins early:[232]

WHEN bright *Orion* glitters in the Skies
In *Winter* Nights, then early we must rise;
The Weather ne'er so bad, Wind, Rain, or Snow,
Our Work appointed, we must rise and go. . . .

(ll. 143–46)

And it ends late:

NOW Night comes on, from whence you have Relief,
But that, alas! does but increase our Grief;
. . . .
Tho' we all Day with Care our Work attend,
Such is our Fate, we know not when 'twill end:
When Ev'ning's come, you Homeward take your Way,
We, till our Work is done, are forc'd to stay. . . .

(ll. 188–97)

Like Duck's threshers, Collier's washerwomen are chided by their employer: hours after the women have arrived and begun work, their mistress arises and comes to inform

> Herself, what Work is done that very Morn;
> Lays her Commands upon us, that we mind
> Her Linen well, nor *leave the Dirt behind*:
> Not this alone, but also to take care
> We don't her Cambricks nor her Ruffles tear;
> And *these* most strictly does of us require,
> *To save her Soap, and sparing be of Fire*;
> Tells us her Charge is great, nay furthermore,
> Her Cloaths are fewer than the Time before.
>
> (ll. 173–81)

The care of these clothes which will adorn the bodies of the rich — "Cambricks and Muslins, which our Ladies wear, / Laces and Edgings, costly, fine, and rare" (ll. 159–60) — literally consumes part of the bodies of the workers:

> Now we drive on, resolv'd our Strength to try,
> And what we can, we do most willingly;
> Until with Heat and Work, 'tis often known,
> Not only Sweat, but Blood runs trickling down
> Our Wrists and Fingers; still our Work demands
> The constant Action of our lab'ring Hands.
>
> (ll. 182–87)

Thus Collier, like Cobbett and Duck, turns back on the comfortable classes the charge of grotesque appetite, and thus these writers fiercely insist both on seeing the laboring-class body whole and on seeing how economic exploitation was affecting that body. In so doing, they indicate eloquently that for these objects of representation, figures of speech could have consequences that were both large and literal. That which was written about the body of the laborer was also, often, written upon that body.

3

"Whilst We Beside You But as Cyphers Stand": Idleness and the Ladies

IN WORKS PUBLISHED ALMOST A CENTURY APART, THE VERY DIFFER-
ent feminists Mary Astell and Mary Wollstonecraft use the same word
to describe the status of women—or, more accurately, of ladies[1]—as
they saw it. In her *Serious Proposal to the Ladies, for the Advancement of their
True and Greatest Interest* (1694), Astell says that since "neither God nor
Nature have excluded them from being Ornaments to their Families
and useful in their generation," women, if better educated, would not
"be content to be Cyphers in the World, useless at the best, and in a
little time a burden and nuisance to all about them."[2] In *A Vindication of
the Rights of Woman* (1792), Wollstonecraft writes, "Riches and hereditary honours have made cyphers of women to give consequence to the
numerical figure. . . ."[3] Further on, she notes that "the laws respecting
woman . . . make an absurd unit of a man and his wife; and then, by the
easy transition of only considering him as responsible, she is reduced to
a mere cypher."[4] This image of the eighteenth-century lady as cipher
seems to me both accurate and rich. Like a cipher, a zero, she was nothing: excluded from the world of work and politics,[5] she was to be passive and silent. Also like a zero, however, as Wollstonecraft points out,
she added to the value of the man to whom she was united.[6] The eighteenth-century lady was a cipher in another sense, also: she was a puzzle, a message in code. Her meaning had to be deciphered.[7] In *The
Proper Lady and the Woman Writer*, Mary Poovey discusses the eighteenth-century notion "that one can interpret a woman's essence by her
context—by her reputation or her 'situation'" ("situation" referring, as
Poovey goes on to explain, both to her [or her father's] position in society and even her physical surroundings).[8] What I want to argue in this
chapter is that this interpretation of a woman's essence, this deciphering, often occurred in observing how she used her time. Idle ladies, who
spent their time in frivolous diversions, marked themselves as lacking
the valuable interiority, the "resources," a lady was supposed to have.
They also, generally, revealed a shameful desire to display themselves,

to be in the public eye. Ladies who spent their time well proved they had no such need for display or diversion; their kingdoms were within. In her poem "On Myselfe," Anne Finch thanks God that she is one of these ladies, "rescu'd from the Love / Of all those Trifles" lesser ladies crave. She will accept "Pleasures, and Praise, and Plenty," if they are given, but

> If they're denied, I on my selfe can Liue,
> And slight those aids, unequal chance does give.
> When in the Sun, my wings can be display'd,
> And in retirement, I can bless the shade.[9]

One project of the conduct books and some of the novels of the eighteenth century is to form such a lady.

I

That a lady's idleness was a sign that she lacked the qualities of a good woman is, of course, ironic, since during the eighteenth century, women above the laboring classes were increasingly relieved—or divested—of work. As workplaces became separated from homes, as traditionally female paid occupations were usurped by men,[10] as the amount of housework middling-rank women had to do decreased due to technological advances and more servants,[11] ladies' leisure grew. Ruth Perry discusses this development in *Women, Letters, and the Novel*, arguing that the eighteenth century saw the formation of "a class in which the men worked and the women were idle. Until then," she explains, "men and women of the leisured classes had entertained themselves in prescribed ways, while people of the laboring classes had worked hard, regardless of sex. Within the growing urban bourgeoisie, however," men increasingly tended to work for their livings and women to be supported by their men.[12] Perry quotes foreign visitors who "were impressed with the leisure of the English women. They neither spun thread nor wove cloth nor brewed spirits nor made candles. They did not usually cook, either, for servants cooked or else food could be provided by taverns, alehouses, cookshops, piemen, foodstalls."[13] One of these visitors remarked of English women that "Their husbands love them to such a point that they do not give them the least domestic work to do. They do not even permit them to suckle their own children."[14]

Pleasant as is this notion that men provided their women with leisure out of sheer love, a more realistic explanation comes from another foreign visitor: "it is become a Qualification now, to be good for no one thing in the World, but to Dance, Dress, play upon the Guitar, to prate in a Visiting-Room, or to play amongst Sharpers at Cards and Dice." "Unbroken leisure for a woman," Perry adds, "was becoming a signifi-cant symbol of the status of her family."[15] As the century advanced, this urban notion of gentility spread, so that the gentility of country-dwell-ers, too, depended on the leisure of the family's women. In *The Female Advocate: An Attempt to Recover the Rights of Women from Male Usurpation* (1810), Mary Ann Radcliffe recalls the days when the wives and daugh-ters of tradesmen "were employed in the domestic concerns of the household" and also in "spinning, knitting, and preparing necessaries for the use of the family." "But were the tradesman, in this refined age," she exclaims, "to employ his wife or daughters in any such low capacity, what would the world suppose, or where would be his credit!"[16] Jane West makes a similar comment in her *Letters to a Young Lady* (1806), noting that "the potent decree of fashion" has "determined it to be unfit for the wife of a man in reputable circumstances to employ herself in domestic arrangements, or useful needle work."[17] As Susan Staves ar-gues in the conclusion of *Married Women's Separate Property in England, 1660–1833*, middle-class men

> made their own claims to gentility increasingly dependent on having wives who were not engaged in productive work outside the home and wives who had leisure to engage in amusements like reading, music, and shopping. Gentility, now a possible aspiration for many manufacturers and retail tradesmen, required the separation of the household economy from the busi-ness and so increasingly excluded the female members of the household not only from knowledge about the business but even from the place where business was conducted.[18]

The importance of female leisure to class status can also be seen in the disapproval with which writers of the time tended to regard the idle-ness of female members of the upstart classes. Class struggle can be read between the lines of the caustic comments on the new fashionable accomplishments of farmers' daughters, who are now in the parlor play-ing the harp, instead of in the dairy making butter, as an 1801 *Gentle-man's Magazine* article complains:

> Now . . . these farmer's daughters . . . instead of dishing butter, feeding poultry, or curing bacon, the avocations of these young *ladies* at home are, studying dress, attitudes, novels, French, and music, whilst the fine ladies their mothers sit lounging in parlors adorned with the fiddle-faddle fancy-work of their fashionable daughters. . . .[19]

A letter in the 1759 *Annual Register* declares with similar tartness of shopkeepers' daughters being overeducated at boarding schools that "it would be of much more consequence they should be well instructed how to wash the floor than how to dance upon it."[20] The accomplishments that women of the rising ranks were increasingly acquiring were status-gaining because they displayed leisure, and writers' complaints about them indicate that those trying to guard the gates, as well as those jostling to join the gentry, knew that a major aspect of class status was female leisure. (Just exactly which classes it is that should not possess leisure is not entirely clear, but it often seems to be the class just below that to which the writer her- or himself belongs.) A letter in Charlotte Lennox's periodical *The Lady's Museum* speaks for many: "I would not be thought to mean," the writer says, "that the polite accomplishments are not very useful and becoming to persons of a certain rank and character," but, she goes on to say, "The polite attainments too frequently give young ladies of middling station an unhappy propensity to dissipation and pleasure, and indispose them to the ordinary and necessary occupations of life."[21]

Another problem, besides the increasing leisure of women and the increasing importance of such leisure to class status, with the insistence that ladies not be idle is that ladies were often viewed as leisure personified, as the ornamental companions of men's nonworking hours. Alice Browne tells us in *The Eighteenth-Century Feminist Mind* that the eighteenth century saw "a strengthening of the association between women, and the frivolous or ornamental aspects of life,"[22] and this observation is borne out by many of the period's conduct books. Male conduct-book authors point out that ladies were put on earth to make men's leisure more pleasant. Thomas Gisborne, for instance, says in his popular *Enquiry into the Duties of the Female Sex* (1797) that the female mind excels in "powers adapted to unbend the brow of the learned, to refresh the over-laboured faculties of the wise, and to diffuse, throughout the family circle, the enlivening and endearing smile of cheerfulness."[23] In another influential conduct book, *A Father's Legacy to his Daughters* (1774), John Gregory spells out a lady's reason for being: ladies are "designed to soften our hearts and polish our manners; and, as Thomson finely says, 'To raise the virtues, animate the bliss, / And sweeten all the toils of human life'."[24] Women writers often emphasize woman's role as companion in order to plead for improvements in women's education. Hannah More says that "when a man of sense comes to marry, it is a companion whom he wants, and not an artist,"[25] Jane West that "we are designed to be the companions as well as the help-mates of man; and it is . . . our duty to render ourselves conversable and agreeable, by enlightening our minds,"[26] and Priscilla Wakefield that "something far beyond the elegant trifler is wanted in a companion for life."[27]

Other, less circumspect, women who wrote about female education complain bitterly of the idea that ladies exist only to please the eyes of men and entertain their leisure. In her *Letters on Education* (1790), for instance, Catherine Macaulay invokes "the judicious Addison" to join her in animadverting "on the absurdity of bringing a young lady up with no higher idea of the end of education than to make her agreeable to a husband," and argues that while "the admiration of the other sex is held out to women as the highest honour they can obtain; and whilst this is considered as their *summum bonum*," women will be liable to the "vices and foibles" that have caused men like Chesterfield to consider them "only children of a larger growth," to be trifled and played with by men.[28] Mary Hays proclaims in her *Appeal to the Men of Great Britain in Behalf of Women* (1798) that women have been kept "in a state of PERPETUAL BABYISM"[29] and laments that women in the higher classes are, therefore, "the ornaments of society, the pleasing triflers, who flutter through life for the amusement of men, rather than for any settled purpose in regard to themselves."[30] Mary Wollstonecraft's *Vindication* also asserts that "trifling employments have rendered woman a trifler"[31] and that woman is considered to have been "created to be the toy of man, his rattle, and it must jingle in his ears whenever, dismissing reason, he choose to be amused."[32]

Wollstonecraft's statement seems to have a basis in truth. Ladies were, a male physician wrote in 1740, "made to serve us as Play-toys after our more serious Occupations."[33] James Fordyce gallantly explains that gentlemen do not object to ladies who seem overfond of their persons or dress, because "we are willing on such occasions, to make more allowance for the imbecility of those who were formed to delight us, not so much by an emulation of intellects, as by external graces and decorations, united with the softer virtues of the heart, and the sprightlier charms of the fancy."[34] This notion that a lady's vocation in life was to please and entertain men meant, of course, that she had carefully to guard her charms, and serious—nontrifling—female activity was sometimes censured on the grounds that it would injure her beauty. Laetitia Matilda Hawkins, for instance, writing in 1793, argues that the evidence that women "were not designed for the exertion of intense thought" can be seen in "the effect it produces on the countenance and features. The contracted brow, the prolated visage, the motionless eyeball, and the fixed attitude, though they may give force and dignity to the strong lines of the male countenance, can give nothing to soft features that is not unpleasant . . . ."[35] Serious, meaningful activity did not accord with a lady's role as ornament, amusement, representation of leisure.

Mentally and morally, as well as physically, ladies were to be passive, not active. Their virtues, as many writers said, were passive or negative;

Jane West, for instance, calls "the passive virtues" women's "natural endowments"[36] and says that while a man who lacks "activity, energy, courage, and enterprise" can "only be a negatively good citizen, and may, indeed, be said to *encumber* rather than *strengthen* the commonwealth," for woman the opposite is true: "the passive virtues, and the christian graces, are her natural dowry."[37] Hannah More advises parents to be sure their daughters are early "inured to contradiction," since "it is a lesson with which the world will not fail to furnish them." Girls should "receive but little praise for their vivacity or their wit, though they should receive just commendation for their patience, their industry, their humility"; the qualities most important to their happiness in life are "a submissive temper and a forbearing spirit."[38] Any sort of active self-assertion—except, of course, in defense of her virtue—must be sternly excised from a lady's character.

Active appetitiveness, also, had to be firmly repressed. To be desired objects, ladies must not be desiring subjects. In *The Proper Lady and the Woman Writer*, Mary Poovey traces notions of female sexual voraciousness, arguing that the strategy increasingly used to counter this feared attribute was "not to allow or to admit to appetites of any kind. Thus women were encouraged to display no vanity, no passion, no assertive 'self' at all."[39] Lack of chastity, as always, was the lapse from which there was no recovery, but now even lawfully wed women were discouraged from displaying too much fondness toward their husbands. This advice, I imagine, may have been more often given than followed—and it was sometimes satirized, as in Henry Fielding's portrait of Lady Booby—but it does crop up fairly often. John Gregory, for instance, warns, "If you love [a man], let me advise you never to discover to him the full extent of your love, no not although you marry him. That sufficiently shews your preference, which is all he is entitled to know. If he has delicacy, he will ask for no stronger proof of your affection, for your sake; if he has sense, he will not ask it for his own," since "violent love cannot subsist, at least cannot be expressed, for any time together, on both sides" without "satiety and disgust." "Nature has in this case," Gregory not surprisingly goes on to say, "laid the reserve on you."[40] Gregory also asserts, however, that ladies are unlikely to feel this sort of love in the first place: "What is commonly called love among you is rather gratitude. . . ."[41] The Wollstonecraftian[42] character Elinor in Frances Burney's last novel, *The Wanderer* (1814), struggles against this convention that ladies not express or perhaps even feel love, asking "Why, for so many centuries, has man, alone, been supposed to possess, not only force and power for action and defence, but even all the rights of taste; all the fine sensibilities which impel our happiest sympathies, in the choice of our life's partners," and why woman's heart "must be

circumscribed by boundaries as narrow as her sphere of action in life,"
her emotions hidden and denied.[43] Wollstonecraft herself, however,
says in her early *Thoughts on the Education of Daughters* (1787) that it is
"sufficient for a woman to receive caresses, and not bestow them";
women should not, after marriage, "give way to fondness, and over-
whelm the poor man with it."[44]

While this ideal of feminine passivity made ladies into ciphers, devoid
of strength, action, and selfhood,[45] passivity was also a lady's one approved path to power: as Nancy Armstrong argues in the introduction
to *The Ideology of Conduct*, "the domestic woman exercised a form of
power that appeared to have no political force at all, because that power
seemed passive."[46] Through it, conduct-book ideology claimed, a lady
could hope to influence both the men within her household and the
larger world without. Most advisers of wives agree with Mr. B's injunc-
tions to his bride in Richardson's *Pamela* (1762). "[Y]ou must not suppose," he tells her,

> whenever I am out of humour, that, in opposing yourself to my passion, you
> oppose a proper check to it; but when you are so good as to bend like the
> slender reed, to the hurricane, rather than, like the sturdy oak, to *resist* it,
> you will always stand firm in my kind opinion; while a contrary conduct
> would uproot you, with all your excellencies, from my soul.[47]

Later in this didactic passage, Mr. B tells Pamela what he has looked
for in a wife: "she must have borne with my imperfections; she must
have watched and studied my temper; and if ever she had any points to
carry, any desire of overcoming, it must have been by sweetness and
complaisance. . . ."[48] Only by submission could a wife gain a degree of
sway.

Passivity also was the answer for a lady's desire to take action in the
world. Ladies could, moralists often said, make a great difference in
their society, but this difference was not achieved by direct action (with
equals, that is; as I will argue later, ladies were allowed to exercise more
direct, active forms of power when dealing with social inferiors), but by
that almost magical property, influence. Thomas Gisborne argues that
one of a lady's purposes in life is to form and improve "the general manners, dispositions, and conduct of the other sex, by society and example."[49] Jane West agrees that ladies are "the refiners of manners, and
the conservators of morals," and, in a remarkable passage steeped in
conservative anxiety at the time of the French Revolution, describes
what happens when women do *not* provide this sort of good example.
She goes so far as to link female virtue and influence with the preservation of nations:

No nation has preserved its political independence for any long period after its women became dissipated and licentious. When the hallowed graces of the chaste matron have given place to the bold allurements of the courtezan, the rising generation always proclaims its base origin. Luxurious self-indulgence; frivolous or abandoned pursuits; indifference to every generous motive; mean attachment to interest; disdain of lawful authority, yet credulous subservience to artful demagogues; the blended vices of the savage, the sybarite, and the slave, proclaim a people ripe for ruin, and inviting the chains of a conqueror. As far as the records of past ages permit us to judge, female depravity preceded the downfall of those mighty states of Greece and Italy which once gave law to the world. We have inspired testimony, that the licentiousness, pride, and extravagence of "the daughters of Sion," during the latter part of her first monarchy, accelerated the divine judgments, and unsheathed the sword of the Babylonish destroyer.[50]

Hannah More seems also to be considering such dire possibilities when she calls on her fellow ladies, at "this moment of alarm and peril"—again, the time of the French Revolution—to "come forward, and contribute their full and fair proportion towards the saving of their country."[51] Lest we think, though, that she is asking women to take an active martial or political role in the struggle, she goes on to explain: "I am not sounding an alarm to female warriors, or exciting female politicians: I hardly know which of the two is the most unnatural and disgusting character."[52] What she is asking of women, rather, can be seen in the heading of her chapter: "On the Effects of Influence."[53] They are, in other words, not to *act* so much as to *be*.[54] Ladies may be, indeed, *should* be, a force for good—able to reform plummeting standards of morality and to shore up tottering empires—but they can only come to this power passively, through their characters, not their actions.

II

It would seem, then, that all these forces—the growing leisure of women above the laboring classes, the importance of this leisure to their and their men's class status, the notion that ladies are personifications of leisure, and the insistence that ladies be physically inactive and mentally and emotionally nondesiring and passive—should combine to require that eighteenth-century gentlewomen be idle. And yet conduct books of the period repeatedly proclaim the evils of idleness. The authors of these works admonish their readers over and over that time is fleeting and must be employed well. Thomas Gisborne, for instance, says that "time spent amiss can never be recalled."[55] Lady Pennington tells her daughters the same thing in stronger terms: time is "invaluable, its loss is irretrievable!—the remembrance of having made an ill use of it must be one of the sharpest tortures to those who are on the brink of eternity!—and, what can yield a more unpleasing retrospect, than whole years idled away in an irrational and insignificant manner."[56] Hannah More's *Strictures* contains many reminders that a woman acting under truly religious principles will not be "contented to spend a large portion of her time harmlessly, it must be spent profitably also."[57] The virtuous use of time was a concern not restricted to ladies; as we will see in my fifth chapter, Samuel Johnson—the great man himself—was obsessed with using his time well.[58] But, given the extreme restrictions on a lady's approved activities, the question of how exactly to employ her time well was, for her, more vexed.

Also more vexed for women was the idea that idleness causes sexual trangression.[59] Priscilla Wakefield, for instance, asserts that "the first false step" toward "some of the unhappy deviations from conjugal fidelity, which of late years have so often given employment to the gentlemen of Doctors Commons," and which have "thrown a public odium upon the [female] sex," could "be found to proceed from the want of energetic employment, an indolent vacuity of mind, which produced a wearisome restlessness, and led to dissipation as a relief." Not even "the boldest seducer," she goes on to declare, "should dare to whisper his unhallowed love in the ear of her, whom he saw devoted to the duties of the conjugal state"; he would realize he had no chance with one "whose mind was so virtuously pre-occupied."[60] In her *Vindication*, Mary Wollstonecraft also connects female idleness with sexual looseness, thus condemning both society's injunction that ladies engage in no meaningful work and the voluntary idleness of which she often finds women guilty. She argues that since "women have seldom sufficient serious employment to silence their feelings" they tend to be "romantic and inconstant,"[61] that women lack true modesty because of their great "mental and bodily indolence,"[62] and that a woman whose husband has ceased to love her is likely to commit adultery because she lacks "sufficient native energy to look into herself for comfort, and cultivate her dormant faculties."[63] Wollstonecraft indicts the whole ethic that ladies should not work as responsible for prostitution, flatly stating that it frequently results from "the state of idleness in which women are educated, who are always taught to look up to man for a maintenance, and to consider their persons as the proper return for his exertions to support them."[64]

These two ideological forces, the one requiring ladies' idleness and the other forbidding it, appear to be in opposition but actually, in many ways, worked together. The nervous attention paid to the problem of female idleness in the eighteenth century clearly came in part from the awareness that women now had greater opportunities to *be* idle. As Nancy Armstrong argues in *Desire and Domestic Fiction* (her quotations are from Gisborne): "When they prohibited female labor, conduct books made many hours available for women to indulge in 'trifling employment.' Because of her 'gay vivacity and quickness of imagination,' however, a future wife could never be left to her own devices." Thus, Armstrong goes on, "the matter of how to occupy a woman's idle hours"—and, I would add, the exhortations for her to *avoid* such idle hours—"commanded as much attention in conduct books as did her economic behavior."[65] Another and perhaps deeper way the two forces worked in tandem is, as I indicated in my introduction, that while her culture made the eighteenth-century lady into a cipher, it also strove to *de*cipher her by scrutinizing her use of time. As not only the conduct books but also many novels of the period indicate, the secret to distinguishing a good, desirable woman from one who might seem attractive, but was not really good-wife material, was increasingly seen to lie in investigating her activities. Since all ladies' activities were so circumscribed, the difference between approved and disapproved ways of spending time could be subtle: as Burney's *The Wanderer* indicates, for instance, playing the harp could be a sign both of excellence and of imperfection. In general, though, as Nancy Armstrong argues, ladies' approved activities often involved their supervising others, and disapproved activities usually included an element of self-display. The merits of a truly desirable woman, one who spent her time correctly, were not displayed, but discovered. And, perhaps most important of all, a desirable woman was one who was never bored, whose interiority was all-sufficient, who possessed inner "resources" that rendered her independent of the public realm.

The conduct books tend to agree on how a lady should be spending her time. Her first duty is to her soul, so she must spend part of her day in devotion. The health of the female soul, though, is dependent on how well she fulfills her duties, so not even religion is an excuse for neglecting them. Thomas Gisborne says, after enumerating the other female obligations, that the "attainment of everlasting felicity" depends on "her conduct during her present probationary state of existence."[66] If a lady has children, one of these important duties is to care for and educate them—"to rear and instruct the subsequent generation," as Jane West puts it in her list of ladies' essential duties.[67] Many conduct books tell women that, unless their delicate health forbids it, they should nurse their own children; to fail to do so is read as a sign of idleness: the non-nursing mother is either coddling her indolence or refusing to part with her dissipated amusements.[68] To educate one's children oneself, also, is always a sign of female merit; Clara Reeve's *Plans of Education*, for instance, contains attractive portraits of good women who have done so. Serinda, though she "was left young a widow," has still "educated six daughters, in the strictest principles of piety and virtue; at the same time, she has given them every advantage in her power in regard to ornamental accomplishments. They were educated in her own house . . . ; she taught them the social and relative duties, and enforced them by her own example." Charinda's ten children have all been "educated under the eyes of their excellent parents, who have devoted themselves to the most useful of employments, that of forming good and useful members of the community." Even the amusements of the children have been "so directed, as to contribute to their improvement."[69] Clearly these are excellent women who use their time properly.[70]

Another way ladies could spend their time was in "improvements," that is in educational reading and study. Conduct-book authors tend to approve of this way of spending time, as long (most of them are careful to say) as it does not interfere with a lady's other duties,[71] or puff her up with vanity,[72] or cause her to become unattractively learned. Mrs. Chapone's *Letters on the Improvement of the Mind*, as its title indicates, is largely concerned with this topic. Lady Pennington advises her daughters to rise early and regulate their time carefully so that they can, without their husbands' objecting, devote part of their day to improvement.[73] Gisborne says that "the habit of regularly allotting to improving books a portion of each day . . . cannot be too strongly recommended" to ladies,[74] and Wakefield ranks "the improvement of the mind" second after "the performance of duties."[75]

The two other main arenas of approved activity for ladies, according to the conduct books, are household management and charity; both of these, significantly, involve supervision. Conduct books are adamant about a lady's duty to attend closely to the running of her household and the welfare and good behavior of her servants. Ladies who are mistresses of households must be always watching, inspecting, overseeing. The importance of a lady's all-seeing eye is made clear by the language of the conduct books. Running a household always requires "an attentive observation";[76] "it is incumbent on [ladies] to inspect the whole" establishment.[77] A mistress of servants "ought in some sense to perform the part of a vigilant observer";[78] she must "overlook" her servants and "be ever watchful over their conduct."[79] Although, as we saw in the previous chapter, conduct books for servants admonish them to avoid "eye-service" and warn them that the Lord is always watching, even when the mistress is not, the conduct books for ladies seem to urge them to take the role of the all-seeing God. In *Desire and Domestic Fiction*, Nancy Armstrong traces the rise of the domestic woman in the eighteenth century and argues that her main duties were supervisory: although her duties "appeared to be active," in reality the main duty of the new housewife was to "supervise the servants who were the ones to take care of these matters."[80] Further on, Armstrong points out that the passive, nondesiring woman described by the conduct books "fulfills her role by disappearing into the woodwork"—becoming a cipher, a blank—"to watch over the household."[81] She adds that this woman's supervision "constituted a form of value in its own right and was therefore capable of enhancing the value of other people and things"[82]—again, I would add, like a cipher, a zero added to other figures.

In her supervisory capacity, a good woman could exercise a less passive form of power, especially when it came to the charitable activities she was constantly urged to engage in. "Charity is the calling of a lady; the care of the poor is her profession," as Hannah More said,[83] and, frequently, "inspection" could be substituted for "care." Wakefield, like many writers, tells ladies that it is important for them to supervise the poor, and not merely to give them alms: "the inspection of workhouses, schools of industry, and cottages, not merely once or twice in a twelvemonth, but so frequently as to become acquainted with the wants and condition of the inhabitants, would enable women of the higher classes to do much good, and to correct many abuses."[84] Since, as we saw in the previous chapter, comfortable-class ideology dictated that only the "deserving" poor should be aided, ladies were encouraged to investigate the objects of charity around them and ascertain which ones were industrious, sick, or old enough to merit assistance.[85] Charity work gave ladies something active they could legitimately *do*; Mary Poovey argues that "in one sense women might be considered the primary beneficiaries of the reform movement, for such work gave both married and unmarried women a constructive vehicle for their talents and, in return, a heightened sense of their ability and self-worth."[86] One has only to picture the supremely ladylike More sisters, posting all over the hills of Cheddar to set up and inspect their schools, to know what an important opportunity for activity and the exercise of power charity work could be.[87]

III

These activities, then—devotions, child rearing, possibly "improvement," household supervision, and charity work—are the ones in which the conduct books agree ladies should be engaging. The books are equally unanimous about what it is ladies should *not* be doing. With the exception of novel-reading, the disapproved female pastimes all include an element of self-display, a need to enter the public realm and be seen there. If the commended activities for ladies tend to involve their over-seeing others, the frowned-upon ones tend to involve their *being* seen.[88] Excessive desire for public diversions is read as a sign of a defective interiority, a lack of sufficient inner depth.

Clara Reeve provides a quick list of disapprobated activities for la-dies in her discussion of bad mothers who are unfit to educate their children themselves[89]: "In truth, if all mothers fulfilled their duties, there would be little occasion for boarding-schools; but if they give up their time and attention to dress, to visiting, to cards, and to public places; it is better that the children should go to school, than that they should converse with the servants, or play in the streets."[90] A letter in *The Lady's Museum* supplies a similar list, saying that the business of "that gay part of my own sex so improperly called fine ladies" is "to dress, to play at cards, to simper in the drawing-room, to languish at an opera, and coquet at a play."[91] Lady Pennington vividly describes the overconcern with dress of "that insignificant set of females, whose whole life . . . is but a varied scene of trifling": they "pass whole morn-ings at their looking-glass, in the important business of suiting a set of ribbands, adjusting a few curls, or determining the position of a patch."[92]

The fashionable world is often presented in conduct books as a scene of hurry and insignificance, its female denizens as wasting their lives in vain trifles: "Gay, elegant, and accomplished, but thoughtless, im-mersed in trifles, and hurrying with impatience, never satisfied, from one scene of diversion to another; how many women are seen floating down the stream of life, like bubbles on which the sun paints a thousand gaudy colours; and like bubbles vanishing, . . . and leaving no trace of usefulness behind!"[93] The diversions and dissipations of public amuse-ments are represented as addictive,[94] even when their pleasures have faded. As Gisborne describes it, "The delights of novelty are past; but the chains of fashion and habit are rivetted."[95] West also depicts the social whirl as enchaining: "Languid and spiritless, the fine lady sets out upon her nightly round, more reluctant than the watchman does on his monotonous task. . . . Observe, *inclination* and *pleasure* are never as-signed as the motives" for her actions; "*compulsion* and *necessity* supply the impetus for motion."[96] Participating in the fashionable whirl signals, again, a defective interiority, an unwillingness to be alone with oneself. Wollstonecraft says that the "pale-faced creatures" filling the "numer-ous carriages that drive helter-skelter about this metropolis in a morn-ing" are "flying from themselves."[97] Gisborne argues that ladies engaging in dissipation find in it "if not a positive satisfaction, yet a re-lief from the dulness of vacancy, and the painfulness of intercourse with [her]self."[98]

Cards come in for particular censure and satire. A letter in *The Lady's Museum* contends that, "in this polite age," ladies consider love, marriage, virtue, wisdom, morality, and wisdom to be trifles: "there is nothing serious but cards"; "tho' there are many other serious affairs, such as balls, operas, concerts, masquerades, and the like, which must claim the attention of persons of rank and fortune, yet all these must yield to cards."[99] A passion for play, like participation in the fashionable world, evinces a lack of inner resources, an interior vacancy which must be filled; as Wollstonecraft says in *Thoughts on the Education of Daughters*, "Cards are the universal refuge to which the idle and the ignorant resort, to pass life away, and to keep their inactive souls awake. . . ."[100] Gisborne considers time spent playing cards "a mere blank; it is cut, as it were, out of life, and consigned . . . to vacuity and oblivion,"[101] but asks "what resource, what possible occupation remains, except cards" for ladies subjected to a stay in the country? "To the unfurnished mind," he concludes, "none."[102]

Novel-reading, even more than card-playing, is a subject of special disapproval by many conduct books. Novels are suspect because they are "at once the *offspring* and the *food* of idleness,"[103] and because "with the increase of a passion for reading novels, an aversion to reading of a more improving nature will gather strength."[104] Most of all, though, the conduct books fear that novels will arouse romantic fantasies and sexual desires: "they are apt to give a romantic turn to the mind, which is often productive of great errors in judgment, and of fatal mistakes in conduct";[105] they "nourish a vain and visionary indolence, which lays the mind open to error and the heart to seduction";[106] they "tend to inflame the passions of youth."[107] Ruth Perry argues in *Women, Letters, and the Novel* that eighteenth-century novels "in their very form . . . carried the cultural message that women's lives were to be spent in idleness, daydreams, and romance";[108] this message was clearly objected to by the conduct books.

The acquisition and enjoyment of "accomplishments" was in some ways the quintessential ladylike way of spending time and seems an answer to the problem of interiority and inner depth; accomplishments often were, after all, a large part of a lady's "resources."[109] Some conduct books regard them with ambivalence, however, because of their connection to display. Writers worry that ladies want to be accomplished in order to be admired, and the desire for admiration is always a cause for concern. Jane West asserts that girls endure "the bodily fatigue, and . . . exercise of patience and attention" required to acquire accomplishments largely "in order to attract the attention of their fellow-creatures."[110] Priscilla Wakefield complains that women spend their best years attaining "shewy superficial accomplishments, polished

manners, and in one word, the whole science of pleasing."[111] Hannah
More, especially, tends to view accomplishments with suspicion, saying
that because of society's emphasis on them, "the life of a young lady . . .
now too much resembles that of an actress; the morning is all rehearsal,
and the evening is all performance."[112] Ladies proud of their accomplishments, again like actresses, tend to crave the limelight: "Talents
which have *display* for their object despise the narrow stage of home:
they demand mankind for their spectators, and the world for their theatre."[113] This comparison between accomplished ladies and actresses
hints at sexual trangression; even more explicitly sexual is her statement
that "in all polished countries an entire devotedness to the fine arts has
been one grand source of the corruption of women," and that among
the ancient Greeks, the women skilled in the fine arts were the courte-
sans.[114]

Display of other sorts is always, in the conduct books, the subject of
censure. The ballroom, of course, as "the stage for displaying the attractions, by the possesssion of which a young woman is apt to be most
elated,"[115] is suspect, but so apparently innocuous an activity as letter-
writing can be problematic also, if ladies let "the desire of shining" draw
them and they become too "ambitious to be distinguished for writing,
as the phrase is, *good* letters."[116] Even the mental improvements urged
upon ladies should not, some authors emphasize, be displayed. Hannah
More, for instance, says that a lady "is to read the best books, not so
much to enable her to talk of them, as to bring the improvement she
derives from them to the rectification of her principles . . . ,"[117] Gisborne
that she should commit to memory "select and ample portions of poetic
compositions, not for the purpose of ostentatiously quoting them in
mixed company, but for the sake of private improvement. . . ."[118]

Other sorts of female speech besides learned quotations are, for many
writers,[119] also problematic. "Silence is the ornament of your sex; and
in silence, if there be not wisdom, there is safety,"[120] writes Maria Edgeworth in "An Essay on the Noble Science of Self-Justification" (1795),
a sentiment echoed by others. The *Treatise on the Education of Daughters*
excerpted in *The Lady's Museum* proclaims, "A young lady should not
talk but as occasion requires, and then with an air of doubt and defer-
ence; nay, as to subjects out of the reach of women in general, she
should not speak upon them at all, though well informed."[121] John
Gregory was an especial proponent of female silence, saying that "modesty, which I think so essential in your sex, will naturally dispose you
to be rather silent in company."[122] Female wit seems especially to alarm
some of the male conduct-book authors: Gregory calls wit "the most
dangerous talent [she] can possess,"[123] and Wetenhall Wilkes, in his *Let-*

ter of Genteel and Moral Advice to a Young Lady (1740), says that "[wit] is the most dangerous companion that can lurk in a female bosom."[124]

Another aspect of female display which seems to concern some male writers is that, if ladies indulge their appetite for self-display, they will soon surfeit the public's appetite for them. The Marquess of Halifax describes fine ladies who "are engaged in a Circle of *Idleness*, where they turn round for the whole Year, without the *Interruption* of a serious Hour." "The Streets," he says, are "so weary of these daily Faces, that *Men's Eyes* are over-laid with them. The *Sight* is glutted with fine things, as the *Stomach* with sweet ones; and when a fair *Lady* will give too much of her self to the World, she groweth luscious, and oppresseth instead of pleasing."[125] John Gregory advises his daughters to avoid "being always in our eye at public places," as this excessive showing of themselves will dispel "the pleasing illusion" and "soon reduce the angel to a very ordinary girl."[126] (This concern with "glutting" the male appetite resembles Gregory's warning that if a married woman reveals too freely her love for her husband, she risks his feeling "satiety and disgust.") Ladies, it would appear, should be neither much heard nor much seen.[127]

This almost-inaudible, almost-invisible proper lady was a cipher in two senses: she was both a blank and, because she said so little, a puzzle. She was desirable, in some sense, *because* she required deciphering: her essence lay below her surface; she possessed depth. This sense that desirable ladies located their value beneath the surface is one reason, I would argue, for the horror with which many in the eighteenth century viewed the lady who had to work for money. The working-class woman was valued (to the extent she was valued at all) for what she did with her body, for how much labor she could perform. The gentlewoman who worked for pay, therefore, not only defied the ideology that proclaimed ladies the representatives of leisure; she was also the site of a clash between systems of value. Perhaps this clash accounts at least in part for the frequent linking of employed ladies and prostitution. Although this linking is logical in one way, since female workers were often paid so little (or found it so difficult to find work) that they were forced to resort to prostitution,[128] the connection seems ideologically surprising, given the connection also made between prostitution and female *idleness*. Writers frequently worried that daughters of the upstart classes would be led by their status-gaining idleness into prostitution, and the idleness of even established ladies was often linked to sexual transgression and even prostitution; and yet the lady who was forced to take money for her work was also sexually suspect. As Wollstonecraft complains in her *Vindication*, "an attempt to earn their own subsistence, a most laudable one! sink[s women] almost to the level of those poor abandoned creatures who live by prostitution. For are not milliners and mantua-makers reckoned the next class?"[129] Mary Ann Radcliffe describes the loss of reputation involved in earning a living in terms that make the sexual danger of the situation apparent, saying that the distressed gentlewoman is persecuted by "the shrill voice of censure, or the destructive whisper of calumny," which breathes "such a poisonous vapor over her character" that "she is despised by all," and "irremediably doomed to sink, never more to rise: for who will admit a woman of lost reputation into their house?"[130] This connecting of ladies' paid work with prostitution seems to me to complicate Nancy Armstrong's discussion in *Desire and Domestic Fiction* of the power middle-class women derived from their control of the domestic realm. While clearly their role as supervisors of the home and inspectors of the poor gave ladies a measure of power (as I discussed earlier), I would also argue that this control of the domestic world was countered by the increasing exclusion of ladies from the public world of work. If entering the public realm as a worker was viewed in some measure as similar to walking the public streets as a whore—which Armstrong herself concedes ("the figure of the prostitute could be freely invoked to describe any woman who dared to labor for money"[131])—surely a lady's power in the world was sharply limited.

A lady without fortune had to contend, then, with the threat that she would lose her reputation, her most important possession. Such unlucky ladies also usually suffered the lowering of another important attribute, class status. As Priscilla Wakefield says, the prejudice "against a woman, of any degree above the vulgar, employing her time and her abilities, towards the maintenance of herself and her family" rose "like an insurmountable barrier"; "degradation of rank immediately follow[ed] the virtuous attempt."[132] She also notes that men are reluctant to marry women who have so humbled themselves: "One of the effects of this ill-directed pride, is to deter young men of liberal prospects, from demeaning themselves, as it is erroneously termed, by marrying a girl who has been trained up to any profitable employment."[133] Thus a third important female possession, a husband, is threatened by a lady's paid employment. Mary Lamb also remarks upon this loss of marriageability entailed upon a working lady, saying that a young lady cannot earn a profit from a trade "but at the expence of losing that place in society, to the possession of which she may reasonably look forward, inasmuch as it is by far the most *common lot*, namely, the condition of a *happy* English wife."[134]

As if these potential losses were not enough, the impoverished gentlewoman had the difficulty of even finding employment in the first place. Trades traditionally practiced by women were, over the course of the century, increasingly becoming dominated by men. (The cultural insistence that ladies should not work seems both to have reinforced, and to have been reinforced by, this usurpation.) Many commented on this problem; Clara Reeve, for instance, says, "There are very few trades for women; the men have usurped two-thirds of those that used to belong to them; the remainder are over-stocked, and there are few resources for them."[135] Thomas Gisborne does not complain about the male appropriation of female employments, but he does urge his readers to be "mindful of the scarcity of modes of employment in which persons of the female sex can properly engage for a subsistence."[136] These few forms of employment, along with their disadvantages, are neatly listed in Wollstonecraft's *Thoughts on the Education of Daughters*. "Few are the modes of earning a subsistence, and those very humiliating,"[137] she begins. "Perhaps to be the humble companion to some rich old cousin, or what is still worse, to live with strangers, who are so intolerably tyrannical, that none of their own relations can bear to live with them, though they should even expect a fortune in reversion." This vocation causes countless "hours of anguish"; the humble companion is "above the servants, and yet always considered by them as a spy, and ever reminded of her inferiority when in conversation with the superiors." The next option is to be a teacher at school, but she is "only a kind of upper servant, who has more work than the menial ones." The third option, being "a governess to young ladies," is "equally disagreeable." She is unlikely to "meet with a reasonable mother," and "the children treat her with disrespect, and often with insolence." The only other options, "the few trades that are left," are, Wollstonecraft concludes, "now gradually falling into the hands of the men, and certainly they are not very respectable."[138] A further difficulty for ladies seeking remunerative employment is that, as Radcliffe explains, many employers "want no gentlewomen, or gentlewomen's daughters."[139] Ladies lacking fortunes were thus beset on all sides: the prohibition against gentlewomen's gainful work was rigorously enforced.

IV

Several eighteenth-century novels focus on this plight of the impoverished gentlewoman, and, more generally, on the whole cultural project of deciphering ladies. In two of the novels I will examine, Mary Brunton's *Discipline* (1814) and Jane Austen's *Emma* (1816), young ladies are set the task of learning the proper use of their time; in the other novels I will look at, Samuel Richardson's *Pamela* (1740), Sarah Scott's *A Description of Millenium Hall* (1762), Hannah More's *Coelebs in Search of a Wife* (1809), and Frances Burney's *The Wanderer* (1814), the true essences of various young ladies are deciphered through examining their use of time. The good, desirable lady, these novels tell us, has no need for frivolous, public amusements; her "resources" keep her content within her own interiority.

The heroines in Brunton's little-known *Discipline* and Austen's famous *Emma* are similar in some respects.[140] Both are beautiful, well-born, somewhat spoiled, and rich; both have dead, virtuous mothers and living, faulty fathers, though faulty in very different ways. Emma's father, Mr. Woodhouse, is a sweet, nervous, unworldly valetudinarian, while Ellen's father, Mr. Percy, is excessively worldly, obsessed with money, and, ultimately, deeply irresponsible: after losing his fortune, he kills himself, leaving his daughter penniless. Both Emma and Ellen have female mother-substitutes, though Ellen's friend Miss Mortimer is more committed to Ellen's moral and spiritual reclamation, while Mrs. Weston, Emma's governess, has a mild temperament that had "hardly allowed her to impose any restraint"[141] upon her charge. Both heroines also have worthy, responsible, older men in their lives—for Ellen, Mr. Mortimer, for Emma, Mr. Knightley—who see the heroines' flaws but nevertheless love them, and who, when the women have matured and seen the error of their ways, marry them. The novels are different in scope, though. Ellen moves from a splendid and fashionable home in London to a thatched cottage in a quiet English village, to a governess's rooms in Edinburgh, to a madhouse, to the slums of Edinburgh, to the castle of a Highland chieftain. Emma never strays farther from her native village of Highbury than the nearby beauty spot Box Hill. The issue of female idleness with which the novels concern themselves is, therefore, fairly subtle in *Emma* and, as its title might indicate, quite overt in *Discipline*.

On the fifth page of *Discipline*, Ellen, its narrator, indicates the story's concern with idleness. She recounts that during her childhood her father had said of her, "no fear of her happiness. Won't she have two hundred thousand pounds, and never know the trouble of earning it, nor need to do one thing from morning to night but amuse herself?" Ellen adds, "by this and similar conversations, a most just and desirable connection was formed in my mind between the ideas of amusement and happiness, of labour and misery."[142] She is sent to a fashionable school where, as she puts it, "at the end of seven years of laborious and expensive trifling, the only accomplishment, perhaps, in which I had attained real proficiency, was music" (81). Having musical abilities "equal to any which the public may command for hire" might be an attribute most fashionable ladies would envy, but Ellen is quick to point out that she is spurred to attain this degree of excellence only by envious emulation of a schoolmate, and that the accomplishment is not worth the time spent on it:

> This acquisition (I blush whilst I write it) cost me the labour of seven hours a day!—full half the time which, after deducting the seasons of rest and refreshment, remained for all the duties of a rational, a social, an immortal being! Wise Providence! was it to be squandered thus, that leisure was bestowed upon a happy few!—leisure, the privilege of Eden! for which fallen man must so often sigh and toil in vain! (82)

Spending seven hours a day on one's music does not sound like idleness, but the converted Ellen knows it is indeed a misspending of time.

Emma, on the other hand, reveals *her* idleness by *failing* to spend this sort of time on her music or her painting. She has a natural talent for both, but lacks the self-discipline to become excellent at either, despite her desire to be so: she "had made more progress, both in drawing and music, than many might have done with so little labor as she would ever submit to. She played and sang—and drew in almost every style; but steadiness had always been wanting; and in nothing had she approached the degree of excellence which she would have been glad to command and ought not to have failed of." Emma's motivation for excellence at her accomplishments is also suspect: "She was not much deceived as to her own skill either as an artist or a musician, but she was not unwilling to have others deceived, or sorry to know her reputation for accomplishment often higher than it deserved" (38). She is, in other words, at least as interested in display as in achievement.

Neither heroine engages much in the activities the conduct books consider virtuous. Since both Ellen and Emma are single and childless, they cannot spend their time educating and tending their children; and although both, as motherless mistresses of their fathers' homes, could spend time in domestic supervision, neither is shown doing very much of this (although Emma at least appears to order the meals and does attend more directly to her father's comfort). Neither woman employs much of her time in "improvement." Emma fails to follow through on the plans she is always making for intellectual growth; the only book we see her actually reading in the course of the novel is the undemanding *Elegant Extracts*.[143] As Mr. Knightley says about her, when Mrs. Weston tells him Emma "means" to read more,

> Emma has been meaning to read more ever since she was twelve years old. I have seen a great many lists of her drawing up at various times of books that she meant to read regularly through—and very good lists they were— very well chosen and very neatly arranged—sometimes alphabetically and sometimes by some other rule. . . . But I have done with expecting any

course of steady reading from Emma. She will never submit to anything
requiring industry and patience and a subjection of the fancy to the under-
standing. (32)

Ellen does not learn until after she has lost her fortune and her place in
society that "the prospect of exhibition is not necessary to the interest
of study" (281) and that time spent in "serious study, reading and often
writing abstracts of what I read,—left no portion of my time for weariness" (273). Austen is fairly quiet on the subject of Emma's devotions,
though the guilty self-examination in which Emma engages only after
her errors are dramatically pointed out to her might indicate that she
falls short in this area, also; the more evangelical Brunton makes clear
that Ellen is guilty of a sinful neglect of her soul. Though at one point
she resolves she will "no longer be an unprofitable servant" (191), she
does not truly take her religious duties seriously until she loses her
money.

Both heroines also fail to fulfill their charitable duties. Ellen's friend
Miss Mortimer points out to her "how your mother's mornings were
spent"—that is, in aiding and instructing the poor inhabitants of the
neighborhood. Ellen, however, despite her tenderness for her mother's
memory, knows her worldly friends would ridicule "the absurdity of a
handsome woman of fashion spending her time teaching cottage girls
mantua-making and morality" and refuses to follow her mother's example: "Ah! my mother was an angel; I must not pretend to resemble her"
(93). Even when Ellen does make an offer of charity, it is, significantly,
the wrong sort. As the conduct books say, merely to give money to the
poor, without animating their industry and supervising their morality,
is not truly to be a virtuous lady. Ellen has offered to give fifty pounds
to a poor girl but refuses the request that would make the girl self-sup-
porting: to wear a dress she has made and thus help her acquire more
customers. "I could part with fifty pounds without inconvenience," she
says, "but to wear a gown not made by Mrs. Beetham, was a humilia-
tion to which I could not possibly submit." Miss Mortimer, who practices the approved brand of charity, "exerted her influence so
successfully, as to procure employment for every hour of the girl's
time," while Ellen's "profuse offer passed from [her] mind, and was forgotten" (128).

Emma visits the poor only once in her novel, and her serious reflections about them are soon driven from her mind by thoughts of match-
making. Her most conspicuous failure to perform a lady's duty is in her
behavior to the Bateses and Jane Fairfax. Thomas Gisborne, like other
authors of conduct books, tells his readers to "examine into the wants
and distresses of the female inhabitants of the neighbourhood,"[144] and

Mrs. and Miss Bates have many wants and distresses. Although their happy temperaments would not indicate how badly off they are, they live "in a very small way" (17), and Miss Bates has to devote her life to "the care of a failing mother and the endeavour to make a small income go as far as possible" (18). That their neighbors send them frequent gifts of food perhaps hints at how close to real destitution they are. Although Emma does send them a hindquarter of pork at one point, the narrator tells us that "she was considered by the very few who presumed ever to see imperfection in her as rather negligent [in visiting them], and as not contributing what she ought to the stock of their scanty comforts" (137). When Miss Bates's niece Jane Fairfax, who has been reared by a wealthy family but is herself poor and doomed to become a governess, comes to stay with the Bateses, Emma has another opportunity, which again she refuses, to aid a woman in bad circumstances. Jane and Emma are the same age; they are intellectual equals; they have known each other since childhood—everyone expects them to be friends, and if they were, Emma would be able to offer many small comforts to Jane. Partly because Emma dislikes Jane's reserve, partly because Emma is envious that, as Mr. Knightley points out, Jane is "the really accomplished young woman which she wanted to be thought herself" (148), Emma never tries to become Jane's friend. Jane is never invited to leave the two cramped rooms she shares with her grandmother and logorrheic though lovable aunt to enjoy a visit in the spacious, quiet, warm rooms of Hartfield. Emma's eventual overtures of friendship to Jane come too late.

Neither Ellen nor Emma, then, spends her time in recommended ways. Ellen, after she leaves school and comes out into fashionable society, plunges into worldly dissipations. "My whole course of life," she says, "was aptly described in a short dialogue with Mr. Maitland. 'Miss Percy,' said he, 'I hope you are not the worse for the fatigues of last night.'-'Not in the least, sir.'-'Well, then, are you any thing the better for them? Do you look back on your amusements with pleasure?'-'No, I must confess, I do not. Besides, I have not leisure to look back, I am so busily looking forward to this evening's opera'"(103). The sketch of Ellen's way of life at this time resembles the descriptions of decadent, idle high life in the conduct books: "I had entered the throng who were in the chase of pleasure, and I was not formed for a languid pursuit. It became the employment of every day, every hour. My mornings were spent at auctions, exhibitions, and milliners' shops; my evenings wherever fashionable folly held her court." Brunton, again like the conduct-book authors, figures the fashionable whirl as an addictive drug: "Miss Mortimer attempted gently to stem the torrent. She endeavoured to remove my temptation to seek amusement abroad by providing it for me at home; but I had drunk of the inebriating cup, and the temperate draught was become tasteless to me" (103).

Two of Ellen's friends at this time could be models for the sort of lady the conduct books deplore. Juliet Arnold, a friend Ellen makes at school, is all empty display; she lacks any sort of valuable depth. "She was," Ellen says, "educated to be married," which does not mean she was "practised in the domestic, the economical, the submissive virtues; that she was skilled in excusing frailty, enlivening solitude, or scattering sunshine upon the passing clouds of life!" Rather, Juliet has been taught "accomplishments which were deemed likely to attract notice and admiration; . . . she knew what to withdraw from the view, and what to prepare for exhibition. . . ." (79–80). Lady St. Edmunds, a wealthy older lady Ellen meets in London, is a deeply bad woman who is conspiring with the wicked Lord Frederick's plan to seduce Ellen. Lady St. Edmunds lures Ellen into her lair, a seductive "boudoir to which only her most select associates were admitted." This room is the embodiment of luxurious, decadent idleness, a place from which all signs of productive or improving work are banished:

> Nothing which taste could approve was wanting to its decoration, — nothing which sense desires could be added to its luxury. The walls glowed with the sultry scenes of Claude, and the luxuriant designs of Titian. The daylight stole mellowed on the eye through a bower of flowering orange trees and myrtles; or alabaster lamps imitated the softness of moonshine. Airy Grecian couches lent grace to the forms which rested on them; and rose-coloured draperies shed on the cheek a becoming bloom. No cumbrous foot-men were permitted to invade this retreat of luxury. Their office was here supplied by a fairy-footed smiling girl, whose figure and attire partook of the elegance of all around. Had books been needful to kill the time, here were abundance well suited to their place; not works of puzzling science or dull morality; but modern plays, novels enriched with slanderous tales or caricatures of living characters, and fashionable sonnets, guarded to the ear of decency, but deadly to her spirit. (222–23)

This "temple of effeminacy" (223) shows how easily the softness and leisure that are associated with woman can slide into reprehensible, sexually corrupting indolence.

Emma's idleness, unlike that of Ellen, Juliet, and Lady St. Edmunds, does not lead to a vortex of fashionable dissipations—no such dissipations are available to her. Emma leads, despite her privilege, an extremely constricted life; she has never seen the sea (91), and we never see her go to London, only sixteen miles away from Highbury, though many of the other characters go there. Frank Churchill, Mr. Weston's son who has been brought up by rich relatives, can travel from Highbury to London and back again just to have his hair cut (and secretly purchase a pianoforte for Jane Fairfax), but Emma has no such freedom. Frank, the only man in *Emma* besides Mr. Woodhouse who has no profession, may be, as Mr. Knightley claims, an idle young man, but he is free to seek his "mere idle pleasure" (134) more or less where he likes. He says, at one point, that he is "tired of doing nothing" (330), but his "nothing" does not begin to compare to Emma's. Emma will not occupy herself with the activities approved by the conduct books, and she is not able to spend her time in the disapproved fashionable frivolity. She believes, as she tells her little friend Harriet Smith, that she possesses "a great many independent resources" (78), but this boast is no more true than the similar one made by the vulgar parvenu Mrs. Elton, who is constantly claiming that her "resources" render society unnecessary to her: "I always say that a woman cannot have too many resources—and I feel very thankful that I have so many myself as to be quite independent of society" (277). Although Mrs. Elton says that "blessed with so many resources within myself, the world [is] not necessary to *me*" (248), she is constantly seeking society and uses her newly married state as an excuse for neglecting the music she "absolutely cannot do without" (248); Emma, similarly, is fooling herself about the sufficiency of her resources to employ and entertain her. What Emma *does* occupy herself with resembles another activity the conduct books censure: novel-reading.

As we have seen, novels are considered by many conduct-book authors to be "at once the *offspring* and the *food* of idleness," and to turn young ladies' minds overmuch toward romantic love. Though Emma does not literally read or write novels during *Emma*, she does read the lives of those around her as if they were novels, inventing aristocratic parents and a splendid marriage for Harriet Smith, an adulterous passion for Jane Fairfax, and, later, a marriage tragically beneath him for Mr. Knightley, as well writing herself and Frank Churchill into a bittersweet love story.[145] Her busy and creative imagination is what really occupies Emma; the plans and schemes, plots and scandals her fancy invents form her true employment. Emma is an "imagist," always "on fire with speculation and forethought" (302), whose fancy, "that very dear part of [her]" (192), affords her pleasure and occupation. And of course her imagination, as the rather erotic sound of those phrases might hint, is most often turned toward romance; as Mr. Knightley rebukes her, when she is taking credit for having brought about the marriage between the former Miss Taylor and Mr. Weston: "Success supposes endeavour. Your time has been properly and delicately spent, if you have been endeavouring for the last four years to bring about this marriage. A worthy employment for a young lady's mind!" (10)

Emma's and Ellen's misspending of their time leads, naturally, to bad results. Emma's attempt to make a match between Harriet and Mr. Elton hurts Harriet, since Harriet obediently falls in love with Mr. Elton but he inconveniently wants to do better for himself and proposes to Emma. Then Emma allows her thoughtless wit (something else the conduct books censure) to wound Miss Bates, thus inviting a sharp reprimand from Mr. Knightley, with whom Emma then realizes she has been in love all along. Ellen, more seriously, finds when she is reduced to penury that her idle and dissipated former life has rendered her unfit for the new, more sober life she now needs and wants to lead. Although she has had a spiritual revelation and realized that because her "talent" has been "buried in the earth" she is in danger of "that more awful sentence which consigns the unprofitable servant to 'outer darkness'" (263), she finds that "the activity of my mind had hitherto been so unhappily directed, that it now revolted from every impulse, except such as was either pleasurable or of overwhelming force." She is trying to lead the life of a truly virtuous lady, but she becomes "sensible of a vacancy,—a wearisome craving for an undefined something to rouse and interest me" (265), which makes it more difficult for her to live as she should. Also, Ellen must now begin to contribute to her own living, which her former idleness makes both shameful and difficult. While she is living with Miss Mortimer, Ellen begins the "manufacture of a variety of ingenious trifles," but she is "ashamed of openly contributing to [her] own subsistence"—her work is "always privately done, and privately disposed of" (272–73), and, since she is "habituated to confound the needful with the desirable" (287), and unused to hard work, she cannot fully support herself. When Miss Mortimer dies and Ellen is thrown entirely on her own resources, her sufferings are intense. Brunton is interested in the plight of the impoverished gentlewoman and shows us how few channels "the customs of society [had] left open to the industry of woman" (295) and how difficult and painful it was to survive by means of these few channels.

Ellen first tries to become a governess, because, although she feels her "thorough knowledge of music, and [her] acquaintance with other arts of idleness" fits her for only "a small part of the education of a rational and accountable being," she seems to have no other alternative (295). Attempting to gain a post as a governess, Ellen meets another bad, idle lady, Mrs. Boswell. Mrs. Boswell, the servants tell Ellen, does not arise until one o'clock. When Ellen goes to see her at that hour she is shown into a breakfast parlor where, "upon a fashionable couch, half sat, half lay, Mrs. Boswell" (342), engaged in bedizening herself from a box of trinkets. Mrs. Boswell hires Ellen but then becomes jealous of her, eventually causing her to be confined in a madhouse and, perhaps more realistically, refusing to give her the money she has earned.[146] Ellen has the same troubles in her next line of endeavor, the making of more "ingenious trifles." The shopman who purchases them from her is rude and unfeeling,[147] and he suddenly and arbitrarily lowers the price he is willing to give for them, plunging Ellen into even greater distress:

> I was thunderstruck at this disaster. My earnings were already barely adequate to our wants, therefore, to reduce my wretched gains, was to incur at once all the real miseries of poverty. After my former experience in the difficulty of procuring employment, the loss of my present one seemed the sentence of ruin; and I, who should once have felt intolerable hardship in one day of labour, could now forsee no greater misfortune than idleness. (415)

Austen, of course, does not directly show these difficulties of the lady who has to earn her way; her novel is smaller in scope and lighter in tone. She is clearly aware of them, though. Teaching, the only career apparently open to ladies in the novel—Mrs. Goddard, Miss Nash, Mrs. Weston, and Jane Fairfax are all current, former, or potential members of this profession—is clearly a job which endangers a lady's class position. Mrs. Goddard, the mistress of a school, visits the Woodhouses, but she is not on an equal footing with them; Miss Nash, a teacher at Mrs. Goddard's school, occupies an even more marginal position, as the information that she thinks her sister "very well married, and it is only a linen-draper" (49) reveals.[148] Mrs. Weston, Emma's former governess, has been lucky in having been a beloved member of the Woodhouse's household and in being now well married, but the delicacy with which her friends refer to her former position, and Mr. Knightley's remark that she is not a person of worldly consequence (134), indicate uneasiness about her class status. The greatest indication, though, of the difficulties inherent in a lady's having a profession is seen in the presentation of Jane Fairfax's plan to become a governess. Her adoptive family, the Campbells, have educated her to educate others, but they and she have been postponing her departure: "The evil day was put off" (146). The narrator calls this delay "a taste of such enjoyments of ease and leisure as must now be relinquished," and refers to Jane's career as a "sacrifice" that will cause a retirement from "all the pleasures of life, of rational intercourse, equal society, peace and hope, to penance and mortification for ever"(147)—strong words. Jane anticipates her fate with horror, comparing the "governess-trade," the sale of human intellect, to the slave trade, the sale of human flesh: "widely different certainly as to the guilt of those who carry it on; but as to the greater misery of the victims, I do not know where it lies" (271). The reader is grateful for her rescue from this fate by marriage to Frank Churchill.

Ellen, also, is eventually rescued by marriage, but not before she has made her way through chapter after chapter of difficulty and has learned the right way to employ her time. As she says in the penultimate chapter of the novel (in a sentence of fine eighteenth-century length),

> almost the earliest work of my renovated judgment had been to impress me with a solemn conviction of the value of time; and when I recollected that, of the few alloted years of man, seventeen had already been worse than squandered; that of the uncertain remainder, a third must be devoted to the mere support of animal existence, —a part given to the harmless enjoyments, a part rifled by the idle fooleries of others, —an unknown portion laid waste of joy and usefulness, by sickness, by sorrow, or by that overpowering languor which palsies at times even the most active spirit;—when I remembered, that the whole is fugitive in its nature as the colours of the morning sky, irreversible in its consequences as the fixed decree of Heaven, I could no longer waste the treasure on the sports of children, or suffer the jewel to slip from the nerveless grasp of an idiot.

Ellen goes on to explain that she has "formed a plan for the distribution of [her] time" to which she faithfully adheres, and that she therefore seldom spends "an hour altogether unprofitably" (456). She now deserves to live happily ever after, and she does, marrying the remarkable Mr. Maitland, who has turned out to be chieftain of a Highland clan, and becoming "the mother of three hardy, generous boys, and two pretty, affectionate little girls" (476). *Discipline* ends with these words attesting to the profound importance of a correct use of time: "Having in my early days seized the enjoyments which selfish pleasure can bestow, I might now compare them with those of enlarged affections, of useful employment, of relaxations truly social, of lofty contemplation, of devout thankfulness, of glorious hope. I might compare them!—but the Lowland tongue wants energy for the contrast" (476).

Emma also gets a happy ending, although her reformation is neither so hard-won nor, perhaps, so convincing as Ellen's. Emma never loses her money or her position in society, but the shame and self-reproach she does endure prompts her to reflect that the outing to Box Hill (where she flirted with Frank Churchill and insulted Miss Bates) was "a morning more completely misspent, more totally bare of rational satisfaction at the time, and more to be abhorred in recollection, than any she had ever passed" and to call the next morning on the Bateses and Jane Fairfax, as the "beginning, on her side, of a regular, equal, kindly intercourse" (341). When she finds out that Harriet has fallen in love with Mr. Knightley and mistakenly believes that this love is requited, she realizes "that it had all been her own work" (383)—the work of her idle imagination in encouraging Harriet to aspire above herself and of her own lack of "resources" in having needed to look to Harriet for friendship in the first place—and forms resolutions "of her own better conduct, and the hope that, however inferior in spirit and gaiety might be the following and every future winter of her life to the past, it would yet find her more rational, more acquainted with herself, and leave her less to regret when it were gone" (384). Significantly, it is shortly after this epiphany and resolution that Mr. Knightley proposes to Emma. Now that this "sweetest and best of all creatures, faultless in spite of all her faults" (393) has at least resolved to employ her mind and time better, she can be rewarded with a marriage which, the narrator tells us at the end of the novel, is one of "perfect happiness" (440).

V

The other four novels I want to discuss here, *Pamela, A Description of Millenium Hall, Coelebs in Search of a Wife,* and *The Wanderer,* do not have as heroines ladies who need to learn not to be idle. Rather, they feature already virtuous ladies whose worth is gradually revealed to the other characters (generally male ones). The valuable essence of these women is deciphered (not, it is important, displayed) by an observation of how they use their time. These women employ their time in the approved ways and truly possess what Mrs. Elton only pretends to have: a rich interiority that renders them independent of idle pastimes.

Although Pamela is confined during much of the course of Richardson's novel and has little to do other than write long journal-letters and attempt to evade the improper advances of her salacious employer, Mr. B., she also clearly understands the value of time. After her impenetrable virtue has finally convinced Mr. B. to make her an honorable offer of marriage, he wonders how she will fill her days since, because of her status as a former servant, she is likely to be shunned by polite society. He asks, "But how will you bestow your *time*, when you will have no visits to receive or pay? No parties of pleasure to join in? No card-tables to employ your winter evenings; and even, as the taste is, half the day, summer and winter?" Pamela instantly responds with a two-page speech listing, in terms right out of a conduct book, how she will spend her time, asserting that the mistress of Mr. B.'s family will easily find "useful employments for her time, without looking abroad for any others." First, she says, she will "look into all such parts of the family management, as may befit the mistress of it to inspect. . . ." Then she will take over the family accounts. Third, she will visit "the unhappy poor in the neighbourhood" and administer charity to them. Fourth, she plans to assist the housekeeper in making ladylike provisions: jellies, sweetmeats, cordials, and the like. Her fifth way of employing her time will be to greet Mr. B. when he comes home and to wait lovingly for him when he is out—"I shall have the pleasure of receiving you with chearful duty; as I shall have counted the moments of your absence"— and to provide company for him: "And I shall have no doubt of so be-having, as to engage you frequently to fill up some part of my time (the sweetest by far that will be) in your instructive conversation." Her sixth duty will be to prepare for and entertain Mr. B.'s guests and the occa-sional "good-humoured lady" who might visit her. Significantly, Pamela says that although she will play cards with guests, she does not much desire to: "Cards, 'tis true, I can play at, in all the games that our sex usually delight in; but they are a diversion that I am not fond of; nor shall I ever desire to play, unless to induce such ladies, as you may wish to see, not to shun your house, for want of an amusement they are ac-customed to." Her seventh way of filling her time will be to practice her music; her eighth way will be to read and write, though her "scribbling" will now be employed only "in the family accounts," and she will read, she is careful to say, "at proper times" and mainly for the purpose of improvement. Last and most important is her "duty to God."[149]

Household supervision, charitable visiting, self-improvement, wifely companionship, religious devotions: Pamela's list would be approved by any conduct-book author. All that the admiring Mr. B. has to add to it is the hope that one day Pamela will also have motherly duties to fulfill. Pamela's perfect employment of her time is a sign of her virtue and de-sirability, as is her eagerness to distribute charitably some of her newly acquired wealth. Shortly after her nuptials, Pamela reflects on "the ex-alted pleasure" that comes from being able "to administer comfort and relief to those who stand in need of it" (388–89). Mr. B. turns over the family's charitable duties to her, allotting two hundred guineas a year for her "to lay out at her own discretion, and without account, in such a way, as shall derive a blessing upon us all: for she was my mother's almoner, and shall be mine, and her own too" (483). Pamela proves her worthiness to hold this post, carefully distinguishing the deserving from the nondeserving poor. In a letter to her parents, she offers to help the worthy poor of their neighborhood, asking for "a list of such honest, industrious poor, as may be true objects of charity, and have no other assistance; particularly such as are blind, lame, or sickly . . . ; and also such families and housekeepers as are reduced by misfortunes, as ours was, and where a great number of children may keep them from rising to a state of tolerable comfort . . ." (490). Although she was not born a lady, Pamela seems innately to possess that mark of a good lady: the ability to supervise.

After their marriage, Mr. B. explains to Pamela what he expects of her as his wife, and, again, much of this discussion has to do with Pamela's management of her time. Complaining that many ladies grow lazy about their looks after they are married, Mr. B. insists that Pamela always "be dressed by dinner-time . . . whether you are to go abroad, or stay at home." He goes on to complain about the bad hours many ladies keep:

> they too generally act in such a manner, as if they seemed to think it the privilege of birth and fortune, to turn day into night, and night into day, and seldom rise till 'tis time to sit down to dinner; and so all the good old family rules are reversed: for they breakfast when they should dine; dine, when they should sup; and sup, when they should retire to rest; and, by the help of dear quadrille, sometimes go to bed when they should rise. (393)

Mr. B. lays out a far different schedule for his Pamela. Unless "hindered by company," they are to be in bed by eleven; he plans to "rise by six, in summer," and will allow her "to lie half an hour after" him. They are to breakfast around nine, dine at three, and sup by nine, and in between these mealtimes Pamela will have "several useful hours . . . to employ [her]self in" (394). As Nancy Armstrong points out, "even though it is no longer permissible for Pamela to labor, her hours are now more rigidly regulated than before. . . ."[150] Mr. B. hopes that their visitors will conform to this model of regularity and that his example may "revive the good old-fashioned rules" in their neighborhood, thereby "answering the good lesson I learned at school—*Every one mend one*" (394). To quote Armstrong again, this passage "dramatizes nothing else so much as the total reorganization of leisure time toward which the conduct books also aspired."[151] The "editor" of Pamela's papers, summing up her virtues on the last pages of the novel, asks "even *ladies of condition*" to learn from "the *economy* she purposes to observe in her elevation" that "there are family employments, in which they may and ought to make themselves useful, . . . and that their duty to God, charity to the poor and sick, and the different branches of household management, ought to take up the most considerable portions of their time."[152] Like Mr. B., the "editor" hopes that Pamela's good use of her time will influence others.

In Sarah Scott's *Millenium Hall*, the next novel I want to consider, ladylike industriousness does indeed influence others. In this utopian and didactic novel, the shining example provided by the virtuous ladies who live in Millenium Hall is responsible for reclaiming a young gentleman from a life of idleness and athesim. Mr. Lamont has, the opening of the novel tells us, laid aside "useful and improving studies" for the "desultory reading" fashionable in the "idle societies" he frequents and has thus become an infidel.[153] Mr. Lamont is making a tour of the north with the book's narrator when their chaise happens to break down. Strolling about while it is being repaired, the two gentlemen happen upon the estate the narrator calls "Millenium Hall," where a number of ladies live together in a harmonious and virtuous sisterhood. A description of the estate and the interpolated tales of its residents form the body of the novel.

Even before the travelers meet the ladies of the Hall, they get a hint of the ladies' worthiness by observing a group of hay-makers, noting their unusual "cleanliness and neatness" and that a number of children "were all exerting the utmost of their strength, with an air of delighted emulation between themselves, to contribute their share to the general undertaking" (5). Clearly these peasants have been taught well the virtues of industry and cleanliness. The ladies, when the gentlemen meet them, are also industriously employed: two are reading, and the other four are painting, drawing, sculpting, or engraving, while a group of young girls under their tutelage are similarly well employed. The two gentlemen spend several days with the ladies, and everything around the estate proclaims the ladies' goodness. An old woman the narrator finds spinning near "a row of the neatest cottages I ever saw" tells him that her happiness, and that of the other residents of the cottages, is "all owing" to the ladies. She and her neighbors had been "half dead for want of victuals" because they "had not things to work with, nor any body to set [them] to work," she says. The ladies have organized these cottagers into various jobs, even finding ways to employ the lame, the deaf, and the old. (As I mentioned in the last chapter, age or infirmity is no excuse for idleness.) If the cottagers "are not idle," the old woman says, "that is all [the ladies] desire, except that we should be cleanly too." To make sure the cottagers *are* cleanly, the ladies inspect them daily, as the woman explains: "There never passes a day that one or other of the ladies does not come and look all over our houses, which they tell us, and certainly with truth, for it is a great deal of trouble to them, is all for our good, for that we cannot be healthy if we are not clean and neat" (12–14).

The ladies aid and supervise other groups of people, too. They have filled a "very large old mansion" with "women, who from scantiness of fortune, and pride of family, have been reduced to become dependent," and who cannot support themselves because, as Mrs. Maynard, one of the ladies of the Hall, says, "they have been educated as it is called, genteelly, or in other words idly" (64). The ladies have "by their examples and suggestions" led these reduced gentlewomen "to industry, and shewed it to be necessary to all stations, as the basis for almost every virtue," says Mrs. Maynard, adding impressively, "An idle mind, like

fallow ground, is the soil for every weed to grow in; in it vice strengthens, the seed of every vanity flourishes unmolested and luxuriant; discontent, malignity, ill humour, spread far and wide, and the mind
becomes a chaos which is beyond human power to call into order and
beauty." Therefore, the ladies "got this sisterhood to join with them in
working for the poor people, in visiting, in admonishing, in teaching
them"—in, in other words, supervising them, as good ladies should.
The ladies of the Hall have also encouraged these impoverished gentlewomen in "gardening, drawing, music, reading, or any manual or mental art" which may prevent "languidness and inactivity" (67–68). But
the ladies' goodness does not stop here. Among other projects, they
sponsor a group of orphaned, poor girls of good birth, educating them
to be housekeepers and governesses. The ladies keep the girls with them
at all times, carefully "inspect[ing]" their "performances" (111–12).
The ladies also watch over the young women of the parish, stocking the
dairies and poultry houses of young brides who have "behaved with
remarkable industry and sobriety" (114) and giving little presents to
young women who behave well. "This encouragement," the Hall's
housekeeper says, "has great influence, and makes them vie with each
other . . . to excel in sobriety, cleanliness, meekness, and industry"
(120). The ladies also run a village school, which teaches the children
ways of earning their livings and "inculcate[s] the purest principles in
their tender minds" (150), and a manufactory, which employs "several
hundreds of people of all ages, from six years old to four score," all of
whom are "busy, singing and whistling," and neatly dressed (201).

The ladies rise early to accomplish all this: "they are always up by
five o'clock, and by their example the people in the village rise equally
early; at that hour one sees them all engaged in their several businesses
with an assiduity which in other places is not awakened till much later"
(152). They also, not surprisingly, forgo frivolous amusements. Miss
Mancel, another of the ladies, explains to the worldly Mr. Lamont that
they feel no need for such amusements:

> You will pity us perhaps because we have no cards, no assemblies, no plays,
> no masquerades, in this solitary place. The first we might have if we chose
> it, nor are they totally disclaimed by us; but while we can with safety speak
> our own thoughts, and with pleasure read those of wiser persons, we are
> not likely to be often reduced to them. We wish not for large assemblies,
> because we do not desire to drown conversation in noise; the amusing fic-
> tions of dramatic writers are not necessary where nature affords us so many
> real delights; and as we are not afraid of shewing our hearts, we have no
> occasion to conceal our persons, in order to obtain either liberty of speech
> or action. (61)

Unlike the idle women we meet in some of the interpolated tales,[154] these women have resources with which to occupy themselves and a profound awareness of the value of time. As Miss Trentham says to Mr. Lamont and his friend, "We might spend our time in going from place to place, where none wish to see us except they find a deficiency at the card-table, perpetually living among those whose vacant minds are ever seeking after pleasures . . . which vanish as soon as possessed"; instead, these ladies choose "the infinite satisfaction of being beheld with gratitude and love, and the successive enjoyments of rational delights, which here fill up every hour" (203–4). Miss Trentham also points out to Mr. Lamont, who has defended "innocent pleasures," that "things are not always innocent because they are trifling. . . . Should a schoolboy be found whipping a top during school hours, would his master forbear correction because it is an innocent amusement? And yet thus we plead for things as trifling, tho' they obstruct the exercise of the greatest duties in life" (204). This conversation, and the example the ladies provide, is instrumental in saving Mr. Lamont from his atheism and trifling ways. By the end of the novel he has been "convinced by the conduct of the ladies of the house that their religion must be the true one" and has "risen at day break" to read the Bible, "that he might study precepts which could thus exalt human nature almost to divine" (206). In this novel, as in the conduct books, the influence of virtuously industrious ladies can save both communities and souls.

The third novel under discussion, Hannah More's *Coelebs in Search of a Wife*, also features a rather utopian community, this time a biological family. Coelebs, the young hero of the piece, is looking for an exemplary lady to become his wife. He goes to visit the Stanley family and finds what he is looking for in the person of Lucilla Stanley, the eldest of the family's several daughters. Before Coelebs even meets Lucilla, he is told of her excellent use of time by the family's housekeeper. Lucilla, she says, "rises at six, and spends two hours in her closet, which is stored with the best books." She then consults the housekeeper about "the state of provisions, and other family matters" and goes over the household accounts. After these activities, she "comes in to make breakfast for her parents, as fresh as a rose, and as gay as a lark." After breakfast, she and her father read "some learned books together," and then she helps teach her five little sisters. One day a week, she works for the poor, and two evenings a week she visits them in their cottages.[155] Here, again, is a woman who spends her time exactly as the conduct books say she should.

Lucilla also declines to spend her time on useless though fashionable accomplishments: "Though she has a correct ear, she neither sings nor plays; and . . . I never saw a pencil in her fingers, except to sketch a seat or a bower for the pleasure-grounds." She knows that life's "duties are too various and important" to allow for any such trifling (2:234). Lucilla delights in gardening, but will not allow herself to spend unlimited time even in this praiseworthy (both Hannah More and Jane West single it out as especially good) activity. Mrs. Stanley tells Coelebs that Lucilla has been made uneasy by how much she loves to garden and has therefore hung her watch on a tree in the garden, to remind her to limit her time there (2:386). She also has found ways to tie her gardening into charitable activities. When she was fourteen, worried "that the delight she took in this employment was attended neither with pleasure nor profit to any one but herself," she decided to begin growing various fruit trees to present to worthy girls from the charity-school she runs when they get married (just as the ladies in *Millenium Hall* give presents to virtuous working-class brides). By this means the girls are encouraged to be virtuous and the village is beautified; the trees "diffuse an air of smiling comfort around [the] humble habitations, and embellish poverty itself." Lucilla also makes sure to fulfill her duty to supervise, and not just to aid, the poor: she makes "periodical visits of inspection to see that neatness and order do not disintegrate" (2:376–77).

Lucilla has been carefully brought up to possess ample "resources," a rich interiority that qualifies her to live happily in retirement and to have no need to display herself. As Mr. Stanley tells Coelebs,

> The girl who possesses only the worldly acquirements—the singer and the dancer—when condemned to retirement, may reasonably exclaim with Milton's Adam, when looking at the constellations, "Why all night long shine these? / Wherefore, if none *behold*." Now the woman who derives her principles from the Bible, and her amusements from intellectual sources, from the beauties of nature, and from active employment and exercise, will not pant for *beholders*. She is no clamorous beggar for the extorted alms of admiration. She lives on her own stock. Her resources are within herself. (2:433–34).

Coelebs falls in love with Lucilla in part because she refuses such display. Her essence is not all on the surface; she requires deciphering. When her father and some other gentlemen are conversing, for instance, Lucilla observes "the most profound silence," but reveals her intelligent interest through her gestures and facial expressions, as Coelebs admiringly notices (2:355). She is behaving exactly as John Gregory says, in his conduct book, ladies should: After saying (as I quoted earlier) that female modesty will dispose women to be silent in company, he adds that "People of sense and discernment will never mistake such silence for dulness. One may take a share in conversation without uttering a syllable. The expression in the countenance shews it, and this never escapes an observing eye."[156] The (presumably male) "observing eye" runs no risk of being "over-laid" and "glutted" by a woman like Lucilla; unlike the idle, self-displaying lady who is "always in our eye at public places," the woman of resources whets male appetite rather than cloying it.

Coelebs is enchanted when one day he happens to observe Lucilla making a pious, charitable visit to a cottager: "What were my emotions when I saw Lucilla Stanley kneeling by the side of a little clean bed, a large old Bible spread open before her, out of which she was reading one of the penitential Pslams to a pale emaciated female figure, who lifted up her failing eyes, and clasped her feeble hands in solemn attention!" (2:412). And his amorous admiration of Lucilla is deepened even further when, walking home with her from the cottage, they talk about *Paradise Lost* (both are big fans of Milton's Eve) and he realizes she has read "the best authors, though she quoted none." Coelebs reflects, "exultingly," that this "is the true learning for a lady; a knowledge that is rather detected than displayed . . ." (2:413). Female excellence, this novel and many other sources say, is most valuable when it is half-hidden, when the observer must discover it for himself.

Frances Burney's *The Wanderer*, the last novel I will be discussing, takes to an extreme this notion of deciphering a lady, for its heroine is truly a cipher. Because of complicated circumstances (including the French Revolution and the private though legal marriage of her parents), Lady Juliet Granville cannot reveal her name or situation to anyone. Her full name is withheld even from the reader for most of the novel's many pages. Having lost her purse in her hasty escape from France to England, Juliet is penniless; she is also, for much of the novel, family-less and nameless. All the usual ways of "placing" a lady are absent here; Juliet must really be judged on her essence. And this essence is, again, revealed to a large extent in her use of time.

In the early part of the novel, the class status of Juliet (as I will call her for clarity, although she is at this point called the Incognita and then Ellis) is a matter of contention, since gentlewomen were not generally found crossing the English Channel unaccompanied, penniless, and disguised. That she is a lady becomes clear as she is discovered to possess all the ladylike attributes. First she is overheard—and I think it is important that she *is* overheard, that her talent is "detected, not displayed"—playing the harp "with uncommon ability."[157] Then Harleigh, who will love her faithfully through nine hundred pages and eventually be rewarded with her hand, reads something she has written and is convinced by "the beautiful clearness of the hand-writing, and the correctness of the punctuation and orthography" that Juliet's "education had been as successfully cultivated for intellectual improvement, as for elegant accomplishments" (83). Next she is seen to dance, and Harleigh is struck "by the measured grace and lightness of her motions, which . . . were equally striking for elegance and for modesty" (84). Next Harleigh finds a sketch she has drawn, "beautifully executed, and undoubtedly from nature," which prompts him to clasp his hands and exclaim, "Accomplished creature! who . . . and what are you?" (88; ellipsis Burney's). Then Juliet is forced to take part in a private theatrical, and though her modest reluctance to act at first causes her to do it badly, her performance after the first scene is "the essence of gay intelligence, of well bred animation, and of lively variety." Her motions are graceful, her voice is expressive, and her face speaks "her discrimination of every word" (94). Finally she is found to be an elegant conversationalist (101) and an excellent player of the pianoforte (115). In the spaces between these activities, Juliet engages diligently in "the useful and appropriate female accomplishment of needle-work" (78). Here is a lady indeed.

Juliet's accomplishments mark her as a lady, and her good use of time marks her as a virtuous one. When, in the last part of the novel, she has some leisure to employ, she employs it as the conduct books recommend. Staying with a working-class family in a remote area, she writes letters to her friend. "This, however, not filling up her time," the narrator says, "the wish of obliging, joined to a constant desire of acquiring, in every situation, the art of being useful, —that art which, more than wealth, or state, or power, preserves its cultivator from wearying either himself or those around him; —led her to bestow the rest of the day" in helping her hostess with "sundry occupations" (661). Staying with another family of rustics, Juliet endears herself to all by her industriousness: "She took pleasant walks, accompanied by the tallest boy and girl; she worked for the grandmother; taught a part of the catechism to some of the children; played with them all, and made herself at once so useful and so agreeable in the rustic dwelling, that she won the heart . . . of all the inhabitants" (672). She mends the clothes of ragged children—"her industry and adroitness soon put their whole little wardrobe in order" (709)—and even, despite her poverty and troubles, manages to engage in some supervision. Visiting a rural school, she "captivated the easy hearts of the little scholars, by the playful manner in which she noticed their occupations, encouraged their diligence, and assisted them to learn their lessons" (695). Even when she is alone, Juliet finds it easy to entertain herself. Unlike idle ladies who need constant diversions to avoid boredom, Juliet can pick up a volume of the *Guardian* and find "in the lively instruction, the chaste morality, and the exquisite humour of Addison, an enjoyment which no repetition can cloy" (508). A lady possessing true virtue is always useful, and she is never bored.

A lady lacking money, however, is forced to work, and in the middle section of the novel Burney takes on the problem of female employment. Juliet tries to earn her living in various ways, all of which are fraught with difficulty and danger. (The alternate title Burney gives for *The Wanderer* is *Female Difficulties*.) She first considers becoming a governess, but finds that impossible without a sponsor to recommend her, so she turns to giving harp lessons. She finds many of her pupils to be less interested in music than in attaining a reputation for accomplishment or in using the harp to display their personal charms. One Miss Brinville, for instance, takes up the harp to impress a baronet for whom she has set her cap and spends her time trying "attitudes and motions" before the glass, rather than practicing the notes (236). Juliet has great difficulty in getting her pupils to pay her; they seem to feel that niceties like harp lessons do not require payment. As one lady says, "this young music-mistress" is not "a butcher, or a baker; or some useful tradesman" (323), and although "singing and dancing, and making images, are ever so pretty, one should not pay folks who follow such light callings, as one pays people that are truly useful" (324).

Juliet has exactly the same problem in her next line of endeavor, doing fine embroidery—her lady clients refuse to pay her: "Her pains and exertions, their promises and fondness, sunk into the same oblivion; and the commonest and most inadequate pay was murmured at, if not contested" (406). Other sorts of work prove equally problematic. When she works in a milliner's shop, she suffers from "the total absence of feeling and of equity, in the dissipated and idle, for the indigent and laborious" (427); she is badly treated and badly paid. When she takes work as a seamstress, her employer, Mrs. Hart, turns out to be a tyrant, demanding that Juliet keep up the too-rapid pace of work with which she unwisely started out. Juliet realizes, "I have thrown away my power of obliging, by too precipitate an eagerness to oblige! . . . All I can perform seems but a duty, and of course; all I leave undone, seems idleness and neglect." But "what," she asks, "is the labour that never requires respite? What the mind, that never demands a few poor unshackled instants to itself?" (453). When she is dismissed from this job, she becomes the "humble companion" of the odious Mrs. Ireton, a remarkably malicious woman who delights in tormenting her inferiors,[158] and whose every speech to Juliet is sarcastic and cruel. Juliet's job description is accurately sketched out in one of Mrs. Ireton's tirades: Mrs. Ireton accuses Juliet of being what, in fact, she is—"a fine lady!"— and says that a humble companion should be "a person who [can] read to me when I [am] tired, and who, when I [have] nobody else, [can] talk to me; and find out a thousand little things for me all day long; coming and going; prating, or holding her tongue; doing everything she [is] bid;

and keeping always at hand" (487–88). The kindly Mr. Giles provides another description when he tells Juliet he hopes she has not turned "toad-eater," and let "yourself out, at so much a year, to say nothing that you think; and to do nothing that you like; and to beg pardon when you are not in fault; and to eat all the offals; and to be beat by the little gentleman [Mrs. Ireton's nephew]; and worried by the little dog" (521).

As if all this were not enough, Juliet faces other problems in her attempts to support herself. At one point, desperate, she reluctantly accedes to a plan the officious and nasty Miss Arbe puts forward: to perform her music for money. Juliet views the prospect of performing in public with horror, and in rehearsal is "seized with a faint panic that disorder[s] her whole frame" and causes her to perform badly (310). Her distress is magnified by Miss Arbe, who uses the money that has been advanced for Juliet to buy a shocking-pink silk dress for her to perform in. This tasteless garment is, Miss Arbe says, "to distinguish us *Dilettanti*" —the ladies with money who have the privilege of performing for applause rather than pay—"from the artists" (314). Things get even worse when Miss Arbe then decides that Juliet is to sing, without the ladies, at the concert a professional (and male) musician is to give and that her name is to be on the advertisements. Juliet at first refuses to perform "at any concert open to the public at large" (327), but then, with great distaste, gives in. Her distaste is matched by Harleigh's. When he hears of her plan he earnestly beseeches her to reconsider, telling her that her "accomplishments should be reserved for the resources of [her] leisure, and the happiness of [her] friends" (338) and implying in a letter that he will be unable to marry her if she goes through with the performance. (She does try to do so, but luckily faints as she is standing up to sing.) This strong aversion to the idea of Juliet's performing in public comes partly from the harm it would do her class status— making public, as it would, her need to earn a living—but also from the sexual impropriety associated with it. To perform publicly, to be paid, in a sense, to be looked at, is, as Harleigh says in his letter, to depart "from the long-beaten track of female timidity" (343) to a suspect sexual realm.

All through the novel, in fact, Juliet encounters difficulties with people's suspecting her to lack sexual virtue. Since she is such a cipher, lacking family, friends, fortune, a history, even a name, people continually try to decode her, but often incorrectly. (The novel's admirable characters, significantly, recognize her true worth.) Although, as Harleigh indignantly and logically points out, "a female, who is young, beautiful, and accomplished" is unlikely to "suffer from pecuniary distress, if her character be not unimpeachable" (149), she is constantly having to fend off the lecherous advances of men and the catty accusations of women.

Her need to support herself makes it even more difficult for her to defend herself from these attacks. When, for instance, she is working in the
milliner's shop, she finds she cannot avoid the ill-intentioned Sir Lyell:
"But how avoid him," the narrator asks, "while she had no other means
of subsistence than working in an open shop?" (448).

Because she is fleeing the pursuit of the unspeakable man who has
forced her into marriage, Juliet has to hide and disguise herself. This
need to hide herself resembles uncomfortably the need of all ladies in
Juliet's society to avoid being too much looked at or talked about, for
fear of besmirching their reputations. As the editor of Lady Sarah Pennington's letters to her daughters says, "the crystalline purity of female
reputation is almost sullied by the breath even of good report."[159] In one
painfully ironic episode, Juliet trades bonnets with a working-class girl
she has met. Feeling safe in this disguise, she is accosted rudely by a
young man who seems to think he knows her, and she realizes she has
been mistaken for this girl. Juliet, gathering from the way the man has
spoken to her "how light a character [the girl] bore," is stricken with
the idea that "danger thus every way surround[s] her" (666). In attempting to escape her persecutors, an attempt that in itself injures her
reputation,[160] Juliet has put on the tainted reputation of another, and
thus opened herself up to further sexual danger. Juliet's pathetic gratitude, at the point of her direst distress, for a bonnet that "offers some
shade for her face, now exposed to every eye" (769) testifies that "female difficulties" were indeed painful. Required to be a cipher—hidden,
silent, passive, coded—she always ran the risk of being misread, deciphered incorrectly. Harleigh's correct deciphering of Juliet, and her
persistence through five volumes of being misinterpreted by most, make
their happy ending, when it finally comes, seem deeply deserved.

The Wanderer and the other novels concerned with the problem of impoverished gentlewomen indicate, I think, some of the limits placed on
the eighteenth-century lady's power. Yes, as Armstrong says, she
gained control over her household and the "objects" of her charity. And
certainly I do not want to underestimate the extent to which domestic
ideology served to naturalize class inequality. But the power Lucilla
Stanley enjoys—to oversee the sexual purity of village girls or inspect
the cleanliness of humble households—must be put alongside the help-
lessness Juliet Granville suffers, unable to earn her living or even exist
safely in the public realm. Lucilla's power as all-seeing eye within her
household and neighborhood must be weighed against Juliet's pained
cringing from the public eye. A lady safely connected to a trustworthy
man may have exercised a fair amount of power, but the same cannot
be said, I think, of every lady in this period. Like a cipher, she could
be wrongly decoded, and she was often worth nothing when she stood
alone.

4

An Empire of Degenerated Peoples:
Race, Imperialism, and Idleness

THE EUROPEAN EIGHTEENTH CENTURY SAW THE ESTABLISHMENT AND expansion of two important and interlinked entities: the British Empire and the systematizing of nature. Mary Louise Pratt's influential book *Imperial Eyes: Travel Writing and Transculturation* traces this systematizing of nature (which she connects to "a new version of . . . Europe's 'planetary consciousness' "[1]), arguing that it had "a deep and lasting impact not just on travel and travel writing, but on the overall ways European citizens made, and made sense of, their place on the planet."[2] She notes that "the systematization of nature coincides with the height of the slave trade, the plantation system, colonial genocide in North America and South America, slave rebellions in the Andes, the Caribbean, North America, and elsewhere"[3] and asks, "what were the slave trade and the plantation system if not massive experiments in social engineering and discipline, serial production, the systematization of human life, the standardizing of persons?"[4] Pratt also remarks that this systematizing is closely connected to accumulation, carrying it to "a totalized extreme."[5] And certainly the accumulation of a bewildering variety of goods was, at least in part, the aim and the result of eighteenth-century Britain's imperialist project. In *The Sense of the People: Politics, Culture, and Imperialism in England, 1715–1785,* Kathleen Wilson tells us that "newspapers in commercial and trading centers . . . coaxed and shaped their readers' involvement, both material and ideological, in war, trade and imperial expansion" and that "the structure and content of these papers reflected and encouraged a mercantilist world view in which trade and the accumulation of wealth appeared to be the highest national and individual good." She notes that fully a third of the content of these papers consisted of reportings on wars in colonial centers and listings of the arrivals and departures of merchant ships, together with advertisements for the goods fought for in these wars and borne in by these ships: "tea, coffee, chocolate and tobacco; calicoes and silks; wines, rum and spirits; fruits and seeds, furs, exotic birds and plants."[6]

The systematizing of nature was intricately bound up with the acquisition and accumulation of these goods.

The lust for both colonies and for categories, for trade and for taxonomies, that fills so much of the writing of this period seems at least partly to spring from the same root—a desire to control, to achieve mastery over the world. And whether the English (and other Europeans) were trying to achieve this goal by building empires or indexes, their attempts often prompted them to travel to other countries and describe what they saw there.[7] These travel accounts were read, plagiarized, anthologized, argued about, and reprinted all through the long eighteenth century;[8] and, to quote Pratt once again, "In the second half of the eighteenth century, scientific exploration was to become a magnet for the energies and resources of intricate alliances of intellectual and commercial elites all over Europe."[9] I might put the date a bit earlier, but I hope in this chapter to examine how the discourse of idleness figures in early categories of the races and in the literature of imperial exploration, which had significance to science, commerce, and empire.[10] This discourse, I want to argue, both supported and undermined imperialist and colonialist ambitions.

I

In 1785, William Guthrie's *New Geographical, Commercial, and Historical Grammar* made a statement that, while seeming to discourage descriptions of African people, neatly sums up many such accounts: "In Africa the human mind seems degraded below its natural state. To dwell long upon the manners of this country, a country so immersed in rudeness and barbarity, besides that it could afford little instruction, would be disgusting to every lover of mankind."[11]

This idea that the African is "degraded" below what should be a "natural state" recurs throughout the century, in literature of empire and of systems. Travel writers represent Africans, and especially the people whom they called Hottentots,[12] as having slid down the chain of being to a spot barely above that of the beasts. John Ovington's 1696 *Voyage to Suratt* claims that

of all People they are the most Bestial and sordid. They are the very Reverse of Human kind . . . , so that if there's any medium between a Rational Animal and a Beast, the *Hotontot* lays the fairest Claim to that Species. They are sunk even below Idolatry, are destitute both of Priest and Temple, and saving a little show of rejoicing, which is made at the Full and the New Moon; have lost all kind of Religious Devotion. Nature has so richly provided for their convenience in the Life, that they have drown'd all sense of the God of it, and are grown quite careless of the next.[13]

John Barrow's 1801 *Account of Travels into the Interior of Southern Africa*, which gives a more modulated description of the Hottentots, says that "their character seems to have been very much traduced and misrepresented," but also that "they are sunk [low] in the scale of humanity."[14]

Scientific theorists on the "varieties of mankind"—what we would now consider the "races"—also viewed Africans as having degenerated; seeing whiteness, as Johann Friedrich Blumenbach says, as "the primitive colour" of humankind, and the other races as degenerations from the Caucasian. Besides color itself, this African "degeneration" is most often figured in two (sometimes overlapping) ways: as the absence of approved, "civilized" features in their society, and as the presence of grotesque, "savage" features in their bodies and the practices associated with their bodies. Notably often, both this absence of civilization and this presence of savagery are attributed to or associated with idleness. While observers disagree on some details of their descriptions (especially when evincing their unseemly fascination with African genitals, spiritedly debating such questions as whether or not Hottentot women sport labial excrescences and whether Hottentot men do indeed lack a testicle and, if so, how they come to lose it), and while descriptions of different African groups do vary a bit in some accounts, most features of these descriptions are ubiquitous. The picture of the African that emerges from these writings is one of stupidity, filth, stench, bestial appetite, improvidence, and, above all, indolence.

One of the features that Europeans saw African, and, more specifically, Hottentot, culture to lack most scandalously is religion, as the passage from Ovington quoted above indicates. Hottentots are said either to have no notion of religion at all, or to practice only a vague, enormously heathen sort of moon-worship in their nighttime dancing. As Peter Kolb's much-read account *The Present State of the Cape of Good Hope* (1731) describes the ceremony,

their Behavior at those Times is indeed very astonishing. They throw their Bodies into a thousand different Distortions; and make Mouths and Faces strangely ridiculous and horrid. Now they throw themselves flat on the Ground, screaming out a strange unintelligible Jargon. Then jumping up on a Sudden, and stamping like Mad (insomuch that they make the Ground shake) they direct, with open throats . . . Addresses to the moon [which] they repeat over and over, accompanying them with Dancing and Clapping of Hands.[15]

Another conspicuous absence is found in their homes, which many writers see as little better than the lairs of animals. In his *New Voyage Round the World* (1691), William Dampier declares,

> The *Hottantots* houses are the meanest I ever did see. They are about nine or ten Foot high, and ten or twelve from side to side. They are in a manner round, made with small Poles stuck into the Ground, and brought together at the top, where they are fastened. . . . They have no Beds to lie on, but tumble down at Night round the Fire. Their Houshold Furniture is commonly an earthen Pot or two to boil Victuals, and they live very miserably and hard. . . .[16]

Francois Leguat's account of his voyage to the Cape in 1698 juxtaposes a declaration of the Hottentot's lowness on the chain of being with a comment on their habitations: "The Cafre Hottentots are extreamly ugly and loathsome, if one may give the name of Men to such Animals. They go in Companies, [and] live in Holes or vile Cottages. . . ."[17]

The Khoekhoe were mainly a pastoral people, whose economy revolved around their herds of sheep and cattle; they supplemented their diet of milk products with gathered roots and meat from animals they occasionally hunted, but they practiced no agriculture. This particular "lack" of their culture really gnawed at European vitals, especially since Africa, like other tropical lands, was thought to produce crops almost spontaneously. Observers attributed this deficiency to savagery and indolence. As Edward Long claims in his *History of Jamaica* (1744), "In many of their provinces they are often reduced to the utmost straights for want of corn, of which they might enjoy the greatest abundance, if they were but animated with the smallest portion of industry."[18] John Matthews says in his *Voyage to the River Sierra-Leone* . . . (1788), "In short, my friend, Nature appears to have been extremely liberal [here], and to have poured forth her treasures with an unsparing hand: but in most cases the indolence of the natives prevents their reaping those advantages, of which an industrious nation would possess themselves."[19]

Descriptions of the Hottentots' economy and food straddle both categories of degradation. Not only do these people lack the civilized practice of agriculture and a decent provision for their needs, but the practices they do have are seen as savage and grotesque. Even their tending of cattle is tainted: several writers express disgust at the reported practice of blowing into the cows' rectums to stimulate milk production. And their choices in food and manner of eating fill many writers with revulsion. "Captain Cowley's Voyage Around the Globe," included in William Hacke's anthology (1699), paints this picture:

> They are a people that will eat anything that is foul; If the *Hollanders* kill a Beast, they will get the Guts, and squeeze the Excrements out, and then

Illustration from *A New Universal Collection of Authentic and Entertaining Voyages and Travels, from the Earliest Accounts to the Present Time,* by Edward Cavendish Drake (London, 1769): "The Cloathing & Arms of the Hottentots inhabiting the Cape of Good Hope in Africa"; "Hottentots Tearing to Pieces a dead Ox & Eating it." Reproduced permission of the University of Michigan Special Collections.

without washing or scraping, lay them upon the Coals, and before they are well hot through, will take them and eat them.[20]

Leguat (1698) has a similar report:

They eat raw Flesh and Fish, finding them, it seems, better, and more savoury so, then when they are boil'd or fry'd: Nay, they trouble the Kitchin so little, that when they find a dead Beast they immediately embowel him, sweet or stinking, and having press'd the Guts a little between their Fingers, they eat the remaining Tripe with the greatest Appetite that can be.[21]

In his *Account of the Cape of Good Hope* (1798), Robert Percival links laziness and voracity:

They are indeed lazy to a great degree; even hunger cannot provoke them to be at any trouble in procuring food; yet when it is procured, they are most disgustingly voracious, and will swallow down at one time an enormous quantity of half broiled meat, or even raw intestines. Any preparation of their food seems indeed to be accounted by them altogether superfluous. Their only luxury consists in eating; and sleeping seems to be the only recreation from which they derive any enjoyment.[22]

Other aspects of Hottentot culture that are seen as grotesque and savage have to do with their dress, bodies, and bodily practices. Nearly everyone who mentions the Hottentots reports on their practice of smearing their bodies with grease, sometimes said to be mixed with soot, dirt, or dung. Europeans are often confounded by this practice, both because of the smell of the fat and, perhaps more deeply, because the practice turns the fairly light skin of the Hottentots much darker. Peter Kolb's account is fairly typical:

What makes the *Hottentots* still a nastier Generation, is a Custom, observ'd from their Infancy, of besmearing their Bodies and apparel . . . with Butter or Sheep's Fat, mix'd with Soot that gathers about their Boiling Pots, in order to make 'em look black, being naturally . . . of a Nut- or Olive-Colour. . . . The meaner Sort of 'em, who are but ill provided, are for the most Part oblig'd to make Use of Butter or Fat that is rank; which renders them offensive to the Nose of a *European*, who may smell them at a considerable distance.[23]

Another form of bodily decoration that most Europeans see as barbaric is face painting. Even Francois Le Vaillant, whose *Travels from the Cape of Good Hope into the Interior Parts of Africa* (1790) is remarkable for its Rousseau-inspired admiration for much of Hottentot culture, says,

Though so much habituated to the sight of these Africans, I could never reconcile myself to the custom they have of painting themselves with a thousand ridiculous marks and figures; to the last, it appeared to me hideous and disgusting. I cannot conceive what grace they can possibly think they receive from this abominable custom, which is not only ridiculous but nasty.[24]

The dress of the Hottentots was of course far unlike European garb and often described as primitive and immodest. Barrow, for instance, notes that the sort of case with which the men covered their genitals is little better than complete nakedness: "If the real intent of it was the promotion of decency, it should seem that he has widely missed his aim, as it is certainly one of the most immodest objects, in such a situation as he places it, that could have been contrived."[25] He also claims that the aprons the women wear over their genitals seem to be designed to "attract notice towards this part of their person."[26] Many writers reported that the Hottentots not only ate guts, but wore them, especially wrapped around their legs. Leguat says that the women have "the loathsom Custom to wear several rounds of raw Guts about their Necks and Legs in lieu of Necklaces and Garters, which being green and corrupted, stink abominably."[27]

The connections made between these "deficiencies"—and even some of the "savagery"—of African societies and idleness make some intuitive sense: as J. M. Coetzee points out in his seminal work *White Writing*,

The charge of idleness often comes together with, and sometimes as the climax of, a set of other characterizations: that the Hottentots are ugly, that they never wash but on the contrary smear themselves with animal fat, that their food is unclean, that their meat is barely cooked, that they wear skins, that they live in the meanest of huts, that male and female mix indiscriminately, that their speech is not like that of human beings. What is common to these charges is that they mark the Hottentot as *underdeveloped*— underdeveloped not only by the standard of the European but by the standard of Man. If he were to develop dietary taboos, ablutionary habits, sexual mores, crafts, a more varied body decoration than a uniform coating, domestic architecture and technology, a language of human articulation rather than animal noises, he would become, if not a Hollander, at least more fully Man. And the fact that he self-evidently does not employ his faculties in developing himself in these ways, but instead lies about in the sun, is proof that it is sloth that must be held accountable for retarding him.[28] (Coetzee's italics)

However, what is not so clear is how we should read perhaps the strongest images of savagery and grotesqueness in these accounts, which ap-

Illustration from *A New Voyage to the East-Indies by Francis Leguat and His Companies,* by Francis Leguat (London, 1708): "A Hottentot Man in his Summer Dress." Reproduced permission of the University of Michigan Special Collections.

pear when Europeans describe the Hottentots' bodies, at least certain portions of them. Many writers comment on the pendulous quality of the women's breasts, observing that mothers can nurse their babies behind their backs by simply flinging a breast over their shoulder. Leguat achieves the most horrifying description of Hottentot breasts I've read:

> But what is yet more frightful, is their Necks; they seem to have two long, half-dry'd, and half-fill'd Hoggs Bladders hanging at them. These nasty Dugs, whose Flesh is black, wrinkled and rough . . . , come down as low as their navels, and have . . . Teats as large as those of a Cow. In truth these swinging Udders have this commodious in them, that you may lead a Woman by them to the Right or Left, forwards or backwards, as you please. For the most part they throw them behind their Shoulders to suckle their Child, who is slung upon their Backs.[29]

Genitals come in for even more horrified fascination. Both the men and the women of the Cape were reported to be different from other human beings in this regard. The men were said to lack a testicle, with various reasons ascribed for this peculiarity. Ovington claims that

> the Male Children at Eight or Ten Years of Age, are Cut in their Privy Parts, and depriv'd of one of their Testicles. [This is done] for prevention of a too Luxuriant Increase by Generation; because when their Children Increase beyond their Desires, and the just number which they design, to prevent a heavier Charge upon the Parents, they dispatch the Supernumaries to the other world, without any Remorse for the horrid Crime, or Consciousness of the execrable Sin of Murther. . . . [30]

Kolb reports testicle-removing as a sort of manhood ritual, giving a lengthy description:

> The Patient being first besmear'd all over with the fat of the Entrails of a Sheep newly kill'd, lies on his Back, at full Length, on the Ground. His Hands are tied together; as are his feet. On each Leg and Arm kneels a Friend, and on his Breast lies another, to keep him down and deprive him of all Motion. Then advances the Operator, with a common Case- or Table-knife, well sharpen'd, (They have no better Instrument,) and laying Hold of the left Testicle, makes an Orifice in the Scrotum of an Inch and a Half long, and squeezes out the Testicle and cuts and ties up the Vessels in a Trice. This he performs, notwithstanding the Clumsiness of the Instrument, with such Dexterity, as would amaze the ablest Artist in Europe. Then taking a little Ball, which he has at Hand, of Sheep's Fat, mix'd with the Powders of salutary Herbs . . . and of the Bigness of the outed Testicle, he crams it into the Scrotum to fill up the Vacancy. This Fat must be of the Sheep, kill'd by the Parents for this Occasion.[31]

Leguat gives an earlier date, and an even more alarming method, for this procedure:

> Some take for a sort of Circumcision what the Mothers do to their New-born Males, whose Right Testicle they always tear away with their Teeth and eat it, but I rather think they do so to render those Children more nimble and proper for Hunting. . . . After these barbarous Mothers have thus maim'd their poor Children, they give them Sea-water to drink, and put Tobacco in their Mouths, believing these two things, in conjunction with what was before done, would render them so robust and supple, that they might overtake a Roe-Buck in his full Course. [32]

The women's genital eccentricity, on the other hand, was reported as an addition rather than a deletion, and as the product of nature rather than culture. Like those of the men's oddity, though, reports differ in some regards. Leguat has one common version of the story:

> The women wear a sort of Petticoat which covers them from their Wasts to their Knees, which however is not necessary, since certain Skins hanging from their upper parts like Furbelo's are sufficient to do that Office. Some have told me they had the Curiousity to look under these Veils, and an end of Tobacco procur'd them that Liberty.[33]

And *The Journal of Wilhelm Ten Rhyne in which is given an account of Saldanha Bay and Dassen Island and principally of the Cape of Good Hope and the natives of that place called the Hottentots* (1685) has the other version:

> The women may be distinguished by the men by their ugliness. And they have this peculiarity to distinguish them from other races, that most of them have dactyliform appendages, always two in number, hanging down from their pudenda. These are enlargements of the Nymphae. . . . If one should happen to enter a hut full of women—the huts they calls kraals in their idiom—then, with much gesticulation, and raising their leathern aprons, they offer these appendages to the view.[34]

These points are debated throughout the period, with later writings claiming that earlier ones were incorrect or exaggerated, but even denials keep attention focused on this area. What are we to make of this fascination with African breasts and genitals? Is simple prurience the cause of so much attention?[35] If so, why are these descriptions so often closely linked to comments about African idleness? In fact, some of the accounts seem to assert that indolence is the *cause* of these bodily "abnormalities," as when one commentator in the Awnsham and Churchill collection says that "the inside of the Womens Privities are so relaxed, that they hang out."[36] Anders Sparrman goes even further when he

Illustration from *A New Voyage to the East-Indies by Francis Leguat and His Companies,* by Francis Leguat (London, 1708): "A Hottentot Woman without her Petticoat." Reproduced permission of the University of Michigan Special Collections.

Illustration from *Travels from the Cape of Good-Hope into the interior parts of Africa,* by François Le Vaillant (London, 1790). Reproduced courtesy of Albion College Archives.

claims that "The women have no parts uncommon to the rest of their sex, but the *clitoris* and *nymphae*, particularly of those who are past their youth, are in general pretty much elongated; a peculiarity which undoubtedly has got footing in this nation, in consequence of the relaxation necessarily produced by the method they have of besmearing their bodies, their slothfulness, and the warmth of the climate."[37]

I wonder if these two areas of obsessive concern—Africans' sexualized body parts and Africans' supposed idleness—are really performing the same sort of cultural work. As I argued in the chapter on the British laboring classes, bodies that are considered idle are also considered grotesque. The grotesqueness assigned to laboring-class bodies in many ways resembles that assigned to African bodies. Both are seen as appetitive, dirty, and uncontainable: consuming disgusting foods, covered in malodorous filth, and uncovered by inadequate clothing. Anomalous genitals might be seen as the ultimate in grotesqueness, and thus they might become associated with the idle body, which is also grotesque. But additionally, genitals might be seen to represent that which is most deeply human (especially since one creature's ability to reproduce with another had been recently established as proof that the two beings were of the same species). Thus, genitals unlike those of other humans would make the African irreducibly "other." (Linda Merians says in her important article "What They Are, Who We Are: Representations of the 'Hottentot' in Eighteenth-Century Britain" that these reports of genital strangeness "suggest how eager European observers were to delimit [Hottentots] from the rest of the human race. Indeed, what more singular proof of marginal humanity could be invented?")[38] As I will argue at greater length later, invincible idleness also constructs the African as "other"—not other than human, given the British comfortable-class insistence on the natural idleness of their laboring classes, but other than the industrious, adventurous, exploring, systematizing, colonizing person who was writing about them.

Certainly, reports of African idleness are even more plentiful than reports of genital anomalies.[39] Almost without exception, accounts of Africans stress over and over that, as Peter Kolb says in his 1731 *Present State of the Cape of Good-Hope*, "They are, without doubt, both in Body and Mind, the laziest People under the Sun. A monstrous Indisposition to Thought and Action runs through all the Nations of 'em: And their whole earthly Happiness seems to lie in Indolence and Supinity."[40] William Bosman speaks similarly of the inhabitants of Africa's Gold Coast in his 1704 *New and Accurate Description of the Coast of Guinea*, saying that they are "so prone" to "Sloth and Idleness" that "nothing but the utmost Necessity can force them to Labour."[41] John Matthews's *Voyage to the River Sierra-Leone, on the Coast of Africa* (1788) says much the same thing about the Africans of this region: "The disposition of the natives is nearly the same every where, extremely indolent, unless excited by revenge."[42] Opinions of African idleness remain firmly fixed throughout the period; William Dampier's claim in his 1697 *New Voyage Round the World* that "they are a very lazy sort of People" who, despite their land's fertility, "choose rather to live as their Fore-fathers, poor and miserable, than be at Pains for Plenty"[43] is neatly echoed by the ringing assertion John Barrow makes in his 1801 *Account of Travels into the Interior of Southern Africa*: "the indolence of a Hottentot is a real disease, whose only remedy seems to be that of terror. Hunger is insufficient to effect the cure. Rather than to have the trouble of procuring food by the chace, or of digging the ground for roots, they will willingly fast the whole day provided they may be allowed to sleep."[44]

Even writers who take a less hateful view of Africans often support the idea of African indolence. In *A Geographical and Topographical Description of the Cape of Good Hope* (1785), O. F. Mentzel observes the despised Hottentots with a kinder eye than most European travel writers, saying that they are "faithful and in their actions upright and honest," not inclined to avarice and incapable of deception,[45] but he also says firmly, "It is quite true that the Hottentot is lazy, idle, improvident, and so forth."[46] William Burchell, who also takes a somewhat sympathetic view of Hottentot culture in his 1822 *Travels in the Interior of Southern Africa*, enjoying their dancing and music-making and praising their acts of generosity, still speaks of the "fit[s] of laziness" that overcome "my Hottentots"[47] and says that he supports their spending their evenings in singing and dancing as the alternative to their lying in "dull inanimate idleness; a state which I believed to be, both disgraceful to themselves, and displeasing to their Creator."[48] The very British captain Robert Percival, whose 1795 *Account of the Cape of Good Hope* is invested in blaming the rival Dutch for many of the Hottentots' bad qualities, admits that, while "their original bad qualities were comparatively but few" before they were exploited by the Dutch, Hottentots by nature are "indeed lazy to a great degree; even hunger cannot provoke them to be at any trouble for procuring food."[49]

Even specifically antiracist and pro-abolitionist works tend to accept without argument the notion that Africans are idle. Henri Gregoire's *Enquiry Concerning the Intellectual and Moral Faculties and Literature of the Negroes*, which debates many racist notions of black inferiority, nevertheless says that "the accusation of indolence" is "not without some degree of truth."[50] James Ramsey's abolitionist work *Objections to the Abolition of the Slave Trade, with Answers*, while arguing that freed blacks *will* work to support themselves, unquestioningly accepts "the indolence of savages."[51] Thomas Clarkson, who also argues for the abolition of slavery in his *Essay on the Slavery and Commerce of the Human Species* (1786), says that one reason slavery is cruel is that the life of a slave presents so sharp a contrast to the life of a free African, which he describes as "a life of indolence and ease, where the earth brings forth spontaneously the comforts of life, and spares frequently the toil and trouble of cultivation."[52] Although Clarkson's attitude toward African indolence differs from that held by most commentators, he concurs entirely with the idea that Africans *are* indolent.

The modern reader, confronted with the pervasiveness of this notion in so many types of discourse, from writers with otherwise differing ideologies, may well wonder from whence it springs. Certainly, one obvious source of the idea is simply the ethnocentrism of eighteenth-century European observers. Certainly, also, Africans had very different ideas about time and time-use than did clock-conscious Europeans.[53] Philip D. Curtin suggests that Europeans failed to understand African agricultural practices, since, unlike European practices, they often centered around dry and rainy seasons: "The dry-season underemployment might look like simple laziness."[54] More recently, Anne McClintock also argues that "complaints about black sloth were as often complaints about different habits of labor."[55] Additionally, the theories of climate and environment that were being circulated to explain racial differences—and, not so incidentally, to suggest that people who lived in moderate climates like that of Great Britain were most likely to develop certain character traits that the British found admirable—tended to reinforce the misunderstanding. As I mentioned earlier, Europeans believed incorrectly that African soil could bring forth bountiful crops if only the natives would make a minimal effort, and they also believed that fertile climates made people indolent. This myth of "tropical exuberance,"[56] coupled with the notion that warm weather causes lassitude, could serve as a self-fulfilling prophecy: if you believe that tropical environments lead to indolence, you may be more likely to observe indolence when visiting such environments. But a further and perhaps more compelling source of this notion of African idleness has to do, as I suggested earlier, with the importance of the notion of idleness to national identity. As I have been arguing, the eighteenth-century British—especially the increasingly powerful middling classes—defined themselves as an industrious people, basing much of their entitlement to empire on this claim, that they deserved to control the land and its wealth because only they possessed the industriousness to make proper use of them. Clearly the willingness of British commentators to buy into the notion of African indolence, even when they refute other negative stereotypes, and the tendency of British writing on southern Africa to accuse the Dutch settlers also of a shameful idleness (especially later in

the century, when Great Britain was struggling with Holland for control of South Africa) argues for the importance to the British of defining
themselves as a non-idle people. And if the British defined themselves
as industrious, defining the African as idle enabled them to separate
themselves from him even more radically, to cast him even more firmly
into the realm of "other." (That we have seen this move before, in comfortable-class writings about the laboring classes, makes especially sus-
picious the frequency with which depictions of Africans, especially in
pro-slavery writings, compare the "idle" Africans unfavorably to the
"hardworking" British poor.)[57]

This centrality of notions of idleness and industriousness to British
national identity, then, accounts at least in part for their seeing African
life as a display of disgusting indolence, rather than, for instance, a pastoral enjoyment of Edenic leisure. The idea of African idleness also, as
I have indicated earlier, had several important benefits for the British
and their colonialist project. While the general construction of Africans
as bestial beings allowed the English to position themselves as markedly
superior to them and therefore entitled to exploit them much as they
would useful animals, the conviction that Africans were *idle* specifically
provided a splendid justification for slavery. J. P. L. Durand is one of
many commentators who argued that "It is an admitted fact, that the
free Negroes never work; it is therefore necessary to employ slaves."
He goes on to explain that "this apprehension is founded on the knowledge I possess of their natural and invincible indolence."[58] Thus to abolish slavery would be to abolish the African's only spur to industry. Lord
Henry Brougham agrees with this idea, asserting in his *Inquiry into the
Colonial Policy of the European Powers* (1803) that "free Negroes are ut-
terly destitute of industry; [and] from their confirmed habits of idleness
they are the pests of society."[59]

Thus, according to eighteenth-century British notions of the evils of
idleness, if the African will not work, then he must be compelled to
work. If he insists on lying supinely in the sun, refusing to exploit the
potential riches of his environment (a scandal that especially vexes
many commentators), then those who have proved their superiority by
their activity and industry are entitled, almost obligated, to force him
into useful labor. Even the outright cruelty of slave owners could, for
some, be palliated by this notion of inveterate African indolence: as
Thomas Atwood explains in his *History of the Island of Dominica* (1791),
"Idleness is so very predominant in negroes, and their dislike of labour
is so great, that it is very difficult to make them work: it is sometimes
absolutely necessary to have recourse to measures that appear cruel, in
order to oblige them to labour."[60] A writer in a 1789 issue of *Gentleman's
Magazine* claims that African blacks are "apparently useless in the great

scale of human society" and that the way to make them useful and to promote their becoming civilized is to introduce them to labor in the West Indies.[61] Edward Long, who claims in his pro-slavery *History of Jamaica* that the African has "no wish but to be idle,"[62] goes on to assert that he *can* be made into a useful being: "It cannot be doubted, but the far greater part of them are more inclined to a life of idleness and ease, than a life of labour: yet the regular discipline to which [slaves] are inured from their infancy, becomes habitual and natural to them. . . ."[63] Thus the British could see slavery as providing two splendid benefits. It provided a labor force necessary to the building of an empire: as Edward Long proclaims, "The true strength of the island [of Jamaica] must originate, not from the number or nature of its lines and bastions, but from a well-regulated spirit of industry, diffused through every part of it."[64] It also could be seen as shining the saving light of industriousness into benighted African souls, reclaiming them from the abyss of habitual idleness.

Whether the people who created these portrayals of "the African" were consciously shaping their accounts to support the slave trade and imperialism or not, these representations certainly did an excellent job of upholding British interests. Since the idea of African idleness brought the British so many benefits, it is not surprising that it was held so firmly and so long. But this idea, like much ideology, was also a double-edged sword. Under slavery and colonialism, native Africans were obviously performing amounts and kinds of labor that the whites in the colonies were not. A tension therefore arises: how were they to retain the degree of leisure that ruling-class Englishmen deemed desirable and suitable for themselves, without slipping into the stigmatized category of "idler" and thus, by their own discursive insistence, of "African"? One response to this problem is the insistence that Europeans are constitutionally incapable of working in the tropics, that they simply have no other choice but to decline to labor, and that therefore their lack of work cannot be called idleness.[65] However, as I will discuss later, other ideas about race that might indicate that the white could slip into the category of "African" were not so easy to dismiss.

II

Africans are not the only nonwhite people stigmatized as idle in this period. Indians, also, are often spoken of as idle, though in a different way. Whereas the indolence of Africans is brutish, prompting them to sprawl bestially in the dirt, the indolence of Indians is effeminate, inclining them to recline on sofas and puff dreamily on hookahs. Thomas

Salmon's *New Geographical and Historical Grammar* (revised edition, 1772) says of Asia that "the warmth of these Eastern climates has doubtless ever contributed to the indolence and effeminacy of its inhabitants; and it may be doubted whether they ever had the industry and active spirits of the inhabitants of Europe, who found the necessity of labour for their support, which the Asiatics had less occasion for, through the luxuriancy of their soil. . . ."[66] Robert Orme, a historiographer to the East India Company, frequently refers to the luxurious indolence of the inhabitants of "Indostan" in his *Historical Fragments of the Mogul Empire* (1805). The Indian sun, he asserts, is "too sultry to admit the exercise and fatigues necessary to form a robust nation;"[67] and he points out that even the originally robust Tartars, who easily conquered the indolent Indians, have succumbed to the climate: "A licentiousness and luxury peculiar to this enervating climate, have spread their corruption. . . . ;"[68] "The climate and habits of Indostan have enervated the strong fibres with which the Tartars conquered it. . . ."[69] In *Representations of India, 1740–1840: The Creation of India in the Colonial Imagination*, Amal Chatterjee also speaks of the idea that the Indian climate can unman even the stalwart Tartar:

> The "placid-lazy" school often "observed" degrees of effeminacy in (male) Indians,[70] an observation surprisingly shared by a former British captive who otherwise complained vociferously of extreme ill-treatment. He was convinced the Indian climate emasculated the men: "In two or three generations, it is observed, the progeny of the Tartarian and Persian conquerors of the plains of Hindostan, are subdued by an enervating climate, and sink down with the effeminate aborigines of the country into sloth and sensuality."[71]

Many commentators assert that the climate causes indolence also because it allows people to survive with almost no work; here we see again the idea of tropical exuberance. Alexander Dow's *Dissertation Concerning the Origin and Nature of Despotism in Hindostan* (1770) says of the Indian that "Other motives of passive obedience join issue with the love of ease. The sun, which enervates his body, produces for him, in a manner spontaneously, the various fruits of the earth. He finds subsistence without much toil; he requires little covering but the shade."[72] The final chapter of Orme's work, entitled "Effeminacy of the Inhabitants of Indostan," also puts forth this idea of indolence caused by tropical exuberance, and it leaves us with this portrait of the emasculated Indian: "Breathing in the softest of climates; having so few real wants; and receiving even the luxuries of other nations with little labour, from the fertility of their own soil; the Indian must become the most effeminate inhabitant of the globe; and this is the very point at which we now see him."[73]

This Indian indolence, many writers assert, has made them ripe for despotism. Dow begins his dissertation by linking climate, indolence, and despotism: "Government derives its form from accident; its spirit and genius from the inherent manners of the people. The languor occasioned by the hot climate of India, inclines the native to indolence and ease; and he thinks the evils of despotism less severe than the labour of being free."[74] Other writers reverse the causality, assigning despotic government as a source of indolence. The Reverend William Tennant makes both these gestures in his *Indian Recreations* (2nd edition, 1804):

> Three causes have been assigned for the small progress made by the Oriental nations in the arts; the tyranny of their despotic governments; the enervating heat of the climate; and their attachment to ancient usages. By a reflecting mind, however, these will be found easily reducible to the second; for if the energies of body and mind are injured by the effects of climate, despotism, the most simple of all forms of government, will of consequence arise. . . .[75]

Thus climate is responsible both for the despotic Indian government and for India's ranking so low on the scale of industrious nations, as Tennant has asserted earlier: "The most indolent nation in Europe far excels in every exertion, whether mental or corporeal, this listless and unambitious race."[76]

Some commentators ascribe Indian indolence to the fixed structure of their society, which precludes rising in status through hard work. In his *Philosophical and Political History of the Settlements and Trade of the Europeans in the East and West Indies* (revised edition, 1783), the Abbe Raynal says that Indians are

> of a weak, mild, and humane disposition, and almost strangers to several of the passions that prevail among us. What motive of ambition indeed could there be among men destined always to continue in the same state? The constant and repeated exercise of the religious ceremonies is the only pleasure most of them enjoy. They love peaceable labour and an indolent life, and often quote this passage of one of their favourite authors: *'Tis better to sit still than to walk; better to sleep than to awake; but death is better than all.*[77] (his italics)

Luke Scrafton says very similarly in his *Reflections on the Government of Indostan* (1743) that Indians

> are almost strangers to many of those passions that form the pleasure and pain of our lives. Love, at least all the violent tumults of it, is unknown to

the Gentoos, by their marrying so young, and by the little intercourse they have with other women; ambition is effectually restrained by their religion, which has, by insurmountable barriers, confined every individual to a limited sphere. . . . But from hence also, they are strangers to that vigor of mind, and all the virtues grafted on those passions which animate our more active spirits. They prefer a lazy apathy, and frequently quote this saying from some favourite book: "It is better to sit than to walk, to lie down than to sit, to sleep than to wake, and death is best of all."[78]

Commentators also discuss characteristics of what we might now call the Indian "lifestyle" as causes of enervation and indolence. Interestingly, Dow looks at two traits often associated, as we have seen earlier, with the grotesque idle body, bodily hygiene and the consumption of alcohol. However, Dow associates excessive cleanliness and the avoidance of alcohol with indolence, thus making the Indian the opposite of grotesque, but still idle:

The frequent bathing inculcated by the Coran, has, by debilitating the body, a great effect on the mind. Habit makes the warm bath a luxury of a bewitching kind. The women spend whole days in water; and hasten by it the approach of age. The indolence of the men, which inclines them to follow every mode of placid pleasure, recommends to them a practice which Mahommed has made a tenet of religion. The prohibition of wine is also favourable to despotisim. It prevents that free communication of sentiment which awakens mankind from a torpid indifference to their natural rights.[79]

Richard Owen Cambridge claims that the indolence induced by the Indians' diet and consumption of opium is the reason for their lack of military prowess: "At the close of the evening, every man eats an inconceivable quantity of rice, and many take after it some kind of soporific drugs; so that about mid-night, the whole army is in a dead sleep: the consequence of these habits is obvious; and yet it would appear a strange proposition to an Eastern monarch, to endeavour to persuade him, that the security of his throne depended upon the regulation of the meals of the common soldier. . . ."[80] In his *History of the Military Transactions of the British Nation in Indostan* (1763), Robert Orme blames the nonviolence and temperance of the Indian religion, as well as diet and climate, for the Indian's indolent effeminacy, and he also indicates that Indians do not make good soldiers:

An abhorrence to the shedding of blood, derived from his religion, and seconded by the great temperance of a life which is passed by most of them in a very sparing use of animal food, and a total abstinence from intoxicating liquors; the influence of the most regular of climates, in which the great heat of the sun and the great fertility of the soil lessen most of the wants to which the human species is subject in austerer regions, and supply the rest without the exertion of much labour; these causes have all together contributed to render the Indian the most enervated inhabitant of the globe.

He shudders at the sight of blood, and is of a pusillanimity only to be excused and accounted for by the great delicacy of his configuration.[81]

III

As I mentioned earlier, differences among the "varieties of mankind" were of considerable interest to many eighteenth-century thinkers. Writers such as George Louis Leclerc Buffon, Johann Friedrich Blumenbach, Samuel Stanhope Smith, and Henry Home, Lord Kames put forth various theories to account for the supposed physical and temperamental differences between the varieties of the human species. These theories are different in some ways, but they share a belief in the strong influence of climate, and of the related "modes of life," on human characteristics. They also share a tendency to form a hierarchy, whether implicit or explicit, of the varieties of mankind, with the white (or, to use the word coined by Blumenbach, the "Caucasian") variety at the top of the hierarchy. The other varieties of mankind, whether these are numbered, as in Carl von Linne's work, as three (leaving out the "wild man") — "American," "Asiatic," and "African," — or, as in Blumenbach's later editions, as four — "Mongolian," "Ethiopian," "American," and "Malay" — have somehow "degenerated" from the Caucasian variety. (This notion of the white variety of man as original and of the other varieties as degenerations of whiteness is, of course, a very convenient support of the important eighteenth-century British project of imperialism. If the nonwhite peoples of the world are in various ways inferior, then it might naturally follow that the white people are meant to rule them.)

Much of this theory-of-race writing also stresses the degenerate state of "the African" and insists that he represents a degradation from an earlier, better, and — more important — whiter state. Thus the eighteenth-century interest in systematizing and categorizing the "varieties of mankind" soon invested the image of the indolent African with scientific authority. In his *General System of Nature through the Three Grand Kingdoms of Animals, Vegetable, and Minerals*, Linnaeus separates the types of humankind into (besides the briefly mentioned "Wild Man") American, European, Asiatic, and African, and he associates each one with a humor: for instance, the European is "Fair, sanguine, brawny" and the Asiatic is "Sooty, melancholy, rigid." Not surprisingly, the African is "Black, phlegmatic, relaxed." In a brief description after each of these headings, each of the four varieties is accorded a list of three adjectives: "obstinate, content, free" for the American, "gentle, acute, inventive" for the European, and "severe, haughty, covetous" for the Asiatic. "Crafty, indolent, negligent" are the three adjectives with which Linnaeus sums up the African.[82] While only the European receives entirely positive adjectives, only the African is defined in terms of laziness. The section on Africa in the *Universal Modern History* (1760) ascribes laziness, along with other negative qualities, to Africans, it exclaims over the "shameful indolence" of the natives of the Congo, and it refutes the idea that the relative frugality of the African diet is an admirable sign of temperance, saying that it "is not so much the result of virtue as laziness, which prevents their going in search of game."[83] The article on "Negroes" in the first American edition of the *Encyclopaedia Britannica*, published late in the eighteenth century, produces a long list of "vices the most notorious" that are "the portion of this unhappy race": at the head of the list is "idleness."[84] Thus the personal "observations" of travelers were hardened into scientific "truth."

Samuel Stanhope Smith's *Essay on the Causes of the Variety of Complexion and Figure in the Human Species* (1787), for instance, not only associates idleness with nonwhite "savagery" but assigns idleness as the *cause* of degeneration from civilization into "savageness": "[T]he primitive nations are, at their first appearance, in history, already civilized. Savagism was an after growth, which took its origin from idle, or disorderly men who, abhorring the constraints of society, sought, in the bosom of boundless forests, that freedom from control, and from labor, which was congenial with their wandering disposition."[85] Smith goes on to assert of "every savage people" that "unless urged by some violent passion, or urged by immediate want, they are always indolent."[86]

While not all theorists assert so clearly that idleness has caused a degeneration from originary civilization into savagery, all seem to link race and behavior with climate. Smith's *Essay* is in part a reply to the *Sketches of the History of Man* (1774) written by Henry Home, Lord Kames. Smith argues against the idea of polygenesis—separate creations of the races of man—with which Kames briefly flirts. Smith argues vehemently that all the races came from a single creation, and he ascribes all racial differences to the influence of climate. Interestingly, then, considering these writers' different views, both Kames and Smith assert the likelihood that people of one race can degenerate into a darker race if they live in a hot climate. Kames says,

[I]nstances are without number of men degenerating in a climate to which they are not fitted by nature; and I know not of a single instance where in such a climate people have retained their original vigour. Several European

colonies have subsisted in the torrid zone of America more than two centuries; and yet even that length of time has not familiarized them to the climate: they cannot bear heat like the original inhabitants, nor like negroes
transplanted from a country equally hot: they are far from equalling in vigour of mind or body the nations from which they sprung. . . . The offspring
of Europeans born in Batavia, soon degenerate. Scarce one of them has talents sufficient to bear a part in the administration. There is not an office of
trust but must be filled with native Europeans. Some Portuguese, who have
been for ages settled on the sea-coast of Congo, retain scarce the appearance
of men.[87]

This picture is certainly alarming to the colonialist project,[88] and Smith
points out reasonably enough that it seems to prove his own idea that
climate causes changes that account for racial difference:

The degeneracy of the human constitution often produced by changes in
climate, [Kames] confirms by the example of a Portuguese colony on the
coast of Congo, 'who, in a course of time, have degenerated so much, that
they scarce retain the appearance of men.'—A fact more to the purpose of
the preceding essay could not be adduced. Apply it to the case of the neigh-
bouring tribes of negroes, and of Hottentots. Although they are now so rude
that scarcely do they retain the appearance of men, does not his own example demonstrate that, in some remote period, they may have descended from
the same original stock with these degenerated Portuguese?[89]

Lord Kames, like many others, asserts that a moderate climate produces the best, most manly citizens, and that denizens both of harsher
and of easier climates fall short:

Were all the earth barren like New Holland, all men would be ignorant and
brutish, like the inhabitants of New Holland. On the other hand, were every
portion of this earth so fertile as spontaneously to feed all its inhabitants,
which is the golden age figured by poets, what would follow? Upon the former supposition, man would be a meagre, patient, and timid animal: upon
the latter supposition, he would be pampered, lazy, and effeminate. In both
cases, he would be stupidly ignorant, and incapable of any manly exertion,
whether of mind or body.[90]

This commonly held theory seems to reserve for the inhabitants of climates like England's such traits as wisdom, civility, courage, industry,
and manliness. Much climate theory focuses mainly on the warmer
countries from which so much of Britain's colonial wealth was pouring
forth, asserting, as we have seen, that tropical climates are responsible
both for nonwhite skin (and other racial features) and for indolence.

IV

The idea that climates like that of Britain spawn wise, industrious, manly citizens, while climates like those of places the British were trying to colonize spawn indolent, weak, bestial, or effeminate natives is of course very useful to would-be imperialists. And yet, as I implied earlier, the notion of racial degeneration, and especially the climatic explanation for it, brings in another possibility that is vastly troubling to the imperialist project. If all races were originally white and degenerated through climate to their varying degrees of darkness and deficiency of character (the two are almost always linked, again, whether implicitly or explicitly), then what might happen to white colonists living in these very same climates? As different as the pictures of African and Indian indolence are, both are often ascribed to climate, and both, therefore, might infect European colonists as they live in the enervating heat and idleness-inspiring fertility of Africa, Jamaica, or India. Might the European, too, degenerate away from superior whiteness? After all, as Blumenbach says, arguing that white was "the primitive colour" of humankind, "it is very easy for that to degenerate into brown, but very much more difficult for dark to become white. . . ."[91] Smith agrees, speaking of "the greater ease with which a dark colour may be stained on a skin originally fair, than effaced from it," asserting that "white is the original ground" of skin color, and cautioning that "the whiteness of skin is to be preserved only by carefully protecting it" from degenerative forces.[92] Sliding down the chain of being, it would seem, is easier than clambering up.[93]

And indeed, some eighteenth-century accounts of white colonists in Africa, the West Indies, and India do imply that such degeneration may be taking place. Some of the portraits of the colonizers and enslavers emerge as troublingly similar to portraits of the colonized and enslaved. The discourse of degeneration focused on these three colonial areas differs in some ways, but all three share an emphasis on idleness and indolence.

Many commentators on Africa, for instance, write of the idleness of the Boers, the Dutch settlers living at the Cape. (This sort of discourse is especially frequent at the end of the eighteenth century and the beginning of the nineteenth, as the British were struggling with the Dutch for possession of the Cape.)[94] John Campbell's *Travels in South Africa* (3rd edition, 1815) reports that, because of the excessive number of servants the Boers employ, they "have no occasion to put their hands to any work, wherefore they sit with their legs across, the better part of the day, or else indulge in sleep." Thus, he says, "in this way their days and years pass on in miserable idleness."[95] Sir James Edward Alexander complains in *An Expedition of Discovery into the Interior of Africa* (1838) that, though the Boers should live long lives, they do not, because they "live grossly; that horrid sheep's tail fat clogs the wheels of the machine. Besides, the men take, in general, little active exercise, and the women less, the former leaving any hard work to slaves . . . while the vrows sit in a corner preparing 'tea-water,' and get fat from inactivity. . . ."[96]

Several commentators make the same complaint about the Boers that is so often made about the Hottentots: that, positioned in the midst of potential plenty, they refuse to exert themselves toward a better life. "Placed in a country where not only the necessaries, but almost every luxury of life might by industry be procured," says John Barrow, the Boer "has the enjoyment of none of them." He drinks no wine, despite an environment perfect for vineyards, his house is primitive and dirty, his windows lack glass, and he has barely any furniture—all because he prefers smoking his pipe and napping after his meals of mutton "swimming in the grease of the sheep's tail."[97] "Unwilling to work, and unable to think; with a mind disengaged from every sort of care and reflexion, indulging to excess in the gratification of every sensual appetite," the Boer lives out his idle life.[98] Captain Robert Percival's *Account of the Cape of Good Hope* (1795) makes a very similar complaint, saying that "though the country abounds with whatever can make life comfortable," the Boer prefers to live in indolent dirt and discomfort. "Smoking all the morning, and sleeping after dinner, constitute the great luxury of the boor; unwilling to work himself, he lords it over his slaves and hired Hottentots. At a middling age he is carried off by a dropsy, or some disease contracted by indolence and eating to excess."[99] Lady Anne Barnard's *Cape Journals* makes the same point more succinctly: "how these people have every thing but possess things so unneatly . . . so indiligently that there is the appearance of *misery* when there ought to be all the *charms* of comfort"[100] (ellipses and italics hers).

These descriptions of the Boers' idleness also echo other features heard in descriptions of the Hottentots. Four of the most often reported practices of the Hottentots are tobacco smoking, brandy drinking, eating large quantities of meat, and smearing the body with grease. The first three of these are also constant features of descriptions of the Boers; and the fourth, grease-smearing, could perhaps find its match in the enormous quantities of grease the Boers were reported to consume. These similarities might certainly prompt the idea that the colonizers were degenerating into people hard to distinguish from the natives, thus presenting an idea deeply troubling to the imperialist project—that the lines between the superior European and the bestial African might not be entirely immutable. This question hovers around several of the commentators' accounts: Percival discusses the "degeneracy" of the

Boers,[101] and O. F. Mentzel worries that if only African-born whites populate the country, it will "degenerate and become uncivilized."[102] Mentzel even goes so far as to claim that African-born whites are almost indistinguishable from the blacks: they have so "accustomed themselves" to "the carefree life, the indifference, the lazy days and the association with slaves and Hottentots," he says, that "not much difference may be discerned between the former and the latter. If, in addition, the sweet little wife has also grown up among slave and Hottentot women, one may easily form a conception of the kind of people their children will eventually be."[103] As troubling as this idea may be to imperialism in general, however, for the British to view the Boers as a degenerated people certainly helped support the claim that England should own the Cape.

Accounts of both black slaves and white colonizers in the West Indies present a picture less brutish than, but equally idle as, accounts of native and colonial Africans, but it is generally the women who are condemned as idle. In his *History of the West Indies*, Bryan Edwards, a staunch supporter of the colonies, defends the Creoles (permanent white residents) against charges of cowardice but says, "indolence, I will admit, is too prevalent among them."[104] He also says that the women, because of their abstemious diets and the "hot and oppressive atmosphere" of the islands, suffer from "a lax fibre, and a complexion in which the lily predominates rather than the rose." They appear to new visitors "as just arisen from the bed of sickness" and their "voice is soft and spiritless, and every step betrays languor and lassitude. With the finest persons, they certainly want that glow of health in the countenance, that delicious crimson . . . which, in the colder countries, enlivens the coarsest set of features, and renders a beautiful one irresistible."[105] John Stewart paints much the same portrait in his *Account of Jamaica* (1808), saying that the Creole women have "a sickly and languid appearance" and "the appearance of languor and indolence," and, although he denies exaggerated reports of their indolence, he admits that "a degree of languor originates in the climate."[106] He also claims that a Creole man seldom becomes "as eminent in his particular walk of life as the native of any other country," because "he is too lively, too volatile, too indolent, and too fond of pleasure for such application."[107] Although a great supporter of English colonies in Jamaica, Edward Long says similarly in his *History of Jamaica* (1774) that the white women, at least, "yield too much to the influence of a warm climate in their listless indolence of life"[108] and are tainted by too much contact with indolent blacks. Like Edwards and Stewart, he reports female languor and lassitude, drawing our attention to

a very fine young woman aukwardly dangling her arms with the air of a
Negroe servant, lolling almost the whole day upon beds or settees, her head
muffled up in two or three handkerchiefs, her dress loose, and without stays.
. . . In the afternoon, she takes her *siesto* as usual; while two of these [black]
damsels refresh her face with the gentle breathings of the fan; and a third
provokes the drowsy powers of Morpheus by delicious scratchings on the
sole of either foot. When she rouzes from slumber, her speech is whining,
languid, and childish. When arrived at maturer years, the consciousness of
her ignorance makes her abscond from the sight or conversation of every
rational creature. Her ideas are narrowed to the ordinary subjects that pass
before her, the business of the plantation, the tittle-tattle of the parish; the
tricks, superstitions, diversions, and profligate discourses, of black servants,
equally illiterate and unpolished.[109]

That such a vicious racist as Long would let whites set the standard of
illiteracy which the black servants then equal is quite remarkable; and
on the next page, he seems to withdraw somewhat from this position,
blaming the ladies' indolence on the inattention of the men: "But it is
chiefly the fault of the men, if they do not assemble till the hour of dinner is served up, or retire from it with the cloth, to doze away an hour
or two, or enjoy a separate *tete a tete* in some adjoining chamber, leaving
the men to their bottle."[110]
    These portraits of white settlers in the West Indies are different from
those of the African Boers, but they certainly might imply that whites
are as susceptible as other races to the degenerative effects of a tropical
climate. The physician Benjamin Mosely, who practiced for several
years in the West Indies, supports this idea in his *Treatise on Tropical
Diseases; on Military Operations; and on the Climate of the West Indies* (1787).
He claims that the mental activities of Europeans "degenerated" in
tropical climates: "There is, in the inhabitants of hot climates . . . , a
promptitude and bias to pleasure, and an alienation from serious
thought and deep reflection."[111] The Abbe Raynal's *Philosophical and Political History of the Settlements and Trade of the Europeans in the East and
West Indies* makes this strong and, for imperialists, troubling statement:
"It would seem that the Europeans, who have been translated into the
American islands, must no less have degenerated than the animals
which they have carried over thither. The climate acts on all living
beings. . . ."[112]
    Colonists in India, also, are often reported as succumbing to the luxu-
rious, effeminizing indolence of that country. Many accounts, as we
have seen, represent the Tartar conquerors of India as having degenerated from their original robust, active manliness. Luke Scrafton's *Reflections on the Government of Indostan* is fairly typical, explaining that
"The last conquerors of India were the Tartars . . . , a fierce and warlike

people, who, in the same century, over-ran China and Persia; but their posterity degenerated into a weak, effeminate race. . . ."[113] Scrafton claims that at first the Tartars "abhor the sensuality and effeminacy" of the country, but "by degrees their native manners wear off, they adopt the luxury they despised," and in a generation or two they "have nothing remaining of their Tartar origin; like our English hounds, [who,] when sent abroad, the first breed of which retains some little of the qualities of a hound, but the next are no better than curs."[114] William Mackintosh, author of the 1782 *Travels in Europe, Asia, and Africa*, presents yet another portrait of white indolence in the colonies, describing a day in the life of a Company-employed Englishman in Calcutta. The passage goes on for several pages, beginning and ending with a "female companion" in the man's bed "to amuse him." An excerpt from the description of this fortunate fellow's morning will give you the idea:

> In about half an hour after undoing and taking off his long drawers, a clean shirt, breeches, stockings, and slippers, are put upon his body, thighs, legs, and feet, without any greater exertion on his own part, than if he was a statue.[115] The barber enters, shaves him, cuts his nails, and cleans his ears. The chillumjee and ewer are brought by a servant, whose duty it is, who pours water upon his hands, to wash his hands and face, and presents a towel.—The superior then walks in state to his breakfasting parlour in his waistcoat; is seated; the consummah makes and pours out his tea, and presents him with a plate of bread or toast. The hair-dresser comes behind, and begins his operation, while the huccabadar softly slips the upper end of the snake or tube of the houcca into his hand. While the hairdresser is doing his duty, the gentleman is eating, sipping, and smoking by turns.[116]

This picture certainly resembles Owen Cambridge's account in *An Account of the War in India* (1761) of the "luxurious indolence" in which native Indians "pass the greater part of their lives": "they sit for the most part (when they are not with their women) upon their sofas, smoking, and amusing themselves with their jewels, [and] taking coffee or sweet-meats, seeing their quails fight,[117] or some such like pastimes. . . ."[118]

A less attractive picture of what happens to Europeans in India comes from Tennant's *Indian Recreations*. Tennant emphasizes the harmful physical effects of the climate, which causes indolence not through languid pleasure, but through sickness: "A sallow and livid complexion is so universal in Bengal, that when you behold a face of the roseate hue, you can pronounce that its owner is newly arrived, nearly with as much certainty as if you heard that part of his history from his own mouth. Even in the ordinary health of persons not supposed to be materially injured by the climate, they are capable of little exertion or fatigue: in the hot season of hardly any at all."[119]

V

While this idea that Europeans in India are incapable of any exertion may serve to make idleness allowable, it also seems to make them unfit for colonial rule, thus undermining the whole project. Also, and perhaps more seriously, it brings up again the question of how climate affects character and behavior, and thus the question of degeneration. These questions threaten to undermine not only one important justification for colonialism—that the white man deserves to control the land and its wealth since he alone possesses the industry to make proper use of them—but even the secure identity of whiteness itself. If white colonists are so quickly being infected by the indolence of the natives, might their very status as whites be called into question? I would like to suggest as my conclusion that one of Britain's responses to these anxiety-provoking concerns, illogical as it might seem in some ways, is to embrace even more vehemently the British national identity of activity, industry, strength, and manliness. Percival claims in a passage immediately following one where he says that "the Dutch have ever held the Hottentots in the greatest contempt"[120] that he used to hold the same opinion, but now has conceived "a more favourable" one.[121] He suggests,

> Should ever the Cape fall permanently into the hands of Great Britain, those people under proper management, may speedily arrive at a great degree of civilization. Their industry may be excited, and be turned to produce the most important advantages to the colony. By instructing them in the arts of husbandry, by accustoming them to a mild and equitable treatment, by granting them those rights which ought to be common to the whole human race, although barbarously withheld from them by the Dutch; the Hottentots would speedily be allured from the remote parts and wilds of the interior of Africa, to colonize the country nearer the Cape. The progress of civilization would soon inspire those already in the colony with confidence in themselves, as a people who have a certain part to act in life, and recover them from that state of utter degradation to which they have been reduced. . . .[122]

This passage seems to claim for the British the ability to reverse the process of degeneration and to boost the lowly Hottentot back up the chain of being. By thus ascribing to empire the power to change systems of nature, Percival demonstrates the close connection between these eighteenth-century obsessions. The subjects of Enlightenment En-

gland's systematizing science, it seems, were apt also to become subjected to her imperial sway.

In *Dandies and Desert Saints: Styles of Victorian Masculinity*, James Eli
Adams argues that the Victorian period saw "the loss of traditional,
more assured forms of masculine identity and authority"[123] and that
"the passing of the 'old ideal of manhood' thus marked the loss of a
central point of identity and social reference for large numbers of
men. . . ."[124] At the same time and as a result of this loss of the traditional
assurance of manhood, the period also saw "the increasingly pointed
and violent social leverage inherent in the authority to designate a man
or an idea 'effeminate'. . . ."[125] Given these current anxieties about masculinity even in England, to cling fiercely to the ideal of an active, industrious manhood is perhaps even more important in the colonies—where
anxieties about degeneration, idleness, and unmanliness are so ram-
pant—than it is at home. The chest-thumpingly masculine and industrious colonial of the nineteenth century, who refuses even a lunchtime
siesta but ventures out in the noonday sun, seems to find his origin in
the eighteenth-century fears of degeneration.

5

"Driving On the System of Life": Samuel Johnson and Idleness

THAT SAMUEL JOHNSON WAS TERRIBLY PREOCCUPIED WITH THE NO-
tion of idleness, that he in fact feared his own idleness would cause him
to be damned, may strike the person standing abashed before his shelf
of writings as odd. Johnson's *Dictionary* alone is a staggering accomplishment; in nine years, unaided except by a few amanuenses, he wrote
the definitions for 40,000 words, and, as W. Jackson Bate describes it,
"illustrated them with approximately 114,000 quotations, drawn from
the entire range of English writing, in every field of learning, from the
mid-sixteenth to the mid-eighteenth centuries."[1] Johnson also, of
course, edited the plays of Shakespeare, wrote the critical biographies
of fifty-two poets, produced 103 issues of the *Idler* and 208 issues of the
Rambler, and did a huge amount of charitable ghostwriting for others
(including prefaces, sermons, and law lectures), not to mention his
poems and *Rasselas*, among other works. And yet a glance at Johnson's
Diaries, Prayers, and Annals will reveal the wrenching guilt he felt over
his indolence and misspent time. Johnson's writing, both personal and
public, and his reported conversation return again and again to the idea
of idleness. Johnson's preoccupation with idleness[2] both testifies to and
was partly prompted by the concern with idleness that, as I have been
arguing, was an important element of his culture. And, since he was one
of the most influential authors of his day, the attention he paid to idleness helped shape and reinforce his culture's focus on it.

Johnson's preoccupation with and guilt about idleness trapped him
in a serpentine maze of vicious circles. As I will discuss more thoroughly below, one reason idleness is so hard to escape is that it leads to
boredom (for which Johnson had a great capacity), which causes an
indolence that prevents occupation, which leads to even greater boredom and indolence. Johnson's late rising—one of the manifestations of
his idleness that most plagued him—was nearly impossible for him to
escape, for a similar reason: his insomnia led to late sleeping, which
made him accomplish little during the day and therefore feel guilty; this

guilt then kept him from sleeping at night. Guilt over misspent time can also lead to resolutions of and dreams about future improvement, but this attention to the future, in removing one's attention from the present, is another cause of idleness, leading to yet another vicious circle. The vicious circle which most trapped and tormented Johnson, however, came from his conviction that the mind needed to be kept occupied to prevent melancholy and excessive imaginings. The trifling activities that will distract the troubled mind, though, do not constitute the meaningful work which, Johnson profoundly believed, was the only means to salvation; and the guilt this trifling caused led to a further need to distract himself, and hence to more trifling and more guilt. In *Bad Behavior: Samuel Johnson and Modern Cultural Authority*, Martin Wechselblatt describes this vicious circle in a different way, pointing out that while in *Idler* 31 "the chief element that makes idleness visible is its antithesis, 'busyness' . . . ," in *Rambler* 47, sorrow "is . . . to be cured by the application of the same bustle and empty 'motion' that *Idler* 31 associates with idleness. . . ."[3] Presumably the busy idleness that is sorrow's cure may then become sorrow's cause, and the circle will spin on.

Johnson's keen awareness of time—its brevity, its elusiveness—was another factor in his concern with idleness. For him, nothing but meaningful work could redeem time from the danger of being unprofitably spent, could anchor the present moment and rescue time from dissolving into nothingness. The final and, I think, most important factor in this preoccupation was Johnson's sense that activity alone keeps everything—society, the mind, the soul, the cosmos itself—organized and moving forward. Without activity, all flies out into chaotic oblivion, into the "vacuity" Johnson mentions so often in his conversation and writings, which both lured and deeply terrified him.

I

The boredom to which idleness often leads is, for Johnson, more than an unpleasantness, for boredom can occasion both sinful behavior and profound misery. That the need the bored feel to "rid themselves of the day," as Johnson puts it more than once,[4] leads them into sinful behavior is a familiar notion. When, in Sermon 26, Johnson calls idleness "the original or parent vice, from which they all have their birth,"[5] when he says in *Rambler* 85 that he likes to see "a knot of misses busy at their needles" because such work provides "a security against the most dangerous ensnarers of the soul, by enabling themselves to exclude idleness from their solitary moments,"[6] when he defends in *Rambler* 177 the activity of a group of virtuosos (activity he has just satirized) by saying,

"Whatever busies the mind without corrupting it, has at least this use, that it rescues the day from idleness, and he that is never idle will not often be vitious,"[7] he is reiterating the oft-repeated idea that idleness is the devil's workshop. Much seventeenth- and eighteenth-century devotional literature stresses this tendency of idleness to lead to vice. For instance, *Holy Living*, by Jeremy Taylor, an author Johnson read and admired,[8] tells us that "to a busy man temptation is fain to climb up together with his business, and sins creep upon him only by accidents and occasions, whereas to an idle person they come in a full body, and with open violence, and the impudence of restless importunity,"[9] and it advises us, as a "remedy against uncleanness," to "Avoid *idleness*, and fill up all the spaces of thy time with severe and useful employment: for lust usually creeps in at those emptinesses where the Soul is unemployed and the body is at ease."[10]

What is more peculiar to Johnson than this idea of idleness as the root of evil is his very strong sense of the *misery* of idleness and its attendant boredom, a misery which seems to disturb him more than the sins boredom occasions.[11] As he says in *Idler* 3, playfully but also, I think, sincerely, "There are certainly miseries in idleness, which the Idler only can conceive."[12] Paul Fussell points out Johnson's own "profound" capacity for boredom[13] and notes that many of Johnson's critical judgments derive from what Fussell calls "the General Theory of Boredom."[14] For instance, Johnson sees Homer and Shakespeare as two of the greatest writers "ultimately and simply" because, "being the most varied, they are the least boring."[15] Much of Johnson's writing portrays boredom as deeply painful. In *Rasselas*, for example, the Happy Valley is unable to make all its residents happy, despite its beauty and the variety of fish, fowl, and beasts it houses, despite the music and revelry with which the inhabitants are entertained. Although the residents of the valley "lived only to know the soft vicissitudes of pleasure and repose, attended by all that were skilful to delight, and gratified with whatever the senses can enjoy,"[16] Rasselas finds himself "pained with want,"[17] although he does not know what it is he wants. His hours are "tedious and gloomy,"[18] and he "repine[s] to see the sun move so slowly towards the western mountain" and "lament[s] when the day breaks and sleep will no longer hide" him from himself.[19] What he wants, of course, is something to do; he is bored.[20] When he begins to search for a way to escape from the Happy Valley, he finds that the search itself makes him happy, even though for months it is unsuccessful:

In these fruitless searches he spent ten months. The time, however, passed cheerfully away: in the morning he rose with new hope, in the evening applauded his own diligence, and in the night slept sound after his fatigue. He met a thousand amusements which beguiled his labor, and diversified his thoughts.[21]

Rasselas is made happy, not only by the prospect of escape, but by the occupation that searching for escape affords him. Johnson's periodical essays are also full of assertions that boredom causes misery. In *Rambler* 42, for instance, Johnson writes as Euphalia, a young lady from the city who is visiting her aunt in the country. Euphalia finds herself terribly bored without urban amusements and laments her situation:

> Thus am I condemned to solitude; the day moves slowly forward, and I see the dawn with uneasiness, because I consider that night is at a great distance. I have tried to sleep by a brook, but find its murmurs ineffectual; so that I am forced to be awake at least twelve hours, without visits, without cards, without laughter, and without flattery. I walk because I am disgusted with sitting still, and sit down because I am weary with walking. I have no motive to action, nor any object of love, or hate, or fear, or inclination.[22]

As different as the frivolous Euphalia is from Prince Rasselas, they employ the same imagery; for both, the day moves slowly, and both greet the dawn with dismay. Dick Linger, the character who describes his plight in *Idler* 21, also finds time dragging:

> Time with all its celerity, moves slowly to him, whose whole employment is to watch its flight. I am forced upon a thousand shifts to enable me to endure the tediousness of the day. I rise when I can sleep no longer, and take my morning walk; I see what I have seen before, and return. I sit down and persuade myself, that I sit down to think, find it impossible to think without a subject, rise up to enquire after news, and endeavour to kindle in myself, an artificial impatience for intelligence of events, which will never extend any consequence to me, but that a few minutes they abstract me from myself.[23]

In Euphalia's and Dick Linger's complaints are the first of the vicious circles I mentioned above: idleness leads to boredom which leads to greater indolence and therefore idleness, causing further disinclination to find something useful to do which may relieve the boredom. Idleness therefore has a self-reproducing quality which makes it even more engulfing.

The portraits of miserable boredom in *Rasselas* and the letters from Euphalia and Dick Linger have their humorous elements, but some of Johnson's writings about boredom are grimmer. The epistle from Dick Linger claims that soldiers often prefer even the horrors of war to the pain of idleness:

I suppose every man is shocked when he hears how frequently soldiers are wishing for war. . . . those who desire it most, are neither prompted by malevolence nor patriotism; they neither pant for laurels, nor delight in blood; but long to be delivered from the tyranny of idleness, and restored to the dignity of active beings.[24]

In the famous *Rambler* 134 about idleness and procrastination (written, of course, as the printer's boy waited at the door),[25] Johnson, while asserting that the miseries of the idle are their own doing, compares them to the pains of Tantalus in hell, certainly a strong image.[26] But probably the most powerful image of the anguish of idleness is found in Johnson's allegorical tale "The Vision of Theodore, the Hermit of Teneriffe." In the next-to-last paragraph is this description of those who "retreated from the heat and tumult of the way, not to the bowers of Intemperance, but to the maze of Indolence":

> They wandered on from one double of the labyrinth to another with the chains of Habit hanging secretly upon them, till, as they advanced, the flowers grew paler, and the scents fainter; they proceeded in their dreary march without pleasure in their progress, yet without power to return; and had this aggravation above all others, that they were criminal but not delighted. The drunkard for a time laughed over his wine; the ambitious man triumphed over the miscarriage of his rival; but the captives of Indolence had neither superiority nor merriment. Discontent lowered in their looks, and Sadness hovered round their shades; yet they crawled on reluctant and gloomy, till they arrived at the depth of the recess, varied only with poppies and nightshade, where the dominion of Indolence terminates, and the hopeless wanderer is delivered up to Melancholy; the chains of Habit are rivetted for ever; and Melancholy, having tortured her prisoner for a while, consigns him at last to the cruelty of Despair.[27]

The horrifying dreariness of this picture, and its position at the end of the tale, make the region of indolence seem the lowest circle in hell.

The mention of melancholy in the quotation from "The Vision of Theodore" leads us to contemplate another terrible effect of idleness Johnson worries about: it leads to melancholy and "vain imaginings" and, through these, to insanity. Johnson prays that idleness will not lay him "open to vain imaginations"[28] and in a journal entry closely associates inactivity with a troubled mind: "I spent the time idly. Mens turbata."[29] In the episode of the mad astronomer in *Rasselas*, Johnson presents one of his strongest, and most famous, depictions of idleness's leading to insanity. The astronomer, who has retired from society to contemplate the heavens and who therefore is frequently alone and unoccupied, has progressed from imagining what he would do if he were able to control the weather — "This contemplation fastened on my mind, and I sat days and nights in imaginary dominion, pouring upon this country and that the showers of fertility, and seconding every fall of rain with a due proportion of sunshine"[30] — to believing that he actually *is* in control of it. The sage Imlac, to whom the astronomer has imparted his secret, muses upon the cause of the man's madness. It begins with the pleasures of imagination:

> To indulge the power of fiction, and send imagination out upon the wing, is often the sport of those who delight too much in silent speculation. . . . He who has nothing external to divert him must find pleasure in his own thoughts, and must conceive himself what he is not; for who is pleased with what he is?[31]

This imaginative process leads to delight — "The mind dances from scene to scene, unites all pleasures in all combinations, and riots in delights which nature and fortune, with all their bounty, cannot bestow"[32] — but also to danger: "By degrees the reign of fancy is confirmed; she grows first imperious, and in time despotick. Then fictions begin to operate as realities, false opinions fasten upon the mind, and life passes in dreams of rapture or of anguish."[33] When they have heard Imlac's explanation, Rasselas, his sister Nekayah, and her handmaiden Pekuah all resolve to discontinue their own favorite imaginings. Pekuah confesses she has imagined herself the queen of Abyssinia, and "exulted in the beneficence of royalty, till, when the princess entered, I had almost forgotten to bow down before her." Nekayah has pretended she was a shepherdess: "I have often soothed my thoughts with the quiet and innocence of pastoral employments, till I have in my chamber heard the wind whistle, and the sheep bleat. . . ." Rasselas claims that his own favorite fancy is "an indulgence of fantastick delight more dangerous than" theirs. He has imagined himself the leader of his country, and now realizes with pain "with how little anguish I once supposed the death of my father and my brothers."[34]

This strong sense Johnson has that imagination is delicious but dangerous comes through clearly in a couple of his periodical essays. In *Idler* 32, he paints a voluptuous picture of the dreamer:

> Many have no happier moments than those that they pass in solitude, abandoned to their own imagination, which sometimes puts sceptres in their hands or mitres on their heads, shifts the scene of pleasure with endless variety, bids all the forms of beauty sparkle before them, and gluts them with every change of visionary luxury.

All this, Johnson goes on to warn, "is a voluntary dream, a temporary recession from the realities of life to airy fictions, and habitual subjection of reason to fancy."[35] This warning gains force when we recall what Imlac says in *Rasselas*: "All power of fancy over reason is a degree of insanity."[36] These "voluntary dreams," then, are willful flirtations with madness. Johnson urged Queeny Thrale, of whom he was very fond, to beware of these flirtations, to encourage in herself "an implacable impatience of doing nothing," even if this means she must sometimes "be busy upon trifles," because if the mind ever "learns to soothe itself with the opiate of musing idleness, if it can once be content with inactivity, all the time to come is in danger of being lost."[37] Idleness is like a seductive drug that causes almost immediate addiction.

In *Rambler* 89, we have another luxuriant portrait of the daydreamer and another comparison of "musing idleness" to opiates: "The dreamer retires to his apartments, shuts out the cares and interruptions of mankind, and abandons himself to his own fancy; new worlds rise up before him, one image is followed by another, and a long succession of delights dances round him." The peril of this abandon is not just that the dreamer "enters peevish into society, because he cannot model it to his own will," but that the "infatuation" with these fancies "strengthens by degrees, and, like the poison of opiates, weakens his powers, without any external symptom of malignity."[38] The almost erotic language used in these passages shows what deep pleasure Johnson finds in the imagination, but to him this pleasure is, like the allurements of laudanum, deeply dangerous. Imagination is a faculty he is always endeavoring to suppress. Boswell tells us that when Mrs. Burney objected to the situation of some new buildings which had been built near Bedlam, saying she could not live there, Johnson replied, "Nay, Madam, . . . it is right that we should be kept in mind of madness, which is occasioned by too much indulgence of imagination. I think a very moral use may be made of these new buildings: I would have those who have heated imaginations live there, and take warning."[39] That he sees this use of the buildings as "moral" perhaps indicates that he considers madness not just a psychological problem, but also a failure of self-control. And this perhaps is a reason insanity is such a horror to Johnson: not only is it to be dreaded for its own sake, but for what it says about the sufferer's ability to control himself.

The cure for this "heated imagination" which leads to madness, as well as for the melancholy which can also lead there, is, of course, activity. The astronomer in *Rasselas* is gently led back to sanity by the efforts of Rasselas and his friends to keep him busy:

> From this time the astronomer was received into familiar friendship, and partook of all their projects and pleasures: his respect made him attentive, and the activity of Rasselas did not leave much time unengaged. Something

was always to be done; the day was spent in making observations which furnished talk for the evening, and the evening was closed with a scheme for the morrow.[40]

The astronomer soon finds that "since he had mingled in the gay tumults of life, and divided his hours by a succession of amusements, he found the conviction of his authority over the skies fade gradually from his mind."[41] Almost as though the mind were a physical space that can only hold so much, the new objects engaging the astronomer's mind have squeezed out the old delusions. Activity, then, can prevent not only boredom—with its potential for misery and sinful behavior—but also madness.

This notion of the mind as a space needing to be filled with harmless activity so that melancholy and mad ideas cannot find a foothold[42] is of course closely connected to the idea that staying busy prevents sin— Jeremy Taylor, as I mentioned above, told people to "fill up all the spaces" of their time. Because of Johnson's preoccupation with "vacuity" (about which I will have more to say later), however, this emphasis on "filling" seems, for him, especially charged. Thus at the center of Johnson's many exhortations to busyness[43]—whether to prevent sin, melancholy, or the "vain imaginings" that lead to madness—is the notion of "vacancy," an intellectual emptiness which must be filled one way or another. Johnson wrote to Boswell, evidently to encourage him to be contented with his profession, that "all the importunities and perplexities of business are softness and luxury, compared with the incessant cravings of vacancy, and the unsatisfactory expedients of idleness."[44] In *Idler* 72, Johnson says, "Employment is the great instrument of intellectual dominion. The mind cannot retire from its enemy into total vacancy, or turn aside from one object but by passing to another. The gloomy and resentful are always found among those who have nothing to do, or who do nothing."[45] The end of *Rambler* 85, one of Johnson's most famous warnings against idleness, warns against vacancy:

> It is certain that any wild wish or vain imagination never takes such firm possession of the mind, as when it is found empty and unoccupied. The old peripatetick principle, that "Nature abhors a Vacuum," may be properly applied to the intellect, which will embrace any thing, however absurd or criminal, rather than be wholly without an object. Perhaps every man may date the predominance of those desires that disturb his life and contaminate his conscience, from some unhappy hour when too much leisure exposed him to their incursions; for he has lived with little observation either of himself or others, who does not know that to be idle is to be vicious.[46]

Johnson seems to have derived the idea of keeping the mind occupied to prevent insanity from Burton's *Anatomy of Melancholy*, a book he greatly admired, saying once that it "was the only book that ever took him out of bed two hours sooner than he wished to rise."[47] In writing to Boswell about Boswell's melancholy, Johnson says, "The great direction which Burton has left to men disordered like you is this, *Be not solitary; be not idle*: which I would thus modify; — If you are idle, be not solitary; if you are solitary, be not idle."[48] While many critics have discussed how influenced Johnson was by Burton and his ideas about idleness, melancholy, and madness,[49] relatively few of the book's 971 pages of text are devoted to this advice. Pages 210 through 214 discuss idleness as a cause of melancholy, and pages 439 through 464 discuss the importance of bodily exercise and mental diversions such as fishing, travel, games, and computation as ways to avoid harmful idleness of body or mind.[50] But these pages form a rather small portion of the work as a whole, which leads me to think that Johnson's having so taken to heart the "Be not idle" advice comes more from a preoccupation of his own than from an impartial reading of the book itself. While Johnson evidently ignored, for instance, much of the advice about diet, such as to avoid milk and fruit,[51] he embraced Burton's rather offhand recommendation to "demonstrate a Proposition in Euclid in his last five Books, extract a square root, or study algebra."[52] Boswell tells us that Johnson was "all his life fond" of computation, "as it fixed his attention steadily upon something without, and prevented his mind from preying upon itself."[53] Mrs. Thrale recounts a striking example of Johnson's use of calculation to steady the mind:

> When Mr. Johnson felt his fancy, or fancied he felt it, disordered, his constant recurrence was to the study of arithmetic; and one day that he was totally confined to his chamber, and I enquired what he had been doing to divert himself; he shewed me a calculation which I could scarce be made to understand, so vast was the plan of it, and so very intricate were the figures: no other indeed than the national debt, computing it at one hundred and eighty millions sterling, would, if converted into silver, serve to make a meridian of that metal, I forget how broad, for the globe of the whole earth, the real *globe*.[54]

Johnson also attempted to busy his mind with scientific experiments. Boswell mentions that he "sometimes employed himself in chymistry, sometimes in watering and pruning a vine, and sometimes in small experiments," adding in Johnson's defense, "at which those who may smile, should recollect that there are moments which admit of being soothed only by trifles."[55] In his *Diaries, Prayers, and Annals* we see Johnson measuring the exact location of a place on his fingernail he had shaved by accident, "that I may know the growth of nails;"[56] shaving his arms "to see how much time would restore the hairs;"[57] and weighing, then drying, leaves "to try what weight they will lose by drying."[58] On more than one occasion he expressed envy towards women for their socially sanctioned ability to employ themselves with trifles like needlework:[59] "Women have a great advantage that they may take up with little things, without disgracing themselves: a man cannot, except with fiddling."[60] (Of course, as I argued in my third chapter, some women felt they were not only allowed to take up "little things," but were restricted to them—and they longed to take part in something larger.)

In his conversation and letters, Johnson constantly advised others to keep busy in order to stay sane. Since Boswell was prone to melancholy, Johnson advised him to occupy himself: "at least resolve, while you remain in any settled residence, to spend a certain number of hours every day amongst your books"; this will chase away "the gusts of imagination."[61] When, in another conversation about melancholy, Boswell tactfully (knowing about Johnson's own chemistry set) asked Johnson if he would not tell a man so afflicted "to take a course of chymistry," he replied, "Let him take a course of chymistry, or a course of rope-dancing, or a course of anything to which he is inclined at the time. Let him contrive to have as many retreats for his mind as he can, as many things to which it can fly from itself."[62] "Employment, Sir," Johnson said ringingly on another occasion, "and hardships, prevent melancholy. I suppose in all our army in America there was not one man who went mad."[63] When a clerk who was "oppressed by scruples of conscience" for having taken paper and packthread from his employer came to Johnson for help, Johnson at first told him to stop worrying about "such airy nothings" (since the employer had told the clerk to take as much as he liked), and then, thinking that "the fellow might be mad perhaps," asked him "When he left the counting-house of an evening?—At seven o'clock, Sir.—And when do you go to-bed, Sir?—At twelve o'clock." "Then," Johnson replied,

> I have at least learned thus much by my new acquaintance;—that five hours of the four-and-twenty unemployed are enough for a man to go mad in; so I would advise you Sir, to study algebra, if you are not an adept already in it: your head would get less *muddy*, and you would leave off tormenting your neighbours about paper and packthread, while we all live together in a world that is bursting with sin and sorrow.[64]

II

Although Johnson recommended busy-work like chemistry and algebra to others and also engaged in it himself, he did not find in such trifling employment a true answer to the problem of idleness. As I mentioned before, he was all too aware of the difference between being busy and actually doing meaningful work. His periodical essays are full of satirical portraits of those who fool themselves by a whirl of activity into thinking they are engaged in important work, when really they are only trifling and wasting their time. These character sketches are among the liveliest and most memorable of the essays; Johnson seems to relish exposing the bustlingly busy as actually idlers.[65] *Rambler* 51, for instance, which describes Lady Bustle, who prides herself on being "the greatest manager in that part of the country" and has taken the domestic arts to ludicrous extremes, gives us cause to question the value of this undeniably active woman's activity:

> It is, indeed, the great business of her life, to watch the skillet on the fire, . . . and the employments to which she has bred her daughters, are to turn rose leaves in the shade, to pick out the seeds of currants with a quill, . . . and to extract bean-flower water for the skin. Such are the tasks with which every day, since I came here, has begun and ended, to which the early hours of life are sacrificed, and in which that time is passing away which never shall return.[66]

In *Idler* 19, Johnson gives us a portrait of Jack Whirler, a man who manages to pass his life "in bustle without business, and in negligence without quiet." Jack "is always to do what he never does," and "cannot stand still because he is wanted in another place, and . . . is wanted in many places because he stays in none."[67] Jack is always running between one place of business and another and therefore contrives to do little business at all; he dines "at full speed,"[68] racing from one dinner table to another, and he always complains about his lack of time. "Thus," Johnson concludes,

> Jack Whirler lives in perpetual fatigue without proportionate advantage, because he does not consider that no man can see all with his own eyes, or do all with his own hands; that whoever is engaged in multiplicity of business must transact much by substitution, and leave something to hazard; and that he who attempts to do all, will waste his life in doing little.[69]

Several other such character sketches enliven the volumes of the *Rambler* and *Idler*,[70] but perhaps the most memorable, and certainly the most poignant, sketch is the one of Sober, in *Idler* 31. Sober is, as Mrs. Thrale informs us, Johnson's self-portrait,[71] and this self-portrait shows how caught Johnson is between his profound sense that the mind needs to be kept busy to avoid its "preying on itself" and his equally deep feeling that the trifling activity to which one turns for distraction is a form of self-deception and a criminal waste of time. Idleness, Johnson says at the beginning of this essay, "is often covered by turbulence and hurry. He that neglects his known duty and real employment, naturally endeavours to croud his mind with something that may bar out the remembrance of his own folly, and does any thing but what he ought to do with eager diligence, that he may keep himself in his own favor."[72] Sober's chief way of "crouding" his mind is by conversation, but when that is unavailable to him,

> the misery of these tiresome intervals, he has many means of alleviating. He has persuaded himself that the manual arts are undeservedly overlooked. . . . From speculation he proceeded to practice, and supplied himself with the tools of a carpenter, with which he mended his coal-box very successfully, and which he still continues to employ, as he finds occasion. He has attempted at other times the crafts of the shoemaker, tinman, plumber, and potter; in all these arts he has failed. . . . But his daily amusement is chemistry. He has a small furnace, which he employs in distillation, and which has long been the solace of his life.[73]

The paragraph ends movingly: "He draws oils and waters, and essences and spirits, which he knows to be of no use; sits and counts the drops as they come from his retort, and forgets that, while a drop is falling, a moment flies away."[74] It is Johnson's misfortune, of course, that he can *not* always forget that the moments were flying away. He comments frequently on the eagerness with which people persuade themselves that they are not idle—"To be idle and to be poor have always been reproaches, and therefore every man endeavours with his utmost care, to hide his poverty from others, and his idleness from himself";[75] "There is no kind of idleness, by which we are so easily seduced, as that which dignifies itself by the appearance of business"[76]—but he is unable to fool himself so comfortably. He is caught in another vicious circle: trivial activities lead to guilt about wasted time, which leads to a need to distract himself by trifling pursuits, which lead to more guilt. He knows all too well how seductive the insignificant can be; as he says in *Rambler* 103, "There is no snare more dangerous to busy and excursive minds, than the cobwebs of petty inquisitiveness, which . . . detain them in a middle state between the tediousness of total inactivity, and the fatigue of laborious efforts, enchant them at once with ease and novelty, and vitiate them with the luxury of learning."[77] However, he cannot forgive himself for failing to spend his time more profitably.

Johnson had an enormously strong sense of the brevity of life. While time may be something the bored (and he himself was often bored) want to get rid of, it is also a superlatively precious and finite resource—not something to be trifled away. Many of Johnson's sermons stress the shortness and uncertainty of this life: "how short a time, at most, is alloted to [man's] earthly duration, and how much of that time may be cut off";[78] "life is called long, not as being, at its greatest length, of much duration, but as being longer than common";[79] "so near may be the end of thy life, that thou mayest never do what is in thy heart";[80] "He, whose life is extended to its utmost boundaries, can live but a little while; and that he shall be one of those, who are comparatively said, to live long, no man can tell";[81] "the first consideration . . . must be the incessant waste of life, the approach of age, and the certainty of death."[82] While this notion of the end's being near was not unusual for sermons of the day, Johnson's mind seems to have dwelt on it almost constantly. Even when composing light extemporaneous verse occasioned by hearing Queeny Thrale trying to decide whether to wear her new hat to a dinner party, he thinks of life's brevity:

> Wear the gown, and wear the hat,
>   Snatch thy pleasures while they last,
> Hadst thou nine lives like a cat,
>   Soon those nine lives would be past.[83]

And when writing a charming tribute to Mrs. Thrale, "On Her Completing Her Thirty-fifth Year," he cannot resist mentioning that "For howe'er we boast and strive / Life declines from thirty-five."[84]

In his prayers and meditations, Johnson frequently bewails the passing of time and the probable shortness of his remaining life: "I have done nothing; the need of doing therefore is pressing, since the time of doing is short";[85] "In life little has been done, and life is very far advanced. Lord have mercy upon me";[86] "I have great fear lest death should lay hold upon me, while I am as yet only designing to live";[87] "Much time I have not left. . . . But much remains to be done";[88] "I am almost seventy years old, and have no time to lose";[89] "Many years are already gone, irrevocably past in useless Misery."[90] One of the three Biblical texts to which he frequently returns, which, in fact, he had engraved on the dial-plate of his watch,[91] is John 9:4: "I must work the works of him that sent me, while it is day: the night cometh, when no man can work." He refers to this text in three of his sermons (4, 25, and 27) and two of his periodical essays (*Idler* 43 and *Adventurer* 125), and he prays not to forget it ("O God, help me to remember that *the night cometh when no man can work.*)[92] The work Johnson will not be able to do when night comes is the working out of his salvation: "The business of our life," as he writes in Sermon 15, "is to work out our salvation; and the days are few, in which provision must be made for eternity."[93]

Further on in the same sermon he reminds us that "the life allotted to human beings is short; and while they stand still in idle suspence, is always growing shorter"; that "as this little time is spent well or ill, their whole future existence will be happy or miserable"; and that "he who begins the great work of his salvation early, has employment adequate to all his powers; and . . . he who has delayed it, can hope to accomplish it only by delaying it no longer."[94] Johnson's problem is, of course, that he feels he *is* constantly delaying this great work, and he is terrified that he has delayed too long. He means "working," I think, in the most literal sort of way; one's fate after death will depend on how much acceptable work one does in one's life.[95] His well-known fear that he would be "sent to Hell, Sir, and punished everlastingly"[96] comes from his fear that he has not done enough work, and his agonized guilt for wasted time from his sense that our time is entrusted to us by God for the purpose of doing His work. As Robert Voitle nicely puts it, Johnson "thinks of time . . . not as hours, or days or years, but as opportunities for work, opportunities which have been or may be profitably used or wasted."[97] In several of his periodical essays, Johnson refers to a person's lifetime in this way: it is "the great deposit of his Creator,"[98] "only deposited in his hands to be employed in obedience" to God;[99] and the time that remains of it is "to be considered as the last trust of heaven."[100]

The financial images in the last sentence—"trust" and "deposit"—are echoed repeatedly in Johnson's prayers and meditations. Over and over he regrets time "unprofitably spent,"[101] agonizes over how much of his life has "stolen unprofitably away,"[102] and prays that "the time which thou shalt yet allow me, may not pass unprofitably away."[103] He prays often that he will be able to "redeem the time misspent,"[104] to "use all diligence in redeeming the time which I have spent in Sloth, Vanity, and wickedness"[105]—"redeem" in the sense of "to buy back." He prays on four New Year's Days that he will be able to "improve the Year to which thou hast graciously extended my life,"[106] "improve the year which I am now beginning,"[107] meaning by "improve," I think, "to use profitably" or "to make more valuable." Even the image of time as something that is "spent" and "misspent" is in one sense a financial one, and Johnson uses these words frequently—at least fourteen times in the *Diaries, Prayers, and Annals*. Time, like money, can be "wasted,"[108] "lavish[ed] away" "on useless trifles,"[109] and "squandered."[110] Of course, this figuring of time as currency is a familiar trope, certainly not peculiar to Johnson, but for him it does seem to have an especially unsettling resonance. Johnson seems almost to see God as some great accountant, calculating his spiritual credits and debits on a celestial adding machine, and he is wretchedly sure that most of his time will have to go in the debit column.[111]

One of the New Testament's best-known financial images is found in Matthew 25:14–30, the second of the texts by which Johnson is haunted—the parable of the talents. The "talents" entrusted by a man to his three servants, two of whom invested and thereby doubled them while the third just "digged in the earth and hid" the one given to him, are pieces of money; but they also represent talents in the more familiar sense: gifts and abilities. Johnson is piercingly aware of his great talents,[112] and is terribly afraid he had failed to invest them properly. The fear of being another "unprofitable servant," condemned to be "cast out into outer darkness" for his "wicked and slothful" failure to invest the talents that were really only given him in trust, troubles him deeply.[113] Johnson makes reference to the parable of the talents in his prayers, praying he "may be received as a good and faithful servant"[114] and that he will be able "to render up at the last day an account of the talent committed to" him.[115] He refers also to the parable in three of his sermons (19, 27, and 28). The most moving reference to this text, though, occurs in his poem "On the Death of Dr. Robert Levet." Levet, who lived with Johnson for many years, was, according to Boswell, an "aukward and uncouth" man,[116] nearly silent in company. Many of Johnson's friends wondered why he wanted to live with Levet, who, as Bate puts it, "with his stiff silence and 'uncouth' manner, seemed the opposite of all that Johnson enjoyed in company."[117] Part of the answer lies in Johnson's almost boundless charity; that Levet was "poor and honest" and needed a home was recommendation enough.[118] But Johnson also found in Levet, as he expresses in his poem, something deeply admirable: "Here was a man," to quote Bate again, "who, despite serious disadvantages, performed a useful and charitable function not impulsively or occasionally but with unwavering constancy."[119] (Levet, who, although originally a servant and waiter, had managed to scrabble together some knowledge of medicine, spent his days walking great distances through London, ministering to the poor "for a small fee or, if they could not afford that, for anything they felt they could give him."[120]) Perhaps it would be worthwhile to quote the last four verses of the poem, although it is so well-known:

> No summons mock'd by chill delay,
>   No petty gain disdain'd by pride,
> The modest wants of ev'ry day
>   The toil of ev'ry day supplied.
>
> His virtues walk'd their narrow round,
>   Nor made a pause, nor left a void;
> And sure th' Eternal Master found
>   The single talent well employ'd.

> The busy day, the peaceful night,
>   Unfelt, uncounted, glided by;
> His frame was firm, his powers were bright,
>   Tho' now his eightieth year was nigh.
>
> Then with no throbbing fiery pain,
>   No cold gradations of delay,
> Death broke at once the vital chain,
>   And free'd his soul the nearest way.[121]

Levet, though his toil supplied only his modest daily wants, though his virtues were narrow and his talent only single, did what Johnson feels so sharply he himself, with all his amplitude of mind and manifold talents, had failed to do: employ well what he had been given.[122] And surely this is why Levet's days and nights glided by "unfelt, uncounted": although the ostensible reason Johnson gives us is Levet's continued strength and good health, the deeper reason must be that Levet had no *need* to feel or count the passing of his days. He had spent them well, to his credit. Johnson, however, fearing his misspent days are irreversibly piling up debits, is all too aware of their flight.

The third biblical text which troubles Johnson is very similar to the parable of the talents. It is part of Luke 12:48: "For unto whomsoever much is given, of him shall be much required." Both Boswell and Mrs. Thrale mention Johnson's preoccupation with this text. Boswell says, in the last few pages of his *Life of Johnson*:

> The solemn text, 'of him to whom much is given, much will be required,' seems to have been ever present to his mind, in a rigorous sense, and to have made him dissatisfied with his labours and acts of goodness, however comparatively great; so that the unavoidable consciousness of his superiority was, in that respect, a cause of disquiet. He suffered so much from this, and from the gloom which perpetually haunted him, and made solitude frightful, that it may be said of him, 'If in this life only he had hope, he was of all men the most miserable.'[123]

Mrs. Thrale says something very similar: "He knew how much had been given, and filled his mind with fancies of how much would be required, till his impressed imagination was often disturbed by them, and his health suffered from the sensibility of his too tender conscience: a real Christian is *so* apt to find his task above his power of performance!"[124] (Mrs. Thrale also makes the remark, interesting to those of us who may be wondering how Johnson managed both to accomplish so much and to be as indolent as he and everyone else seems to have thought he was, that "whatever work he did, seemed so much below his powers of performance, that he appeared the idlest of all human beings."[125]) In *Rambler* 78, Johnson expounds on this text: "Those, whom God has favored with superior faculties, and made eminent for quickness of intuition, and accuracy of distinctions, will certainly be regarded as culpable in his eye, for defects and deviations which, in souls less enlightened, may be guiltless."[126] Surely he is thinking of himself here, as he is in *Rambler* 154, when he says, "He that neglects the culture of ground, naturally fertile, is more shamefully culpable than he whose field would scarcely recompence his husbandry."[127] Those gifted with extraordinary abilities will be judged even more harshly than the ordinary if they trifle away their time. Johnson seems to have derived from the knowledge of his great talents more torture than pleasure.

III

The fault, besides general misspending of time, for which Johnson most tortures himself is sleeping too late. One can open the *Diaries, Prayers, and Annals* almost at random and find poor Johnson resolving yet again to get up earlier; in his list of resolutions always seems to be "To rise early. Not later than six if I can, I hope sooner, but as soon as I can";[128] "To rise at eight every morning. . . . I purpose to rise at eight because though I shall not yet rise early it will be much earlier than I now rise, for I often lye till two";[129] "To try to rise more early";[130] "To rise in the morning."[131] Literally dozens of times Johnson expresses his desire to rise earlier, and his guilt for repeatedly failing to do so: "The other day looking over old papers, I perceived a resolution to rise early always occurring. I think I was ashamed or grieved to find how long and how often I had resolved, what yet for about one half year I have never done."[132] The logical reason Johnson finds it so difficult to rise early is that he goes to sleep so late; his chronic insomnia frequently keeps him from sleeping when he is in bed, and the fear of not sleeping makes him dread even *going* to bed. Mrs. Thrale gives an account of how inconvenient Johnson's dread of bedtime often was:

Mr. Johnson loved late hours exceedingly, or more properly hated early ones. Nothing was more terrifying to him than the idea of retiring to bed, which he would never call going to rest, nor suffer another to call so. 'I lie down (said he) that my acquaintance may sleep; but I lie down to endure oppressive misery, and soon rise again to pass the night in anxiety and pain.' By this pathetick manner, which no one ever possessed in so eminent a degree, he used to shock me from quitting his company, till I hurt my own health not a little by sitting up with him when I was myself far from well. . . .[133]

Johnson is well aware that his insomnia made early rising very difficult for him; he records in his diary that "one great hindrance is want of rest; my nocturnal complaints grow less troublesome towards morning, and I am tempted [to] repair the deficiencies of the night."[134] But this knowledge does not help him forgive himself his morning slumbers. He is caught in yet another vicious circle, as Voitle notes:

> Anxiety or the physical discomfort he suffered for most of his life keeps him awake. When day comes he is indolent because of fatigue and accomplishes nothing, and this in turn arouses guilt and the fear that the experience will be repeated. If, by chance, he is able to fall asleep before morning and is "tempted to repair the deficiencies of the night," the time lost while he dawdles in bed also breeds guilty anxieties, which do their work the next night.[135]

I would add, though, that Johnson's dawdling in bed seems to occur almost daily, judging from his diaries and prayers.

Part of the seemingly excessive guilt[136] Johnson suffered for rising late may be attributable to the influence of William Law, whose *Serious Call to a Devout and Holy Life* impressed Johnson deeply.[137] As he told Boswell, "When at Oxford, I took up Law's *Serious Call to a Holy Life*, expecting to find it a dull book (as such books generally are) and perhaps to laugh at it. But I found Law quite an over-match for me; and this was the first occasion of my thinking in earnest of religion, after I became capable of rational inquiry."[138] Law is a resolute enemy to slugging abed; for several pages of *A Serious Call* he proclaims its sinfulness. When writing of the importance of early morning prayer, he says, "I take it for granted that every Christian that is in health is up early in the morning; for it is much more reasonable to suppose he is up early because he is a Christian than because he is a laborer, or a tradesman, or a servant, or has business that wants him."[139] He goes on to proclaim "how odious we must appear in the sight of Heaven if we are in bed shut up in sleep and darkness, when we should be praising God,"[140] and that he who chooses morning sleep over morning prayer "chooses that state which is a reproach to mere animals rather than that exercise which is the glory of angels."[141] Law never entirely explains why praying at 5 A.M. is better than praying at midnight, but he does argue that the person who cannot sacrifice the indulgence of a morning bed "can have no reason to think that he has taken up his cross and is following Christ."[142] Late sleeping "gives a softness and idleness to all our tempers,"[143] and "a softness and idleness to your soul."[144] Finally, early rising will "dispose your mind to exactness, and be very likely to bring the remaining part of the day under rules of prudence and devotion."[145] If

Johnson did not already feel guilty for late rising by the time he was at Oxford, reading Law would probably have convinced him to do so.

But there is a deeper reason, I think, both for Johnson's tremendous desire to rise early and for his equally tremendous inability to do so. For Johnson, sleep, along with daydreaming and indolence, represents a sort of oblivion, a terrifying but also attractive cessation of activity and control. He postpones bedtime as long as he can because he is afraid, even more than of not sleeping, of sleep. I agree with Bate that Johnson was "unable to let go his clutch at objective reality as the sole means of steadying his mind, unable not to keep all guards posted and retain 'self-management' rather than to relapse into the unconsciousness that another part of him (a part he feared) deeply craved."[146] In *Idler* 33, Johnson says that by sleep "the mind and body are . . . chained down in irresistible stupefaction,"[147] and that sleep is, like death, the universal leveler: "There is reason to suspect that the distinctions of mankind have more shew than value, when it is found that all agree to be weary alike of pleasures and of cares, that the powerful and the weak, the celebrated and the obscure, join in one common wish, and implore from nature's hand the nectar of oblivion."[148] While he can in another essay call sleep "the chief of all earthly blessings,"[149] and while his inability to wrench himself from sleep once it had claimed him shows how attractive it is to him on one level, on another level it is a frightening "insensibility,"[150] an enchaining stupefaction, an appalling oblivion. This fear is the reason, I would speculate, that Johnson never makes, in his dozens of resolutions to rise earlier, the obviously necessarily concomitant resolution to go to bed earlier. (Only once does he even mention an earlier bedtime, and that is fairly early in his life and only applies to Saturdays.[151]) Sleep, while something he deeply yearns for and knows he needs, is still to be avoided as far as possible. During the one half-year period when he did succeed in early rising, Johnson wrote to Bennet Langton: "and what is greater still, I have risen every morning since New-year's day, at about eight; when I was up, I have indeed done but little; yet it is no slight advancement to obtain for so many hours more, the consciousness of being."[152]

Like sleep, idleness seems to remove "the consciousness of being," or at least the consciousness of having been, and this is another reason, I think, Johnson finds idleness so disturbing. If his time could not be marked by deeds done, his past seems to disappear, to dissolve into oblivion. The anguished remarks he makes in his diaries and prayers about his idle past attest to this feeling of blankness, dreamlikeness, dissolution.

My indolence, since my last reception of the Sacrament, has sunk into grosser sluggishness, and my dissipation spread into wilder negligence. . . .

A kind of strange oblivion has overspread me, so that I know not what has become of the last year, and perceive that incidents and intelligence pass over me without leaving any impression.[153]

Since the last Easter I have reformed no evil habit, my time has been unprofitably spent, and seems as a dream that has left nothing behind. My memory grows confused, and I know not how the days pass over me.[154]

How the last year has past I am unwilling to terrify myself with thinking.[155]

How the last [year] has past, it would be in my state of weakness perhaps not prudent too solicitously to recollect.[156]

When I survey my past life, I discover nothing but a barren waste of time with some disorders of body, and disturbances of the mind very near to madness. . . . Grant O God that I may no longer resolve in vain, or dream away the life which thy indulgence gives me, in vacancy and uselessness.[157]

Days and months pass in a dream, and I am afraid that my memory grows less tenacious, and my observation less attentive.[158]

In reviewing my life from Easter—77, I find a very melancholy and shameful blank; so little has been done that days and months are without any trace.[159]

I am now to review the past year, and find little but dismal vacuity.[160]

It is as though activity, for Johnson, is all that holds time together, that gives it meaning. Without meaningful activity, the days pass over him in a dream, leaving only a shameful blank. Idleness causes his life to be dissipated, not just in the moral sense of that word, but in the chemical or physical senses.

Not only does idleness make the past a blank and therefore painful to contemplate, contemplation of the past or future can cause idleness, by removing one's attention from the duties of the present moment. (Here we have, of course, an additional vicious circle.) Johnson was well aware that, as he wrote to Boswell, "Life is not long, and too much of it must not pass in idle deliberation how it shall be spent."[161] Much of *Rasselas*, in fact, is about how overconcern about the future can cause idleness in the present: "It seems to me," says Imlac to Rasselas, who is trying to decide the best way to spend his life, "that while you are making the choice of life, you neglect to live."[162] Johnson makes a point in the beginning of *Rambler* 2 about the human tendency to neglect the present by dwelling on the future: "the mind of man is never satisfied with the objects immediately before it, but is always breaking away from the present moment, and losing itself in schemes of future felicity; and . . . we forget the proper use of the time now in our power, to provide for the enjoyment of that which, perhaps, may never be granted us"[163]; and he makes a similar statement at the end of *Rambler* 29: "in proportion as our cares are imployed upon the future they are abstracted from the present, from the only time which we can call our own, and of which if we neglect the duties, to make provision against visionary attacks, we shall certainly counteract our own purpose. . . ."[164] In his Sermon 15, Johnson warns us against neglecting the duties of the present by dreaming about what reforms we will make in the future: people who do this "know that their present state is dangerous, and therefore withdraw from it to a fancied futurity, in which whatever is crooked is to be made straight; in which temptations are to be rejected, and passions to be conquered; in which wisdom and piety are to rule the day; in which every hour shall have its proper duty."[165]

The present, although it is "the only time which we can call our own," is, Johnson says more than once, seldom enough to hold our attention. "So few of the hours of life," he writes in *Rambler* 41, "are filled up with objects adequate to the mind of man, and so frequently are we in want of present pleasure or employment, that we are forced to have recourse every moment to the past and future for supplemental satisfactions, and relieve the vacuities of our being, by recollection of former passages, or anticipation of events to come."[166] In *Rambler* 203, he says almost exactly the same thing: "It seems to be the fate of man to seek all his consolations in futurity. The time present is seldom able to fill desire or imagination with immediate enjoyment, and we are forced to supply its deficiencies by recollection or anticipation."[167] And of course Imlac's remark in *Rasselas* that "no mind is much employed upon the present; recollection and anticipation fill up almost all our moments"[168] is a restatement of this same idea. The problem for Johnson with this inadequacy of the present moment to hold our attention is not just that it causes us to neglect what we should do,[169] but that it is another demonstration of the vacuity of life. We are always wishing the present would hurry up and become the past — "Such is the emptiness of human enjoyment, that we are always impatient of the present" — so that we can arrive at the joys we have imagined will happen in the future. Once we get there, however, we find that "attainment is followed by neglect, and possession by disgust."[170] We allow our time to pass over us unmarked by the meaningful activity that would rescue it from the void, and when we arrive at the future good we have longed for we find it vacant, also. We then, of course, distract ourselves from our disappointment by looking toward the future again. In Sermon 14, Johnson eloquently discusses the futility of this constant striving for what can never be reached:

> when one pursuit has failed of affording them that satisfaction which they expected from it, [they] apply themselves with the same ardour to another equally unprofitable, and waste their lives in successive delusions, in idle schemes of imaginary enjoyment; in the chace of shadows which fleet before them, and in attempts to grasp a bubble, which, however it may attract the eye by the brightness of its colour, is neither solid nor lasting, but owes its beauty only to its distance, and is no sooner touched than it disappears.[171]

The present, in a way, eludes our grasp as much as the schemes of imaginary enjoyment; as soon as we think we have caught it, it becomes the past. This sense of the present's ungraspability can be seen in the number of times in his *Rambler* essays Johnson refers to time with slippery words. "Many of the few moments allotted us will slide imperceptibly away,"[172] he says; and life "steal[s] from us"[173]; we suffer it negligently to "slide away."[174] Many people "let their own days glide away"[175]; "time slips imperceptibly away"[176]; "the moments cre[ep] imperceptibly away"[177]; and "day glides after day."[178] For Johnson, then, the past is a blank, the future a bubble, and the present is infinitely elusive.[179] Only meaningful activity, difficult as it is to achieve, can rescue time from this circle of void and vacuity.

Mrs. Thrale was probably the first writer to discuss Johnson's preoccupation with vacuity:[180]

> The vacuity of life had at some earlier period of his life struck so forcibly on the mind of Mr. Johnson, that it became by repeated impression his favorite hypothesis, and the general tenor of his reasonings commonly ended there, wherever they might begin. Such things therefore as other philosophers often attribute to various and contradictory causes, appeared to him uniform enough; all was done to fill up the time, upon this principle. . . . One man, for example, was profligate and wild, as we call it, followed the girls, or sat still at the gaming-table. 'Why, life must be filled up (says Johnson), and the man who is not capable of intellectual pleasures must content himself with such as his senses can afford.' Another was a hoarder: 'Why, a fellow must do something; and what so easy to a narrow mind as hoarding halfpence till they turn into sixpences.'[181]

It is difficult to read many pages of Johnson without coming across the word "fill," as Bate has noticed; the recognition of life as a series of vacuities to be filled

> appears in the phrasing of almost every page, sometimes with comic impatience and more usually with charity: riches fail to '*fill up* the vacuities of

life'; *fill* the day with petty business'; . . . *'filling the vacuities* of his mind with the news of the day'; literary quarreling gratifies the malignity of readers or 'relieves the vacancies of life' for them.[182]

In *Rambler* 8, Johnson speaks of "how many chasms" even an active man, reviewing his past life, "would find of wide and continued vacuity, and how many interstitial spaces unfilled" there would be.[183] If this is so for the active person, how much wider and more threatening are the vacuities in the life of the idle. When Johnson writes about idleness, he uses images of stasis and stagnation, dissolution and death. Curiosity, he says in *Rambler* 118, may be "congealed by indolence"[184]; carrying the same image further, he speaks of "freez[ing] in idleness,"[185] and "freezing in perpetual inactivity."[186] Euphalia, the bored young lady of *Rambler* 42 we met earlier, says that in her boredom "the current of youth stagnates," and she is "languishing in a dead calm"[187]; in *Idler* 30, Johnson says that "the idle and the luxurious find life stagnate."[188] Imlac, in *Rasselas*, also speaks of idleness as stagnation: "Do not suffer the current of life to stagnate; it will grow muddy for want of motion: commit yourself again to the current of the world."[189] Idleness is figured as dissolution in, besides Johnson's diaries and prayers, his Sermon 14 and one of his short poems. In the sermon, he says that the idle "lull themselves in an enervate, and cowardly dissipation"—and here also I think he means the word in its chemical, as well as its moral, sense—"and, instead of being happy, are only indolent."[190] The didactic poem "The Ant" asks, "How long shall sloth usurp thy useless hours, / Dissolve thy vigour, and enchain thy powers?"[191] But perhaps the most striking images of idleness as the cessation of motion and dissolving of self occur in Act 3 of *Irene* and in *Idlers* 31 and 24, all of which figure sloth as a sort of living death. In the seraglio, Aspasia says, Irene will be "Immur'd, and buried in perpetual sloth. . . ."[192] *Idler* 31 says, after a description of people whose "whole labour it is to vary the postures of indulgence":

These are the true and open votaries of idleness, for whom she weaves the garlands of poppies, and into whose cup she pours the waters of oblivion; who exist in a state of unruffled stupidity, forgetting and forgotten; who have long since ceased to live, and at whose death the survivors can only say, that they have ceased to breathe.[193]

Idler 24 gives a harsher picture of this living death: "He that lives in torpid insensibility, wants nothing of a carcase but putrefaction."[194] For Johnson, activity alone keeps things in motion, intact and alive. When Boswell, "in a low-spirited fit, was talking to him with indifference of the pursuits which generally engage us in a course of action, and inquiring a *reason* for taking so much trouble; 'Sir, (said he, in an animated tone) it is driving on the system of life.' "[195]

Johnson's preoccupation with idleness, then, stems from the same place as does his insomnia and his famous and terrible fear of death (which seems to have been a fear of annihilation as much as a fear of hell[196]): in idleness we cease driving on the system of life, leading to stagnation, dissolution, annihilation — vacuity. Johnson strove heroically to keep driving life on, despite his natural indolence, despite the despair to which his torturing guilt often led him. Some of his many eccentricities were probably attempts to keep driving, to maintain a grasp on ordering activity — for instance, his gargantuan appetite and his tics and compulsions. Alvin Kernan argues that the "single-minded intensity" with which Johnson ate was part of "the enormous biological determination of life itself to survive, simply to be"[197] that was in him. Sir Joshua Reynolds made the perceptive observation that Johnson's convulsive movements seemed an attempt to force his mind to stay engaged in the present.[198] Kernan agrees, saying Johnson's tics and ordering compulsions "such as turning around before going through a door, measuring his steps to place his foot on a crack in the floor or sidewalk, touching every post between the tavern and his house" were "attempts to construct at a very rudimentary level an arbitrary but meaningful order in the midst of what was felt as chaos or empty space."[199]

Johnson seems, judging from his diaries and prayers, to have found some peace with God at the end of his life, and some forgiveness of himself for all his misspent time.[200] This is a comfort to those who are saddened to think of him hating himself and fearing hell — a man who was so radically charitable that he gave much of his income away (handing out pocketsful of change to beggars and slipping pennies into the hands of sleeping homeless children so they could buy breakfast when they awakened), even when he himself was terribly poor; a man who took into his house a collection of poor misfits who were often irritable and hard to get along with (Voitle says eloquently: "He must also have patience, humility, and a strong sense of duty, who will remain faithful to the peevish and perverse, the ungrateful and the ignorant"[201]). But even in his newfound peace, Johnson fiercely tried to keep driving life on, saying, as he was dying, "I will be *conquered*; I will not capitulate."[202] Action, even if only the action of the will, was the only earthly thing to cling to, to keep vacuity at bay. And in thinking about Johnson's struggle against idleness and the vacuity it lets flood in, we might consider how much room the activity of writing he forced himself to engage in filled, and continues to fill, in the minds of those who read him. When Johnson died, William Gerard Hamilton said, "He has made a chasm, which not only nothing can fill up, but which nothing has a tendency to fill up."[203] This would be true, except that we still have his writings.

6

Under the Great Taskmaster's Eye:
William Cowper and Idleness

THE MENTAL, EMOTIONAL, AND SPIRITUAL PROBLEMS WITH WHICH William Cowper struggled for most of his life are well known, probably better known today than the poetry he began writing to distract himself from these problems. Several causes have been suggested for his episodes of madness, including an inherited tendency to melancholy, a genital deformity, an overdose of Evangelical religion, and, most recently, the early loss of his mother. While I think that Cowper's problems can probably not be traced to any one cause, I would like to suggest a factor that I believe played into his difficulties, one he tried to work out in much of his poetry, especially *The Task*: his complicated relation to work and idleness. Cowper thought of himself as a leisured gentleman, yet had little money of his own to support a life of genteel idleness; he had the family connections to acquire a sinecure which would allow him a comfortable income requiring little work, yet lived in a time when such arrangements were being called into question; he embraced a religion that proclaimed works useless to salvation, but that sternly disapproved of idleness; he knew that occupation was essential to his maintaining any hold on sanity, yet was disqualified by his instability from any sort of work in the world; he disdained and censured trifling, yet thought of everything he did, even, at times, the writing of poetry, as trifling. Cowper's letters, poems, and, I would argue, life attest to his tense and complicated connections to idleness and industry, leisure and labor; and from this tension came some of his most interesting poetry.

I

Cowper was born into an illustrious family. His father, the Reverend John Cowper, chaplain to the king, boasted a father who was a judge, an uncle, the first Earl Cowper, who was twice lord chancellor of Great Britain, and various relatives who enjoyed the rank of baronet. Cowper's mother, Ann Donne, claimed descent by four different lines from King Henry III, and was supposed to be descended from the poet John Donne, though probably collaterally. Cowper was given a classical, upper-class education at Westminster, where, to quote James King, "above all, he learned . . . to be a gentleman."[1] Cowper's immediate family, however, was not wealthy enough to allow him to be only a gentleman; a profession was necessary for him, and his father decided he should go into law. Cowper himself was not much interested in the law; as he later wrote to his friend Mrs. King, it was "a Profession to which I was never much inclined, and in which I engaged rather because I was desirous to gratify a most indulgent Father, than because I had any hope of success in it myself."[2] And during the fifteen years (1748–63) he spent as a member of the Temple, including the three years (1750–53) he was articled to the solicitor Mr. Chapman, he apparently conducted himself more like a leisured gentleman than a lawyer. In a 1789 letter exhorting his young friend Samuel Rose to work hard at his law studies, Cowper refers to his own legal career as "three years mis-spent in an attorney's office . . . followed by several more equally mis-spent in the Temple" (23 July 1789; 3:305); and in an earlier letter to the same person, he says he "devoted . . . all the earlier part of my life to amusement only" (14 February 1788; 3:100). As Charles Ryskamp tells us,

> From 1748 to 1753 he had not kept the terms of the Middle-Temple year, nor was he present at the formal exercises which were imposed on its members. He took no part in the ancient customs of the Temple; never argued in the moots with the other students before the benchers. He merely paid the fines at the time of his call to the bar, and satisfied the requirements of a token obedience.[3]

After his call to the bar in 1754, he had to fulfill a few requirements for three years, and then he could move to the Inner Temple, which lacked even the few requirements of the Middle Temple. To quote Ryskamp again, "By November 1757 he had sold his old chambers and had begun a life of increased leisure, free from any small struggles which he had previously encountered with the rules."[4]

Many of Cowper's biographers have commented on his lack of industry during these years. Robert Southey asserts, "that he had taken no pains to qualify himself for his profession is certain, and it is probable that he had as little intention as inclination to pursue it, resting in indolent reliance upon his patrimonial means, and in the likely expectation that some official appointment would be found for him in good time."[5] Lord David Cecil devotes several pages to Cowper's "failure as a lawyer," saying he had "never tried to work at it properly" and claiming that years of idleness removed his ability to work, even when he tried: "He had followed the idle bendings of his inclination so long, had become such a slave to chance desire, that he could not make himself work regularly. . . ."[6] Both Walter Bagehot and Gilbert Thomas suggest that Cowper's early idleness was at least partly responsible for his uncle's refusal, in 1753 or '54, to let him marry his cousin Theadora.[7] Certainly few of the extant Cowper letters from this period show him taking his profession very seriously. In an undated letter to Chase Price, probably written sometime in 1754, he writes: "Dancing all last Night; In bed one half of the Day & Shooting all the other half, and now going to—what? To kill a boding Screech Owl perch'd upon a—Walnut Tree just by my Window, have at you old Wise Acre!" (1:74–75). In a Latin letter to Clotworthy Rowley, Cowper tells him, "Dum tu Rhadamanthum tuum, quicunque is est, per villas atque oppida sectaris, majori, ut ais, opere quam lucro; ego, neque laborans, neque lucrum sperans, otiosam, ideoque mihi jucundissimam vitam ago . . ."[8] (August 1758; 1:82).

Cowper's lack of application to the law was caused in part by his dislike of it, and partly by his tendency toward indolence,[9] but it was also caused, I would argue, by his sense of professional ambition as ungentlemanly.[10] Working hard at anything simply did not fit the image of the leisured gentleman. And in a strange way, Cowper's dilettantish habits may not have been altogether a misuse of the Temple's resources. For, as Ryskamp tells us, "Cowper and his friends were not in the Temple for the law alone. Since ancient times the Inns of Court had as their function not only the learning of law, but also all things to qualify young men as leaders in the affairs of the kingdom. They were the final testing and training places of gentlemen."[11] Cowper never, of course, became a leader in the affairs of the kingdom, but he did always think of himself as, perhaps first and foremost, a gentleman. His adoption of a largely middle-class religion and his own relative poverty seem not to have undermined this sense of himself, although they contributed to the conflict he suffered.[12] As King says, "it was the life of a 'mere gentleman' that Cowper pursued. He dressed 'with exactest order & neatness, and look[ed] like an old nobleman'."[13] The villagers of Olney always called him "Sir Cowper" or "The Squire," and he accepted this elevation as his due.[14]

Cowper also accepted as his due the financial support his family and friends provided him. After his 1763 breakdown and retirement from London and the law, he resigned his office as Commissioner of Bankrupts, worth about sixty pounds a year. "By this means," he writes in Adelphi, his spiritual autobiography, "I reduced myself to an income scarcely sufficient for my maintenance, but I would rather have been starved in reality than have deliberately offended against my Saviour."

(Cowper felt his "ignorance of the law" would make him unable to take the oath to do his duty faithfully, and he was unwilling to return to London.) He goes on to say,

> In His great mercy to me the Lord has since raised me up such friends as have enabled me to enjoy all the comforts and conveniences of life and I am well assured that while I live, by means which the Almighty best knows, He will so dispose and order my circumstances that bread shall be given me and my waters shall be sure, according to His gracious promise. (1:41)

In a 1772 letter to Joseph Hill, Cowper again expresses his enviable confidence that the Lord will provide:

> I suppose you are sometimes troubled upon my Account, but you need not. I have no doubt it will be seen when my Days are closed, that I served a Master who would not suffer me to want any thing that was good for me. He said to Jacob, I will surely do thee Good—And This he said, not for His sake only, but for Ours also if we trust in him. This thought releives [*sic*] me from the greatest part of the Distress I should else suffer in my present Circumstances, and enables me to sit down peacefully upon the wreck of my Fortune. (27 June 1772; 1:254–55).

Joseph Hill was, in fact, one of the main providers of Cowper's funds. He managed the little money Cowper possessed on his own, and he made up from his own pocket the difference between what Cowper had and what he asked for. Mrs. Unwin, with whom Cowper lived from 1765 until her death in 1796, pooled her income with Cowper's; her daughter, Susanna Powley, claimed that her mother spent eighteen hundred pounds as a result of merging her fortune with Cowper's.[15] Several of Cowper's relatives provided other financial help at various times.[16]

Thomas makes the reasonable remark that these relatives of Cowper's must sometimes have been galled "to hear him so airily ascribe their generosity to the Lord."[17] But airiness always characterized Cowper's attitude toward money. One might think that after he developed the conviction that he was damned, he would have lost his faith that he would be provided for, but he seems never, once he retired from the world of work after his 1763 breakdown, to have worried about money or to have felt the need to try to earn his living.[18] In 1789 he wrote cheerfully to his cousin Maria Cowper, "I was born to subsist at the expence of my friends; in that, and in that alone, God knows, resembling my Lord and Master" (21 January 1789; 3:333). King ascribes Cowper's unblushing financial dependence on others to the sense of deprivation the early loss of his mother caused him: "Having suffered acute deprivation as a child, he acted childishly in such matters. He thought he had an inalienable right to the largess of others."[19] Early deprivation may have been part of the cause of Cowper's nonchalance about money, but I would argue that his deep sense of himself as a gentleman was also a cause. He was a gentleman; gentlemen lived in a certain way; and if he could not pay for this sort of life himself, then someone else should. Cowper was neither greedy nor, by gentlemanly standards, extravagant, but it was clearly out of the question for him not to live as a gentleman, not to have a reasonable number of servants and nicely tailored clothes.[20] He says in an early letter to Clotworthy Rowley, "Upon the whole my dear Rowley, there is a degree of Poverty that has no Disgrace belonging to [it, th]at degree of it I mean in which a man enjoys clean Linnen and good Company, & if I never sink below this degree of it, I care not if I never rise above it" (2 September 1762; 1:91). His friends and relatives made sure that he never did sink below this clean-linen standard, and he felt it was right they do so.

Cowper's gentlemanly self-image also affected his attitude towards his poetry. Until he began his translation of Homer, about which I will have more to say later, he never spoke of his writing as a professional activity. He earned no money from the two volumes of verse he published before he began working on the Homer, and he usually spoke of his writing as on a par with gardening, sketching, or light carpentry— gentlemanly amusements meant to keep away melancholy. His letters are full of such explanations for his poetry, such as this one to William Unwin: "Amusements are necessary in a Retirement like mine, & especially in such a State of Mind as I Labour under. The Necessity of Amusement makes me sometimes write Verses—it made me a Carpenter, a Bird Cage maker, a Gardener, and has lately taught me to draw. . . ." (6 April 1780; 1:329).[21]

It is hard to know exactly how seriously to take these protestations. Certainly, Cowper did find the writing of poetry therapeutic; like Samuel Johnson, he needed to keep his mind engaged to prevent melancholy thoughts. But his determination to present his poetry as nothing more than bird cage-making or fiddling also, I think, had to do with his desire not to be seen as ungenteelly professional. As William Norris Free says, "Cowper's lack of high seriousness about what we would now consider a vocation undoubtedly sprang in part from his gentlemanly disdain for what a greater commitment would entail."[22] When his poetry was published, Cowper made a point of asserting that his motivation was neither to make money nor to gain fame: a 1781 letter to John Newton says, "[T]hough I have no Objection to lucrative consequences if any such should follow, they are not my Aim; much less is it my Ambition to exhibit myself to the world as a Genius." His motive

for writing, he says, is amusement and occupation, and he plans to publish because "if I did not publish what I write, I could not interest myself sufficiently in my own Success to make an Amusement of it" (18
March 1781; 1:459).[23] Cowper also, again until he was in the midst of
the Homer translation, devoted relatively few hours a day to his writing: he wrote *The Task*, he told Newton, by "writing sometimes an hour
in a day, sometimes half a one, and sometimes two hours (30 October
1784; 2:291).

Cowper's readers have, to a significant extent, accepted his position
as an amateur, a gentleman poet. In the introduction to his bibliography
of Cowperian Studies, Lodwick Hartley says that studies of Cowper's
poetic techniques are fairly rare, because "he has been regarded so long
as a charming amateur that systematic analysis of his work has too often
seemed pointless."[24] Further on, Hartley adds,

> It is, of course, possible to regard Cowper simply as the literary amateur *par
> excellence*. Certainly he never wrote for material gain; moreover, his indepen-
> dence of literary fashions makes his removal from Grub Street seem far
> more remote than his removal from other aspects of the world from which
> he had 'retired.' Writing for him was for a long time a combination of gentle-
> manly amusement and occupational therapy.[25]

In his book on Cowper's poetry, Bill Hutchings says more than once
that Cowper was not just a dabbling dilettante;[26] such protest implies a
general impression to the contrary.[27]

At odds with this view of himself as a gentleman playing with verse
is the strong Evangelical disapproval Cowper held toward "trifling."
Particularly in the moral satires, the most Evangelically flavored of his
poems, Cowper repeatedly censures trifling and wasting time. In "The
Progress of Error," he satirizes fashionable pastimes:

> Oh the dear pleasures of the velvet plain,
> The painted tablets, dealt and dealt again.
> Cards, with what rapture, and the polish'd die,
> The yawning chasm of indolence supply!
> Then to the dance, and make the sober moon
> Witness of joys that shun the sight of noon.[28]

He goes on to refer to these frivolities as "venerable time / Slain at the
foot of pleasure"(ll.181–82; 21) and to imply that this slaying of time is
a crime. In "Hope," Cowper paints a long and comic portrait of Jonquil, a fashionable trifler whose life is "without a plan, / As useless as
the moment it began" (ll. 95–96; 61), whose only activity is

> To rise at noon, sit slipshod and undress'd,
> To read the news, or fiddle, as seems best,
> Till half the world comes rattling at his door,
> To fill the dull vacuity till four;
> And, just when ev'ning turns the blue vault grey,
> To spend two hours in dressing for the day. . . .
>
> (ll. 75–80; 61)

This passage seems quite Johnsonian, with its disapproval of late rising, its mention of filling "vacuity," and its emphasis on the misery of such an idle life, which is, Cowper says, "so tediously the same, / So void of all utility or aim" (ll. 87–88; 61), that poor Jonquil wishes for death. A few lines on there is a strong image of the inescapable, painful boredom of this life:

> Oh! weariness beyond what asses feel,
> That tread the circuit of the cistern wheel;
> A dull rotation, never at a stay,
> Yesterday's face twin image of today;
> While conversation, an exhausted stock,
> Grows drowsy as the clicking of a clock.
>
> (ll. 99–104; 61)

Also reminiscent of Johnson are Cowper's assertions that not only the fashionably idle, but also the apparently busy, may be triflers. In "Charity," he chides the learned man who can discuss "the space between the stars and us" and "measure earth, compute the sea, / Weigh sun-beams, carve a fly, or spit a flea," reducing him to

> The solemn trifler, with his boasted skill,
> Toils much, and is a solemn trifler still:
> Blind was he born, and his misguided eyes
> Grown dim in trifling studies, blind he dies.
>
> (ll. 352–58; 83–84)

"Tirocinium: Or, A Review Of Schools" criticizes modern education, claiming that "Truths that the learn'd pursue with eager thought / Are not important always as dear bought" (ll. 73–74; 244), and emphasizing that men are not meant to "trifle life away / Down to the sun-set of their latest day" (ll. 81–82; 244). The poem urges fathers to make sure that their sons' activities, even their recreations, are profitable, and "T' impress a value, not to be eras'd, / On moments squander'd else, and running all to waste" (ll. 613–14; 255).

   Some of Cowper's minor poems also emphasize the sinfulness of trifling and of wasting time. The short "A Comparison" neatly, if not too originally, discusses the similarities between time and rivers, saying that both proceed irrevocably and undissuadably, and that "a wide ocean swallows both at last" (l. 6; 304). The poem ends by pointing out the difference between the two:

> Streams never flow in vain; where streams abound,
> How laughs the land with various plenty crown'd!
> But time that should enrich the nobler mind,
> Neglected, leaves a dreary waste behind.
>
> (ll. 9–12; 304)

The verses Cowper wrote several times for the annual bill of mortality also, reasonably enough, emphasize time's passing, especially the one written for the year 1788. In this poem Cowper imagines a grim but interesting situation: that the bill cannot just list those who have died in the past year, but also predict who will die in the year to come. If this were true, he says, the person who read his name there would quickly stop trifling:

> Time then would seem more precious than the joys
> In which he sports away the treasure now,
> And prayer more seasonable than the noise
> Of drunkards or the music-drawing bow.
>
> Then, doubtless, many a trifler, on the brink
> Of this world's hazardous and headlong shore,
> Forc'd to a pause, would feel it good to think,
> Told that his setting sun would rise no more.
>
> (ll. 9–16; 366)

In "The Moralizer Corrected," Cowper writes of a hermit musing, as eighteenth-century hermits are wont to muse, on the vanity of human wishes. An angelic guide appears and tells him that whether the time someone spends in pursuing a desire is wasted depends on what "call'd his ardour forth." The guide cautions against chasing trifles: "Trifles pursued, whate'er th' event, / Must cause him shame or discontent . . ." (ll. 44–46; 401).

This strong sense Cowper expresses of the evils of trifling sits uneasily with his many assertions that he himself is only trifling in verse. (Thus Cowper, like Johnson, is caught in a dilemma about trifling.) In "Table Talk," another of the moral satires, Cowper writes of the importance of serious subjects for poetry:

> To dally much with subjects weak and low
> Proves that the mind is weak, or makes it so.

> Neglected talents rust into decay,
> And ev'ry effort ends in push-pin play.
> The man that means success should soar above
> A soldier's feather, or a lady's glove;
> Else, summoning the muse to such a theme,
> The fruit of all her labour is whipt-cream.
>
> (ll. 544–51; 12)

A glance at Cowper's collected works, though, will show that he did fairly often dally with seemingly light or trivial subjects. Goldfinches dying of starvation or bullfinches eaten by rats, cats accidently shut in drawers or mock-heroically saved from vipers, arguments between spectacles and noses or lilies and roses, the ill-fated travels of a linen-draper and his runaway horse or a poet and his lady-friend stuck in the mud—all of these topics, charming as they are, could well be regarded as whipped cream. In his poem "Beau's Reply," a companion piece to "On A Spaniel Called Beau Killing A Young Bird," Cowper amusingly but (considered in context) poignantly points this out. In the first poem, Cowper has censured his dog Beau for killing a young bird, "Against my orders, whom you heard / Forbidding you the prey" (ll. 7–8; 425). In his "Reply," Beau pleads that nature impelled him to the deed, and that he has in the past overcome natures's urgings and forborne to kill his master's pet linnet. "Let my obedience then excuse / My disobedi-ence now" (ll. 21–22; 426), he says, and then turns Cowper's reproach against him:

> If killing birds be such a crime,
>   (Which I can hardly see)
> What think you, Sir, of killing Time
>   With verse address'd to me?
>
> (ll. 25–28; 426)

This reproof, funny though it is, reveals Cowper's unease with the way he spends (or, more violently, "kills") his time. Hutchings says of the poem,

> if we recall Cowper's statements about how verse-writing acts for him as a therapeutic diversion of the mind from horrific personal contemplations, we can see that this conclusion is a piece of savage self-indictment on Cowper's part. The moralizer is simply moralizing to waste time. Thus the central mo-tivation of Cowper's poetic career is called into agonizing question.[29]

Cowper cannot win: he writes to divert his thoughts from his sense of guilt and separation from God; but he sins in so wasting time, and therefore he compounds his guilt and furthers his separation.[30]

II

If writing as a gentleman-trifler causes guilt and conflict, then the answer might seem to be to write instead as a professional. And for a while, perhaps, this worked for Cowper. When he began his translation of Homer in November 1784, he also began, I would argue, to think of himself as a professional writer. For the first time he seemed to think of his writing as labor, and for the first time he became concerned with being paid for it. In a letter to William Unwin, he says that if he lives, he "will surely publish" his translation, explaining,

> In the whole, I shall have composed about 40,000 Verses, about which 40,000 Verses I shall have taken great pains, on no occasion suffering a slovenly line to escape me. I leave you to guess therefore, whether, such a labour once atchieved [*sic*], I shall not determine to turn it to some account, and to gain myself profit if I can, if not, at least some credit for my reward. (22 October 1785; 2:388)

In a letter to Lady Hesketh, Cowper explicitly makes a connection between the time and labor the translation has cost him and the money it should therefore cost the bookseller: "The 21st. of this Month I shall have spent a year upon it, and it will cost me more than another. I do not love the Booksellers well enough to make them a Present of such a labour, but intend to publish by Subscription" (9 November 1785; 2:395). Arguing to Newton that the price of his proposed volume is not too high, Cowper again equates his labor with money and explicitly calls his translation a commodity and a product:

> That the price should be thought too high, I must rather wonder. The immense labour of the work considered, & the price of Pope's first Edition also considered, which was seven guineas, it does not appear to me extravagant. I question if there is a Poet in the three Kingdoms or in any Kingdom who would sell such a commodity for less. (1 April 1786; 2:507)

Still arguing, five years later, for the fairness of the translation's price, Cowper again connects his labor and his readers' money: "I am no very good arithmetician, yet I calculated the other day in my morning walk, that my two volumes, at the price of three guineas, will cost the purchaser less than the seventh part of a farthing per line. Yet there are lines among them that have cost me the labour of hours, and none that have not cost me some labour" (24 March 1791; 3:488).

Cowper went so far as to quarrel with Joseph Johnson, his publisher, about how much he should receive for the translation. Johnson had first proposed an arrangement that Cowper found unfair,[31] and, as

Cowper told Lady Hesketh, "His first proposal, which was to pay me with my own money, or in other words, to get my copy[right] for nothing, not only dissatisfied but hurt me, implying, as I thought, the meanest opinion possible for my labours. For that for which an intelligent man will give nothing, can be worth nothing" (11 July 1791; 3:542). The problem was resolved amicably, but it is remarkable that Cowper, the gentlemanly dabbler in poetry who was born to subsist at the expense of his friends, had become a professional author who considered his writing labor, a commodity which should fetch a fair price. I would speculate that Cowper could make this move to professionalism without worrying about his status as a gentleman because, in choosing to translate Homer, he was returning from the middle-class values of Evangelicalism to the gentlemanly values of his youth. In embracing Evangelicalism, Cowper had to some extent renounced his youthful devotion to the classics. As he wrote to Newton in a 1781 letter,

> When you married I was 18 years of age, and had just left Westminster School. At that time I valued a man according to his proficiency & Taste in classical Literature, & had the meanest opinion of all other Accomplishments unaccompanied by that. I lived to see the Vanity of what I had made my pride, and in a few years found that there were other attainments which would carry a man more handsomely through Life than a mere knowledge of what Homer & Virgil had left behind them. In measure as my Attachment to these Gentry wore off, I found a more welcome reception among those whose acquaintance it was more my Interest to cultivate. (18 February 1781; 1:446–47)

When his interest in the classics resurfaced, Cowper turned away from Newton and his world back to the world of his family and his friends from Westminster and the Temple.[32] He reestablished contact with many people with whom he had not corresponded for years, including his former friends Walter Bagehot, George Coleman, Clotworthy Rowley, Robert Smith, and Edward Thurlow,[33] and, most notably, his cousin Lady Hesketh.[34] These friends and family members were probably the more eager to become reacquainted with Cowper since he was now the successful author of the much-admired *Task* and "John Gilpin," but their support both encouraged his project and, I think, enabled him to be comfortable taking a stance as a professional writer.

This new professional self-image did to some extent keep Cowper from reproaching himself for trifling. The letters he wrote during the six years he spent translating the *Iliad* and the *Odyssey* frequently assert the all-engrossing nature of the occupation and claim it as a valid reason for not engaging in other activities. Typical is this remark to Lady Hesketh, explaining why he had little light verse to send her: "Fine things indeed I have few. He who has Homer to Translate may well be contented to do little else" (18 January 1788; 3:86). Similarly, he wrote a little poem to Walter Bagot, excusing his tardiness in responding to Bagot's letter:

> It is a maxim of much weight
>   Worth conning o'er and o'er,
> He who has Homer to translate
>   Had need do nothing more.
>
> (26 February 1791; 3:469)

Ultimately, however, professionalism was not the answer to Cowper's problems. It kept him from seeing himself as a trifler in verse, but it did not resolve the larger problem of his relationship with God. In 1786 he wrote to Newton,

> Thus far therefore it is plain that I have not chosen or prescribed to myself my own way, but have been providentially led to it. Perhaps I might say with equal propriety, compelled and scourged into it. For certainly, could I have made my choice, or were I permitted to make it even now, those hours which I spend in poetry, I should spend with God. (20 May 1786; 2:548)

To some extent, certainly, Cowper was here saying what Newton wanted to hear, but I think he also meant it—or at least a part of him did. Poetry might keep his mind pleasantly occupied, it might even bring him fame and the admiration of others, but it could not bring him what he felt he most desperately lacked: salvation.

And here we come to what I see as one of Cowper's central struggles, a struggle that circled around the question of what a person's true life-work is. Cowper was caught between two conflicting traditions. On the one hand was the Evangelical religion he had chosen to embrace, which saw personal salvation as the real work of human life, a work that paradoxically could be achieved only through faith, not works.[35] On the other hand was the Augustan tradition he was reared with, which prized public duty and usefulness to society and which stigmatized as self-centered idleness the sort of contemplative retirement Cowper found most conducive to salvation.[36] In "Retirement" and *The Task*, the two poems most concerned with contemplative retirement as salvation, Cowper wrestles with these two conflicting traditions. While he is never able comfortably to resolve the tension between Evangelical and Augustan values in these poems, the strategies he employs in the attempt make for interesting poetry.

In letters, Cowper said that he wrote "Retirement"

to direct to the proper use of the opportunities [retirement] affords for the cultivation of a Man's best Interests; to censure the Vices and the follies which people carry with them into their Retreats, where they make no other use of their leisure than to gratify themselves with the Indulgence of their favorite appetites, and to pay themselves by a life of pleasure for a life of Business. (25 August 1781; 1:512)

The Task, he said, was written "to discountenance the modern enthusi-asm after a London Life, and to recommend rural ease and leisure as friendly to the cause of piety and virtue" (10 October 1784; 2:285). These statements point up one of the differences between the two poems: "Retirement," the earlier poem, takes the attractions of retire-ment more as a given, and it concerns itself with outlining what sort of people should and should not retire and with how retirement should be employed, while *The Task* devotes more energy to arguing for the plea-sures and virtues of retirement itself.[37] The poems have important simi-larities, however: both are clearly written from the standpoint of the retired gentleman, and both name the writing of poetry, along with gar-dening and a few other pursuits, as an admirable occupation for the retired. Thus leisure is not only the topic of both poems, but the pro-ducer of them (and indeed the discursive, meandering nature of the poems does seem the result of leisure), which gives them a self-referen-tial quality. Most essential to my discussion here, though, is that both poems are concerned, more or less explicitly, with defending the retired man against charges of idleness and uselessness. Cowper does some of this defending quite straightforwardly, especially in parts of *The Task*; at other times he employs more subtle strategies.

One feature of both "Retirement" and *The Task* which strikes me as defensive is their use of paradox, both in theme and phrasing. Since Cowper is in these poems seeking to recommend ease and leisure with-out laying himself open to accusations of idleness, he tries to portray leisure as somehow difficult and labor-requiring. In "Retirement," he gives a funny sketch of a statesman who attempts retirement but, lack-ing the necessary inner resources for a life away from the bustle and flash of the world, soon becomes bored and must return:

> He chides the tardiness of ev'ry post,
> Pants to be told of battles won or lost,
> Blames his own indolence, observes, though late,
> 'Tis criminal to leave a sinking state,
> Flies to the levee, and, receiv'd with grace,
> Kneels, kisses hands, and shines again in place.
>
> (ll. 475–80; 119)

By making a self-accusation of indolence and neglect of civic duty nothing but the excuse this man uses to flee a life he cannot handle, Cowper indirectly defends the retired man against having these charges leveled at him. Cowper also presents retirement as something only the few can master, a difficult state requiring hard work. He reiterates this idea later in the poem, saying, "few that court Retirement are aware / Of half the toils they must encounter there" (ll. 609–10; 122). In a bold move, he claims that profit-generating work in the world is easy, while retirement requires real skill:

> Lucrative offices are seldom lost
> For want of pow'rs proportion'd to the post:
> Give e'en a dunce th' employment he desires,
> And he soon finds the talents it requires;
> A business with an income at its heels
> Furnishes always oil for its own wheels.
> But in his arduous enterprise to close
> His active years with indolent repose,
> He finds the labours of that state exceed
> His utmost faculties, severe indeed.
> 'Tis easy to resign a toilsome place,
> But not to manage leisure with a grace;
> Absence of occupation is not rest,
> A mind quite vacant is a mind distress'd.
>
> (ll. 611–24; 122)

Some lines later, Cowper again emphasizes the necessity of the retired man's having a strong mind, ready to ponder life's most important questions:

> A mind unnerv'd, or indispos'd to bear
> The weight of subjects worthiest of her care,
> Whatever hope a change of scene inspires,
> Must change her nature, or in vain retires.
>
> (ll. 677–80; 123)

Thus, again, he presents retirement's ease as, paradoxically, a hard job for which only the strongest few are fit.

One of the great paradoxes of *The Task* is apparent right from the beginning.[38] The first words of the poem, "I sing the SOFA" (l. 1; 129), set up an opposition between the idea of work implicit in the title of the poem and the idea of leisure and laziness implicit in the image of the sofa, that haven for languid ladies and gouty gentlemen. Four lines later, after mentioning some of his recent, serious poetic accomplishments, Cowper declares his intent to "seek repose upon an humbler theme" (l. 5; 129); again, this notion of seeking repose—whether upon a humble theme or a sofa—is at odds with the idea of a task. In Book 3, Cowper uses a paradoxical phrase which seems to sum up how he wants us to think of his life in retirement: "laborious ease" (l. 361; 172). In Book 4, he uses the phrase "easy force" (l. 11; 220), another paradox which is, as Martin Priestman points out, "a flat reversal of . . . 'laborious ease'," and which echoes the paradoxical " 'gentle force' [l. 115; 166] with which Christ removed the darts from the stricken deer in 'The Garden'."³⁹ This use of paradox allows Cowper to encompass both the pleasant, gentlemanly leisure and ease he wants to claim for his life and the admirable work he wants to insist he is doing.

Another strategy Cowper employs for his defense of the retired man in these two poems is to cast others, those usually seen as busy and well-employed, as actually idlers. In "Retirement," he insists that the man of business is the true trifler, interested only in personal gain. Cowper takes this tack right from the beginning: in the first few lines of the poem, he says that the "statesman, lawyer, merchant, man of trade / Pants for the refuge of some rural shade" (ll. 5–6; 109), so that

> He may possess the joys he thinks he sees,
> Lay his old age upon the lap of ease,
> Improve the remnant of his wasted span,
> And, having liv'd a trifler, die a man.⁴⁰
>
> (ll. 11–14; 109)

Thus the man of affairs is pictured as a trifler, whose life of business is "a wasted span" which can be improved only by rural retirement—quite a different view of him than the Augustan one which sees statesmen and merchants as doing their civic duty and increasing the wealth of the nation. Perhaps the most powerful image of urban business as useless acquisitiveness comes in the allegorical vision of "this life of man" as "a little isle" (l. 148; 112); the vision also presents the retired as truly beloved and rewarded by God, though scorned by man:

> The busy race examine and explore
> Each creek and cavern of the dang'rous shore,
> With care collects what in their eyes excels,
> Some shining pebbles, and some weeds and shells;
> Thus laden, dream that they are rich and great,
> And happiest he that groans beneath their weight:
> The waves o'ertake them in their serious play,
> And ev'ry hour sweeps multitudes away;
> They shriek and sink, survivors start and weep,
> Pursue their sport, and follow to the deep.

A few foresake the throng; with lifted eyes
Ask wealth of heav'n, and gain a real prize—
Truth, wisdom, grace, and peace like that above,
Seal'd with his signet whom they serve and love;
Scorn'd by the rest, with patient hope they wait
A kind release from their imperfect state,
And, unregretted, are soon snatch'd away
From scenes of sorrow into glorious day.

(ll. 151–68; 112–13)

The Task is not so concerned as "Retirement" with accusing the unre-
tired of avarice, but it contains several portraits like the one above,
showing worldly business as nothing more than collecting pebbles or
catching smoke. As he did in some of the moral satires, Cowper satirizes
the wasted lives of the fashionable; they

Waste youth in occupations only fit
For second childhood, and devote old age
To sports which only childhood could excuse.
There they are happiest who dissemble best
Their weariness; and they the most polite
Who squander time and treasure with a smile,
Though at their own destruction.

(Book 2, ll. 636–42; 159)

As in "The Progress of Error," fashionable amusements such as cards
and billiards are seen as "tricks" conceived by idleness "To fill the void
of an unfurnish'd brain, / To palliate dulness, and give time a shove"
(Book 4, ll. 209–10; 187). "The world's time is time in masquerade"
(l. 213), Cowper says, and he visualizes time dressed in emblems from
games:

Ensanguin'd hearts, clubs typical of strife,
And spades, the emblem of untimely graves.
What should be and what was an hour-glass once,
Becomes a dice-box, and a billiard mast
Well does the work of his destructive scythe.
Thus deck'd, he charms a world whom fashion blinds
To his true worth, most pleas'd when idle most;
Whose only happy are their wasted hours.

(Book 4, ll. 218–25; 187)

Here, reversing the usual notion of time as the changer and destroyer,
fashionable amusements change and distort time. In Book 6, Cowper
again censures billiards, calling it an "idle sport" (l. 272; 225) involving

"trivial toys" (l. 274); he also includes chess in his disapproval, as well as recreational shopping and auction-attending.

More scholarly pursuits also come in for their share of disapprobation as being ultimately trifling, as they do in "Charity." In the famous "stricken deer" passage in Book 3, Cowper presents a grand vision of all men as wanderers, "lost / In chase of fancied happiness" (ll. 125–26; 166–67), vainly pursuing dreams. "Rings the world / With the vain stir" (ll. 129–30; 167), he says Miltonically, and then calculates,

> I sum up half mankind,
> And add two thirds of the remaining half,
> And find the total of their hopes and fears
> Dreams, empty dreams.
>
> (ll. 130–33; 167)

Millions flit gaily like short-lived flies, he says, and "The rest are sober dreamers, grave and wise, / And pregnant with discov'ries new and rare" (ll. 137–38; 167). Historians, biographers, geologists, and astronomers—all spend "The little wick of life's poor shallow lamp / In playing tricks with nature, giving laws / To distant worlds, and trifling in their own" (ll. 164–66; 167). Their activities are not only useless— chasing smoke and bubbles—but potentially damnable:

> Ah! what is life thus spent? and what are they
> But frantic who thus spend it? all for smoke—
> Eternity for bubbles, proves at last
> A senseless bargain. When I see such games
> Play'd by the creatures of a pow'r who swears
> That he will judge the earth, and call the fool
> To a sharp reck'ning that has liv'd in vain;
> And when I weigh this seeming wisdom well,
> And prove it in th'infallible result
> So hollow and so false—I feel my heart
> Dissolve in pity, and account the learn'd,
> If this be learning, most of all deceiv'd.
>
> (Book 3, ll. 173–84; 168)

Even the monumental employments of the great and powerful are, in Cowper's view, mere triflings:

> Great princes have great playthings. Some have play'd
> At hewing mountains into men, and some
> At building human wonders mountain-high.
> Some have amus'd the dull, sad years of life
> (Life spent in indolence, and therefore sad)

With schemes of monumental fame; and sought
By pyramids and mausolean pomp,
Short-lived themselves, t' immortalize their bones.
Some seek diversion in the tented field,
And make the sorrows of mankind their sport.

(Book 5, ll. 177–86; 204)

Thus Cowper dismisses as trifling the activities of the fashionable, the studious, even the royal, and thus, if the best defense is an offense, he defends himself against a charge of being useless or idle.

When Cowper moves to describing the (presumably nontrifling) occupations he himself engages in in his retirement, however, it is not always entirely clear why they are preferable to those he has been denouncing. Near the close of "Retirement" he claims that "Religion does not censure or exclude / Unnumber'd pleasures harmlessly pursu'd" (ll. 783–84; 126), but the pleasures he names number only three: gardening, landscape painting, and poetry writing. In Book 3 of *The Task*, he mentions "Friends, books, a garden, and perhaps his pen" (l. 355; 171), as well as walks in nature (ll. 357–58; 172), as things with which the retired man may busy himself without reproach. In Book 4, he lists books, music, "the poet's toil" (l. 262; 188), the gardening-related activity of "weaving nets for bird-alluring fruit" (l. 263; 188), and winding thread for ladies. He also gives a pleasant picture of himself staring at the fire, his fancy, "ludicrous and wild," soothing him "with a waking dream of houses, tow'rs, / Trees, churches, and strange visages, express'd / In the red cinders" (ll. 286–89; 188–89).

While it may be obvious that these activities are harmless and innocent, it is not so apparent why they, unlike the frivolous or scholarly pursuits Cowper has earlier denounced, "are arts pursu'd without a crime, / That leave no stain upon the wing of time" ("Retirement," ll. 799–800; 126); why he can say that "Time, as he passes us, has a dove's wing, / Unsoil'd, and swift, and of a silken sound . . ." (*The Task*, Book 4, ll. 211–12; 187). After all, he has denounced the other activities not so much for being harmful (an argument he could have made about warfare and gambling, at least), but for being vain and trifling: for wasting time. So why do these activities in which he engages not stain or soil the wing of time?

III

Cowper cannot, I believe, really answer this question,[41] which is one reason for the tension surrounding questions of work and idleness in these two poems. And a larger question emerges when we wonder what might make one activity nontrifling while another is vain: the question of what exactly a person's true lifework *is*. Is it the soul-searching that will lead to salvation, as Cowper indicates early in "Retirement," where he says that retirement is admirable because it makes one more likely

> To bid the pleadings of self-love be still,
> Resign our own and seek our Maker's will;
> To spread the page of Scripture, and compare
> Our conduct with the laws engraven there;
> To measure all that passes in the breast,
> Faithfully, fairly, by that sacred test;
> To dive into the secret hopes within,
> To spare no passion and no fav'rite sin,
> And search the themes, important above all,
> Ourselves and our recov'ry from our fall.
>
> (ll. 129–38; 112)

Or is it service to others, as we might gather from Book 3 of *The Task*, when Cowper claims he tries to improve, or

> At least neglect not, or leave unemploy'd,
> The mind he gave me; driving it, though slack
> Too oft, and much impeded in its work
> By causes not to be divulged in vain,
> To its just point—the service of mankind.
>
> (ll. 368–72; 172)

We might attribute this difference to a change in Cowper's philosophy between the composition of these poems, but immediately following the lines just quoted are these, which complicate the matter:

> He that attends to his interior self,
> That has a heart, and keeps it; has a mind
> That hungers, and supplies it; and who seeks
> A social, not a dissipated life;
> Has business; feels himself engag'd t' achieve
> No unimportant, though a silent, task.
>
> (ll. 373–78; 172)

That this passage about the "business" of attending to the interior self immediately follows one claiming the "just point" as "the service of mankind" surely indicates a conflict in Cowper's mind. The Evangelical religion that Cowper never renounced, although he felt himself excluded from it, saw personal salvation (and the self-examination leading to it) as the essential work of life. The more public-spirited Augustan tradition that he was reared in and really, I would argue, felt more comfortable with, saw as essential some sort of usefulness to society.[42] Thus Cowper was caught in a conflict, not only between two views of life's work, but between what could be seen as his own failure to live up to *either* view: despite his own retirement, and the opportunity it gave him to examine his interior self and to contemplate eternity, he was convinced he was damned (and therefore found self-examination and thinking about eternity infinitely painful); and, despite his desire to serve society, his retirement made it difficult for him to do so in the usual Augustan ways. Although he tries to make his retired occupations look productive, exclaiming before the lines about friends, books, a garden, and his pen: "How various his employments, whom the world / Calls idle; and who justly, in return, / Esteems that busy world an idler too!" (Book 3, ll. 352–54; 172), it is true, as P. M. S. Dawson says, that "To point to the *variety* of his occupations is no answer to the charge; and the final 'too' virtually concedes the case, however 'justly' Cowper might retort with his *tu quoque*."[43] Cowper goes on to ask, after listing some of his pleasant occupations, "Can he want occupation who has these? / Will he be idle who has much t' enjoy?" (ll. 359–60; 172); the answer, as Newey points out, "must in fact be yes, unless one takes a very restricted view of 'occupation'. For friends, books, a garden, and a pen seem to have more to do with leisure, personal satisfaction, and passing the time than with being productive."[44] And while the number of occupations he has to enjoy may mean Cowper is unlikely to be idle in the sense of doing nothing, the very word "enjoy" seems also to imply more about personal pleasure than useful labor. And yet Cowper did want to be useful.[45] One of the more poignant indications of Cowper's wish to be useful can be seen in the letter he wrote to Lady Hesketh after the sudden death of William Unwin, Mrs. Unwin's only son and his close friend. King notes that Cowper "was strangely reticent about Unwin's death in his letters," and he calls this letter to Lady Hesketh "a severely restricted, not callous, tribute to the man he had seen as both a son and a brother."[46] What is most remarkable to me about this letter is the way Cowper focuses, not on his grief or even that of Mrs. Unwin, but on Unwin's great usefulness:

> He had attained to an Age when, if they are at any time useful, men become most useful to their families, their friends, and the world. His parish began to feel and to be sensible of the advantages of his ministry. The Clergy around him were many of them awed by his example. His children were thriving under his own tuition and management, and his Eldest boy in particular is likely to feel his loss severely, being by his years in some respect

qualified to understand the value of such a parent. . . . The removal of such
a man in the prime of life, of such a character and with such connexions,
seems to make a void in society that never can be filled. (4 December 1786;
2:606)

That Cowper specifically mourns here the void Unwin's death will
cause in society, rather than the void it will make in his own life, may
be partly due to a fear of increasing his sorrow; but I think also it shows
how much value Cowper placed on social usefulness, and how much he
feared he was of little use to his family, his friends, or the world.

Another indication of Cowper's unhappy sense of uselessness may be
his concern with the story of the barren fig tree.[47] Recounting in *Adelphi*
his 1763 breakdown and suicide attempt, he writes of his agonizing
sense that he was damned: "One moment I saw myself, as I thought,
shut out from mercy by one chapter, and the next by another." The
story of the fig tree especially haunted him:

I particularly remember the barren fig tree was to me a theme of inconceivable misery, and I applied it to myself with a strong persuasion upon my
mind that when Our Saviour pronounced a curse upon it He had me in
His eye and pointed that curse directly at me. I turned over all Archbishop
Tillotson's sermons in hopes of finding one upon that subject and consulted
my brother upon the true meaning of it, desirous if possible to arrive at a
gentler interpretation of the passage than my evil conscience would suffer
me to fasten upon it.[48]

Twenty-two years later, the story seemed still to be on Cowper's mind.
In a letter to Newton, he says,

Of myself who had once both leaves and fruit, but who have now neither, I
say nothing; or only this. That when I am overwhelmed with despair, I repine at my barrenness and think it hard to be thus blighted. But when a
glimpse of hope breaks in upon me, I am contented to be the sapless thing I
am, knowing that he who has commanded me to wither, can command me
to flourish again when he pleases. (25 June 1785; 2:357)

One cannot be sure why this particular Bible story so struck Cowper,[49]
but I think it at least possible that he associated his own lack of useful
productivity with the fig tree's fruitlessness, and feared he was cursed
for it, as Jesus cursed and withered the tree for not bearing fruit.

Poetry, of course, was the main form Cowper's productivity took
after his 1763 breakdown, and in some of his letters he asserts his desire
to do some good with his writing. "My pieces are such as may possibly
be made usefull," he wrote to Newton while preparing his first volume

of verse in 1781, adding, "The more they are approved, the more likely they are to spread, and consequently the more likely to attain the end of usefullness, which as I said once before, except my present amusement, is the only end I propose" (16 August 1781; 1:508). A couple of months later he wrote to William Unwin: "The Critics cannot deprive me of the pleasure I have in reflecting that so far as my leisure has been employed in writing for the public, it has been conscientiously employed, and with a view to their advantage" (6 October 1781; 1:528). I think he was sincere in the wish of usefulness he expresses in these letters, but his linking of usefulness with his own amusement, and his saying that his *leisure* (rather than he himself) has been employed, does create some tension in his declarations. In 1785, shortly after his second volume of verse was published, Cowper again told Newton of his hope to be useful, but here his tones seem more defensive, possibly because of the rather lukewarm reception of his first volume:

> God gave me grace also to wish that I might not write in vain. Accordingly I have mingled much truth with much trifle, and such truths as deserved at least to be clad as well and as handsomely as I could cloath them. If the world approve me not, so much the worse for them, but not for me. I have only endeavour'd to serve them, and the loss will be their own. (6 August 1785; 2:367)

In *The Task* and "Retirement," Cowper makes a claim for the usefulness of his poetry. In "Retirement," he asks nature to be his muse, "That I may catch a fire but rarely known, / Give useful light though I should miss renown" (ll. 205–6; 114); and he ends the poem, after describing gardening and painting, two of the activities the retired man may pursue "without a crime" (l. 799; 126), by saying,

> Me poetry (or, rather, notes that aim
> Feebly and vainly at poetic fame)
> Employs, shut out from more important views,
> Fast by the banks of the slow winding Ouse;
> Content if, thus sequester'd, I may raise
> A monitor's, though not a poet's praise,
> And while I teach an art too little known,
> To close life wisely, may not waste my own.
>
> (ll. 801–8; 126)

On one level, it makes perfect sense that by teaching others how not to waste their lives, Cowper is making good use of his. But a difficulty arises when one realizes that poetry writing is the only socially useful activity for the retired that Cowper has actually mentioned. He is serving society by encouraging others to leave society and attend to their interior selves. But by so doing, the others, unless they also happen to be poets, will be withdrawing from public usefulness to achieve personal salvation. When we recall that Samuel Johnson said that in retirement one could do "no good," and that he called it "a civil suicide,"[50] it seems clear that, by Augustan standards, Cowper is avoiding this civil suicide himself by encouraging it in others.[51] In *The Task*, Cowper makes one rather more straightforward claim for his poetry; after a passage asserting the virtues of animals, he says,

> And I am recompens'd, and deem the toils
> Of poetry not lost, if verse of mine
> May stand between an animal and woe,
> And teach one tyrant pity for his drudge.
>   (Book 6, ll. 725–28; 235)

And indeed he did write against cruelty to animals, and against slavery, both in *The Task* and elsewhere.[52] But his larger claim to the status of useful, public poet seems to be more subtle. In Book 2, after a particularly public passage proclaiming his love of England ("England, with all thy faults, I love thee still, / My country" [ll. 206–7; 150]), saying that although "To shake thy senate, and from heights sublime / Of patriot eloquence to flash down fire / Upon thy foes, was never meant my task" (ll. 216–18; 150–51), he can feel England's fortunes and censure her follies like any "thund'rer" (l. 221; 151), he suddenly turns from discussing Wolfe and Chatham, France and America, to say,

> There is a pleasure in poetic pains
> Which only poets know. The shifts and turns,
> Th' expedients and inventions, multiform,
> To which the mind resorts, in chase of terms
> Though apt, yet coy, and difficult to win —
> T' arrest the fleeting images that fill
> The mirror of the mind, and hold them fast,
> And force them sit till he has pencil'd off
> A faithful likeness of the forms he views;
> Then to dispose his copies with such art,
> That each may find its most propitious light,
> And shine by situation, hardly less
> Than by the labor and the skill it cost;
> Are occupations of the poet's mind . . .
>   (ll. 285–98; 152)

While he begins this passage by speaking of the "pleasures" of writing poetry, his positioning it immediately after a section discussing England in a very public voice, and his way of describing the poetic process, making it sound like some sort of manly sport—outrunning and out-wrestling the images of the mind—seem to place the poet Cowper in the same public arena as the national heroes Wolfe and Chatham. The emphasis he places on the labor and skill poetry costs tips the balance away from the pleasure of poetry back towards its "pains." Tipping the balance back again in the next few lines, Cowper goes on to describe how "pleasing" (l. 299) the poet's occupations are and how they make his anxieties retire, then switches the balance back with a reproachful comment that his readers are "Aware of nothing arduous in a task / They never undertook" and that "they little note / His dangers or escapes . . ." (ll. 307–9; 152). Continuing the seesaw motion, he finishes the sentence with, "and haply find / There least amusement where he found the most" (ll. 309–10; 152). Then he moves back again:

> But is amusement all? Studious of song,
> And yet ambitious not to sing in vain,
> I would not trifle merely, though the world
> Be loudest in their praise who do no more.
>
> (ll. 311–14; 152–53)

The seesawing back and forth in this passage is, I think, the result of Cowper's trying both to be honest about the personal, therapeutic value poetry writing holds for him and also to claim for himself some sort of public usefulness: like Chatham and Wolfe, he is willing to undergo la-bors and dangers, to win by his skill something difficult to win; and, like them, he is not a trifler.

Another passage showing Cowper winning by his skill something dif-ficult, though this time on a less heroic level, is the famous georgic pas-sage in Book 3 detailing the growing of cucumbers. Though the cucumbers in question are presented quite realistically—we are given very specific instructions for raising them—it is hard not to see them as also metaphorical and to think that Cowper is linking the production of poetry with the tricky production of these vegetables.[53] He sets this link up in the beginning of the passage, where, after claiming poetic prece-dence for trivial subjects, he asks the "sage dispensers of poetic fame" (l. 457; 17) to pardon

> Th' ambition of one, meaner far, whose pow'rs,
> Presuming an attempt not less sublime,
> Pant for the praise of dressing to the taste
> Of critic appetite, no sordid fare,
> A cucumber, while costly yet and scarce.
>
> (ll. 458–62; 174)

This pleasantly playful association of poem and cucumber might seem
to work toward Cowper's presentation of his poetry writing as a useful
activity; after all, what could be more useful than the producing of
food?[54] But the picture darkens when Cowper addresses those who will
actually consume the cucumbers:

> Grudge not, ye rich, (since luxury must have
> His dainties, and the world's more num'rous half
> Lives by contriving delicates for you)
> Grudge not the cost. Ye little know the cares,
> The vigilence, the labour, and the skill,
> That day and night are exercis'd, and hang
> Upon the ticklish balance of suspense,
> That ye may garnish your profuse regales
> With summer fruits brought forth by wintry suns.
>
> (ll. 544–52; 176)

A food raised only to "garnish" the already abundant feasts of the rich
does not seem especially useful; and, after detailing the many ills that
can befall the cucumber plant before it produces edible fruit, he says he
will not tell of "th' expedients and the shifts" (l. 559) he must devise to
protect his charge, because

> The learn'd and wise
> Sarcastic would exclaim, and judge the song
> Cold as its theme, and, like its theme, the fruit
> Of too much labor, worthless when produc'd.
>
> (ll. 562–65; 176)

Thus Cowper's poetry is in danger of being an expensive delicacy, not
really worth the pains he has taken to produce it. And if it, like the
cucumber, is to be consumed by the idle rich he censures, Cowper is
doing what he has earlier told poets not to do; in "Table Talk," he says,

> For, after all, if merely to beguile,
> By flowing numbers and a flow'ry style,
> The taedium which the lazy rich endure,
> Which now and then sweet poetry may cure;
> . . . .
> How are the pow'rs of genius misapplied!
>
> (ll. 740–49; 16)

In *The Task*, it seems, Cowper is uneasily aware (at least at points) that
he may be misapplying his powers in just this way. His claim to usefulness, as a gardener or a poet, dissolves into indirect self-reproach.[55]

Perhaps because of this uneasiness about the usefulness of his poetry, Cowper's largest, and final, claim to usefulness in *The Task* is for his spiritual activities, rather than his poetic ones. Near the end of Book 6, the last book in the poem, he figures "the world" as a haughty woman who scorns him, the retired man, and he makes a last bid to see the occupations of the world as trifling:

> She scorns his pleasures, for she knows them not;
> He seeks not her's, for he has prov'd them vain.
> He cannot skim the ground like summer birds
> Pursuing gilded flies; and such he deems
> Her honors, her emoluments, her joys.
>
> (ll. 919–23; 239)

Then he moves to a very specific defense of himself against charges of idleness and uselessness—"Not slothful he, though seeming unemploy'd, / And censur'd oft as useless" (928–29; 239)—and to claim as his labor his spiritual struggles:

> Ask him, indeed, what trophies he has rais'd,
> Or what achievements of immortal fame
> He purposes, and he shall answer—None.
> His warfare is within. There unfatigu'd
> His fervent spirit labours. There he fights,
> And there obtains fresh triumphs o'er himself,
> And never with'ring wreaths, compar'd with which
> The laurels that a Caesar reaps are weeds.
>
> (ll. 932–39; 239)

In Book II, Cowper seemed to be attempting to connect his poetry with the nationally useful activities of Wolfe and Chatham. Here he is declaring that his interior warfare will reap rewards far greater than those won by the public warring of a Caesar. And lest we think this means he has abandoned his claim to public usefulness in favor of personal, albeit spiritual, gains, he moves to make a startlingly grand assertion:

> Perhaps the self-approving haughty world,
> That as she sweeps him with her whistling silks
> Scarce deigns to notice him, or, if she see,
> Deems him a cypher in the works of God,
> Receives advantage from his noiseless hours,
> Of which she little dreams. Perhaps she owes
> Her sunshine and her rain, her blooming spring
> And plenteous harvest, to the pray'r he makes,
> When Isaac like, the solitary saint

Walks forth to meditate at even tide,
And think on her, who thinks not for herself.

(ll. 940–50; 239–40)

As if aware, however, that this claim that his prayers keep the world's agricultural cycles running smoothly will scarcely be believed, Cowper again argues, in the next twenty-one lines, that he is not a useless burden on society:

> Forgive him, then, thou bustler in concerns
> Of little worth, an idler in the best,
> If, author of no mischief and some good,
> He seek his proper happiness by means
> That may advance, but cannot hinder, thine.
> Nor, though he tread the secret path of life,
> Engage no notice, and enjoy much ease,
> Account him an incumbrance on the state,
> Receiving benefits, and rend'ring none.
> His sphere though humble, if that humble sphere
> Shine with his fair example, and though small
> His influence, if that influence all be spent
> In soothing sorrow and in quenching strife,
> In aiding helpless indigence, in works
> From which at least a grateful few derive
> Some taste of comfort in a world of woe,
> Then let the supercilious great confess
> He serves his country, recompenses well
> The state, beneath the shadow of whose vine
> He sits secure, and in the scale of life
> Holds no ignoble, though a slighted place.

(ll. 951–71; 240)

Although Priestman says that this "defence, that he performs charitable 'works', seems overspecialized,"[56] it is at least believable; Cowper did provide for many of the poor lace-makers in Olney "some taste of comfort in a world of woe." The claim, though, is a fairly drastic reduction of the earlier one about the efficacy of his prayers, and he goes on to reduce his defense even further:

> The man, whose virtues are more felt than seen,
> Must drop indeed the hope of public praise;
> But he may boast what few that win it can —
> That if his country stand not by his skill,
> At least his follies have not wrought her fall.

(ll. 972–76; 240)

This final reduction of his defense seems rather bathetic; Cowper has gone from saying he may be responsible for keeping the world going to saying at least he has done no harm; and as he then goes on to congratulate himself for refusing to smoke and to follow base fashions, the bathetic effect is increased. Dustin Griffin, in his interesting article "Redefining Georgic: Cowper's *Task*," says, "By redefining labor—with help from the Bible and from Milton—as a virtually spiritual activity, and shifting his attention from the public sphere to the private, Cowper reaffirms, though he significantly modifies, the traditional georgic values of steady dedication to a homely and unspectacular task."[57] Although Cowper does seem to be redefining labor in this passage as a spiritual activity, I think his constantly reducing in scope his defensive claims for himself shows an unease with this shift to the private sphere. As I said earlier, Cowper seems caught between his desires to live out of the world and somehow to speak for it. Richard Feingold puts the problem well, I think: "despite his choice of rural retirement, it was not without great effort that Cowper relinquished the posture of the public poet. *The Task* needs to be understood, not as a simple and sentimental statement of the pleasures of retirement, but as a tortured, and often self-contradictory attempt to speak in a public voice."[58] He wants to be publicly useful, even if, in the end, all he can surely say for himself is that his follies have not wrought his country's fall.

Before I turn away from the question of public usefulness, I would like to consider for a moment Cowper's attitude toward, and insistence on separating himself from, the people whom one might see as living away from the "world" but still participating usefully in it: the rural working class. Cowper largely leaves them out of the picture in *The Task*, and when he does portray them, he tends to distance them and to ignore their part in supplying the ease and leisure he enjoys. In Book 1, for instance, he shows himself and the "dear companion" (l. 144; 132) of his walks pausing upon an eminence to admire a prospect:

> Thence with what pleasure have we just discern'd
> The distant plough slow moving, and beside
> His lab'ring team, that swerved not from the track,
> The sturdy swain diminished to a boy!
>
> (ll. 159–62; 132)

As Patricia Meyer Spacks says of this passage, "The sturdy swain, visually diminished to a boy, therefore need not be considered as a suffering, striving human being. The pleasures of perspective make it unnecessary to contemplate hard realities."[59] Cowper also does not have to consider that the plowman is working to produce the food he and

Mrs. Unwin eat; he can see him as only a producer—along with the
river, the plains, and the cattle—of aesthetic pleasure for those above
him (literally and figuratively). A similar distancing and ignoring take
place later in Book 1, where Cowper shows a thresher at work:

> The grove receives us next;
> Between the upright shafts of whose tall elms
> We may discern the thresher at his task.
>
> . . . .
>
> Come hither, ye that press your beds of down
> And sleep not: see him sweating o'er his bread
> Before he eats it.—'Tis the primal curse,
> But soften'd into mercy; made the pledge
> Of cheerful days, and nights without a groan.
>
> (ll. 354–66; 137)

Not only does Cowper choose to show this worker at a distance and, as
Priestman points out, "carefully framed between elm-trees, so that he
becomes a pictorial emblem not of the community at work, but of the
individual,"[60] but he also chooses to ignore that the thresher is sweating
to produce not only his own bread, but Cowper's. The thresher's labor
does not just afford him cheerful days and sound sleep (and in making
that claim Cowper is, like some of the comfortable-class writers I discussed in my second chapter, constructing labor as something the rich
might envy); it affords the gentry food.[61]

Cowper does another sort of distancing of labor in the gardening passage of Book 3. Although at one point in the cucumber-georgic episode
he seems to come close to identifying himself with the world's workers,
apparently numbering himself among "the world's more num'rous half"
who "lives by contriving delicates" for the rich (Book 3, ll. 545–46;
176), at other points in the same passage he takes pains to separate himself from actual laborers. The aesthetic arranging of a garden, he insists,
is something of which a mere worker is incapable:

> Strength may wield the pond'rous spade,
> May turn the clod, and wheel the compost home;
> But elegance, chief grace the garden shows,
> And most attractive, is the fair result
> Of thought, the creature of a polish'd mind.
>
> (ll. 636–40; 178)

And, although he then says he does not just oversee his laborers, but
does much himself, he is quick to qualify what sort of work this entails:

> No works indeed
> That ask robust tough sinews, bred to toil,
> Servile employ; but such as may amuse,
> Not tire, demanding rather skill than force.
>
> (ll. 404–7; 172–73)

Thus Cowper both characterizes manual laborers as insensitive wielders of brute strength,[62] and insists that he himself is *not* such a wielder of strength, but rather an artist of sorts. His remark that he chooses work that "may amuse, / Not tire" may rather undermine his claim that this activity actually is work, rather than play, but it seems to be more important here for him to separate himself sharply from the lubbard laborers. He seems bent on insisting that, though he may be getting his hands a little dirty, he is still a gentleman.

IV

We can see, then, that Cowper was trying, in these poems, to work out some of his anxieties about leisure and labor and to find a comfortable place for himself between the demands of Evangelical values, Augustan values, and his own personality. While he may have been able to find an uneasy balance between these demands in his poetry, in his life, I would argue, Cowper found them more difficult to resolve. Although probably many factors contributed to his breakdowns, I believe that an important element of them was that Cowper's extreme passivity led to his tendency to see demands on him as "tasks," the failure to accomplish which was somehow unforgivable. In a tragic progression, the pressure he felt from these demands caused an inability to work, which in turn led to failure—and thence to breakdown.

Cowper's passivity, especially regarding his writing, is apparent in many of his letters. He seems to have viewed the composition of poetry as something almost beyond his control, as though he literally believed in the muse. When in the midst of writing "Retirement," for instance, he wrote doubtfully to his publisher, Joseph Johnson, "I am now writing, but whether what I write will be ready for the present volume should you choose to insert it, I know not. I never write except when I can do it with facility, and am rather apprehensive that the Muse is about to forsake me for the present. . . ." (3 September 1781; 1:516). After he finished the poems in his first volume, and before he began *The Task*, Cowper wished to be composing again, but felt it out of his control; to Newton he wrote, "I wish, and have often wished since the [writing] Fit left me, that it would seize me again. But hitherto I have

wished it in vain" (16 February 1782; 2:20).[63] In 1784, in a letter to
Unwin, Cowper asserted his lack of control over the speed with which
he wrote; calling himself the rider of "a Parnassian steed," he said, "If
he [the steed] be disposed to dispatch, it is impossible to accelerate his
pace, if otherwise, equally impossible to stop him" (10 November 1784;
2:297). Certainly, most writers must feel that writing comes more easily
at some times than at others, but the complete lack of control over his
writing Cowper expresses seems remarkable.

Cowper also was passive about choosing the topics of his poems;
most of them seem to have been suggested to him by another. John
Newton got Cowper to write the *Olney Hymns*, and Mrs. Unwin suggested he write on "The Progress of Error," which led to the composition of the other moral satires, too.[64] Lady Austen, of course, made the
suggestion that led to *The Task*, and she told Cowper the story of "John
Gilpin." She also encouraged Cowper to translate Homer.[65] Cowper's
editing of Milton, which was never finished, was the suggestion of Joseph Johnson. As Lord David Cecil says, Cowper "was hard-working
and enthusiastic once he had got something to do; but timid and unen-
terprising about getting it."[66] It was almost as though he had to be
jump-started to write.

King, Cowper's most recent biographer, attributes his passivity to the
early loss of his mother, which made him see God as an overwhelming
and "encroaching force."[67] Whatever the cause of it, Cowper certainly
seemed to view himself as entirely passive in relation to God. In his
poetry, Cowper frequently speaks of God as action, movement, work.
In Book 6 of *The Task*, for instance, he says,

> Nature is but a name for an effect,
> Whose cause is God. He feeds the secret fire
> By which the mighty process is maintain'd,
> Who sleeps not, is not weary; in whose sight
> Slow circling ages are as transient days;
> Whose work is without labour . . .
>
> (ll. 221–28; 224)

In other words, God is eternal motion, action, work. His action keeps
the universe in existence; all things are forms of his work: "there lives
and works / A soul in all things, and that soul is God" (Book 6; ll.
184–85; 223). Earlier in the poem, in Book 1, Cowper also asserts this
principle of universal motion:

> By ceaseless action all that is subsists.
> Constant rotation of th' unwearied wheel
> That nature rides upon maintains her health,

Her beauty, her fertility. She dreads
An instant's pause, and lives but while she moves.
Its own revolvency upholds the world.

(ll. 367–72; 137)

With this view of God and nature, it is easy to see why Cowper felt
such anxiety about idleness: to stop working would be to be separated
from God and his world of action. But one can also see that thinking of
God as the acting principle in all things could make one feel infinitely
passive: if God is responsible for all action, one is unable to act for oneself.[68] The brighter side of this religious passivity is the unworried assurance of the Evangelical Christian that he will be cared for, as in
Cowper's letters about sitting peacefully on the wreck of his fortune,
knowing the Lord will provide. The darker side can be seen, I think, in
Cowper's breakdowns.

Cowper had five major periods of depression in his life, in 1753, 1763,
1773, 1787, and 1794. All but the first caused some degree of insanity.
I think that certainly the last four, and possibly the first, of Cowper's
depressions had something to do with his being asked to perform some
sort of task, tasks he felt essentially unable to accomplish. His breakdowns were in part, I would argue, responses to these failures. The
word "task" implies a job which is assigned to one— Johnson's *Dictionary* says it is work "imposed by another"—and the word seems to have
had a particular resonance for Cowper.[69] His naming his most famous
poem *The Task* is on one level, of course, a reference to the playful as-
signment Lady Austen gave him, as he explained in a letter to Newton:

> As to the Title, I take it to be the best that is to be had. It is not possible
> that a book including such a variety of subjects, and in which no particular
> one is predominate, should find a title adapted to them all. In such a case, it
> seemed almost necessary to accommodate the name to the incident that gave
> birth to the poem. Nor does it appear to me, that because I performed more
> than my task, therefore the Task is not a suitable Title. (11 December 1784;
> 2:309)

And certainly within the poem itself, Cowper uses "task" to refer to
many different sorts of activities, from the employments of the retired
man ("The morning finds the self-sequester'd man / Fresh for his task,
intend what task he may" [Book 3, ll. 386–87; 172]), including cucumber growing ("when now November dark / Checks vegetation in the
torpid plant / Expos'd to his cold breath, the task begins" [Book 3, ll.
467–69; 174]), to the "female industry" of needlework ("the needle
plies its busy task" [Book 4, l. 150; 186]), to contemplation ("Who then,
that has a mind well strung and tun'd / To contemplation, and within

his reach / A scene so friendly to his fav'rite task" [Book 6, ll. 262–64;
225]).

But on the deepest level, I think, Cowper means by "task" a work
imposed by God, a work it will be fatal to fail to do. William Norris
Free says that the word "task" "became a metaphor for the struggle for
salvation"[70]; this is essentially true, but "struggle" seems almost too active a word here. I think Griffin expresses the situation more closely
when he says, "it is perhaps not unreasonable to speculate that entitling
his poem *The Task* obliquely invoked a world, like Milton's, where God,
a severe 'task-master,' laid tasks on the poet."[71] I believe that Cowper's
deep passivity caused some part of him to look at demands upon him
as "tasks" in this sense, and failures to accomplish them were literally
maddening.

Little is known about Cowper's first period of depression, in 1753;
the only information we have is what he tells us in *Adelphi*. There he
says that when he was twenty-one, he "became in a manner complete
master of myself and took possession of a set of chambers in the
Temple . . ." Then,

> it pleased my all-merciful Father in Christ Jesus to give a check to my rash
> and ruinous career in wickedness at the very outset. I was struck not long
> after my settlement in the Temple with such a dejection of spirits as none
> but they who have felt the same can have the least conception of. Day and
> night I was on the rack, lying down in horrors and rising in despair. (1:8)

This depression was suddenly lifted one day when Cowper was visiting
the seaside town of Southampton. Given the sketchy information, it is
impossible to be sure what caused Cowper's depression; King attributes
it to his awareness that his relationship with his cousin Theadora was
doomed.[72] This may be true, in part, but I wonder if another part of the
cause was that Cowper, in becoming the "complete master" of himself,
was leaving the world of childhood and was anxious about the new demands—"tasks"—that would be placed upon him. Of course, as I mentioned earlier, the life of the young Templer turned out to be none too
demanding—that is, until 1763, when Cowper, having run out of
money and been given the appointment of Clerkship of the Journals by
his uncle, Ashley Cowper, was called upon to defend his appointment
at the Bar of the House of Lords. The prospect of a public examination
was terrifying to him, both because, as he says in *Adelphi*, "a public exhibition" of himself was "mortal poison" (1:15), and, I would argue, because he was well aware that he had not done the past work that would
fit him for the position. There seemed no way out of the ordeal: "the
interest of my friend," he says, "the honour of his choice, my own repu-

tation and circumstances all urged me forward; all pressed me to under-
take that which I saw to be impracticable" (1:15). He was given several
months to prepare for the examination, and the journal books were
thrown open to him. He was quite unequal to the task of preparation,
however:

> perhaps a man in health and with a head turned to business might have
> gained all the information he had wanted. But it was not so with me. I read
> without perception and was so distressed that had every clerk in the office
> been my friend it would have availed me little, for I was not in a condition
> to receive instruction, much less to elicit it out of a number of manuscripts,
> some without direction. Many months went over me thus employed—
> constant as to the use of the means, despairing as to the issue. (1:16)

Thus Cowper's anxiety about his task made it impossible for him to
accomplish it. The result was, of course, his suicide attempts and subsequent madness, which he details in *Adelphi*.[73]

Cowper's next breakdown occurred ten years later, when Cowper
was living in Olney with Mrs. Unwin and acting as sort of a disciple to
John Newton. I think it was brought on, at least in part, by Newton's
demands on him. "Newton's great idea," as Bagehot says, "was that
Cowper ought to be of some use. . . . Accordingly he made him a paro-
chial implement; he set him to visit painful cases, to attend at prayer-
meetings, to compose melancholy hymns, even to conduct or share in
conducting public services himself."[74] The visiting and public speaking
must have put a terrible strain on a man as shy and reluctant to "exhibit
himself" as Cowper; and the hymn-writing, especially painful for him
because he was beginning to lose the faith that had so comforted him
and had helped bring him out of his first attack of madness, was to be
the task he could not complete. Maurice J. Quinlan tells us that when
Newton and Cowper began to write the *Olney Hymns*, "Each of the
friends was to contribute approximately the same number of selections,
but because Cowper's second attack of insanity interfered, the collection, which was published in 1779, contained only 67 hymns by Cowper
and 281 by Newton."[75] Writing sixty-seven hymns seems a significant
accomplishment, but Cowper could see only that he had not written as
many as his task required. Lady Hesketh wrote to William Unwin that
the "idea [of working on the hymns] never quitted [Cowper] night or
day, but kept him in a *constant fever*. . . ."[76] This fever led to madness and
another attempt at suicide.

Before I go on to Cowper's fourth serious depression, I must say
more about his attempted suicide in 1773, because it was to haunt him
later. Southey quotes Newton as explaining that Cowper tried to kill

himself because "the enemy" had impressed "upon his disturbed imagination that it was the will of God, he should, after the example of Abraham, perform an expensive act of obedience, and offer not a son, but himself."[77] Cowper's failure to perform this act—this task he thought God had set him—was one of the main reasons he ever afterwards felt himself shut out from God's mercy. As Southey explains it, "He believed that when the will of Heaven was made known to him, power to accomplish the act of obedience had at the same time been given; but having failed to use it, he had been sentenced to a state of desertion and perpetual misery, of a kind peculiar to himself."[78] After this incident, he ceased attending any sort of public or private worship, even going so far as to refrain from bowing his head when grace was said before meals. Though he recovered from this bout of insanity, he was always to believe he was damned. In his harrowing spiritual diary, written in 1795, during the final episode of madness that tortured him until his death in 1800, Cowper expresses his anguish over his failure to commit suicide in 1773 and refers to the suicide specifically as a "task" that was assigned him:

> What opportunities of Suicide had I, while there was any Hope, except a miserable, a most miserable moment, in 73? that moment lost, all that follow'd was as sure as necessity itself could make it. How are such opportunities to be found where the intention is known, watch'd and guarded against? Oh monstrous dispensation! I cannot bear the least part of what is coming upon me, yet am forc'd to meet it with my eyes open'd wide to see its approach, and destitute of all means to escape it.

> I perish as I do, that is, as none ever did, for non-performance of a task, which I know by after-experience to have been *naturally* impossible in the first instance . . . .[79]

In this passage, God appears a terrible taskmaster indeed; and Cowper's punishment for failing to perform his task will, he believes, be infinite.

But before the final, dreadful breakdown during which the spiritual diary was written was the milder one of 1787 (which was preceded, mercifully, by a number of fairly peaceful and productive years). This depression is not well-documented; it occurred while Cowper was translating Homer, and his collected letters barely refer to it. The breakdown interrupted his work on Homer for ten months, and there are no extant letters from January to July of 1787. William Unwin's death late in 1786 probably contributed to Cowper's depression, but I think another contributing factor was his publisher's having engaged the Swiss artist Henry Fuseli to read and comment on his translation.

Although Fuseli was not being paid for his services, his interest in Homer, as King says, "was far from that of a dilettante. He read the translation with great care, comparing it at every step with the Greek original, and wherever pertinent, suggesting readings closer or cleaner than the ones Cowper had adopted. He was a relentless critic of sloppy translations and feeble expressions. . . ."[80] Although in his letters Cowper asserted his gratitude to Fuseli for keeping him up to the mark, his remarks often contain an undertone of resentment and exhaustion. To Lady Hesketh, for instance, after he had attended to the first bout of corrections and suggestions, he said that he had

> just escaped from such a storm of trouble occasioned by endless remarks, hints, suggestions, and objections as drove me almost to despair, and to the very edge of a resolution to drop my undertaking forever. With infinite difficulty I at last sifted the chaff from the wheat, . . . but not 'till the labour and anxiety had undone nearly the whole of all that Kerr [his doctor] has been doing for me.

He went on to say optimistically, "Though Johnson's friend [Fuseli] has teazed me sadly, I verily believe that I shall have no more such cause to complain of him" (11 February 1786; 2:478). While it is true that Cowper did not *complain* again of Fuseli, his praise of him is ominous at points. Writing to Joseph Johnson, his publisher, Cowper told him to ask Fuseli to send along "his strictures." Then he said that he now understands what Fuseli "requires in a translation of Homer" (2 September 1786; 2:588). The words "strictures" and "requires" seem to intimate that Cowper felt somewhat put-upon, that he was being forced to do something. In another letter to Lady Hesketh, he said he has sent Fuseli the present of a hare in gratitude for his help, but added that he hoped this civility would not cause Fuseli to "become at all less rigorous in his demands, or less severe in his animadversions," and that he has corrected the ninth book according to "two sheets filled with his strictures" (11 December 1786; 2:614). Again, rigorous demands, severe animadversions, and strictures seem to imply some resentment on Cowper's part, some sense of being tasked—indeed, overtasked. The 1787 breakdown began just a month or so after this last letter; and I would speculate that this sense of being tasked—of having something required of him he feared he could not achieve—was part of the cause. His translation of Homer was enormously important to Cowper, and I think the demands he placed on himself to do it well (better than Pope did), combined with Fuseli's unasked-for demands, made up a task that was too much for him.

Cowper's last depression began in the fall of 1792, when he was struggling with his edition of Milton. Joseph Johnson suggested the project to him. As Cowper described it to Samuel Rose, "A Milton that is to rival, and, if possible, to exceed in splendor, Boydell's Shakespeare, is in contemplation, and I am in the Editor's office. Fuseli is the Painter. My business will be to select notes from others, and to write original notes, to translate the Latin and Italian poems, and to give a correct text" (14 September 1791; 3:572). For a while he proceeded happily in the work, thinking it an appropriate one to follow his Homer. As he wrote to James Hurdis: "my veneration for our great countryman is equal to what I feel for the Grecian; and consequently I am happy, and feel myself honourably employed whatever I do for Milton" (10 December 1791; 3:597). Soon, however, he was having doubts; two months later he wrote to the same correspondent, "To the labours of versifying I have no objection, but to the labours of criticism I am new, and apprehend that I shall find them wearisome" (21 February 1792; 4:18). The situation worsened considerably with Mrs. Unwin's deteriorating health. She had recovered well from the paralytic stroke she had in December 1791, but in May 1792 she had a second one and thereafter required considerable care. Cowper devotedly ministered to her, which cut substantially into his working time. His worry about losing her, as well as the loss of her taking care of him, added to the difficulties he had in working. Soon he was writing to Joseph Johnson,

> Day, weeks, and months escape me and nothing is done, nor is it possible for me to do any thing that demands study and attention in the present state of our family. I am the Electrician [Mrs. Unwin was being treated with electricity], I am the Escort into the Garden, I am wanted in short on a hundred little occasions that occur every day in Mrs. Unwin's present state of infirmity, and I see no probability that I shall be less occupied in the same indispensible duties for a long time to come. The time fixt in your Proposals for publication meanwhile steals on, and I have lately felt my engagement for Milton bear upon my spirits with a pressure, which, added to the pressure of some other private concerns, is almost more than they are equal to. . . . I cannot bear to be waited for, neither shall I be able to perform my part of the work with any success if I am hunted . . . . (8 July 1792; 4:144)

To Lady Hesketh he expressed his distress more strongly: "I am crazed with having much to do and doing nothing. Every thing with me has fallen into arrear to such a degree that I almost despair of being able by the utmost industry to redeem the time that I have lost" (21 July 1792; 4:151). Clearly his sense of guilt over his failure to accomplish this task added another terrible strain to the ones he was already under.

Cowper was afforded some temporary relief by Johnson's giving him more time, but soon he was again trying and failing to work and finding that the failure made him reluctant to try again. He wrote to his new friend William Hayley,

> Yesterday was a day of assignation with myself; the day of which I said for some days before it came, when that day comes I will begin my Dissertations. . . . But partly from one cause and partly from another, chiefly however from distress and dejection, after writing and obliterating about six lines, in the composition of which I spent near an hour, I was obliged to relinquish the attempt. An attempt so unsuccessful could have no other effect than to dishearten me, and it has had that effect to such a degree that I know not when I shall find courage to make another. (2 October 1792; 4:206)

Three weeks or so later he still had not made another attempt and was afraid to do so, although as he said, again to Hayley, he did plan to: "I purpose in a day or two to make another attempt, to which however I shall address myself with fear and trembling, like a man who having sprain'd his wrist, dreads to use it. I have not indeed like such a man injured myself by any extraordinary exertions, but seem as much enfeebled as if I had." He went on to say that he had other neglected work on his hands, besides his "unaccomplish'd task," and that it all troubled him sorely: "The consciousness that there is so much to do and nothing done, is a burthen that I am not able to bear. Milton especially is my grievance, and I might almost as well be haunted by his ghost, as goaded with such continual self reproaches for neglecting him" (28 October 1792; 4:225). Cowper was aware that the misery occasioned by the unaccomplished task made him even less fit for accomplishing it; as he wrote to Samuel Rose, "it seems to me that a consciousness of that unperform'd engagement has no small share in disqualifying me for the performance of it, by depressing my spirits to a degree they would not otherwise sink to" (9 November 1792; 4:232–33). He also knew that *Paradise Lost* was not the happiest work for a man afraid he was going to hell to dwell upon: "The First Book of the Paradise Lost is in truth so terrible and so nearly akin to my own miserable speculations in the subject of it, that I am a little apprehensive, unless my spirits were better, that the study of it might do me material harm" (25 November 1792; 4:242). But none of these reasons allowed him to excuse himself from the work.

With this new task, Cowper felt responsible not only to Johnson and the others involved in the project, but, more explicitly than before, to God. Before he agreed to the task, he had consulted Samuel Teedon, an odd schoolmaster neighbor of his who was given to spiritual predictions. Cowper had formerly laughed at Teedon, but now, snatching comfort where he could, was willing to listen to him. Teedon had assured him that God smiled on the project—which meant, to Cowper, that to fail to complete it would be to disobey God.[81] The more he failed at his task, the more unlikely success became, but the more desperately he needed it; there seemed to be no way out. Writing to Lady Hesketh, he called the commentary project his "Miltonic trammels" (1 December 1792; 4:248), to William Hayley, "this Miltonic trap" (26 December 1792; 4:265). Notes to Samuel Teedon express even more oppression: "Milton is still a mountain on my shoulders" (21 December 1792; 4:264); "Time presses, I have many things to do, one of them arduous indeed, I mean Milton. God is silent, prayer obtains no answer, one discouragement treads on the heels of another, and the consequence is that I do nothing but prognosticate my own destruction" (11 January 1793; 4:273–4).

The mountain of Milton was removed only by Johnson's finally canceling the project at the end of 1793; Cowper was never able really to begin, much less finish, his commentary. Although he did manage to revise his translation of Homer in the last years of his life, the task of editing Milton was one he failed to accomplish; and his prediction of his own destruction (in this world, though not, one hopes, the next) was all too accurate: he never recovered from the terrible depression he entered in 1794. Although clearly the illness of Mrs. Unwin, the person he most loved, and his own aging and approach to what he thought would be eternal torment had much to do with his last breakdown, I think his failure to perform this task played some part in it also. It was yet another proof of his inability to do what God required.

In Cowper's last, terrible years, the friends who tended him were the ones to assign him tasks—small projects to keep him busy and, they hoped, to assuage his misery a bit. In 1797, Johnny Johnson, Cowper's primary caretaker in these years, suggested that he write his name in ten of his books a day. As he had four hundred books, this would take forty days. "To this he readily agreed," Johnson reported, "though for an odd reason, Dear Soul—viz. because he thought that he *must* live till they were all finished."[82] This delusion seems a poignant testimony to the profound importance Cowper placed on the notion of tasks. Much of his life was a struggle to balance the complicated and conflicting ideas put forth by his era, class, religion, and personality about leisure, labor, industry, and idleness. Although he could not finally hold all these ideas steady in his life, the effort to do so produced some of his best poetry. The real task of *The Task* was perhaps to make a poem capacious enough to contain them all. Here, at least, he succeeded.

7

Conclusion

I

I WOULD LIKE TO END THIS LONG WORK ABOUT IDLENESS BY CONSID-
ering briefly what effect the discourse of idleness had on the next century. To the extent that this discourse helped issue in the cult of
domesticity by insisting on the work that comfortable-class women
must do to make themselves and their homes the embodiment of time
spent away from work—leisure—it clearly shaped nineteenth-century
middle-class life profoundly. I think it is no coincidence that two of the
writers I discuss at greatest length here, William Cowper and Hannah
More, are singled out by Leonore Davidoff and Catherine Hall as the
two writers most beloved by the nineteenth-century middle classes they
study in *Family Fortunes*.[1] Davidoff and Hall argue that these readers
seem to find in Cowper's and More's disapproval of aristocratic vice
and their celebration of quiet domesticity an expression of the readers'
own emerging values. I would agree, but I would also argue that these
writers' preoccupation with idleness is part of the attraction the middle
classes feel towards them.

The middle-class embrace of Cowper is in part ironic, however, because in his rejection of the world of work, he opposed one of the most
important middle-class ideas that emerged from the discourse of idleness: that a man must work.[2] Many writers have commented that the
eighteenth and early nineteenth centuries saw a profound shift in the
way work was viewed. As Clifford Sisken describes the change,

> Two hundred years ago, a job was "petty, piddling work," or a "low, mean,
> lucrative, busy affair," and it certainly did not make absolute sense of per-
> sonal identity, morality, or fate. For that to happen, the concept of work had
> to be rewritten from that which a true gentleman does not have to do, to the
> primary activity informing adult identity . . . .[3]

I would add the word "male" before the word "identity," since, as we
have seen, not working for pay was a requirement of middle-class fe-

217

male identity. Davidoff and Hall discuss the "moves towards masculine identification with occupation," moves that occurred increasingly over the nineteenth century and that were codified in official documents like the census.[4] Cowper's status as a man of leisure, therefore, might seem problematic for his middle-class audience. Presumably his celebration of domesticity was so attractive as to outweigh his unmanly idleness,[5] or perhaps some men, already weary of the world of work, found pleasant escape in Cowper's verse.[6] Or perhaps a nineteenth-century audience would have seen Cowper's status as a writer as profession enough, since writing was seen much more as a professional activity by the end of the nineteenth century than it was at the end of the eighteenth. Sisken notes that "at the end of the first three decades of the nineteenth century, . . . only four hundred respondents classified themselves as professional authors, whereas more than thirteen thousand did so by the century's close."[7] This enormous increase in number does not mean that the period saw a huge increase in the number of people who became writers, but rather that writing had become considered work, a professional occupation.

Perhaps if this view of writing as a profession had been more general in the eighteenth century, Johnson and Cowper would have been spared some of the struggles with idleness that I have delineated in the previous two chapters. Samuel Johnson, less highborn and touchy about his class status than William Cowper, freely admitted that writing is work, asserting that no one but a blockhead ever did it, except for money, but he clearly did not consider it work enough to rescue him from charges of idleness. Cowper, on the other hand, presented his writing as a gentlemanly form of occupational therapy, but worried that he was a sinful trifler. Both these men spent their lives writing, and both were desperately searching for the meaningful work which might, in a way, redeem their lives. Both men seemed to feel—Johnson more explicitly and consciously, Cowper more subtly and confusedly—that the right sort of work could somehow arrest time's flight, could somehow make mortality endurable. Cowper, of course, was tragically convinced he was beyond literal redemption, but he clung to work as his only hold on sanity, even, as we see in the pathetic detail of his thinking he would live until a small task he had been given was completed, his only hold on life. Johnson thought he could be redeemed through work, but always, until the very end of his life, feared that he had fallen far short of the work required of him, that he was failing to work out his salvation; and he, too, clung to work as all that could anchor him in the moment, could keep time from washing over him in a meaningless rush. The work of writing in which both men engaged was thus their only hope for coping with time and death, but it also somehow was not work enough, or enough work, or the right sort of work. Perhaps it was un-fortunate for them that they wrote at a time when work was so fraught a subject and when it was unclear to what degree writing was work. Unlike many who achieve fame or hope to achieve it, neither Johnson nor Cowper, despite the anguished contemplation of death in which both spent so much of their lives, seemed to derive very much comfort from the idea that their writing, their work, might live on when they were gone. But finally all we can know about the degree to which their work of writing did succeed in sheltering them from time's ever-rolling stream (in this world, that is; I will not speculate about their fate in another realm) is that we still read their writing. The power of their work has managed, thus far, to defy time, if not, within their lifetimes, to rescue them from the tortures of idleness.

II

In positioning themselves as the industrious members of eighteenth-century British society, then, middle-class men were, as I hope I have demonstrated, making a claim for themselves, positing a moral and po-litical basis for their challenge to leisured aristocracy. And in so doing, as again I hope I have shown, they assigned to other groups the attri-bute of idleness. The laboring classes were constructed as inherently idle, as requiring the sharpest spurs to incite them to the industrious work they had to perform if the comfortable classes were to remain comfortable. And the presumed idleness of the laboring classes was figured as unendurably grotesque and shameful. The "idleness" of the native peoples coming under Britain's imperial sway in this period was represented as even more grotesque than that of the laboring classes (in fact, as we have seen, the laboring classes suddenly become industrious in writings about the sloth of the natives). Idleness was made part of their racial identity, and it provided an excuse for the British to force them into unpaid labor and to usurp their land and its resources. It also provided a way for the British to separate themselves, at least for a time, from the darker races they deemed inferior. This aspect of the discourse of idleness seems to remain important into the nineteenth century, as I indicated in my fourth chapter. In *Romantic Imperialism*, Saree Makdisi discusses the crucial shift "taking place at this time in British paradigms of empire and attitudes towards non-Europeans. . . ." He goes on to say (in a sentence whose length and complexity rivals that of the sentence from Burke with which I began this book) that these people were viewed as making the uneasy transition from a wretched state of static pre-modernity to the beginning of their apprenticeship in modernization, in which their social, cultural, and economic practices would be transformed . . . from custom to law; from communal, clan, tribal, or despotic forms of property to private property; from heterogeneous and irregular ("casual") forms of labor to the rigors of a wage economy; from customary forms of payment and compensation to the strictly monetary remuneration of the hourly wage; from archaic, seasonal, irregular temporal practices to the regular practice of modern clock-time; . . . from highly skilled artisanal craftsmanship to an increasingly automated system of production relying only on that flow of quantified and regulated energy-in-time that would eventually come to be called "unskilled labor" but that first was broken down in William Petty's "political arithmetick" into a stream of labor-power that could (ideally) be smoothly distributed across a highly diversified production process, subject only to the forms of resistance that this appropriation of energy might encounter from the possessors of labor-power themselves. . . .[8]

As the reference to William Petty indicates, this shift was also occurring within the laboring classes. Both groups were being forced into new ways of working, and often into working for the profit of others, not themselves. My argument here is that the discourse of idleness helped enable this shift.

III

Like the laboring classes, comfortable-class women were both associated with idleness and urged to avoid it. The idleness associated with ladies was, of course, quite different from that attached to the lower orders or to the nonwhite races: feminine idleness was painted as attractive, alluring, delicious. The feminized space of idleness could be a dangerous temptation, a siren-call the virtuous man must resist. The Castle of Indolence, with its quilts on quilts, its endless pillows that make a room seem one full-swelling Bed, and its languorous denizens clad in airy gowns that every flowing Limb in Pleasure drowns, was one example of such a space; the boudoir belonging to Lady St. Edmunds in *Discipline*, with its fragrant orange trees, its softly glowing alabaster lamps and rose-colored draperies, and its fairy-footed smiling serving girl, was another. A more virtuous feminized space of idleness—though here it should be called leisure, since men enjoyed it after coming home from a good day's work—was, of course, the well-ordered home, the warm hearth which is tended by a smiling, companionable woman whose role was, as Thomas Gisborne puts it, to "unbend the brow of the learned, to refresh the over-laboured faculties of the wise, and to diffuse, throughout the family circle, the enlivening and endearing smile of cheerfulness." Even this pleasant and wholesome feminized space of idleness, however, was not a place a good middle-class man could stay; he came home to it for relaxation, but he always had to leave it again. And when he left it, it was, in the words of Rudyard Kipling, writing at the very end of the nineteenth century, to take up "the white man's burden":

> Take up the White Man's burden—
>   The savage wars of peace—
> Fill full the mouth of Famine,
>   And bid the sickness cease;
> And when your goal is nearest
>   (The end for others sought)
> Watch sloth and heathen folly
>   Bring all your hopes to nought.

While Kipling might, in the imperial moment of 1899, have seen the British white man's manly industriousness being defeated by the "sloth" of racial others, the discourse of idleness allowed him to place himself, and his nation, above all others that he fixed on his great map of mankind.

Notes

1. INTRODUCTION

1. Adam Smith, *An Inquiry into the Nature and Causes of the Wealth of Nations* (Oxford: Clarendon Press, 1976), 2 vols., 1:13.

2. Ibid., 1:23. John Barrell also quotes this sentence in *The Birth of Pandora and the Division of Knowledge*, explaining that its "strategy and structure" have "the effect of instantiating precisely the transcendent form of knowledge which is taken to characterise the subject of the discourse of the division of labour" ([Philadelphia: University of Pennsylvania Press, 1992], 94).

3. John Barrell, *English Literature in History 1730–80: An Equal, Wide Survey* (New York: St. Martin's Press, 1983).

4. Edmund Burke, "An Appeal From the New to the Old Whigs," in *The Works of the Right Honourable Edmund Burke*, 12 vols. (Boston: Little, Brown, and Co., 1884), 4:175.

5. Barrell, *The Birth of Pandora*, xiv–xv.

6. Barrell, *Equal, Wide Survey*, 24.

7. Linda Colley, *Britons: Forging the Nation, 1707–1837* (New Haven: Yale University Press, 1992), 1.

8. Ibid., 5.

9. Ibid., 368.

10. I am grateful to Anne Mellor's *Mothers of the Nation: Women's Political Writing in England, 1780–1830* for clarifying for me some of the details in the print (Bloomington: Indiana University Press, 2000, 143–44).

11. Colley, 5.

12. Ibid., 6.

13. Kathleen Wilson, *The Sense of the People: Politics, Culture and Imperialism in England, 1715–1785* (New York: Cambridge University Press, 1995), 25.

14. Paul Langford, *A Polite and Commercial People: England, 1727–1783* (New York: Oxford University Press, 1989), 62.

15. Ibid.

16. Ibid., 66.

17. For more on the sin of sloth in medieval thought, see Siegfried Wenzel's *The Sin of Sloth: Acedia in Medieval Thought and Literature* (Chapel Hill: University of North Carolina Press, 1967). For more on all seven deadly sins in medieval literature, see Morton W. Bloomfield's *The Seven Deadly Sins: An Introduction to the History of a Religious Concept, with Special Reference to Medieval English Literature* (Michigan: Michigan State College Press, 1952).

18. Stanford M. Lyman, *The Seven Deadly Sins: Society and Evil* (New York: St. Martin's Press, 1978), 5.

19. Ibid., 6.

20. Aldous Huxley, "Accidie" in *On the Margin* (New York: George H. Doran Co., 1923), 25–26.

21. Lyman, 10.

22. In *A Polite and Commercial People: England 1727–1783*, Paul Langford comments that "contemporaries thought the growing wealth and importance of the middle orders of society the most striking of developments" (61).

23. Leonore Davidoff and Catherine Hall, *Family Fortunes: Men and Women of the English Middle Class, 1780–1850* (Chicago: University of Chicago Press, 1987), 30.

24. Ibid., 110.

25. Ibid., 30.

26. For more about occupation and manhood, see chapter 5, "'A Man Must Act': Men and the Enterprise," in Davidoff and Hall.

27. And, as Davidoff and Hall point out, the ideology of female leisure meant that the work women *did* do was constructed as not-work: "women's domestic tasks which took place in the private sphere of the home have been unacknowledged as *work*" (33).

28. Douglas Chambers, *The Reinvention of the World: English Writing 1650–1750* (New York: St. Martin's Press, 1996), 50.

29. Clifford Siskin, *The Work of Writing: Literature and Social Change in Britain, 1700–1830* (Baltimore: The Johns Hopkins University Press, 1998), 6. Siskin also discusses the technological and social changes involved in the spread of print culture in this period. He remarks that "the year 1700 is the marker for a cluster of turn-of-the-century events which helped to accelerate Britain's transformation into a print culture," including "the lapsing of the Print Act," the beginning of "the modern system of copyright," and "the entry of the printers and booksellers of Ireland and Scotland into a print world that had been dominated by London." He also mentions the increase in women's authorship and the spread of newspapers and periodicals, concluding that "one has a strong case for using the roundness of 1700 to highlight the onset of significant change in the form, content, and contexts of writing" (11).

30. Maynard Mack, *Alexander Pope: A Life* (New York: W.W. Norton & Co., 1985), 367.

31. Ibid., 270.

32. Sloth is still considered especially to bedevil writers; as Thomas Pynchon, writing on sloth for the *New York Times Book Review* says,

> Writers of course are considered the mavens of Sloth. They are approached all the time on the subject, not only for free advice, but to speak at Sloth Symposia, head up Sloth Task Forces, testify as expert witnesses at Sloth Hearings. The stereotype arises in part from our conspicuous presence in jobs where pay is by the word, and deadlines are tight and final—we are presumed to know from piecework and the convertibility of time and money. In addition, there is all the glamorous folklore surrounding writer's block, an affliction known sometimes to resolve itself dramatically and without warning, much like constipation, and (hence?) finding wide sympathy among readers. (Thomas Pynchon, "Nearer, My Couch, to Thee," *The New York Times Book Review* [June 6, 1993]: 3)

33. Siskin, 2.

34. Ibid., 45.

35. For instance, writers such as E. P. Thompson, in his seminal article "Time, Work-Discipline, and Industrial Capitalism"(*Customs in Common: Studies in Traditional Popular Culture* [New York: The New Press, 1991]), Henry Abelove, in his much-discussed "Some Speculations on the History of Sexual Intercourse during the Long Eighteenth Century in England" (*Genders* 6 [Fall 1989]), and Stuart Sherman, in his excellent book *Telling Time: Clocks, Diaries, and the English Diurnal Form, 1660–1785* (Chi-

cago: Chicago University Press, 1997), all discuss productivity and time-discipline in this period without much specific attention to the discourse of idleness and its spread throughout many aspects of eighteenth-century British society.

36. James Thomson, *The Castle of Indolence and Other Poems*, edited by Alan Dugald McKillop (Lawrence, Kansas: University of Kansas Press, 1961).

37. Lisa M. Steinman, *Masters of Repetition: Poetry, Culture, and Work in Thomson, Wordsworth, Shelley, and Emerson* (New York: St. Martin's Press, 1998), 9.

38. For instance, Douglas Grant says the first canto is "by far the finer of the two" (*James Thomson: Poet of 'The Seasons,'* [London: The Cresset Press, 1951], 256). Patricia Meyer Spacks mentions "a series of . . . effects which contribute importantly to the 'atmosphere' of *The Castle* but directly contradict the poem's explicit moral, that effort is superior to indolence. Morally, of course, the superiority of effort is readily apparent; emotionally, as this poem fully demonstrates, indolence has far richer appeal" (*The Poetry of Vision: Five Eighteenth-Century Poets* [Cambridge: Harvard University Press, 1967], 53). She goes on to make a similar claim: "the richness of the first canto suggests that in emotional force the Enchanter must triumph; the domain of the Knight of Arts and Industry is more theoretical, less attractive, than that of the Wizard. In this respect particularly the poem cannot resolve its conflict of values . . ."(62). Morris Golden agrees: "As everyone has pointed out, the second canto is far more the product of will and moral intentions than of poetic congeniality" ("The Imagining Self in the Eighteenth Century" in *Eighteenth-Century Studies* 3 [1969], 16). John Sitter calls the work "Thomson's most starkly ambivalent poem" (*Literary Loneliness in Mid-Eighteenth-Century England* [(Ithaca: Cornell University Press, 1982], 93), and argues that "the world of reverie and retreat [in Canto I] looks not only comfortable but potentially noble" (95). Christine Gerrard, while refusing to dismiss the importance of the second canto, admits that the poetry of Canto I is "undoubtedly superior" ("*The Castle of Indolence* and the Opposition to Walpole" in *Review of English Studies* 41 [1990], 60). James Sambrook quotes early and more recent readers to prove that "from the beginning, most readers found the first canto more appealing than the second" (*James Thomson 1700–1748: A Life*, [Oxford, Clarendon Press, 1991], 275). The major opponent of the view that the first canto is superior to the second is Donald Greene, who reads the poem as an expression of the miseries of indolence, which he considers synonymous with accidie, spleen, melancholy, and neurosis ("From Accidie to Neurosis: The Castle of Indolence Revisited," *English Literature in the Age of Disguise*, edited by Maximillian E. Novak [Berkeley: University of California Press, 1977], 131–56).

39. Thomson, *The Castle*, II xlix. Subsequent quotations from this work are cited parenthetically in the text.

40. James Thomson, *James Thomson (1700–1748): Letters and Documents*, edited by Alan Dugald McKillop (Lawrence, Kansas: University of Kansas Press, 1958), 155.

41. Sir Harris Nicolas, "Memoir of Thomson," in *The Poetical Works of James Thomson* (London: William Pickering, 1847), cxix.

42. Grant, 160.

43. Ibid., 239–40.

44. For instance, Sambrook quotes from a letter Richard Savage wrote to Solomon Mendez while Savage was visiting Thomson in May 1737: "Savage also tells Mendez that, at the time of writing, Thomson is still abed, and 'is quite ashamed with regard to you.—He calls himself names about it; and accuses and curses his evil genius for laying a spell upon him in regard to writing letters.' Though Savage promised that Thomson would write 'in a post or two', it was not until 21 July that a typically apologetic letter was sent" (166).

45. Grant, 161.

46. Sambrook, 243.

47. Samuel Johnson, *Lives of the English Poets*, vol 2. (London: Oxford University Press, 1949), 375.

48. Hesther Lynch Thrale Piozzi, *Autobiography, Letters and Literary Remains of Mrs. Piozzi (Thrale)*, edited by A. Hayward, Esq. (London: Longman, Green, Longman, and Roberts, 1861), 87. Sambrook recounts this story, saying the *Public Advertiser* of 16 April 1790 tells it also, locating the scene "with greater probability, in Bubb Dodington's garden" (208).

49. Thomson, *Letters*, 136.

50. Sambrook, 212. Lisa M. Steinman quotes a poem that the Reverend Thomas Morell wrote in 1742 in which he "playfully suggests that Thomson has been seduced by his own descriptions of leisure and rural retreats" (33–34).

51. For instance, Morris Golden sees Thomson in *The Castle* making a personal statement about the nature of poetry:

> In Thomson's fable the selves are divided, objectified, and opposed: the imaginative, delusive, Faustian, and yet inwardly drawn magician against the soberly universal spokesman for fertility, social justice, fulfilling sympathy. Thomson's success with the temptation to drown within the imagination and his relative failure in the self-admonitory second canto suggest again that poetic intensity rises most naturally from the poet's self-centered reveries. (142–43)

52. Sambrook, 274.

53. James Thomson, "To the Memory of the Right Honourable the Lord Talbot," in *The Complete Poetical Works of James Thomson*, edited by J. Logie Robertson (London: Oxford University Press, 1951), ll. 39–67.

54. Ibid., "Hymn on Solitude," ll. 1–8.

55. Ibid., ll. 33–40.

56. Ibid., "Autumn" from *The Seasons*. Subsequent quotations from this work are cited parenthetically in the text.

57. Gerrard notes that "the close correspondence between certain aspects of the life-style enjoyed by the Castle's inhabitants and that of the Knight of Arts and Industry in Canto II suggests that such pleasures are not wrong in themselves" and goes on to argue that "it all depends on the spirit into which they are entered"(155). This claim may be true, but it seems a rather subtle distinction for a didactic poem, one which does not erase the poem's ambiguity.

58. And we notice that when the tidings of the Wizard's evil deeds reach the Knight, he is not in his garden, but on his couch (Thomson, *Castle*, II xxxi).

59. Barrell also notes the venerability of these arguments: "the wizard is not ashamed to present this life of easy pleasure as a moral life, and a religious one: for 'What', he asks, 'is Virtue but Repose of Mind?'—a question that has been asked so often before, by so many poets of rural life, that it may threaten the eventually industrious moral of the poem . . ." (*Equal, Wide Survey*, 81).

60. Ibid., 89.

61. Ibid., 86.

62. Ibid., 87.

63. Ibid., 87–88.

64. Sambrook mentions this passage and Thomson's dissatisfaction with both the patron and the market, the writer's traditional role and his new one:

> The poet is reflecting upon his own status. Though Millar treated him generously by booksellers' standards of the day and was a personal friend, Thomson distrusted the market; he believed that high art should not be subject to commercial considerations. Patronage could be a better

guarantee of good poetry, but the servility that patronage often entailed at this period must sometimes have irritated a man even of Thomson's easy-going nature. (271)

65. Steinman discusses the closely related problem of whether poetry should count as public action: "In *The Castle of Indolence* Thomson tries to define writing poetry as a form of action when he has his Druidic bard sing, 'Who does not act is dead.' Yet elsewhere his writing shows that even for him poetry did not easily count as public action" (43).

66. Margaret Anne Doody, "Whig Dreams" in *London Review of Books*, 27 February 1992: 11.

2. SIX DAYS SHALT THEY LABOR

1. Daniel Defoe, *Giving Alms No Charity*, 1704, in *The Shortest Way with Dissenters and Other Pamphlets* (Oxford: Basil Blackwell, 1927), 186.

2. Bernard de Mandeville, *The Fable of the Bees: Or, Private Vices, Publick Benefit*, 1714, 1723, 2 vols. (Oxford: Clarendon Press, 1924), 1:192.

3. John Clayton, *Friendly Advice to the Poor; Written and Publish'd at the Request of the Late and Present Officers of the Town of Manchester* (Manchester: Jos. Harrop, 1755), 5.

4. Joseph Townsend, *A Dissertation on the Poor Laws. By a Well-Wisher to Mankind*, 1786 (Berkeley: University of California Press, 1971), 23.

5. Ibid., 29–30. These quoted examples constitute only a small percentage of the eighteenth century's assertions of laboring-class idleness. Defoe, for instance, goes on in the remarks I have quoted to claim that " 'Tis the Men who *wont work*, not the Men that *can get no work*, which makes the numbers of our Poor," and that he could produce "above a Thousand Families in *England* . . . who go in Rags, and their Children wanting Bread, whose Fathers can earn their 15 to 25*s. per* Week, but will not work, who may have Work enough, but are too idle to seek after it, and hardly vouchsafe to earn any thing more than bare Subsistance, and Spending Money for themselves," (187). Many articles in *Gentleman's Magazine* also assert that idleness is responsible for the poor's misery. A 1736 essay warns against giving alms to beggars, "as it serves only to encourage and confirm [them] in a Habit of Idleness"(Letter, *Gentleman's Magazine* 6 [1736], 26). "Among these vagabonds, whose number is incredible, two thirds of them may fairly be computed capable of getting their own living; but from a habit of laziness, and want of a sense of shame, they prefer such a profligate life, to a life of labour and honest industry," says a 1761 essay (D.D., Letter, *The Gentleman's Magazine* 31 [1761], 592). A 1765 essay assures its readers that only the "*lazy* poor" are suffering from the high price of provisions: "There are thousands in and near this metropolis, and a still greater number dispersed throughout the kingdom, who make the high price of provisions a pretence for their idleness, and who rather chuse to complain and to beg, than apply themselves to honest labour . . ." (Y.D., Letter, *Gentleman's Magazine* 35 [1765], 613). William Temple was also attached to the idea of the laboring classes' basic idleness, saying in his 1739 pamphlet *The Case as It Now Stands, Between the Clothiers, Weavers, and Other Manufacturers, with Regard to the Late Riot, in the Country of Wilts*:

It may be laid down, as an incontestable Truth, that the Poor, in the manufacturing Countries, will never work any more Time in general, than is necessary just to live, and support their weekly *Debauches*. If the Manufacturer can acquire in two Days, by high Wages, enough to keep him drunk the other five, you may find him all that time rendevouzing in a Tipling-house; or, in the Summer-time, carousing under a Hedge, but never in his Occupation: all that time he shall be celebrating the *Orgies* of *Bacchus*, instead of pursuing the *Arts* of *Minerva*. ([New York: Arno Press, 1972], 41–42)

An Essay on Trade and Commerce, published anonymously in 1770 (tentatively attributed to James Cunningham), claims that "our poor, in general, work only for the bare necessities of life, or for the means of a low debauch; which when obtained, they cease to labour till roused again by necessity" ([London: S. Hopper, 1770], 15).

6. I adopt this phrase to avoid the cumbersome repetition of "upper- and middling-class." In his *Enquiry into the Causes of the Late Increase in Robbers*, Henry Fielding says that the poor are those who "have no estates of their own to support them, without Industry; nor any Profession or Trade, by which, with Industry, they may be capable of gaining a comfortable Subsistence" ([Oxford: Clarendon Press, 1998], 108). "Comfortable-class" seems to me a useful way to designate that minority of people who *did* have these things and who thus were at little risk of having to turn to the parish for relief if they could not immediately find work that would afford them a living wage or if they became incapacitated for labor.

7. Charles Hall, *The Effects of Civilization on the People in the European States*, 1805 (London: Routledge/Thoemmes Press, 1994), 24.

8. Douglas Hay, "Poaching and the Game Laws on Cannock Chase," in *Albion's Fatal Tree: Crime and Society in Eighteenth-Century England*, edited by Douglas Hay et al. (New York: Pantheon, 1975), 191.

9. John Hassell, *Memoirs of the Life of the Late George Morland, with Descriptive Observations on the Whole of His Works Hitherto Before the Public* (London: Albion Press, 1806), 118.

10. "Of Publick Cricket-Matches," *Gentleman's Magazine* 13 [1743], 486. As Peter Linebaugh says in *The London Hanged: Crime and Civil Society in the Eighteenth Century*, "The concept of idleness was . . . independent of skill or constancy in completing a task. Idleness meant the refusal of discipline, subordination or obedience" ([New York: Cambridge University Press, 1992], 14). Further on, he adds, " 'Idleness' is both a moral category and an economic one: it is the refusal to accept exploitation" (428).

11. Mandeville, 1:288.

12. Henry Home, *Sketches of the History of Man. Considerably Enlarged by the Last Additions and Corrections of the Author*, 4 vols. (Edinburgh: William Creech, 1788), 3: 94.

13. As I take a rather negative view of More's work with the laboring classes in this chapter, I should mention an important recent challenge issued to the view of More as self-interested and intent on keeping the lower classes in their place. In her chapter on More in *Mothers of the Nation: Women's Political Writing in England, 1780–1830*, Anne Mellor argues against "the leading historians of eighteenth- and nineteenth-century England" who, because of their training in "Marxist or left-wing socialist ideologies," "*hate* Hannah More" ([Bloomington: Indiana University Press, 2000],15; emphasis Mellor's). While admitting that "More's program for the reform of Britain's social culture was not egalitarian" (24), Mellor finds More to be more democratic than often thought, arguing that she also criticized the aristocracy and that, "in effect, she told the workers, you can have the material rewards your employers have; you can become the middle class" (22). I agree that More criticized the aristocracy, locating industriousness and moral virtue in the middle classes, but I suspect that her promises to the workers were more of a ploy to prevent discontent than an honest desire for them move into her class.

14. Martha More, *Mendip Annals: Or, A Narrative of the Charitable Labours of Hannah and Martha More in Their Neighbourhood*, edited by Arthur Roberts (London: James Nisbet and Co., 1859) Introduction, 6.

15. Hannah More, *The Complete Works of Hannah More*, 2 vols. (New York: Harper & Brothers, 1843), 1:171.

16. Mary R. Mahl and Helene Koon, editors, *The Female Spectator: English Women Writers Before 1800* (Bloomington: Indiana University Press, 1977), 278.

17. Donna Landry, *The Muses of Resistance: Laboring-Class Women's Poetry in Britain, 1739–1796* (New York: Cambridge University Press, 1990), 21.

18. Arthur Roberts, Introduction, M. More, *Mendip Annals*, 7.

19. For more on Yearsley and her relationship with Hannah More, see the section "The unhappy alliance of Ann Yearsley and Hannah More: a parable for feminism" in Landry's *Muses of Resistance* (16–22); Linda Zionkowski's "Strategies of Containment: Stephen Duck, AnnYearsley, and the Problem of Polite Culture," (*Eighteenth-Century Life* 13 [1989]: 91–108; Moira Ferguson's "Resistance and Power in the Life and Writings of Ann Yearsley" (*The Eighteenth Century: Theory and Interpretation* 27 [1986]: 247–48); and Mary Waldron's "Ann Yearsley and the Clifton Records" (in *The Age of Johnson: A Scholarly Annual* 3 [1990]: 301–29).

20. Zionkowski, 91–92.

21. Landry, 1.

22. Elizabeth Hands, *The Death of Ammon. A Poem, with an Appendix: containing Pastorals, and other Poetical Pieces*. Coventry: N. Rollason, 1789, 47 (ll. 11–12).

23. Ibid., 48 (ll. 21–24).

24. Ibid., 49 (ll 45–52).

25. 25. Mary Leapor, *Poems, Upon Several Occasions*, 2 vols. (London: J. Roberts, 1748–51). In "The Ten-Penny Nail," for instance, Leapor refers to "us rhyming sinners" (ibid., 1:125, l. 3); in "Advice to Myrtillo," she tells a fellow-poet that he is devoting his "Time / To the lean Study of delusive Rhyme," "content to slumber out [his] Days, / To dream of Dinners, but to feed on Praise," and that she herself is "one long practis'd in the darling Sin" (ibid., 1:167, ll. 1–6). "The Universal Dream" opens with a "considerate" friend's telling her to "Give o'er your Whims" and "Retrieve the fleeting Hours you idly spend" in writing (ibid., 1:177, ll. 1–2), and it closes with Leapor's plea that she be allowed to enjoy her "visionary World : / To this glad bosom hug the dear Mistake," asking "If Dreams are Blessings, who wou'd wish to wake?" (ibid., 1:179, ll. 32–34). *Crumble-Hall* also opens with a friend "frown[ing] on" Leapor's poems and "Sad *Mira*"—Leapor's poetic name—vowing "to quit the darling Crime"; however, she "takes her Farewel, and repents, in Rhyme" (ibid., 2:111, ll. 1–6).

26. Ibid., 2:54, ll. 154–62.

27. Landry, 102.

28. Leapor, 2:xxix–xxx.

29. In a sad and ironic postscript to this struggle, her book did bring profit after all, but to her father, not to her: Leapor, as Freemantle says, "unfortunately did not live to receive that Benefit by it, which has since accrued to her Father" (Leapor, 2:xxiii).

30. Landry, 104.

31. John Barrell, *The Dark Side of the Landscape: The Rural Poor in English Painting, 1730–1840* (Cambridge: Cambridge University Press, 1980), 83.

32. Mandeville, 1:288.

33. Ibid., 1:317. Those who did, unlike Mandeville, believe in giving the poor some education generally agreed with him about the need to inculcate industrious habits in them. Donna T. Andrew's *Philanthropy and Police: London Charity in the Eighteenth Century* tells us that not only did most charity schools provide vocational training, but that "their general curriculum was constructed for the formation of a more sober and hard-working laboring class. It was hoped that by the imposition of work discipline at an early age, whether in the workhouse or the school, succeeding generations would not only have the needed skills, but also those habits equally necessary to persevere at a job" ([Princeton: Princeton University Press, 1989], 29).

34. Cunningham, 267.

35. "Remarks on the Poor Laws; with some Proposals for the Amendment of them" *Gentleman's Magazine* 67 (1790), 440.

36. Hannah More, "The Shepherd of Salisbury Plain," in *The Complete Works*, 1:190. Another tract character says in the tale "Sorrowful Sam," "Bringing up Children in laziness is the root of all evil," (Cheap Repository Tracts; Entertaining, Moral and Religious [Boston: E. Lincoln, 1803], 240). A 1751 *Gentleman's Magazine* article agrees, proclaiming: "The poor become wicked by not having learned any honest employment when young . . . ," ("Substance of a Proposal for the Employment of the Poor," *Gentleman's Magazine* 21 [1751], 559). The Reverend William Fleetwood, in his 1705 conduct book *The Relative Duties of Parents and Children, Husbands and Wives, Masters and Servants*, urges laboring-class parents to remember their "inuring" duty: "It is certain, that the Poor can never discharge the Duty of Parents well to their Children, without inuring them to labour and hardship . . ." (Marriage, Sex, and the Family Series [New York: Garland Publishing, Inc., 1985], 123). Evidently, though, not all members of the laboring classes were convinced of the benefits of constant and early labor for their children at all costs. Edgar S. Furniss notes in *The Position of the Laborer in a System of Nationalism* that "surprise was expressed by one writer that schemes such as [that of William] Temple's, intended for the laudable purpose of keeping the children employed 'at least twelve hours a day' did not appear 'agreeable and entertaining' to the parents of the children. . . ." Furniss quotes from Richard Wakefield's 1802 *Letter to the Landowners*: "Parents in general from whom to take for time [*sic*] the idle, mischievous, least useful and most burdensome part of their family to bring them up without any care or expense to themselves in habits of industry and decency is a very great relief; are very much adverse to sending their children to the houses of industry; from what cause, it is difficult to tell" ([New York: Kelley & Millman, Inc., 1957], 115).

37. William Temple, *A Vindication of Commerce and the Arts: Proving They Are the Source of the Greatness, Power, Riches and Populousness of a State*, 1758, Classic English Works on the History and Development of Economic Thought (New York: Johnson Reprint Corporation, 1971), 17.

38. For instance, John Clayton similarly says: "The Commandment of God is positive *six Days shalt thou labour, and do all that thou hast to do* . . ." (Clayton, 8). A 1768 article in *Gentleman's Magazine* asserts, again in very similar terms, "SIX *days shalt thou labour*. This is as positive a part of the commandment as that which says, *the* SEVENTH *day thou shalt rest* . . ." (Medius, Letter, *Gentleman's Magazine*, 38 [1768], 157). James Cunningham, who is extremely concerned that the poor be forced to work six days a week, says, "If the making every seventh day a holiday is supposed to be of divine institution, as it implies the appropriating the other six days to labour, surely it will not be thought cruel to enforce it" (Cunningham, 41).

39. Henry Fielding, *An Enquiry*, 80.

40. The classic discussion of this doctrine is found in chapter 6, "The Doctrine of the Utility of Poverty," in Furniss's *The Position of the Laborer in a System of Nationalism* (see note 37 this chapter). The notes contain a staggering list of statements of the doctrine. In his essay "Leisure and Wages in Theory and Practice," Peter Mathias gives a list of "commentators in this vein": "Bernard Mandeville, John Weyland, Thomas Manly, John Houghton, William Petty, Josiah Child, John Law, David Hume, Jonas Hanway, John MacFarland, William Temple, Pollexfen, Joshua Gee, John Gary, Daniel Defoe (in some places, but not in others), William Allen, Josiah Tucker, Francis Fauquier, Henry Fielding, Bishop Berkeley, Roger North" (*The Transformation of England: Essays in the Economic and Social History of England in the Eighteenth Century* [New York: Columbia University Press, 1979], 150–51). Some modern writers, like Max

Weber, seem to agree with the doctrine, at least to some extent. In *The Protestant Ethic and the Spirit of Capitalism*, Weber writes that, in an attempt to speed up production, employers will often raise piece-rates. "But," he adds,

> a peculiar difficulty has been met with surprising frequency: raising the piece-rates has often had the result that not more but less has been accomplished in the same time, because the worker reacted to the increase not by increasing but by decreasing the amount of his work. . . . The opportunity of earning more was less attractive than that of working less. He did not ask: how much can I earn in a day if I do as much work as possible? but: how much must I work in order to earn the wage, 2 1/2 marks, which I earned before and which takes care of my traditional needs? . . . A man does not "by nature" wish to earn more and more money, but simply to live as he is accustomed to live and to earn as much as is necessary for that purpose. (trans. Talcott Parsons [New York: Charles Scribner's Sons 1958], 59–60)

Other writers have questioned the logic of the idea that unless workers are kept at a bare subsistence wage, they will indulge in idleness *and* drunkenness or other forms of recreation that cost money. Mathias speaks of "two strongly held views" that "are to be reconciled only by a joint moral condemnation rather than by any economic logic" — namely, "the double complaint that higher wages involved greater absenteeism but also were associated with the poor indulging in extravagences, forgetting their due station in life and aping their betters in diet, clothing, and pleasures" (161–62). He concludes that "In economic terms such commentators cannot have it both ways—having one's leisure and consuming it, so to speak" (162). In *The Experience of Labour in Eighteenth-Century English Industry*, John Rule also notices this "paradox":

> If workers were spending their time in brandy shops, gin shops or ale-houses to a greater extent than usual, then they were exercising not only a leisure preference, but also increasing their consumption of non-essentials. There is a conflict between the complaints of a leisure preference coming into play *as soon* as wages moved above subsistence level and the accompanying complaints on the increasing 'luxury' expectations of the labouring poor, which were equally used to justify a cut in wage rates. Tea, tobacco, sugar, dress styles which 'aped their betters', as well as spirit drinking were all roundly condemned by those seeking to establish that the poor lived above their station. ([New York: St. Martin's Press, 1981], 54)

41. Mandeville, 1:194.

42. Temple, *A Vindication of Commerce*, 56–57. Temple also says in *The Case As It Now Stands* that "Necessity is the best Spur to Industry, and is the Mother of *Diligence*, as well as *Invention*. When there is nothing but a Prospect of starving without Industry and Providence, this will make the Poor frugal, diligent, and provident" (29). Similarly, Townsend claims that "in proportion as you advance the wages of the poor, you diminish the quantity of their work. All manufacturers complain of this, and universally agree, that the poor are seldom diligent, except when labour is cheap, and corn is dear" (29).

43. Arthur Young, *A Six Months Tour through the North of England*, 4 vols., 1771, Reprints of Economic Classics (New York: Augustus M. Kelley Publishers, 1967), 3:193. Cunningham's *Essay on Trade and Commerce* is full of similar statements, for instance: "it would be better for the labourer, as well as for the state, that he should work six days for six shillings, than that he should receive the same sum for labouring four days, for both the labourer and his family would be made the happier by it; an habit of sobriety and industry would be hereby acquired and confirmed . . ." (31). Cunningham also says, "I think it clearly appears that nothing but an immediate prospect of distress will operate powerfully enough to produce labour and industry among the generality of our labouring populace" (272).

44. G. E. Mingay, editor, *Arthur Young and His Times* (London: MacMillan Press, Ltd., 1975), 140.

45. John Bellers, *Proposals for Raising a College of Industry* in *John Bellers 1654–1725: Quaker, Economist and Social Reformer*, edited by A. Ruth Fry (London: Cassell and Company, 1935), 124. Many other eighteenth-century texts also make this point that the poor labor for the benefit of the rich. For instance, Mandeville's *Fable of the Bees* says, "It is impossible that a Society can long subsist, and suffer many of its Members to live in Idleness, and enjoy all the Ease and Pleasure they can invent, without having at the same time great Multitudes of People that to make good this Defect will condescend to be quite the reverse, and by use and patience inure their Bodies to work for others and themselves besides" (1:286). A 1743 *Gentleman's Magazine* article arguing against the selling of spiritous liquors to the poor points out that "all the Advantages which high Stations or large Possessions can confer, are derived from the Labours of the Poor," and adds that "to the Plow, and the Anvil, the Loom and the Quarry, Pride is indebted for its Magnificence, Luxury for its Dainties and Delicacy for its Ease" ("Debates in the Senate of Lilliput,"*GM* 13, 565). A 1768 article, in the course of trying to argue that *"our labouring poor receive annually the whole of the clear revenues of the nation"* (and therefore should receive no aid or raise in wages), says that the "habitation, furniture, cloathing, carriages, food, ornaments, and everything in short that [the rich], or their families use and consume, is the work or produce of the labouring poor" (Medius, Letter, *GM* 38, 157). Fielding's *Enquiry* argues that "persons of Fashion and Fortune" should concern themselves with preventing idleness in the poor, "that the Labour and Industry" of the poor "may administer to their Pleasures, and furnish them with the Means of Luxury" (84).

46. H. More, *Complete Works*, 2:372.

47. Edmund Burke, "Thoughts and Details on Scarcity" in *The Writings and Speeches of Edmund Burke*, vol. 9, edited by R. B. McDowell (Oxford: Clarendon Press, 1991), 121.

48. In *Life and Labour in England, 1700–1780*, Robert W. Malcolmson mentions this comfortable-class tendency to proclaim that the poor are as happy as, or even happier than, the rich:

> The poor, then, had no reason to be discontented with their lot in life. Indeed, it was often said that their lowly circumstances brought them certain important advantages, usually advantages of a spiritual nature. For labouring people were spared the anxieties, the pressing responsibility and the moral temptations which were imposed on men of property. They were said to enjoy more peace of mind than their betters. ([New York: St. Martin's Press, 1981],160)

49. Mandeville, 1:311. A few pages later, he embarks on an even more self-contradictory flight of fancy. Supposing that "the meanest and most unciviliz'd Peasant" and "the greatest King" could change places with each other, the peasant, although he "might pick out several Things he would like for himself," would ultimately find "a great many more" circumstances which "he would wish for his part to have immediately alter'd or redress'd, and which with Amazement he sees the King submit to" (1:315). And while the king would find some of the peasant's life—his labor, "Dirt and Squalor, his Diet and Amours, his Pastimes and Recreations"—abominable," he would also find great charm in the peasant's "Peace of Mind, the Calmness and Tranquillity of his Soul," and in his freedom from the cares of state (1:315–16). "Was impartial Reason to be Judge between real Good and real Evil," Mandeville sums up, "and a Catalogue made accordingly of the several Delights and Vexations differently to be met with in both Stations, I question whether the Condition of Kings would be at all preferable to

that of Peasants, even as Ignorant and Laborious as I seem to require the latter to be" (1:316).

50. Townsend, 35. Like Mandeville, he concludes with a comparison of peasantry and royalty: "The peasant with a sickle in his hand is happier than the prince upon his throne" (35–36).

51. Fleetwood, 384–85.

52. *A Present for Servants, From Their Ministers, Masters, Or Other Friends*, 1787, Marriage, Sex, and the Family Series (New York: Garland Publishing, Inc., 1985), 60–61. Even Eliza Haywood's *A Present for a Servant-Maid. Or, The Sure Means of Gaining Love and Esteem* (1743), which is more concerned with the practicalities of a servant's life and less intent on reforming her morals than many of these texts, says of a servant's labor that, "if you consider the Difference of Education, it is no more to you than those Exercises which are prescribed to your Superiors for the Sake of Health" (Marriage, Sex, and the Family Series [New York: Garland Publishing, Inc., 1985], 32).

53. One can hear this fear in the anxious way some comfortable-class writers talk about "equality." In "Reasons for Contentment," for instance, William Paley says,

> If any public disturbance should produce, not an equality (for that is not the proper name to give it), but a jumble of ranks and professions amongst us, it is not only evident what the rich would lose, but there is also this further misfortune, that what the rich lost the poor would not gain. I (God knows) could not get my livelihood by labour, nor would the labourer find any solace or enjoyment in my studies. If we were to exchange conditions to-morrow, all the effect would be, that we both should be more miserable, and the work of both would be worse done. Without debating, therefore, what might be very difficult to decide, which of our two conditions was better to begin with, one point is certain, that it is best for each to remain in his own. (*The Works of William Paley, D.D.* vol. 7 [London: S. Hamilton, 1816], 195)

Edmund Burke's "Thoughts and Details on Scarcity," arguing that a small rise in the price of labor may "absorb the whole of what [the employer] possesses," says in that this case, "A perfect equality will indeed be produced;—that is to say, equal want, equal wretchedness, equal beggary, and on the part of the partitioners, a woeful, helpless, and desperate disappointment." Burke goes on to assert, "Such is the event of all compulsory equalizations. They pull down what is above. They never raise what is below: and they depress high and low together beneath the level of what was originally the lowest" (Burke, *The Writings and Speeches*, 126–27). Earlier in the essay he claims that the number of rich people "is so extremely small, that if all their throats were cut, and a distribution made of all they consume in a year, it would not give a bit of bread and cheese for one night's supper for those who labour. . . ." Explaining that, because of the trickle-down effect, "every thing returns, deducting some very trifling commission and discount, to the place from whence it arose," he adds: "When the poor rise to destroy the rich, they act as wisely for their own purposes as when they burn mills, and throw corn into the river, to make bread cheap" (121).

54. William Cobbett, *The Autobiography of William Cobbett: The Progress of a Plough-Boy to a Seat in Parliament*, edited by William Reitzel (London: Faber and Faber Limited, 1947), 186.

55. H. More, *Complete Works*, 1:191.

56. Joseph Hanway, *Virtue in Humble Life*, 2 vols. (London: n.p., 1785), 1:184.

57. Ibid., 1:414.

58. Ibid., 1:419.

59. Ibid., 1:429.

60. Ibid., 1:431.

61. As we will see in my next chapter, though, writing addressed to the comfortable

(or at least to the *women* of these classes) enjoins them from engaging in too much or the wrong kind of play—thus assuming that they do have a choice in the matter. Whether the rich are portrayed as choosing their activities or as compelled into them seems to vary according to the intended audience of the portrayal.

62. Paley, 179.

63. Ibid., 184.

64. Ibid., 191.

65. Ibid., 191–92.

66. Ibid., 192. John Barrell quotes this passage in *The Dark Side of the Landscape*, comparing it to the pastoral paintings of Gainsborough's London period: "these pictures, . . . in their imagery, in the actions they depict and in the values they seem to endorse, . . . are strikingly similar to the essays, tracts, sermons, and treatises on the poor, and often addressed to them, which became suddenly much more numerous in the 1780s, as the rich became more aware of the threat the poor represented to the good order of England" (67). In his chapter on Gainsborough, Barrell examines "the social and political implications of this new, and invariably *domestic* idyll" (68).

67. Paley, 194.

68. For more on this move toward the domestic realm, see chapter 6, "The Undermining of Popular Recreations," in Robert W. Malcolmson's *Popular Recreations in English Society, 1700–1850* (New York: St. Martin's Press, 1981) and chapter 3, "Public Leisure and Private Leisure," in *Leisure in the Industrial Revolution*, by Hugh Cunningham (New York: St. Martin's Press, 1980).

69. Arthur Young, *A Six Weeks Tour, Through the Southern Counties, of England and Wales*, 2nd edition (London: W. Strahan, W. Nicoll, B. Collins, and J. Balfour, 1769), 332.

70. H. More, *Complete Works*, 1:170. Similarly, in "The Way to Plenty, or the second part of Tom White. Written in 1795, the year of scarcity," More's hero tells one of his workmen that he should put aside a few shillings and "with this I would get a bushel of malt, and my wife should brew it, and you may take a pint of your own beer at home of a night, which will do you more good than a gallon at the Red Lion" (ibid., 1:229).

71. Hanway, 1:55.

72. "Sorrowful Sam," Cheap Repository Tracts, 244.

73. Letter, *GM* 6, 25.

74. For a more compendious list of quotations expressing this notion, see chaper 2, "The Doctrine of the National Importance of the Laborer," in Furniss, especially pages 22–23.

75. Bellers, 38.

76. Mandeville, 2:187.

77. Laurence Braddon, *An Humble Proposal for Relieving, Reforming and Employing the Poor. And Herein By Vertue of One New General Law, Instead of Near Forty Statutes, Relating to the Premises. We May Comfortably Maintain all th' Impotent Poor, Judiciously Employ all the Capable Poor . . .* (London: Tho. Warner, 1729), 24.

78. Bellers, 111.

79. Ruth K. McClure, *Coram's Children: The London Foundling Hospital in the Eighteenth Century* (New Haven: Yale University Press, 1981), 111. Braddon and Hanway both performed other calculations of the cash value of an industrious laborer. In his *Corporation Humbly Propos'd, For Relieving, Reforming, and Employing the Poor. Herein There Will Be More Private Gain to the Subscribers, and More Publick Good to Great Britain, than by All Unparliamentary Subscriptions Already Taken. In a Letter to A Justice of the Peace of Middlesex* (1720), Lawrence Braddon asserts that "were it possible for us to purchase, *Ten Millions* of Children, at Ten Pounds *per* Head, we should thereby purchase (what in

Twenty Years) might put us in a *Capacity,* of *giving Laws to all Europe"* ([London: Thomas Warner, 1720], 16). In another text written in 1766, Hanway, to quote Donna Andrew's summary, "computes that the cost of raising an average number of children (allowing for three out of five to die before the age of apprenticeship) to the age of thirteen to be £85.16.0 each, while the worth of their labor, assuming an average life span of only thirty-six years, would be £269.19.3, 'a gain of £184.3.3'" (Andrew, 102).

80. Linebaugh, *The London Hanged,* 49.

81. In his introduction to Henry Fielding's *Enquiry into the Causes of the Late Increase of Robbers and Related Writings,* Malvin R. Zirker also notes this tendency to see the idle as potential wealth for the nation: "The mercantilist saw the idle, extravagant, and criminal poor as a vast store of potential energy and whoever would harness this potential source of wealth and make these people 'sound and useful Members of the Commonwealth, would deserve so well of the Publick, as to have his Statue set up for a Preserver of the Nation'" (lxiii–lxiv; Zirker, of course, is quoting from Swift's "Modest Proposal"). M. G. Jones, in *The Charity School Movement,* mentions that this view of the idle as stores of potential wealth was behind the move to turn charity schools into workhouses: "Political arithmeticians worked out the sums which would accrue to the national income if the restless energy of the children were harnessed in this way to industry. Visions of gold and silver mines appearing in every county of England, if the literary schools were turned into working schools, gripped the public imagination . . ." [London: Frank Cass and Co. Ltd., 1964], 91).

82. Bellers, 125.

83. Defoe, 172.

84. Bellers, 129.

85. Tom Meanwell, Letter, *Gentleman's Magazine* 4 (1734), 199. Another article quotes "Doctor Davenant," who has worked out that there are 1,330,000 idle souls in the kingdom, and says, "To make as many as possible of these 1,330,000 Persons . . . who now live chiefly upon others, get themselves a large Share of their Maintenance, would be opening a new Vein of Treasure of some Millions Sterling *per Annum"* (*GM* 6, 26). A 1751 article recommending forced employment for poor children reckons that at least "60,000 children are maintained by [poor] rates in idleness," and figures, "If the labour of these children can upon an average be made to produce 3*d. per* day, reckoning 300 working days to the year, the annual savings in the poors rates only will amount to 225,000*l.* besides that 60,000 hands will be always at work in such low manufactures as foreigners are now paid for carrying on. . ." ("Substance of a Proposal for the Employment of the Poor," *GM* 21, 559).

86. Jones, 91. In *The Position of the Laborer in a System of Nationalism,* Edgar S. Furniss quotes several other such calculations. Joshua Gee's *Trade and Navigation* (4th edition 1738) contains this bit of math: "Suppose that one million of people were put upon manufacturing . . . rough materials and each person earned but a penny a day and allowing but three hundred working days in a year, it would mean one million two hundred and fifty thousand pounds" (Furniss, 44). Sir Walter Harris, in his 1691 *Remarks,* and Sir Henry Pollexfen, in his 1700 *Discourse of Trade,* both calculated the loss to the nation occasioned by the excessive holidays of the labouring people. Harris supposes

> the working people of England to be but four millions and that the labor of each person be valued at but 6*d.* per day, their work for one day amounts to one hundred thousand pounds: which for twenty-four days that they keep in a year more than the twenty-nine days observed by the Church of England amounts to two millions and four hundred thousand pounds sterling per annum which of itself is sufficient to . . . enrich the nation. (Furniss, 45)

Pollexfen asks "whether the many holidays now kept may not be a great load upon the nation may be considered; for if but 2 million of working people at 6*d.* a day comes to 500,000*l.* which upon due inquiry whence our riches must arise, will appear to be so much lost to the nation by every holiday that is kept" (Furniss, 44).

87. For instance, Defoe says the nation is "burthen'd with a crowd of clamouring, unimploy'd, unprovided for poor People, who make the Nation uneasie, burthen the Rich, clog our Parishes, and make themselves worthy of Laws, and peculiar Management to dispose of and direct them . . ." (162). Sir Frederick Morton Eden's 1797 *State of the Poor; Or, An History of the Labouring Classes in England, From the Conquest to the Present Period* quotes a speech of King William's which says, "if you can find proper means of setting the Poor at work, you will ease yourselves of a very great burthen . . ." (3 vols., 1797 [London: Frank Cass and Co. Ltd., 1966], 1:248). An article from an 1801 issue of *Gentleman's Magazine* says that those "who are too idle or too poor to work are of no other use in the world than to increase the enormous burden of the poor-rates, and, like the drones in a bee-hive, prey on the industrious" (*GM* 89, 491–92).

88. "Remarks on the Poor Laws; with some Proposals for the Amendment of them," *Gentleman's Magazine* 67, 440. In a reversal of this notion, Fielding says that spending time in "Temples of Idleness" will convert "the Artificer, the Handicraft, the Apprentice, and . . . the common Labourer" from "useful Members of the Society" to "a heavy Burden or absolute Nuisance to the Public" (82).

89. Cunningham, 18.

90. Ibid., 87.

91. Neil McKendrick, "Josiah Wedgwood and Factory Discipline," *The Historical Journal* 4 (1961): 53.

92. E. P. Thompson, "Time, Work-Discipline, and Industrial Capitalism," in *Customs in Common: Studies in Traditional Popular Culture* (New York: The New Press, 1991), 61.

93. Ibid., 73.

94. Ibid.

95. Malcolmson, *Popular Recreations*, 99. This traditional tendency toward irregular work habits is discussed in several social history texts; see, for instance, chapter 2 of John Rule's book *The Experience of Labour in Eighteenth-Century English Industry* and chapter 5 of his *Labouring Classes in Early Industrial England, 1750–1850* (London: Longman, 1986). Robert W. Malcolmson also mentions this preference for irregular work habits: in *Life and Labour in England 1700–1780* he says that for an eighteenth-century laborer independence meant, in part, "setting his own rhythms of work (starting and stopping partly at his own pleasure)" (133).

96. As Peter Linebaugh says, "In the seventeenth century watches were toys, ornaments, insignia of power or stores of wealth. In the eighteenth century the watch assumed new functions; it became a measure of labour time or a means of quantifying 'idleness' " (*The London Hanged*, 225).

97. Samuel Richardson, *The Apprentice's Vade Mecum*, 1734, edited by Alan Dugald McKillop (Los Angeles: Augustan Reprint Society, 1975), 7.

98. Ibid., 26.

99. R. Campbell, *The London Tradesman*, 1734 (Devon: David and Charles Reprints, 1969), 313.

100. Ibid., 314. A *Gentleman's Magazine* article complaining of "the Diversion of Cricket" says that it "brings together Crowds of Apprentices and Servants, whose Time is not their own" (*Gentleman's Magazine* 13, 486).

101. *A Present for Servants, From Their Ministers, Masters, Or Other Friends*, 35.

102. Haywood, 13. In the "Duty of Servants to Masters" section of his *Relative Duties*

of Parents and Children, Husbands and Wives, Masters and Servants, William Fleetwood makes the same point rather more prolixly:

> A Servant, when he enters into Service, gives up his Time and Labour, by agreement, to his Master, in consideration of what Wages, Keeping, and Protection he expects from him: And therefore he would be unjust to waste that Time, and spare that Labour, that is truly none of his; they are his Masters by his Contract, and his Master ought to have the advantage of them; it is defrauding People of what is their due, it is keeping back part of what is already sold them, and agreed for, and it would be full as just for a Master to detain part of his Servants Wages, contracted for, at the years end, as it is for a Servant to waste a great deal of that Time, and spare a great deal of that Labour, that was his Masters by Agreement. . . . (352)

Three more reminders of this principle occur in the section. The story of an exemplary female servant in Jonas Hanway's *Virtue in Humble Life* tells us that "She was as careful not to defraud them of her time, as of any other property belonging to them" (1:281). "Some Thoughts for the New Year," a Cheap Repository Tract, tells the reader who is a servant that idleness implies "some injustice to your employer: you have agreed with him to give him so much work for so much pay, but if you have secretly wasted in idleness, or turned to your own use a part of that time which you engaged to give your master, you have then robbed him of his due . . ." (106).

103. *A Present for Servants*, 35. Haywood's conduct book also warns against "being what they call an Eye Servant" (15), as does Richardson's *Vade Mecum*: "It will even behove [*sic*] you to double your Diligence in his Absence; for no one can well have a worse Character than he that deserves the Name of an Eye-Servant . . ." (27).

104. "The Good Mother's Legacy," in Cheap Repository Tracts, 337. Not surprisingly, some other Cheap Repository Tracts also mention eye-service. In "The Two Shoemakers," a virtuous master preaches on the text to a remiss apprentice, and "it did more towards curing him of idleness than the soundest horse-whipping would have done" (H. More, *Complete Works*, 1:206). "Some New Thoughts for the New Year" asks its reader "whether you may not have been more or less an *eye servant?*" (*Cheap Repository Tracts*, 105).

105. E. P. Thompson, *The Making of the British Working Class* (New York: Vintage Books, 1966), 369.

106. "What servants, journeymen, labourers, carpenters, bricklayers do as they would be done by? Which of them does as much work as he can?" asked the Wesleyan Conference Minutes of 1766, adding, "Set him down for a knave that does not . . . and the Methodist knave is the worst of all knaves" (Wellman J. Warner, *The Wesleyan Movement in the Industrial Revolution* [New York: Russell & Russell, 1930], 147).

107. A few exceptional people did manage to rise from quite humble beginnings through talent and hard work. Francis Place, for instance, who was born in poverty and apprenticed to a breechesmaker, worked constantly to open his own tailorshop and was able eventually to retire comfortably and become a radical reformer. William Cobbett rose from being a poor plowboy to, as he says in the title of his autobiography, "a seat in Parliament." Both these men emphasize the part extreme industry and self-sacrifice played in their success. Cobbett, for instance, speaks repeatedly in his autobiography of his early rising, saying he owed much of his success in life to his habit of arising "in summer, at daylight, and in winter at four o'clock" (*Autobiography*, 32). Place says that for a long period he and his wife "worked full sixteen and even eighteen hours a day sundays and all. . . . We turned out of bed to work and turned from our work to bed again" (*The Autobiography of Francis Place*. Edited by Mary Thale. [Cambridge: Cambridge University Press, 1972], 123). While Cobbett does recommend early rising

to others, both he and Place seem to realize how unusual their ability to labor so unceasingly was and how precarious laboring-class success generally was.

108. Sean Shesgreen, "Hogarth's *Industry and Idleness*: A Reading" in *Eighteenth-Century Studies* 9 (1976), 582.

109. A great deal of cultural energy was expended on trying to keep apprentices from becoming idle; as Linebaugh says, the "idle apprentice" was "a social figure every much as threatening to the established order as the 'sturdy rogue' of the sixteenth century, or the 'sectary' of the seventeenth century or the 'factory proletarian' of the nineteenth century" (*The London Hanged*, 9). Shesgreen's "Hogarth's *Industry and Idleness*: A Reading" provides a useful discussion of the threat of the idle apprentice. Shesgreen tells us:

London was continually threatened by the disorderly conduct of its apprentices in the eighteenth century. In reaction to the use of female and child workers, the employment of Irish labor, poor wages, trade fluctuations, and chronic unemployment, apprentices had rioted in the first half of the century in a manner which alarmed the city to the point where these disorders were perceived as a threat to London's entire fabric of peace and order. . . . Among the various groups of London apprentices, the weavers [the apprentices depicted in Hogarth's series] were the most violent and the most radical. (590)

110. Ronald Paulson, *Hogarth: High Art and Low, 1732–1750* (New Brunswick: Rutgers University Press, 1992), 292. The advertisement for the series said "This little Book ought to be read by every 'Prentice in England, to imprint in their hearts these two different examples . . . and is a more proper Present to be given by the Chamber of London, at the binding and enrolling an Apprentice than any other Book whatever" (Frederick Antal, *Hogarth and His Place in European Art*, [New York: Basic Books, 1962], 12). Paulson tells us "the prints sold especially well at Christmas, when masters gave their apprentices sets as Christmas gifts" (290).

111. Shesgreen argues that "there emerges from Hogarth's method a level of meaning which often challenges the didacticism of the progress's subject matter and the moralistic shape which that subject matter assumes" (582); Paulson says that the "essential reading experience [of the series] is arrived at not through sophisticated inference drawn by the 'men of greater penetration,' who read down, but by the popular or 'plebeian' audience who immediately perceived a meaning that questioned the status quo" (309).

112. Paulson, 311.

113. Shesgreen, 582.

114. Ibid., 583.

115. Ibid.

116. Paulson, 309–10.

117. Shesgreen, 585.

118. Ibid., 584.

119. Ibid., 585.

120. Ibid.

121. Ibid., 589.

122. The odd and anonymous little pamphlet *The Effects of Industry and Idleness Illustrated; in the Life, Adventures, and Various Fortunes of Two Fellow-'Prentices of the City of London* (1748) is even clearer about, although entirely uncritical of, the class difference in the two apprentices. Although the pamphlet purports to be "an Explanation of the Moral of Twelve Celebrated Prints, lately published, and Designed by the Ingenious Mr. Hogarth," it does very little explaining of the prints and instead spins its own narrative, supposedly the real-life story on which the series is based. The pamphlet has the

industrious apprentice born to the "second Son to Sir *Jonathan Careless*," a baronet, and "*Martha*, sole Heiress of Sir *Humphry West*, of *Derbighshire* Knight . . ." ([London: C. Corbett, 1748], 12). The family loses its money due to its loyalty to Charles the First and the ingratitude of Charles the Second, and "*John West* the second Son, the Hero of this Part of our Work" is apprenticed to a relative, Nathaniel West. Although the author of the pamphlet claims that poor John had "nothing else but his Business and Industry in it to depend on" (17), clearly his gentle birth and cousinhood with his master are also helpful. John writes in a letter to his aunt that the master and his wife "use me very kindly, and are always giving me good Counsel . . . The Servants are not allow'd to be familiar with me, for all that I am a 'Prentice; and the Workmen in the Shop, if they meet me any where out of it, always pull off their Caps, and call me Master *West*" (20). No such special treatment is accorded the idle apprentice, to whose story only seven of the pamphlet's forty-eight pages are devoted. Tom Randal, as he is called, has a bit of money, but he is the son of a silversmith, not the grandson of a baronet. He is certainly idle and full of bad behavior, and John is clearly industrious and full of virtue, but one wonders how much lacking or possessing the kinship and favor of the master, or the love of the master's daughter (which John also secures, and which might also be seen as partly a result of his high class status), has to do with the different fates of the two lads.

123. "The Two Shoemakers," in H. More, *Complete Works*, 1:201.

124. Ibid., 1:203.

125. Ibid.

126. Ibid., 1:205.

127. "Sorrowful Sam," in Cheap Repository Tracts, 239.

128. Ibid., 257.

129. Maria Edgewood, *Idleness and Industry Exemplified; in the History of James Prescott and Lazy Lawrence* (Philadelphia: J. Johnson, 1804), 8.

130. Ibid., 35.

131. Ibid.

132. As Paulson says, in Plate 5 the nooses have "now moved from the decorative border into Idle's world" (295).

133. Supposedly nonfictional accounts of criminals whose lives ended on the gallows also frequently cast idleness as the first link in a chain of sin. Linebaugh says that all three contemporary biographies of Jack Sheppard, a notorious eighteenth-century criminal, present "idleness [as] a decisive concept in what are otherwise differing inter-pretations of the origins of his criminality" (*The London Hanged*, 14).

134. Paulson, 317.

135. George Lillo, *The London Merchant*, edited by William H. McBurney (Lincoln: University of Nebraska Press, 1965). Richardson's *Vade Mecum*, while arguing at length that the theater is no fit place for apprentices, makes an exception for Lillo's play: "I know of but one Instance . . . where the Stage has condescended to make itself useful to the City-Youth. . . . I mean, the Play of *George Barnwell*, which has met with the success that I think it well deserves; and I could be content to compound with the young City Gentry, that they should go to this Play once a Year. . . ." (16).

136. William Harlin McBurney, Introduction, Lillo, xxi–xiii.

137. David Wallace, "Bourgeois Tragedy or Sentimental Melodrama? The Signifi-cance of George Lillo's *The London Merchant*" in *Eighteenth-Century Studies* 26 (1991–92), 129.

138. Shesgreen, 591. Shesgreen adds that the similarity between *The London Merchant* and Hogarth's *Industry and Idleness* series (on its didactic level) is "in both works' con-scious spiritual kinship as uniquely purposeful examples of bourgeois didacticism and

crusading, and as records of as well as reactions to social and economic phenomena of vital concern to a middle class that now needed to defend and conserve [its] power and influence . . ." (592).

139. Lillo, *The London Merchant*, act I, sc. v, lines 64–66.

140. Ibid., act I, sc. v, lines 84–86.

141. And it is worth noting that Trueman, the other, nontransgressing, apprentice in the play, is explicitly spoken of as industrious several times: Thorowgood, for instance, tells him "I commend your diligence" (ibid., act III, sc. iii, line 30) on one occasion and later says to him, "Trueman, you, I am sure, would not be idle on this occasion" (ibid., act IV, sc.vii, line 6).

142. Ibid., act III, sc. vii, lines 34–43.

143. Ibid., act II, sc. ii, lines 93–94.

144. Edgewood, 12.

145. Ibid., 33.

146. Ibid., 63.

147. "The Two Shoemakers," H. More, *Complete Works*, 1:203.

148. Ibid., 1:214.

149. Ibid., 1:218.

150. "Black Giles the Poacher," H. More, *Complete Works*, 1:258.

151. "The Good Mother's Legacy," Cheap Repository Tracts, 342.

152. *A Present for Servants* also warns that a servant's neglect of duty will lead to greater crimes: "They that are unfaithful in their Master's Work, will not (it is to be feared) make much Conscience of defrauding him in his Estate. How quickly does the Devil teach an ungodly Servant to make bold with his Master's Money . . . ; till they who made nothing to trample on God's Law for a Penny, came afterwards to Pounds and higher Robberies?" (36).

153. "Sorrowful Sam," Cheap Repository Tracts, 246.

154. Ibid., 255.

155. "Wild Robert," Cheap Repository Tracts, 427.

156. *The Relative Duties of Parents and Children* says that "many poor People" are "extremely guilty of" allowing their children to "continue lazy, idle, and doing nothing," which is "a Mistake not only mischievous to the Commonwealth, but of most pernicious consequence to their Children, the unkindest thing they can do to them; for though it please them for the present, yet it entails on them perpetual misery, and very often untimely Death, by engaging them in wicked courses, the sure and ready road to ruin . . ." (Fleetwood, 124).

157. I will be using the word "grotesque" in its more ordinary sense, but it is interesting to note that in *The Politics and Poetics of Transgression* Peter Stallybrass and Allon White say that "idleness" is one of the "demonized terms for the topology which [Mikhail] Bakhtin celebrated, from the perspective of the low, as the grotesque" ([Ithaca: Cornell University Press, 1986], 34). And indeed the list they present of the "discursive norms" of the grotesque body includes many qualities complained of in eighteenth-century discussions of the idle poor, especially, "impurity (both in the sense of dirt and mixed categories) . . . , exorbitancy, clamour, decentered or eccentric arrangements, a focus upon gaps, orifices and symbolic filth . . . , [and the] physical needs and pleasures of the 'lower bodily stratum' " (ibid., 23).

158. "Debates in the Senate of Lilliput," *Gentleman's Magazine* 13, 566.

159. Fielding, *An Enquiry*, 90.

160. Townsend, 30.

161. Mathias, 161.

162. Temple, *Case As It Now Stands*, 19.

163. Temple, *A Vindication of Commerce and the Arts*, 31.

164. Ibid., 32.

165. In fact, Peter Linebaugh points out in *The London Hanged: Crime and Civil Society in the Eighteenth Century* that tea is sort of an anti-gin: "Tea, on the other hand, was sobering, its caffeine was conducive to work discipline, and it became the drink of the weekly meetings of the small Methodist bands" (215).

166. Furniss, 154.

167. Young, *Six Months Tour through the North of England*, 3:261–62.

168. H. More, "The Two Shoemakers" in *Complete Works*, 1:207.

169. H. More, "Shepherd of Salisbury" in *Complete Works*, 1:195.

170. Ibid., 1:196.

171. Ibid.

172. As Elizabeth Kowaleski-Wallace says in her interesting chapter on Hannah and Martha More in *Their Father's Daughters*, this choice shows the shepherd's "tremendous control over his bodily appetites" ([New York: Oxford University Press, 1991], 77); the tale "celebrate[s] the binding . . . of desire" (79). Kowaleski-Wallace focuses more than I am doing here on the gendered aspects of this attention to the grotesque body: "by assuming control over the symbolic body of an infantalized, working-class 'Other,' the Evangelical woman defined herself in relation to what she was not; her supreme bodily self-discipline became the identifying mark of her class privilege" (74).

173. M. More, *Mendip Annals*, 61–62.

174. More goes so far as to give recipes in some of her writings for "cheap dishes." Kowaleski- Wallace makes the excellent point that these recipes

> literalize the concern with "appetite" that pervades More's Evangelical discourse. If, for example, the poor can be taught to satisfy themselves with economical stews, made from cheap cuts of meat left over from the pots of wealthier citizens, it is not likely their unruly appetites will provoke them into acts of insurrection. While cheap stews literally fulfill the appetite, they also metaphorically contain the rampant desire for more than the status quo will provide. (85)

175. "The Hubbub," Cheap Repository Tracts, 154–55.

176. Ibid., 157.

177. Ibid., 155.

178. Ibid.

179. "Black Giles the Poacher," H. More, *Complete Works*, 1:251.

180. "The Shepherd of Salisburt Plain," 1:196.

181. Ibid., 1:191.

182. Hanway, 1:60.

183. John Clayton, 34–35.

184. Barrell, *The Dark Side*, 76. Barrell adds, "The successful suppliant, then, will keep up appearances, . . . for the rich know perfectly well that those who *look* like beggars are ragged only through idleness, idle only through inclination, and that rags and tatters are a sort of rhetoric adopted only to solicit our concern" (77).

185. Townsend, 69.

186. Clayton, 3.

187. Ibid., 41.

188. Ibid., 4.

189. Ibid., 34.

190. Ibid., 35.

191. As Carol Houlihan Flynn, in *The Body in Swift and Defoe*, quotes Defoe as doing, especially in regard to the plague and its "purgative quality, its ability to empty a teeming city of 'useless mouths,' the bodies of the poor" ([New York: Cambridge University

Press, 1990], 133; see also 78 and 148). Fielding's *Proposal for Making an Effectual Provision for the Poor* (1753) says (quoting Nathaniel Bacon) that the kingdom will never be enriched "so long as many Mouths are fed upon the main Stock, and waste the same in Idleness and Prodigality" (in *An Enquiry into the Causes of the Late Increase in Robbers and Related Writings*, 261). Sir Frederick Morton Eden's *The State of the Poor* (1797) quotes "Dr. Davenant" as saying that "he who does not some way serve the commonwealth" is a "mouth" that does not "profit a country" (Eden, 1:231).

192. In his *Proposal*, Fielding uses the phrase in reference to "the Vagabonds" who "ought clearly to be banished"; he is quoting "that most wonderful young Prince" Edward VI (227).

193. As Dr. Thomas Bray puts it in a pamphlet (Andrew, 59).

194. *A Present for Servants*, 16–17.

195. Bellers, 47–48.

196. Laurence Braddon, *To Pay Old-Debts without New-Taxes, by Charitably-Relieving, Politically-Reforming, and Judiciously-Employing the Poor . . .* (London: Thomas Warner, 1723), 6. Hannah More's "Village Politics. Addressed to All the Mechanics, Journeymen, and Labourers, in Great Britain" (1792) represents a clever twist on the "body politic" metaphor. The story presents a dialogue between Jack Anvil, a blacksmith, and Tom Hod, a mason, which at first appears to be turning the metaphor upside down. Tom says, "I don't see why we are to work like slaves, while others roll about in their coaches, feed on the fat of the land, and do nothing." Jack answers with a fable "between the belly and the limbs": "The hands said, I won't work any longer to feed this lazy belly, who sits in state like a lord and does nothing. Said the feet I won't walk and tire myself to carry him about; let him shift for himself; so said all the members; just as your levellers and republicans do now." More does not let the levellers have the last word, of course:

> And what was the consequence? Why the belly was pinched to be sure, and grew thin upon it; but the hands and the feet, and the rest of the members, suffered so much for want of their old nourishment, which the belly had been all the time administering, while they accused him of sitting in idle state, that they all fell sick, and would have died, if they had not come to their senses just in time to save their lives. (H. More, *Complete Works*, 1:59)

197. Cultivator, Letter, *Gentleman's Magazine* 21 (1751), 206. This figure of speech abounds in eighteenth-century writing. The following examples represent a small percentage of the available instances. Daniel Defoe's *Giving Alms No Charity* says more than once that "there is more Work than Hands to perform it" (166; also 163). Bernard de Mandeville's *Fable of the Bees* calculates that if the laboring people in one country work longer hours and more days than those in another, "the one is obliged to have Nine Hands for what the other does with Four" (1:313), and that "the hard and dirty Labour throughout the Nation requires three Millions of Hands" (2:352). In his *Distilled Spirituous Liquors the Bane of the Nation* (1736), Thomas Wilson says that "that Part which is the Strength and Riches of every Country" is "the Laborious Hands" ([London: J. Roberts, 1736], ix.). An *Essay on Trade and Commerce* argues that any method "that will enforce labour and industry, will have the same effect as increasing the number of hands" in a state (Cunningham, 18). Arthur Young's *Six Months Tour through the North of England* claims that "Industrious hands are not bred by the idle" (4:413). Sir Frederick Morton Eden's *State of the Poor* (1797) quotes a bit of "his Majesty's speech" saying that to find "proper means of setting the Poor at work" would "add so many useful hands to be employed in our manufactures" (1:248).

198. Young, *Six Months Tour through the North of England*, 1:175.

199. Wedgewood, McKendrick, 46.

200. Clayton, 3.

201. Meanwell, Letter, *GM* 4, 198.

202. "The Hubbub" in Cheap Repository Tracts, 158.

203. "The Shepherd of Salisbury Plain," H. More, *Complete Works*, 1:194.

204. *A Corporation Humbly Propos'd, For Relieving, Reforming, and Employing the Poor. Herein There Will Be More Private Gain to the Subscribers, and More Publick Good to Great Britain, than by All Unparliamentary Subscriptions Already Taken. In a Letter to A Justice of the Peace of Middlesex* (London: Thomas Warner, 1720), 14–15. Malvin R. Zirker, quoting this sentence, adds drily, "One is grateful that not much force was required" (lxxviii).

205. Flynn, 168.

206. William George Maton, *Observations Chiefly Relative to the Natural History, Picturesque Scenery, and Antiquities, of the Western Counties of England, Made in the Years 1794 and 1796*, 2 vols. (Salisbury: J. Easton, 1797), 1: 233.

207. Bernard Ramazzini, *A Treatise of the Diseases of Tradesmen, Shewing the Various Influence of Particular Trades Upon the State of Health; With the best Methods to avoid or correct it, and useful Hints proper to be minded in regulating the Cure of all Diseases incident to Tradesmen* (London: Andrew Bell, 1705), 30. I have quoted from the English translation of the original Latin text written in 1700.

208. William Pryce, *Mineralogia Cornubiensis; A Treatise on Minerals, Mines, and Mining* . . . (London: James Phillips, 1778), 176.

209. John Fletcher, *An Appeal to Matter of Fact and common Sense. Or a rational Demonstration of Man's corrupt and lost Estate* (Bristol, William Pine, 1772), 53.

210. In *The Vital Century: England's Developing Economy, 1714–1815* (London: Longman Group, 1992), John Rule says that "Manufacturing, declared one pamphleteer, was the equal of war in producing 'a mournful procession of the blind and lame, and of enfeebled, decrepit, asthmatic, consumptive wretches, crawling half alive upon the surface of the earth' " (209–210). For more about occupational injuries and diseases, see chapter 3 of Robert W. Malcolmson's *Life and Labour in England, 1700–1780*, chapter 3 of John Rule's *Experience of Labour in Eighteenth-Century English Industry*, and chapter 5 of Rule's *Labouring Classes in Early Industrial England, 1750–1850*.

211. Later, during the brief reign of William IV, the "Dead-body Bill" was passed (2 and 3 Wm. IV, c. 75, sec. 7), which enacted that the unclaimed bodies of those dying in hospitals and workhouses could also be delivered over for dissection. (William Cobbett, the radical M.P. who began life as a plowboy, campaigned against this bill, to no avail [J. M. Cobbett, "Preface," *A Legacy to Labourers*, (London: Charles Griffin and Company, 1872), viii–ix].) Since the workhouse was thought to be full of idle people, this bill provided another way for the idle to end up under the dissector's knife.

212. Linebaugh, "The Tyburn Riot Against the Surgeons," Hay et al. 65–117.

213. Hanway, 1:xvi. He amends this statement slightly when speaking specifically of laboring-class women: their "only dowry is their *virtue* and *ability* to labour" (1:xvii).

214. Eden, 1:413. This ability to labor is, many writers assert, the "patrimony" of the poor. *The Relative Duties of Parents and Children* tells laboring-class parents that what they have to hand down to their children is a habit of labor and industry: " 'Tis certain that the poorest Parents in the World, are oblig'd to provide for their Children, according to the best of their Abilities, and as certain, that they can provide for them no otherwise, than by accustoming them to Labour, and industry, and therefore 'tis certain, that they are oblig'd to provide thus for them" (Fleetwood, 123–24). Hannah More's ballad "The Honest Miller of Gloustershire" tries to tell the poor this patrimony is equal to that of richer folk:

And though no wealth he has, except

> The labour of his hands;
> Yet honest Industry's as good
> As houses or as lands.
>
> (Complete Works, 1:56, ll. 13–16)

215. Fielding, 228.

216. Eden, 1:5.

217. William Cobbett, *A Legacy to Labourers*, 1834, edited by J. M. Cobbett (London: Charles Griffin and Company, 1872), 33.

218. William Cobbett, "The Rights of the Poor, and the Punishment of Oppressors," *Cobbett's Monthly Sermons* (London: C. Clement, 1821), 88.

219. Cunningham, 16.

220. Burke, "Thoughts and Details on Scarcity," 122.

221. William Cobbett, "The Rights of the Poor, and the Punishment of Oppressors," 93.

222. William Cobbett, "Legacy to Labourers," 107. For an interesting examination of some of the ways these threats that Cobbett refers to were carried out, see *Crime, Protest, and Popular Politics in Southern England, 1740–1850*, by John Rule and Roger Wells (London: Hambledon Press, 1997).

223. Flynn, 133. Defoe, she says further on, tells a tale "he keeps on telling, using in other versions of mortal need the figure of the cannibal to uncover the complicated workings of a consumer society that devours its own children" (148).

224. Ibid., 161.

225. William Cobbett, "The Rights of the Poor, and the Punishment of Oppressors," 93.

226. Ibid., 96.

227. Cobbett also uses such images of sweat and blood. In his autobiography, for instance, he criticizes "the Pitt system of government" for "draw[ing] the produce of labour into unnatural channels" and then "deal[ing] it back again in driblets, under the name of relief, or of charity, just to support the life of those from whose pores it had been drained" (*Autobiography*, 94), and later he speaks of "wretches, who, being too lazy to work, wished to make fortunes out of the sweat; and, if necessary, the blood of the people" (197). In "The Punishment of Oppressors," he compares the conduct of oppressive employers to that of Judas Iscariot, "for, to rob men of their blood differs only in degree from robbing them of their sweat; and, in some respects, the former is less cruel than the latter" (94).

228. Stephen Duck, *The Thresher's Labour*, 1736, in *The Thresher's Labour and The Woman's Labour* (Los Angeles: Augustan Reprint Society, 1985), ll. 246–58. Subsequent quotations from this poem will be cited internally.

229. These "sweaty" passages can be compared to a passage from John Gay's *Rural Sports*. The earlier version of the poem contains these lines:

> But when th'Ascent of Heav'n bright *Phoebus* gains
> And scorches with fierce Rays the thirsty Plains;
> When sleeping Snakes bask in the sultry Sky,
> And Swains with fainting Hand their Labours ply,
> With naked Breast they court each welcome Breeze,
> Nor know the shelter of the shady Trees:
> Then to some secret Covert I retreat,
> To shun the Pressure of th'uneasie Heat;
> Where the tall Oak his spreading Arms entwines,
> And with the Beech a mutual Shade combines;
> Here on the Mossy Couch my Limbs I lay,

And taste an Ev'ning at the Noon of Day.

(John Gay, *Poetry and Prose*, edited by Vinton A. Dearing and Charles E. Beckwith, Vol 1 [Oxford: Clarendon Press, 1974], 43; ll. 269–80 in the earlier version)

Gay does here show some of the workers' sufferings—they work with "fainting Hand" and do not "know" shelter and shade—but in a modulated tone, and from a distance. The focus is on the leisured poet who has the privilege of escaping the heat, who can watch work from his comfortable couch, far enough away to avoid seeing the sweat that work costs the workers. (And in the revised version of the poem, which is the main text in the Oxford edition—the early version appears only in the notes—the swains disappear altogether; only heifers populate the plains [ibid., 43].) John Barrell argues that Gay's poem, like many eighteenth-century landscape paintings, serves to naturalize the contrast between the hardworking laborers and the leisured poet: "we are likely to feel . . . that because the two sorts of opposed relationship with nature, a gentle pastoral idleness or a rustic georgic industry, can each be represented as a mode of peaceful harmony with nature, each must be in harmony also with the other, and the apparent division between those who bend and work, and those who lie and rest, is unimportant" (Barrell, *Equal, Wide Survey*, 46). He notes later, however, that "the harmony of life in nature may not be equally evident to those who at high noon must keep on working if sportsmen and poets are to relax" (ibid., 47); Duck's poem supports this point, and provides a voice for those whose work allows others to be idle.

230. In *The Muses of Resistance: Laboring-Class Women's Poetry in Britain, 1739–1796*, Donna Landry says that Collier takes "Duck's refusal to 'see' women's agricultural labor as, in fact, productive, to be a violation of class loyalty rather than chivalry, good manners, or even good sense" (63).

231. Mary Collier, *The Woman's Labour*, 1739, in *The Thresher's Labour and The Woman's Labour* (Los Angeles: Augustan Reprint Society, 1985), ll. 57–58. Subsequent quotations from this poem will be cited internally.

232. The radical tailor Francis Place wrote of his mother, who had for a time to work as a laundress: "Often did she labour till twelve o clock at night, and rise again at four in the morning to pursue her occupation" (99). In her introduction to Collier's poem, Moira Ferguson says, "A modern historian acknowledges that 'among the longest hours of outworkers were those of the wretched women who went out to wash by the day.' Often they began at one in the morning and worked a day and a half for a day's wages" (Ferguson, Introduction, *The Thresher's Labour*, viii).

3. "Whilst We Beside You But as Cyphers Stand"

1. As Astell's title indicates, her proposal is addressed to *ladies*, and Wollstonecraft also is largely writing to and about middle- and upper-class women: women with some degree of education (however faulty) who were not expected to support themselves by their labor. If lack of fortune meant these women did have to work, this was felt, as I will discuss later, to be a profound degradation.

2. Mary Astell, *A Serious Proposal to the Ladies, for the Advancement of their True and Greatest Interest*, 1694 (New York: Source Book Press, 1970), 6.

3. Mary Wollstonecraft, *A Vindication of the Rights of Woman*, volume 5 of *The Works of Mary Wollstonecraft*, edited by Janet Todd and Marilyn Butler, 7 vols. (New York: New York University Press, 1989), 44.

4. Ibid., 331.

5. Anne Mellor has recently issued an important challenge to this idea that women

were restricted to the private sphere in this period. In *Mothers of the Nation: Women's Political Writing in England, 1780–1830*, she argues that "Habermas's conceptual limitation of the public sphere in England between 1780 and 1830 to men of property is historically incorrect. During the Romantic era woman participated fully in the public sphere as Habermas defined it." She goes on to say, "Not only did women participate fully in the discursive public sphere, but their opinions had definable impact on the social movements, economic relationships, and state-regulated policies of the day" ([Bloomington: Indiana University Press, 2000], 2–3). Mellor's argument is compellingly made and an important correction to the notion of women as entirely removed from public life. However, I would emphasize that, as Mellor herself admits, many women who did attempt this participation were "widely attacked" (10), indicating that many disapproved of this public activity. Also, the discursive power Mellor examines so well is still not an official sort of power—it relies on persuasion, rather than force, and so could be argued to be within the realm of the "influence" that, as I discuss below, was the approved form of participation for women. Certainly, however, Mellor demonstrates well that women like Hannah More did not always observe the silence and passivity that they recommended to others.

6. Mary Poovey also makes this point in *The Proper Lady and the Woman Writer*:

> In that society [eighteenth-century England] a woman was often metaphorically described as a "cypher." Etymologically, this word means "empty" or "a void," and by extension it means "a nonentity"; but a cypher is also, numerically, a zero, and this figure has properties that are almost magical. Like the number that is no number, a woman could increase or decrease the value of other figures (and herself) simply by her relationship to them. . . . ([Chicago: University of Chicago Press, 1984], 45)

7. The *Oxford English Dictionary* lists all three of these definitions of "cipher" (or "cypher"). The first definition begins, "An arithmetical symbol or character (0) of no value in itself, but which increases or decreases the value of other figures according to its position." The dates of the examples given to illustrate this definition of the word go from 1399 to 1827. The second definition gives the figurative use of this mathematical meaning: "A person who fills a place, but is of no importance or worth, a nonentity, a 'mere nothing'." The examples of this definition date from 1579 to 1852. The fifth definition the *OED* gives for the word is "A secret or disguised manner of writing . . . ; a cryptograph. Also anything written in cipher, and the key to such a system." These dates of the examples illustrating this definition range from 1528 to 1885.

8. Poovey, 24.

9. Anne Finch, *Selected Poems of Anne Finch, Countess of Winchilsea*, edited by Katharine M. Rogers (New York: Frederick Ungar Publishing Co., 1979), 18, ll. 9–12.

10. A development some contemporary writers deplored, as I will discuss later.

11. Alice Browne says in *The Eighteenth-Century Feminist Mind*, "technological advances meant much less household work for upper- and middle-class women to do; foreign visitors were struck by English women's sloth" ([Detroit: Wayne State University Press 1987], 31). Patricia Meyer Spacks discusses this lack of work for women in *Boredom: The Literary History of a State of Mind*: "Recent social historians have conclusively demonstrated . . . that England's 'modernization' entirely deprived many middle-class women of meaningful occupation" ([Chicago: University of Chicago Press, 1995], 63). In her introduction to *Eighteenth-Century Women: An Anthology*, Bridget Hill discusses the desire of the newly wealthy middling ranks to rise in status: "One way to establish membership of the middle class was by the employment of domestic servants. The number you employed determined your exact social standing. Such social aspirations were to lead to a steady withdrawal from labour and a deliberate cultivation of a

life of leisure" ([London: George Allen & Unwin, 1984], 4). Nancy Armstrong notes in *Desire and Domestic Fiction: A Political History of the Novel* that eighteenth-century conduct books "represent the woman of the house as apparently having nothing to do. Ideally servants would perform most, if not all, of the work specified for maintaining the household" ([Oxford: Oxford University Press, 1987], 79).

12. Ruth Perry, *Women, Letters, and the Novel* (New York: AMS Press, 1980]. In *Married Women's Separate Property in England, 1660–1833*, Susan Staves notes that this increasing association of women with leisure occurred in the upper classes, also: "not only in the middle classes but also in the gentry and the aristocracy, genteel femininity increasingly became dissociated from active and direct personal involvement in household management and household production and increasingly became associated with the possession of leisure time for amusement, consumption, and travel away from the home" ([Cambridge: Harvard University Press, 1990], 225).

13. Perry, 38.

14. Ibid., 39.

15. Ibid.

16. Mary Ann Radcliffe, *The Female Advocate*, 1810 (New York: Garland Publishing, Inc., 1974), 431.

17. Jane West, *Letters to a Young Lady, in Which the Duties and Character of Women Are Considered*, 1806, 3 vols. (New York: Garland Publishing, Inc., 1974), 1:142.

18. Staves, 224. Other writers have also commented on the importance of female leisure to male status at this period. For instance, Vivien Jones argues in her introduction to *Women in the Eighteenth Century: Constructions of Femininity* that "In a developing consumer economy to have, or to become, a 'leisured' wife was a measure of social success, underwriting the dependence of that economy on the isolated unit of the nuclear family, serviced by an invisible working class" (Vivien Jones, editor [London: Routledge, 1990] 10); and Katharine M. Rogers notes in *Feminism in Eighteenth-Century England* that "The active participation of wives in their husbands' businesses, encouraged by writers such as Defoe, became less common as tradesmen aimed at gentility and furnished their daughters only with useless fashionable accomplishments" ([Chicago: University of Illinois Press, 1982], 19). In *Family Fortunes: Men and Women of the English Middle Class, 1780–1850*, Leonore Davidoff and Catherine Hall do not so explicitly discuss the implications for class status of female leisure, but they remark on its increasing prevalence and on the insistence on separate spheres for men and women ([Chicago: University of Chicago Press, 1987]).

19. Hill, 185.

20. Ibid., 63.

21. Charlotte Lennox, *The Lady's Museum* (London: J. Newbury, n.d.), 1:183. Many writers express concern that women of the aspiring classes will lose their "usefulness." In her *Plans of Education* (1792), for instance, Clara Reeve speaks of girls of these classes who are educated above themselves, full of "improvements and accomplishments" and "unable or unwilling to work for themselves": "far the greater number" of these, she predicts, will "become useless, and some, mischievous members of society" ([New York: Garland Publishing, Inc., 1974], 61–62). Jane West snorts that "the village madam" who "hopes her showy array, and fastidious scrupulosity, will convince you that her husband cannot be a farmer" thinks "that it is very vulgar to be thought useful" (1:165). In "The Two Wealthy Farmers; Or, The History of Mr. Bragwell," one of her "Stories for Persons of the Middle Rank," Hannah More tells of another farmer's wife who thinks this: Mrs. Bragwell's "whole notion of gentility was, that it consisted in being rich and idle . . . To be well dressed, to eat elegantly, and to do nothing, or nothing of which is of any use, was what she fancied distinguished people in genteel

life" (*The Complete Works of Hannah More*, 2 vols. [New York: Harper & Brothers, 1843], 1:130).

The quest for class status through female leisure could, some writers worried, have a consequence even direr than uselessness: prostitution. In *Reflections on the Present Condition of the Female Sex* (1798), Priscilla Wakefield says that "false notions of enjoyment, and a dangerous taste for elegance, acquired at boarding-school, have been the unhappy means of casting many women" who have grown "too proud for the lowly occupations of their parents" into "the abyss of prostitution" ([New York: Garland Publishing, Inc., 1974], 60). Clara Reeve, like Wakefield, blames the class-climbing parents of these "young women who are turned loose upon the world, over educated" and therefore ripe for seduction and betrayal into "shame and poverty": the women are "the victims of their parents [*sic*] pride and vanity" (119–20).

22. Browne, 123.

23. Thomas Gisborne, *Enquiry into the Duties of the Female Sex*, 1797 (New York: Garland Publishing, Inc., 1974), 22.

24. John Gregory, *A Father's Legacy to His Daughters*, 1774 (New York: Garland Publishing, Inc., 1974), 6–7.

25. Hannah More, *Strictures on the Modern Systems of Female Education*, 1799, 2 vols. (New York Garland Publishing, Inc., 1974), 1:98.

26. West, 2:420.

27. Wakefield, 31.

28. Catherine Macaulay, *Letters on Education*, 1790 (New York: Garland Publishing, Inc., 1974), 208–9.

29. Mary Hays, *Appeal to the Men of Great Britain in Behalf of the Women*, 1798 (New York: Garland Publishing, Inc., 1974), 97.

30. Ibid., 160.

31. Wollstonecraft, *Vindication*, 168.

32. Ibid., 66. Wollstonecraft, however, seems more than Macaulay or Hays to blame women as well as society for this situation. She chides women repeatedly for being content to "loiter life away merely employed to adorn her person, that she may amuse the languid hours, and soften the cares of a fellow-creature who is willing to be enlivened by her smiles and tricks, when the serious business of life is over" (55–56).

33. Jones, 82.

34. James Fordyce, *The Character and Conduct of the Female Sex, and the Advantages to Be Derived from the Society of Virtuous Women* (London: T. Cadell, 1776), 54.

35. Laetitia Matilda Hawkins, *Letters on the Female Mind, Its Power and Pursuits* (London: Hookham and Carpenter, 1793), 7. Much earlier in the century Anne Finch complained of this sort of censuring in her poem "The Introduction," saying of women "who attempt the pen":

> They tell us, we mistake our sex and way;
> Good breeding, fassion, dancing, dressing, play
> Are the accomplishments we shou'd desire;
> To write, or read, or think, or to enquire
> Wou'd cloud our beauty, and exaust our time,
> And interrupt the Conquests of our prime. . . .
>
> (Finch, 5, ll. 13–18)

36. West, 1:128.

37. Ibid., 3:219–20.

38. H. More, *Strictures*, 1:142–43. Although Mrs. Chapone argues in her *Letters on the Improvement of the Mind* (1773) against an affectation of weakness and excessive sen-

sibility, she agrees with West and More that "The same degree of active courage is not to be expected in woman as in man; and, not belonging to her nature, it is not agreeable in her"; she should aspire instead for "passive courage—patience, and fortitude under sufferings—presence of mind, and calm resignation in danger" ([London: John Sharpe, 1822]), 54–55).

39. Poovey, 21.

40. Gregory, 88.

41. Ibid., 80.

42. In *Frances Burney: The Life in the Works*, Margaret Anne Doody calls Elinor an "apparently doctrinaire feminist of the Wollstonecraft school" ([New Brunswick, NJ: Rutgers University Press, 1988], 333).

43. Frances Burney, *The Wanderer*, edited by Margaret Anne Doody, Robert L. Mack, and Peter Sabor (Oxford: Oxford University Press, 1991), 177.

44. Mary Wollstonecraft, *Thoughts on the Education of Daughters*, vol. 4 of *The Works of Mary Wollstonecraft*, 32.

45. In *Women, Letters and the Novel*, Ruth Perry quotes a 1696 pamphlet that claims women want to please men more than anything else and that "this desire, which is so innate to the Sex, makes them live without action." Perry adds, "Women were instructed to treat themselves as mirrors, to reflect others rather than to have any self" (149).

46. Nancy Armstrong and Leonard Tennenhouse, *The Ideology of Conduct* (New York: Methuen, 1987), 9.

47. Samuel Richardson, *Pamela: Or Virtue Rewarded* (New York: Penguin Books, 1985), 462.

48. Ibid., 465.

49. Gisborne, 12–13.

50. West, 1:56–57.

51. H. More, *Strictures*, 1:4.

52. Ibid., 7.

53. As Mary Poovey glosses this passage, "More is calling on women to support the traditional system of English values through an even more emphatic performance of their traditional offices; they are to continue to act indirectly: through the influence that radiates outward from the home" (33).

54. Mellor seems to disagree with this idea that More wants women to be, rather than to act. She claims that "More effectually defined women as the best managers of the national estate, as the true patriots" (29). I will agree that More herself exercised a power that was more direct than mere influence and that she paved the way for other women to do so, but her many direct statements that women should not try to be "politicians" seems to indicate that she feels this power should at least be veiled.

55. Gisborne, 140.

56. Lady Sarah Pennington, *A Mother's Advice to Her Absent Daughters*, 1817 (New York: Garland Publishing, Inc., 1974), 22.

57. H. More, *Strictures*, 2:185.

58. In fact, Jane West's choice of words when she asserts that talents "are not bestowed to rust in inactivity" (1:50), and that those who misemploy their talents will find that "life glides from them; the opportunity of improving lost time ceases; and at the bar of a just God they will be questioned for sins of *omission*" (1:333) is remarkably similar to Johnson's.

59. Spacks notes that "women risk the miserable state of being 'lost' if they try to avoid the miserable state of being bored" (*Boredom*, 66).

60. Wakefield, 44–45. And indeed, in Elizabeth Inchbald's play *Wives As They Were*

And Maids As They Are (1797), a virtuous, industrious (though the couple are aristocrats, her husband makes her get up at five every morning and dress his hair) wife deflates the passions of a would-be seducer by sitting down to knit a pair of stockings. "By heaven she looks so respectable in that employment, I am afraid to insult her," the poor rake cries (*The Plays of Elizabeth Inchbald*, edited by Paula R. Backscheider, 2 vols. [New York: Garland Publishing, Inc., 1980], 2:78).

    61. Wollstonecraft, *Vindication*, 163.

    62. Ibid., 293.

    63. Ibid., 51–52.

    64. Ibid., 156.

    65. Armstrong, *Desire and Domestic Fiction*, 99.

    66. Gisborne, 13.

    67. West, 1:35.

    68. The reasons Gisborne assigns for transferring "to a stranger, as modern example dictates, the office of nurturing your child, when your health and strength are adequate to the undertaking" are "that your indolence may not be disturbed, or that your passion for amusement may not be crippled in its exertions" (363–64). Mary Wollstonecraft's *Female Reader* quotes Sarah Trimmer as agreeing when she asks, "If pleasure is the object, where can a woman find one, in the whole circle of public amusements, to compensate for the loss of that a fond mother feels while she nourishes her infant with the food which is its natural right, and sees a succession of human beings thriving in their native soil under her own immediate culture?" (vol. 4 of *The Works of Mary Wollstonecraft*, 125). *The Ladies Dispensatory or, Every Woman her own Physician* (1740) is equally convinced that the failure of healthy ladies to nurse their own children comes from a dislike of work and a preference for frivolous amusements: "The objections of *Trouble* and *Restraint* which *nursing* lays on Women of high Rank," the anonymous author thunders,

> are altogether insufficient. As to the Trouble, no Person can be discharg'd from any Duty on that Account, since God, who made it a Duty, forsaw the Trouble of it when he made it so. And as to the Restraint, it can only restrain from spending the Morning in superfluous Dressing, the day in formal and impertinent Visits, the Evening at lascivious Plays, and much of the Night in Gaming and Revelling. ([London: James Hodges, 1740], xi)

    69. Clara Reeve, *Plans of Education*, 1792 (New York: Garland Publishing, Inc., 1974), 113–15.

    70. Other authors also emphasize the importance of direct, active care of one's family. Hannah More mentions admiringly ladies who put their children before the exercise of their own talents: "And the writer of this page is intimately acquainted with several ladies who, excelling most of their sex in the art of music, but excelling them also in prudence and piety, find little leisure or temptation, amidst the delights and duties of a large and lovely family, for the exercise of this talent. . . ." (*Strictures*, 1:99). Mary Wollstonecraft "views with pleasure" the domestic idyll of "a woman nursing her children, and discharging the duties of her station with, perhaps, merely a servant maid to take off her hands the servile part of the household business," and her heart "throb[s] with sympathetic emotion" at the sight of the husband returning home to "smiling babes and a clean hearth" (*Vindication*, 325).

    71. Both Hannah More and Catherine Macaulay defend intellectual improvement on the grounds that it is far less likely to interfere with a lady's duties than is dissipation: "those hours which are spent in studious retirement by learned women, will not in all probability intrude so much on the time for useful avocation, as the wild and spreading dissipations of the present day" (Macaulay, 202); "if families *are* to be found who are

neglected through too much study in the mistress, it will probably be proved to be Hoyle, and not Homer, who has robbed her children of her time and affections" (H. More, *Strictures*, 2:150).

72. Pennington claims that a sensible woman will not become vain of her learning, since she "will soon be convinced, that all the learning her utmost application can make her a mistress of, will be, from the difference of education, in many points, inferior to that of a school-boy:—this reflection will keep her always humble . . ." (29–30).

73. Ibid., 41–42.

74. Gisborne, 213.

75. Wakefield, 89. Many women who wanted to engage in such improvement, however, found it hard to find the uninterrupted time to do so. Although a lady's whole life in one sense consisted of leisure, in another sense her time was frequently not her own. As Jane West says, explaining that "profound or abstruse learning" does not suit the female sex, "our duties in life, . . . though comparatively less important than those of men, are hourly recurring" (2:423–24). In her essay "On Needle-work" (1815), Mary Lamb laments this situation. *"Real business* and *real leisure,"* she says, "make up the portion of men's time—two sources of happiness which we certainly partake of in a very inferior degree." Women's duties, unlike men's business, have no "consoling importance attached," and women's "leisure" often consists of necessary minutiae which prevent them from even "one quarter of an hour's positive leisure." When men come home, they are fully at ease; women never are (vol. 1 of *The Works of Charles and Mary Lamb*, 7 vols. [London: Methune & Co., 1903], 177). In her letters to Elizabeth Carter, Catherine Talbot frequently complained of this eating-up of her time. "And when one looks back upon a long winter," writes Miss Talbot, "which has been filled up with unavoidable trifles that left one at the time with no leisure to reflect what they were, and to what use, the mind is presented with . . . a mere blank" (Elizaberth Carter and Catherine Talbot, *A Series of Letters Between Mrs. Elizabeth Carter and Miss Catherine Talbot, from the Year 1741 to 1770*, 1809, 4 vols. [New York: AMS Press, n.d.], 2:25). In another letter, she exclaims, "our noblest faculties, how tied down to petty attentions! and our invaluable hours, how wasted . . . upon matters of no importance, no improvement in themselves, though of the greatest when submitted to as making up the daily round of duty . . ." (2:50–51). She remarks wistfully that "sometimes I fancy solitude and leisure is all my mind wants to expand a pair of eagle's wings, and soar away nobody knows whither" (2:84–85), and she complains of required visits, when "a whole afternoon's conversation is wasted on the most uninteresting trifles" (2:217). In her poem "Petition for an Absolute Retreat," Anne Finch longs for a place free from time-wasting visitors: "No Intruders thither come! / Who visit, but to be from home . . ." (ll. 8–9). Spending their time in commended ways, it would seem, was not always for ladies a mere matter of will.

76. Pennington, 30–32.

77. Wakefield, 81–82.

78. West, 1:47.

79. Chapone, 117–18.

80. Armstrong, *Desire and Domestic Fiction*, 67.

81. Ibid., 80.

82. Ibid., 81.

83. H. More, *Complete Works*, 581.

84. Wakefield, 83.

85. Mrs. Chapone warns that those who are "willing to give money," but will not "bestow their time and consideration," often "hurt the community when they mean to do good to individuals," presumably by giving to the undeserving; and she explains

that, generally, "charity is most useful when it is appropriated to animate the industry of the young, to procure some ease and comfort to old age, and to support in sickness those whose daily labour is their only maintenance in health" (124). Similarly, Lady Pennington asserts that "the giving trifling sums *indiscriminately,* to such as appear necessitous, is far from being commendable—it is an injury to society—it is an encouragement to idleness, and helps to fill the streets with lazy beggars. . . ." "The proper objects of charity," she goes on to explain, are distressed gentlefolk and tradesmen, and "those, who, by their utmost industry, can hardly support their families above the miseries of want—or, who, by age or illness, are rendered incapable of labour. . . ." (88–89).

86. Poovey, 9.

87. Charity work also allowed a lady, without risking loss of caste, to engage in more productive labor; useful, non-ornamental sewing, for instance, was fine if done for the poor. Nancy Armstrong notes that "in allowing women to produce goods for charity when it was no longer respectable for them to produce goods for their own kin, much less for purposes of trade, the conduct books fostered a certain form of power relations that would flourish later as the welfare institutions of a modern culture developed" (*Desire and Domestic Fiction,* 92).

88. In *Familiar Violence: Gender and Social Upheaval in the Novels of Frances Burney,* Barbara Zonitch notes, "As objects of display, [women] not only brought a potentially hazardous attention to themselves; they might also learn to crave the seductive public gaze, thus sacrificing their supposedly natural proclivity for domestic life" ([Newark: University of Delaware Press, 1997]), 29).

89. Some writers express concern that fashionable dissipations render ladies unfit to be mothers in a more physical way; Wakefield, for instance, says: "The manners of our women of fashion, are but ill calculated to prevent the degeneracy of the species; . . . crowded rooms, late hours, luxurious tables, and slothful inactivity, must contribute to the production of a puny offspring, inadequate to the noble energies of patriotism and virtue" (15–16). Catherine Macaulay blames these amusements for fashionable mothers' inaptness to nurse their babies: "Can you expect that a fine lady should forgo all her amusements and enter into the sober habits of domestic life, in order to enable her to nourish her offspring with wholesome food? Can you expect that she should part with her luxuries, for fear of endangering the being she has undertaken to support?" (33).

90. Reeve, 112.

91. Lennox, 311.

92. Pennington, 38–39.

93. Gisborne, 202.

94. Other writers also represent dissipation as addictive. Hannah More, for instance, says: "It is . . . an error to fancy that the love of pleasure exhausts itself by indulgence, and that the very young are chiefly addicted to it. The contrary appears to be true. The desire grows with the pursuit . . ." (*Strictures,* 2:159). Lady Pennington warns that when amusements are pursued to excess, "they then give a distaste to every valuable employment—and, by a sort of infatuation, leave the mind in a state of restless impatience from the conclusion of one, till the commencement of another . . . " (23).

95. Gisborne, 312.

96. West, 1:269–70.

97. Wollstonecraft, *Vindication,* 334.

98. Gisborne, 312.

99. Lennox, 242.

100. Wollstonecraft, *Education of Daughters,* 45.

101. Gisborne, 197.

102. Ibid., 195.

103. West, 2:453.

104. Gisborne, 217.

105. Pennington, 45.

106. H. More, *Strictures*, 1:166.

107. Chapone, 148. Similarly, Gisborne claims that novels create "a susceptibility of impression and a premature warmth of tender emotions" (217), and Macaulay contends, "many trips to Scotland [i.e., elopements] are undoubtedly projected and executed, and many unfortunate connections formed, from the influence which novels gain over the mind" (144).

108. Perry, x.

109. And many writers do admit the value of accomplishments in fighting boredom. Maria Edgeworth, for instance, while she says somewhat scornfully that accomplishments "are supposed to increase a young lady's chance of a prize in the matrimonial lottery," says that their role as "resources against ennui" "deserves to be considered with respect," since "women are peculiarly restrained in their situation, and in their employments" (Maria Edgeworth and Richard Lovell Edgeworth, *Practical Education*, 2 vols. [London: J. Johnson, 1798], 1:522–23). Gisborne says that accomplishments are useful for supplying a lady's "hours of leisure with innocent and amusing occupations" (80); and Mrs. Chapone that "it is of great consequence to have the power of filling up agreeably those intervals of time which too often hang heavily on the hands of a woman, if her lot be cast in a retired situation" (137).

110. West, 1:292–94.

111. Wakefield, 30.

112. H. More, *Strictures*, 1:105.

113. Ibid., 2:160.

114. Ibid., 1:73–75.

115. Gisborne, 181.

116. Ibid., 112.

117. H. More, *Strictures*, 2:2.

118. Gisborne, 218.

119. Mrs. Chapone is a notable exception here: "Many are of the opinion that a very young woman can hardly be too silent and reserved in company," she notes, and grants that "certainly, nothing is so disgusting in youth as pertness and self-conceit. But," she goes on to add, "modesty should be distinguished from an awkward bashfulness, and silence should only be enjoined when it would be forward and impertinent to talk" (131).

120. Maria Edgewood, "An Essay on the Noble Science of Self-Justification," in *Letters for Literary Ladies* (London: J. Johnson, 1795), 44–45.

121. Lennox, 846.

122. Gregory, 28.

123. Ibid., 50.

124. Wetenhall Wilkes, *A Letter of Genteel and Moral Advice to a Young Lady* (Dublin: E. Jones, 1740), 107.

125. Marquess of Halifax, *Advice to a Daughter*, in *The Complete Works of George Saville, First Marquess of Halifax*, edited by Walter Raleigh (Oxford: Clarendon Press, 1912), 45.

126. Gregory, 42–43.

127. As Nancy Armstrong says in *Desire and Domestic Fiction*, "a woman's participation in public spectacle . . . injures her, for as an object of display, she always loses value as a subject" (77).

128. In *A Double Singleness: Gender and the Writings of Charles and Mary Lamb*, Jane Aaron discusses the problem of employment for "unfortunate daughters struggling to retain a foothold in the middle classes, and the possibility of marriage within that class," by becoming seamstresses, "even though they were thus reduced to worse material circumstance than they would have endured had they sought factory employment or domestic service. The tragic irony of the situation," she explains,

> was that the difficulty of ensuring a subsistence as a needlewoman meant that many were forced, through lack of employment, from the lower-middle-class status of an independent milliner or mantua-maker to the working-class position of a plain sewer or 'slop-worker' employed by a mistress, and often from thence, particularly in the middle years of the century, to prostitution, and its concomitant entire and irremediable loss, in their society's eyes, of all character and status. ([Oxford: Clarendon Press, 1991], 76–77)

129. Wollstonecraft, *Vindication*, 338.

130. Radcliffe, 436–37.

131. Armstrong, *Desire and Domestic Fiction*, 79.

132. Wakefield, 67–68.

133. Ibid., 72.

134. Lamb, 179. Aaron notes that historical evidence backs up Lamb's assertion: "Historical studies of the period do indeed indicate that a practical education would have detracted from a woman's opportunities in the upper- and middle-class marriage market: to be trained for any profession would have entailed a loss in status and marital appeal in an age in which it was considered an 'affront against nature', and an indication of her 'moral and spiritual degradation', for a woman to earn her own wages" (76).

135. Reeve, 119–20. Radcliffe censures "the vile practice of men filling such situations as seem calculated, not only to give bread to poor females, but thereby to enable them to tread the paths of virtue, and render them useful members" (409), and declares that it is "past a joke, when poor, unfortunate females are compelled to go without clothing, in order to support an army of Herculian figures at the back of a counter, displaying the beauties of a lady's bandeau, or commenting upon the device of a fan" (428).

136. Gisborne, 319.

137. Wollstonecraft, *Education of Daughters*, 25. Wollstonecraft makes the same point in her *Vindication*: "The few employments open to women, so far from being liberal, are menial . . ." (338).

138. Wollstonecraft, *Education of Daughters*, 25–26.

139. Radcliffe, 457.

140. In her study of *Mothers of the Novel: 100 Good Women Writers Before Jane Austen*, Dale Spender also comments on the similarities between these heroines, noting that in Ellen Perry, too, "the author was creating a heroine whom 'no one but myself would much like' " ([London: Pandora, 1986], 335. See pages 335–36 for a comparison of the two novels).

141. Jane Austen, *Emma* (Oxford: Oxford University Press, 1991), 3. Subsequent references to this work will be cited parenthetically in the text.

142. Mary Brunton, *Discipline* (London: Richard Bentley, 1849), 67. The pagination includes a sixty-three-page memoir of Brunton. Subsequent references to this work will be cited parenthetically in the text.

143. Several conduct-book writers specifically condemn the use of extracts, probably because they feared the readers of such volumes wanted to display a degree of learning they did not actually possess.

144. Gisborne, 220.

145. Many critics have called Emma a sort of novelist; for instance, "Emma is, admittedly, acting like a bad novelist" (Joseph Litvak, "Reading Characters: Self, Society, and the Text in *Emma*," *PMLA* 100 [1985], 767); "Emma is a bad 'novelist' who is the central subject of a great novel" (Tony Tanner, *Jane Austen* [Cambridge: Harvard University Press, 1987], 203); "Match-making is for Austen simply another word for fiction-making" (Armstrong, *Desire and Domestic Fiction*, 143); and "In *Emma* therefore an artist is portrayed in the process of creating art, the art of fiction" (Darrel Mansell, *The Novels of Jane Austen: An Interpretation* [London: Macmillan, 1974], 153).

146. Brunton's description of the shame and embarrassment Ellen suffers in trying to get her employer to pay her resembles the difficulties of the Wanderer in Burney's novel.

147. As, again, are many from whom the Wanderer seeks work.

148. Mary-Elisabeth Fowkes Tobin quotes this remark, and says it indicates "much about how Miss Nash feels about being a spinster struggling to earn her living as a teacher" (Mary-Elisabeth Fowkes Tobin, "Aiding Improverished Gentlewomen: Power and Class in *Emma*," *Criticism* 30 [1988], 69).

149. Richardson, *Pamela*, 298–300. Subsequent quotations from this work will be cited parenthetically in the text.

150. Armstrong, *Desire and Domestic Fiction*, 126.

151. Ibid.

152. This quotation is from an afternote by the "editor" which is not present in all editions of *Pamela*. It is not present in the Penguin edition from which I have been quoting, but I have found it in numerous editions of *Pamela*, for instance the two-volume 1741 London edition printed for C. Rivington, listed as the 5th edition (where the quoted lines are in volume 2, on page 395); the four-volume 1742 London edition, printed for Richardson, listed as the fourth edition, corrected (where the quoted lines are in volume 3, page 395); and the four-volume 1902 London edition, published by William Heinemann (where the quoted lines are in volume 2, on page 282).

153. Sarah Scott, *A Description of Millenium Hall* (New York: Penguin Books, 1986), 3. Subsequent quotations from this work are cited parenthetically in the text.

154. Lady Sheerness, for instance, the aunt of one of the ladies, provides a contrast to them and a catalog of bad, worldly, idle behavior. A "victim to dissipation and the love of fashionable pleasures," and "destitute of any stable principles," Lady Sheerness was "carried full sail down the stream of folly. In the love of coquetry and gaming few excelled her; no one could exceed her in the pursuit of every trifling amusement . . ." (126). Even when she was "seized with a lingering, but incurable disorder," Lady Sheerness employed her time exclusively in trifles, insisting on playing cards constantly, lest she be left "a moment's time for reflection" (140). "[S]eized with a fainting-fit at the card-table," Lady Sheerness died—"departed to a world of which she had never thought and for which she was totally unprepared" (142). Another idle lady, it is interesting to note, expires similarly in *Discipline*. Ellen meets her former friend Juliet, now reduced to poverty (through an unwise private marriage to an unscrupulous gentleman), abandoned, and consumptive, and takes her in. Juliet, even as she lies dying, refuses to employ her time or mind seriously. Ellen attempts to turn Juliet's attention toward higher thoughts: "I had seen the inanity of her life; I had, alas! shared in her mad neglect of all the serious duties, of all the best hopes of man; and I did not dare to see her die in this portentous lethargy of soul" (430). Ellen is unable to undo the habits of an idle and frivolous lifetime, though, and poor Juliet sinks unredeemed into her grave.

155. H. More, *Complete Works*, 2:333. Subsequent references to this work will be cited parenthetically in the text.

156. Gregory, 28.

157. Burney, 73. Subsequent quotations from this work are cited parenthetically in the text.

158. Zonitch makes the interesting point that Mrs. Ireton is also cruel to her slave, threatening to ship him back to the West Indies "to face brutal punishment." Zonitch argues that through her treatment of Juliet and of the slave, Mrs. Ireton shows herself to support "the principles of patrilineage and colonialism, in short, institutions that victimize the other" (120).

159. Pennington, vii.

160. As Jane West says, "Adventures *rarely* happen to a prudent woman, and *never* without injury to her reputation" (2:450).

4. AN EMPIRE OF DEGENERATED PEOPLES

1. Mary Louise Pratt, *Imperial Eyes: Travel Writing and Transculturation* (London: Routledge, 1992), 16.

2. Ibid., 24.

3. Ibid., 36.

4. Ibid.

5. Ibid.

6. Kathleen Wilson, *The Sense of the People: Politics, Culture and Imperialism in England, 1715–1785* (New York: Cambridge University Press, 1991), 38.

7. I should point out here that, while some of the texts to which I will be referring in this chapter were written by non-British writers, all were quickly translated into English and published in England, and ideas and influences moved between European countries quite readily.

8. Or, as Mary Louise Pratt says more poetically of the writings about the La Condamine expeditions, "Oral texts, written texts, lost texts, secret texts, texts appropriated, abridged, translated, anthologized, and plagiarized; letters, reports, survival tales, civic description, navigational narrative, monsters and marvels, medicinal treatises, academic polemics, old myths replayed and reversed—the La Condamine corpus illustrates the varied profile of travel-related writing on the frontiers of European expansion at mid-eighteenth century" (23).

9. Ibid.

10. Anne Fausto-Sterling describes well this tangled relationship between science, commerce, and empire:

> The investigations were, to be sure, part of the history of biology and, especially, a component of the movement to catalogue and classify all the living creatures of the earth. But this movement was in turn embedded in the process of European capitalist expansion. Not only did traders and conquerors, by collecting from around the world, create the need for a classification project, they also required the project to justify continued expansion, colonialism, and slavery. Further entangling the matter, the vast capital used to build the museums and house the collections came for the economic exploitations of non-European goods—both human and otherwise. ("Gender, Race, and Nation: The Comparative Anatomy of 'Hottentot' Women in Europe, 1815–1817," in *Deviant Bodies: Critical Perspective on Difference in Science and Popular Culture*, edited by Jennifer Terry and Jacqueline Urla [Bloomington, IN: Indiana University Press, 1995], 39–40)

11. William Guthrie, *A New Geographical, Historical, and Commercial Grammar; and Present State of the Several Kingdoms of the World* (London: Charles Dilly, 1785), p. 9 of the preface.

12. "Hottentot," was, of course, a name that Europeans gave to the people who lived near the Cape of Good Hope—the people who called themselves the Khoekhoe, which means, in their language, "men of men." "Hottentot" is now considered an offensive term, but, since it was the one used in the eighteenth century and carries important connotations, I will be using it in this essay.

Eighteenth-century usage was rather imprecise, and so the term "Bushman" was sometimes used interchangeably with "Hottentot," although some writers make a distinction between the two groups. The "Bushmen," more correctly known as the Khoisan or !Kung, were, as Anne Fausto-Sterling explains in her article "Gender, Race, and Nation: The Comparative Anatomy of 'Hottentot' Women in Europe, 1815–1817," "a physically similar but culturally distinct people who lived contiguously with the Khoikhoi" (22). Since I am writing not about these peoples as they were but as they were constructed by European writers, I will accept the terms the writers used, although they may be inaccurate.

For more information about the Khoekhoe, see also Linda Merians, "What They Are, Who We Are: Representations of the 'Hottentot' in Eighteenth-Century Britain," in *Eighteenth-Century Life* 17.3 (1993), especially pages 16–17, and Merian's full-length study of "Hottentots," *Envisioning the Worst: Representations of "Hottentots" in Early-Modern England* (Newark: University of Delaware Press, 2001), especially the introduction. *Envisioning the Worst* (which came out just as my book was going to press) is an extremely interesting study of how the early-modern British constructed the "Hottentot" as "humanity's worst" and and how this construction helped them to construct "themselves as humanity's best" (Merians, *Envisioning*, 14).

13. John Ovington, *A Voyage to Surat in the Year 1689*, 1696, edited by H. G. Rawlinson (London: Oxford University Press, 1929), 284. I am grateful to Merians's article "What They Are, Who We Are" for drawing my attention to this text.

14. John Barrow, *An Account of Travels into the Interior of Southern Africa in the Years 1797 and 1798*, 1804, 2 vols. (New York: Johnson Reprint Co., 1968), 1:151.

15. Peter Kolb, *The Present State of the Cape of Good-Hope, Or, A particular Account of the Several Nations of the Hottentots . . .*, translated by "Mr. Medley," 1731, 2 vols. (New York: Johnson Reprint Corp., 1968), 1:97. For an interesting and informative discussion of the reception and influence of Kolb's *Present State*, see Merian's *Envisioning the Worst*, pp. 152–67.

16. William Dampier, *A New Voyage Round the World*, 1697 (London: Argonaut Press, 1927), 360.

17. Francois Leguat, *The Voyage of Francois Leguat of Bresse to Rodriguez, Mauritius, Java, and the Cape of Good Hope*, 1698, edited by Captain Pasfield Oliver, 2nd edition, 2 vols. (London: Printed for the Hakluyt Society, 1891), 2:287.

18. Edward Long, *The History of Jamaica*, 3 vol., 1744 (London: Frank Cass & Co., Ltd., 1970), 2:378.

19. John Matthews, *A Voyage to the River Sierra-Leone, on the Coast of Africa* (London: Printed for B. White and Son, 1788), 63.

20. William Hacke, *A Collection of Original Voyages*, 1699 (Delmar, NY: Scholars' Facsimiles and Reprints, 1993), 36.

21. Leguat, 2:288.

22. Robert Percival, *An Account of the Cape of Good Hope*, 1795 (New York: Negro Universities Press, n.d.), 85.

23. Kolb, 1:49–50.

24. Francois Le Vaillant, *Travels from the Cape of Good-Hope into the Interior Parts of Africa . . .*, 1790 (London: Johnson Reprint Corp., 1972), 50. For more on Le Vaillant's "noble savage" view of the Hottentot's see Merian's *Envisioning the Worst*, p. 171.

25. Barrow, 1:154.

26. Ibid., 1:155.

27. Leguat, 2:291.

28. J. M. Coetzee, *White Writing: On the Culture of Letters in South Africa* (New Haven, CT: Yale University Press, 1988), 22. Italics Coetzee's.

29. Leguat, 2:292.

30. Ovington, 287–88.

31. Kolb, 1:112–15.

32. Leguat, 2:289–90.

33. Ibid., 2:292.

34. William Ten Rhyne, *An Account of the Cape of Good Hope and the Hottentots* . . . in *A Collection of Voyages and Travels* . . . , 1685, edited by Awnsham and John Churchill, vol. 4 (London: Awnsham and Churchill, 1704), 115.

35. Merians points out also that descriptions of the women's sexual "abnormalities" might be intended to discourage Europeans from having sex with them ("What They Are, Who We Are," 28–29). In *Imperial Leather: Race, Gender, and Sexuality in the Colonial Context*, Anne McClintock says, "By the nineteenth century, popular lore had firmly established Africa as the quintessential zone of sexual aberration and anomaly" ([New York: Routledge, 1995], 22).

36. Merians, "What They Are, Who We Are," 28.

37. Andrew [Anders] Sparrman, *A Voyage to the Cape of Good Hope . . . from the Year 1772, to 1776*, 1786, 2 vols. (New York: Johnson Reprint Corp., 1971), 1:182.

38. Merians, "What They Are, Who We Are," 24.

39. Anthony J. Barker mentions that "laziness [is] mentioned in virtually every work on Africa" (Anthony Barker, *The African Link: British Attitudes to the Negro in the Era of the Atlantic Slave Trace, 1550–1807* [London: Frank Cass and Co. Ltd., 1978], 98).

40. Kolb, 1:46.

41. William Bosman, *A New and Accurate Description of the Coast of Guinea*, 1705 (New York: Barnes and Noble, n.d.), 117.

42. Matthew, 96.

43. Dampier, 362.

44. Barrow, 1:152.

45. O. F. Mentzel, *A Geographical and Topographpical Description of the Cape of Good Hope*, trans. H. J. Mandelbrote, 1785, 2 vols. (Cape Town: Van Riebeeck Society, 1925), 2:264.

46. Ibid., 2:276.

47. William J. Burchell, *Travels in the Interior of Southern Africa*, 1822, edited by J. Schera, 2 vols. (London: Batchworth Press, n.d.), 2:48.

48. Ibid., 2:205.

49. Percival, 85.

50. Henri Gregoire, *An Enquiry Concerning the Intellectual and Moral Faculties and Literature of Negroes* . . . , 1810, trans. D. B. Warden (College Park, MD: McGrath Publishing Co., 1967), 90.

51. James Ramsey, *Objections to the Slave Trade, with Answers* (Miami, FL: Mnemosyne Publishing Co., 1969), 51.

52. Thomas Clarkson, *An Essay on the Slavery and Commerce of the Human Species, Particularly the African* . . . , 1786 (Miami, FL: Mnemoysne Publishing Co., 1969), 92–93.

53. See Mark M. Smith's interesting book *Mastered by the Clock: Time, Slavery, and Freedom in the American South* for a discussion of African concepts of time (Mark M. Smith, *Mastered by the Clock: Time, Slavery, and Freedom in the American South* [Chapel Hill, NC: University of North Carolina Press, 1997], 132–33).

54. Philip D. Curtin, *The Image of Africa: British Ideas and Action, 1780–1850* (Madison: University of Wisconsin Press, 1964), 224. See Barker for a discussion of the difficulty of year-round agricultural work in most areas of Africa ([London: Frank Cass and Co. Ltd., 1978], 111–12).

55. McClintock, 253. McClintock also makes the important point that "the discourse on idleness was not a monolithic discourse imposed on a hapless people. Rather it was a realm of contestation, marked with the stubborn refusal of Africans to alter their customs of work as well as by conflicts within the white communities" (ibid.). In this way as well as in others, the racial discourse of idleness resembles the class discourse of idleness that I discuss in my second chapter.

56. For more on this notion of "tropical exuberance" and its effects on beliefs about Africans, see chapter 3 of Curtin's *The Image of Africa* (58–87).

57. For just one example among many, see John Stewart's *Account of Jamaica, and Its Inhabitants*: "As to labour, the fact is, that a poor peasant or labourer in Great Britain, performs twice the quantum usually performed by an able Negro. But when we come to compare their respective situations (and keep but the name and idea of slavery out of the question), that of the latter has in many respects decidedly the preference" (John Stewart, *An Account of Jamaica, and Its Inhabitants* [London: Longman, Hurst, Rees, and Orme, 1808), 218).

58. J. P. L. Durand, *A Voyage to Senegal: Or, Historical, Philosophical, and Political Memoirs . . .* (London: Printed for Richard Phillips by J. G. Barnard, 1806), 87–88.

59. Lord Henry Broughham, *An Inquiry into the Colonial Policy of the European Powers*, 1803, 2 vols. (New York: Augustus M. Kelley, Publishers, 1970), 2:415.

60. Thomas Atwood, *The History of the Islands of Dominica . . .*, 1791 (London: Frank Cass and Co. Ltd., 1971), 272.

61. Barker, 160.

62. Long, 3:353.

63. Ibid., 3:404–5.

64. Ibid., 3:7.

65. For a discussion of this notion of white incapacity for labor in hot climates see Barker (62 and 165).

66. Thomas Salmon, *A New Geographical and Historical Grammar; Containing the True Astronomical and Geographical Knowledge of the Terraqueous Globe . . .* (London: C. Bathurst et al., 1772), 430.

67. Robert Orme, *Historical Fragments of the Mogul Empire* (London: F. Wingrave, 1805), 409.

68. Ibid., 423.

69. Ibid., 425.

70. For more about this school of thought that saw Indians as passive and lazy, see Chatterjee (Amal Chatterjee, *Representations of India, 1740–1840: The Creation of India in the Colonial Imagination* [New York: St. Martin's Press, 1998], 149–52 and 155).

71. Ibid., 152. For a further discussion of ideas about the Indian climate and its enervating effects, see Marshall and Williams, chapter 5: "Asia and the Progress of Civil Society" (P. J. Marshall and Glyndwr Williams, *The Great Map of Mankind: British Perceptions of the World in the Age of Enlightenment* [London: J. M. Dent & Sons Ltd., 1982] 128–54).

72. Alexander Dow, "A Dissertation on the Origin and Nature of Despotism in Hindostan," in *The History of Indostan*, vol. 3, 1770 (New Delhi: Today and Tomorrow's Printers and Publishers, 1973), viii.

73. Orme, *Historical Fragments*, 472.

74. Dow, vii.

75. William Tennant, *Indian Recreations: Consisting Chiefly of Strictures on the Domestic and Rural Economy of the Mahomedans and Hindoos*, 2nd edition (London: Longman, Hurst, Rees, and Orme, 1804), 297.

76. Ibid., 102–3.

77. The Abbe Raynal, *A Philosophical and Political History of the Settlements and Trade of the Europeans in the East and West Indies*, 14 books, trans. J. O. Justamond (London: A Strahan and T. Cadell, 1783), Book 1, vol. 1, 93.

78. Luke Scrafton, *Reflections on the Government of Indostan* (London: G. Kearsley and T. Cadell, 1770), 16.

79. Dow, xvi.

80. Richard Owen Cambridge, *An Account of the War in India, Between the English and French, on the Coast of Coromandel, from the Year 1750 to the Year 1760* (London: T. Jeffrey, 1761), xiii.

81. Robert Orme, *A History of the Military Transactions of the British Nation, in Indostan, from the Year MDCCXLV* (London: John Nourse, 1763), 5.

82. Richard H. Popkin, "The Philosophical Basis of Eighteenth-Century Racism," *Studies in Eighteenth-Century Culture*, vol. 3 (Cleveland: Press of Case Western Reserve University, 1973), 248.

83. Marshall and Williams, 238; Barker, 111–12.

84. Popkin, 249.

85. Samuel Stanhope Smith, *An Essay on the Causes of the Variety of Complexion and Figure in the Human Species*, 1810 (Cambridge, Mass.: Belknap Press, 1965), 21.

86. Ibid., 61.

87. Henry Home, Lord Kames, *Sketches of the History of Man*, 1774 (Edinburgh: William Creech, and Bell and Bradfute, 1813), 16–17.

88. Also alarming to the colonialist project, and perhaps more largely to capitalism, is Kames's statement that "Riches produce another lamentable effect: they enervate the possessor, and degrade him into a coward" (334). Although Kames has earlier praised private property and money, since "Without private property there would be no industry, and without industry, men would remain savages for ever" and "Money prompts men to be industrious" (97), his claim that a lot of money enervates might unnerve the many who go to the colonies in order to amass a fortune. Not only is the climate likely to render them indolent, but so even is their financial success. His many associations of indolence and savagery throughout the work (see 276–77, for instance), also, makes disturbing the idea that riches cause indolence: does that mean that riches might cause savagery? Kames recommends a sort of golden mean, praising as ideal that climate that is neither barren (which will render the inhabitants "meagre, patient, and timid") nor overfertile (which will make the inhabitants "pampered, lazy, and effeminate") (400). However, colonialism (and capitalism in general) seeks not moderation, but accumulation.

89. Smith, 190.

90. Kames, 400.

91. Johann Friedrich Blumenbach, *On the Natural Varieties of Mankind*, 1775 (New York: Bergman Publishers, 1969), 269.

92. Smith, 106n.

93. Buffon is the only major theorist I have found who suggests otherwise: he claims that "if a colony of Negroes were transplanted into a northern province, their descendants of the eighth, tenth, or twelfth generation would be much fairer, and perhaps as white as the natives of that climate" (Comte de [Georges-Louis Leclerk] Buffon, "From *A Natural History, General and Particular*," in *Race and the Enlightenment: A Reader*, edited by Emmanuel Chukwudi Eze [Cambridge, MA: Blackwell Publishers,

1997], 24). However, the idea of racial instability is still troubling to people who want to see their racially superior identity as immutable.

94. Also, often, these late-period accounts represent the Hottentots as having degenerated, not from a long-ago white level of refinement, but from the state they were in before the Dutch colonized their land. Writers like Barrow and Percival tend to blame many of the shortcomings of the Hottentots on the degrading influence of the Dutch. Even when reporting the small ethnographic details earlier writers often focused on, these later writers see a decline from earlier, purer Hottentot culture. Reporting on the rings worn round the women's legs, for instance, Barrow (after claiming that they never were made of guts) says that now, instead of simple leather, women want ones made of beads, and he links this to European-inspired degeneration. He laments that this "immoderate rage for dress" has "accelerated the ruin of their husbands, which they themselves had brought on by as strong a rage for ardent spirits and tobacco" (which were, of course, European introductions) (154).

95. John Campbell, *Travels in South Africa*, 1815 (Cape Town: C. Struik Ltd., 1974), 81.

96. Sir James Edward Alexander, *An Expedition of Discovery into the Interior of Africa*, 1838, 2 vols., (New york: Johnson Reprint Co., 1967), 1:28.

97. Barrow, 1:76–77.

98. Ibid., 1:77–78.

99. Percival, 204–5.

100. Anne Barnard, *The Cape Journals of Lady Anne Barnard 1797–1798*, edited by A. M. Lewin Robinson, Margaret Lenta, and Dorothy Driver (Cape Town: Van Riebeeck Society, 1994), 356.

101. Percival, 232.

102. Mentzel, 2:120.

103. Ibid., 2:115.

104. Bryan Edwards, *The History, Civil and Commercial, of the British Colonies in the West Indies*, 4 vols. (Dublin: Luke White, 1793), 4:15.

105. Ibid., 4:12.

106. Stewart, 156.

107. Ibid., 167.

108. Long, 2:280.

109. Ibid., 2:279. In his essay "Reluctant Creoles: The Planters' World in the British West Indies," Michael Craton says that this idea of the indolent Creole lady does not end with Long: "Many commentators echoed Edward Long in denigrating the indolence, inanity, and drawling accents of the planters' ladies . . ." (in *Strangers With the Realm: Cultural Margins of the First British Empire*, edited by Bernard Bailyn and Philip D. Morgan [Chapel Hill, NC: University of North Carolina Press, 1991], 354).

110. Long, 2:280.

111. Benjamin Moseley, *A Treatise on Tropical Diseases; on Military Operations; and on the Climate of the West-Indies*, 1787 (London: T. Cadell, 1792), 80–81.

112. Raynal, Book 11, vol. 5:339–40.

113. Scrafton, 30.

114. Ibid., 21.

115. Kate Teltscher makes the astute observation that in this sentence "Macintosh's grammar begins to break down: there is no subject and the verb is unexpectedly passive; a construction which serves to highlight the sense of an unmanly loss of agency" (*India Inscribed: European and British Writing on India 1600–1800* [Delhi: Oxford University Press, 1995], 163).

116. William Mackintosh, *Travels in Europe, Asia, and Africa*, 2 vols. (London: J. Murray, 1782), 2:215–16.

117. Teltscher cites this scene, as I do, as an example of "effeminate degeneracy." She also makes the amusing point that quail-fights are "a kind of eastern parody of cock-fights, particularly because of the cowardly associations of the birds' names" (112).

118. Cambridge, xxviii.

119. Tennant, 78.

120. Percival, 92.

121. Ibid., 93.

122. Ibid., 93–94.

123. James Eli Adams, *Dandies and Desert Saints: Styles of Victorian Masculinity*, (Ithaca, NY: Cornell University Press, 1995), 5.

124. Ibid., 6.

125. Ibid., 4.

5. "DRIVING ON THE SYSTEM OF LIFE"

1. W. Jackson Bate, *The Achievement of Samuel Johnson* (Chicago: University of Chicago Press, 1995), 24.

2. Given how often this concern with idleness appears in Johnson's writing and conversation, it seems odd that (to my knowledge, at least) there are no sustained discussions of Johnson and idleness. Martin Wechselblatt's recent *Bad Behavior: Samuel Johnson and Modern Cultural Authority* does devote part of a chapter to a section titled "Idleness and Vacuity," but as it is only six pages long, it does not go into the subject very thoroughly, although it makes some interesting points ([Lewisburg: Bucknell University Press, 1998], 143–49).

3. Ibid., 146–47.

4. See, for instance, *Rambler* 147 (Samuel Johnson, *The Rambler*, 3 vols. [New Haven: Yale University Press, 1969], 5:18) and *Rasselas* chapter xxvi (Samuel Johnson, *Rasselas and Other Tales* [New Haven: Yale University Press, 1990], 16:98). The numerals before the colons in the citations refer to volumes of the Yale edition of the works of Johnson.

5. Samuel Johnson, *Sermons* [New Haven: Yale University Press, 1978], 14:282.

6. Johnson, *Rambler*, 4:86.

7. Ibid., 5:172.

8. Johnson quotes him in the *Dictionary* (see "scruples") and discusses him with Boswell (James Boswell, *Life of Johnson*, 6 vols. [Oxford: Oxford University Press, 1987], 4, 294).

9. Jeremy Taylor, *The Rule and Exercises of Holy Living*, 1650 (London: Bell and Daldy, 1857), 7.

10. Ibid., 100.

11. Robert Voitle also notes this in *Samuel Johnson the Moralist*: "The thought of this boredom, this vacuity of life which always must be filled, often was in itself more appalling to Johnson than some of the vices bred by it" ([Cambridge, MA: Harvard University Press, 1961], 137).

12. Johnson, *The Idler and the Adventurer* (New Haven: Yale University Press, 1963), 2:11.

13. Paul Fussell, *Samuel Johnson and the Life of Writing* (New York: Harcourt, Brace, Jovanovich, 1971), 236.

14. Ibid., 237.

15. Ibid.

16. Johnson, *Rasselas*, 16:11.

17. Ibid., 16:13.

18. Ibid.

19. Ibid., 16:16.

20. Patricia Meyer Spacks notes that "Johnson's fullest exploration of boredom . . . occurs in *Rasselas*" (*Boredom: The Literary History of a State of Mind* [Chicago: University of Chicago Press, 1995], 46). She also makes the good point that, for Johnson, "the tendency to be bored despite the abundant stimulation the world provides, despite the need to labor for a reward in heaven, becomes a manifestation of fundamental human perversity" (ibid., 50).

21. Johnson, *Rasselas*, 16:21.

22. Johnson, *Rambler*, 3:230.

23. Johnson, *Idler*, 2:67.

24. Ibid.

25. See Mrs. Thrale's *Anecdotes of Dr. Johnson* (Hester Lynch Thrale Piozzi, *Anecdotes of the Late Samuel Johnson, LL.D.*, 1786 [London: Oxford University Press, 1974], 76).

26. Johnson, *Rambler*, 4:347.

27. Johnson, *Rasselas*, 16:211–12.

28. Samuel Johnson, *Diaries, Prayers, and Annals* (New Haven: Yale University Press, 1958), 1:47.

29. Ibid., 1:316.

30. Johnson, *Rasselas*, 16:146.

31. Ibid., 16:151–52.

32. Ibid., 16:152.

33. Ibid.

34. Ibid., 16:153.

35. Johnson, *Idler*, 2:101.

36. Johnson, *Rasselas*, 16:150.

37. Henry William Edmund Petty Fitzmaurice, 6th Marquis of Lansdowne, editor, *The Queeney Letters: Being Letters Addressed to Hester Maria Thrale by Doctor Johnson, Fanny Burney, and Mrs. Thrale-Piozzi* (London: Cassell and Company, 1934), 35.

38. Johnson, *Rambler*, 4:106.

39. Boswell, 4, 208.

40. Johnson, *Rasselas*, 16:161.

41. Ibid., 16:161–62.

42. For a discussion of the history of this notion see chapter 4 of Arieh Sachs's *Passionate Intelligence* (Baltimore: Johns Hopkins University Press, 1967).

43. And indeed these exhortations are numerous. Even in a sweet letter to a child Johnson stresses the importance of continual occupation; in writing to Jenny Langton, his seven-year-old godchild, he says: "I am glad, my dear, to see that you write so well, and hope that you mind your pen, your book, and your needle, for they are all necessary. Your books will give you knowledge, and make you respected; and your needle will find you useful employment when you do not care to read" (Boswell, 4, 271).

44. Ibid., 2, 2.

45. Johnson, *Idler*, 2:226–27.

46. Johnson, *Rambler*, 4:86–87.

47. Boswell, 2, 121.

48. Ibid., 3, 415.

49. See, for instance, Bate (*Achievement*, 48), Sachs (14 and 59–61), Alkon (Paul K. Alkon, *Samuel Johnson and Moral Discipline* [Evanston, IL.: Northwestern University Press, 1967] 100–4), Irwin (George Irwin, *Samuel Johnson: A Personality in Conflict* [New

Zealand: Auckland University Press, 1971], 72–74), and Charles E. Pierce, Jr., *(The Religious Life of Samuel Johnson* [Hamden, CT.: Archon Books, 1983], 91).

50. Robert Burton, *The Anatomy of Melancholy*, 1621 (New York: Tudor Publishing Co., 1968).

51. Johnson evidently took milk in his tea, since he speaks of not doing so on fast days, and he wrote in a letter that he had "a voracious delight in raw summer fruit" (Boswell, 4, 353).

52. Burton, 460.

53. Boswell, 1, 72.

54. Piozzi, *Anecdotes*, 87.

55. Boswell, 3, 398.

56. Johnson, *Diaries*, 1:118–19.

57. Ibid., 1:278.

58. Ibid., 1:362.

59. Although at another time Johnson acknowledges that trifles are not always sufficient in times of real trouble; when the Thrales's only son dies suddenly, he says that Mr. Thrale will recover from his grief before Mrs. Thrale: "No, Sir, Thrale will forget it first. *She* has many things that she *may* think of. *He* has many things that he *must* think of" (Boswell 2, 470).

60. Ibid., 3, 242.

61. Ibid., 1, 474.

62. Ibid., 2, 440.

63. Ibid., 3, 176.

64. Piozzi, 135–36.

65. Jeremy Taylor also notes that busyness may cover idleness: "For a man may be very idly busy, and take great pains to so little purpose, that in his labors and expense of time he shall serve no end but of folly and vanity" (9).

66. Johnson, *Rambler*, 3:275–76.

67. Johnson, *Idler*, 2:60.

68. Ibid., 61.

69. Ibid., 62.

70. For instance, see *Rambler* 82, for a letter from the virtuoso Quisquilius, who has spent his life (and his entire fortune) collecting such treasures as "the longest blade of grass upon record" (4:67), "a snail that has crawled upon the wall of China" (4:69), and "sand scraped from the coffin of King Richard" (ibid.); and *Idler* 33, for a bit of the diary of an academic, recording activities like "Mended a pen. Looked at my weather glass again" (2:102), and "Returned home, and stirred my fire" (2:103), and such pithy observations as "Too much water in the soup. Dr. Dry always orders the beef to be salted too much for me" (ibid.). See also *Idler* 35, recounting the "pernicious activity" of an inveterate "buyer of bargains" (2:109), whose life's "great care" it is "that the pieces of beef should be boiled in the order in which they are bought; that the second bag of pease shall not be opened till the first are eaten, that every feather-bed shall be lain on in its turn, that the carpets should be taken out of the chests once a month and brushed," and so on (2:110–11).

71. Piozzi, 76.

72. Johnson, *Idler*, 2:96.

73. Ibid., 2:97–98.

74. Ibid., 2:98.

75. Johnson, *Idler* 17, 2:54.

76. Johnson, *Idler* 48, 2:150.

77. Johnson, *Rambler*, 4:187.

78. Johnson, *Sermon* 4, 14:44.
79. Johnson, *Sermon* 10, 14:113.
80. Johnson, *Sermon* 11, 14:125.
81. Johnson, *Sermon* 15, 14:161.
82. Johnson, *Sermon* 25, 14:263.
83. Johnson, *Poems*, 6:306.
84. Ibid., 6:293.
85. Johnson, *Diaries*, 1:81.
86. Ibid., 1:152.
87. Ibid., 1:160.
88. Ibid., 1:224.
89. Ibid., 1:296.
90. Ibid., 1:305. Note also the poignant scene in Boswell's *Life*, when Johnson's friends were urging him to publish a book of prayers; he called out "in great agitation," "Do not talk thus of what is so aweful. I know not what time God will allow me in this world. There are many things which I wish to do." Some of them still persisted, and Johnson cried, "Let me alone, let me alone; I am overpowered." Then he "put his hands before his face, and reclined for some time upon the table" (4, 294).
91. Boswell, 2, 57.
92. Johnson, *Diaries*, 1:118.
93. Johnson, *Sermons*, 14:161.
94. Ibid., 14:164.
95. In *The Religious Life of Samuel Johnson*, Charles E. Pierce Jr. also notes the literal way Johnson thinks of working out his salvation: "The aim of human life, as Johnson came to understand it, was . . . to work out his salvation, in the literal sense of that phrase" (109).
96. Boswell, 4, 299.
97. Voitle, 167.
98. Johnson, *Rambler* 41, 3:225.
99. 99. Johnson, *Rambler* 127, 4:315.
100. Johnson, *Rambler* 71, 4:11. In *Rambler* 108, Johnson gives a more secular version of this notion: "An Italian philosopher expressed in his motto, that 'time was his estate'; an estate, indeed, which will produce nothing without cultivation, but will always abundantly repay the labors of industry . . ." (4:214).
101. Johnson, *Diaries*, 1:49.
102. Ibid., 1:225.
103. Ibid., 1:125.
104. Ibid., 1:70.
105. Ibid., 1:38; also see 64 and 99.
106. Ibid., 1:42.
107. Ibid., 1:48; also see 49, 262, and 358.
108. Ibid., 1:48, 107, 306.
109. Ibid., 1:48.
110. Ibid., 1:111.
111. It is interesting to note that Sir Matthew Hale, whom Johnson discussed with Boswell (Boswell 2, 158 and 2, 344), wrote a devotional work entitled "The Great Audit."
112. Paul Fussell also notes Johnson's awareness of his abilities: "From the beginning, he knew that he was extraordinarily gifted with literary talent" (94). So also does Charles E. Pierce Jr.: "And Johnson had realized from an early age, owing largely to the reactions of his parents and teachers, that he did possess remarkable abilities, not

the least of which were a near photographic memory, extraordinary powers of concentration, great intellectual curiosity, and an admirable capacity to grasp abstract principles" (105).

113. For other discussions of Johnson and the parable of the talents see Fussell, pages 94–102, 130, and 253; and Pierce, pages 105–9. Bate also mentions Johnson's preoccupation with it: "throughout his life he was always thinking of the parable of the talents in the Bible" (*SJ*, 232).

114. Johnson, *Diaries*, 1:41.

115. Ibid., 1:50.

116. Boswell, 3, 22.

117. Bate, *SJ*, 271.

118. Boswell, 1, 417.

119. Bate, *SJ*, 271.

120. Bate, *SJ*, 271. For more information about Levet and a good discussion of the poem, see chapter 6 of John Wiltshire's interesting and useful *Samuel Johnson and the Medical World: The Doctor and the Patient*, (Cambridge: Cambridge University Press, 1991), 195–222.

121. Samuel Johnson, *Poems* (New Haven: Yale University Press, 1964), 6:314–15.

122. Fussell also feels Johnson is contrasting in this poem Levet's and his own use of talents: "What this glance at the Parable of the Talents implies is Johnson's awareness of the multiplicity of his own talents, which contrast so strikingly with Levet's single one" (130).

123. Boswell, 4, 427.

124. Piozzi, 68.

125. Ibid.

126. Johnson, *Rambler*, 4:44.

127. Ibid., 5:57.

128. Johnson, *Diaries*, 1:82.

129. Ibid., 1:92–93.

130. Ibid., 1:106.

131. Ibid., 1:146.

132. Ibid., 1:158–59.

133. Piozzi, 101.

134. Johnson, *Diaries*, 1:143.

135. Voitle, 139.

136. Boswell argues that Johnson's guilt was excessive, quoting the same passage about his "nocturnal complaints" as "surely a sufficient excuse" for late sleeping, and adding, "Alas! how hard it would be if this indulgence were to be imputed to a sick man as a crime." Boswell goes on to say that he feels early rising was "very difficult, and in my opinion almost constitutionally impossible" for Johnson, and that Johnson "had fair ground enough to have quieted his mind on this subject, by concluding that he was physically incapable of what is at best only a commodious regulation" (2, 143).

137. For a discussion of Law's influence on Johnson, see Katherine C. Balderston's "Doctor Johnson and William Law," *PLMA* 75 (1960): 382–94.

138. Boswell, 1, 68.

139. William Law, *A Serious Call to a Devout and Holy Life*, 1729 (New York: Paulist Press, 1978), 189.

140. Ibid.

141. Ibid., 190.

142. Ibid., 192.

143. Ibid., 191.

144. Ibid., 195.

145. Ibid., 196.

146. Bate, *SJ*, 377.

147. Johnson, *Idler*, 2:99

148. Ibid., 2:100.

149. Johnson, *Idler* 40, 2:351.

150. Johnson, *Idler* 33, 2:100.

151. Johnson, *Diaries*, 1:56.

152. Boswell, 2, 17.

153. Johnson, *Diaries*, 1:77–78.

154. Ibid., 1:92.

155. Ibid., 1:119.

156. Ibid., 1:121.

157. Ibid., 1:264.

158. Ibid., 1:267.

159. Ibid., 1:291–92.

160. Ibid., 1:294.

161. Boswell, 2, 22.

162. Johnson, *Rasselas*, 16:111.

163. Johnson, *Rambler*, 3:9.

164. Johnson, *Rambler*, 3:162. Johnson makes comic use of this notion in *Rasselas*, when he has Rasselas, upset that he has wasted time, spend "four months in resolving to lose no more time in idle resolves" (16:20).

165. Johnson, *Sermons*, 14:163.

166. Johnson, *Rambler*, 3:221.

167. Johnson, *Rambler*, 5:291.

168. Johnson, *Rasselas*, 16:112.

169. As Alkon puts it, it is a "culpable violation of the obligation, imposed upon us by God, to carry out our share of the tasks of this world" (152).

170. Johnson, *Rambler* 207, 5:310.

171. Johnson, *Sermons*, 14:150.

172. Johnson, *Rambler* 89, 4:105.

173. Johnson, *Rambler* 111, 4:227.

174. Johnson, *Rambler* 108, 4:211.

175. Johnson, *Rambler* 180, 5:184.

176. Johnson, *Rambler* 201, 5:286.

177. Johnson, *Rambler* 204, 5:298.

178. Johnson, *Rambler* 207, 5:310.

179. Sachs makes the good point that "our natural need to stop time, to rest in an immutable X that will not slip through our fingers, leads us to idealize scenes of the past in precisely the way we imaginatively transform the future 'prospects' of expectation into seemingly absolute satisfactions" (43).

180. And many modern critics have also commented on Johnson and vacuity. For instance, see the first chapter of Sachs's *Passionate Intelligence* and pages 98 through 101 in Isobel Grundy's *Samuel Johnson and the Scale of Greatness*, where she makes the point that Johnson gives the impression he "was more strongly repelled by the idea of passing our time in nothingness than in wickedness" ([Leicester: Leicester University Press, 1986], 100).

181. Piozzi, 111.

182. Bate, *Achievement*, 64.

183. Johnson, *Rambler*, 3:41.

184. Johnson, *Rambler*, 4:268.
185. Johnson, *Rambler* 134, 4:348.
186. Johnson, *Idler* 3, 2:11.
187. Johnson, *Rambler*, 3:231.
188. Johnson, *Idler*, 2:93.
189. Johnson, *Rasselas*, 16:127.
190. Johnson, *Sermons*, 14:150.
191. Johnson, *Poems*, 6:264.
192. Ibid., 6:165.
193. Johnson, *Idler*, 2:96.
194. Johnson, *Idler*, 2:77.
195. Boswell, 4, 112.
196. For discussions of this fear, see Pierce, pages 37 and 38; Voitle, pages 164 to 167; and Watkins, pages 80 to 84 (W. B. C. Watkins, *Perilous Balance* [Princeton: Princeton University Press, 1939]).
197. Alvin Kernan, *Samuel Johnson and the Impact of Print* (Princeton: Princeton University Press, 1987), 145.
198. Sir Joshua Reynolds, *Portraits*, edited by Frederick W. Hilles (New York: McGraw-Hill, 1952), 78–79.
199. Kernan, 146. Bate also notes this ordering tendency of Johnson's tics and compulsions (*SJ*, 382).
200. His last prayer mentions his "late conversion" (Johnson, *Diaries*, 1:418), meaning by "conversion," as the Yale editor tells us, "Change from reprobation to grace, from a bad to a holy life" (ibid.). This prayer is also one of the few times he mentions "redemption," not in the context of his need to redeem his time, but in the redemption of his soul already accomplished by Christ.
201. Voitle, 124.
202. Bate, *SJ*, 597.
203. Bate, *SJ*, 599.

6. UNDER THE GREAT TASKMASTER'S EYE

1. James King, *William Cowper* (Durham: Duke University Press, 1986), 12.
2. William Cowper, *The Letters and Prose Writings of William Cowper*, edited by James King and Charles Ryskamp, 4 vols. (Oxford: Oxford University Press, 1979–84), 3 March 1788; 3:120–21. Subsequent quotations from letters in this work are cited parenthetically in the text.
3. Charles Ryskamp, *William Cowper of the Inner Temple, Esq.* (Cambridge: Cambridge University Press, 1959), 65.
4. Ibid., 66.
5. Robert Southey, *The Life of William Cowper, Esq.*, 2 vols. (Boston: Otis, Broaders, and Co., 1839), 1:22.
6. Lord David Cecil, *The Stricken Deer* (London: Constable and Co., 1944), 45.
7. Bagehot says, "Probably the old gentleman thought the young gentleman by no means a working man, and objected, believing that a small income can only be made more by unremitting industry,—and the young gentleman, admitting this horrid and abstract fact, and agreeing, though perhaps tacitly, in his uncle's estimate of his personal predilections, did not object to being objected to" (Walter Bagehot, "William Cowper," *Literary Studies*, 3 vols. [London: Longmans, Green, and Co., 1898], 1:100). Thomas says, somewhat more gently, "And it may have been Cowper's seeming lassi-

tude, rather than the fact of his close relationship to Theodora [*sic*], that determined his uncle's opposition" (Gilbert Thomas, *William Cowper and the Eighteenth Century* [London: Ivor Nicholson and Watson, 1935], 94).

8. Translation: While you are following your Rhadamanthus with more pains, as you tell me, than profit, I, who neither take pains nor hope for profit, am leading an idle, and therefore what is to me a most agreeable life . . . (Thomas Wright's translation, Cowper, *Letters*, 81).

9. Several times in his letters Cowper describes himself as naturally indolent; for instance, "my natural Indolence" (11 February 1766; 1:130); "the natural Indolence of my Disposition" (26 November 1780; 1:412); "my love of Indolence" (8 April 1781; 1:462).

10. I agree with William Norris Free's statement that "Cowper had what might be called a gentlemanly disdain for the goals and means by which such ambition expressed itself" (*William Cowper* [New York: Twayne Publishers, Inc., 1970], 23).

11. Ryskamp, 68.

12. As Norman Nicholson puts it, "His religion and morality were those of the middle classes, but his conception of society was largely that of the aristocrat" (*William Cowper* [London: John Lehman, 1951], 52).

13. King, 77; quoting a letter from Maria Cowper to Penelope Maitland.

14. King, 97 and Thomas, 60.

15. King, 59.

16. Cowper's exact finances are difficult to ascertain. King reports that "until he sold his stock in 1790, Cowper had presumably retained £300 in stocks from 1772. During the Olney years, his only other income would have been £20 per year for the rental of his Inner Temple chambers (which his tenant gave Hill a great deal of trouble in collecting) and an annual grant of £20 from the Earl Cowper. . . ." The stock, King says, would have generated fairly little interest, and so Hill, with the assistance of the Cowper family, "obviously subsidized the average yearly request of the poet for £100." In 1786, Lady Hesketh arranged an annuity of £100 for Cowper, provided by her, her sister Theadora, the Earl Cowper, and another William Cowper, the poet's cousin (ibid., 59). Both Thomas (Thomas, 134–35) and Cecil (Cecil, 106) report that Cowper's relatives were annoyed when he, on leaving Dr. Cotton's asylum for Huntington in 1765, brought with him a servant and a boy he felt he was rescuing from a drunken father and a degenerate future. Their annoyance indicates that they were paying Cowper's debts. Cowper also was the recipient of many small presents throughout his life, especially after Lady Hesketh renewed her relationship with him. His collected letters are full of charming thanks for gifts of oysters and desks, wine and snuffboxes, halibut and bedcovers.

17. Thomas, 134.

18. He certainly did not follow the breezy advice he gives in "The Progress of Error": "if you yourself, too scantily supplied, / Need help, let honest industry provide. / Earn, if you want . . ." (William Cowper, *The Poetical Works of William Cowper*, edited by H.S. Milford, fourth edition [London: Oxford University Press, 1934], ll. 251–53; 22–23).

19. King, 59.

20. Ryskamp agrees that Cowper "indulged in many unnecessary expenses—which he deemed necessary for a gentleman," but goes on to say that "in truth, they were rarely beyond the standards of the simplest *gentle* folk" (166). Rsykamp also makes the good point that, although "Cowper's easy dependence on friends and relatives is not one of the delightful qualities in his character," it should be viewed in context: Cowper "should be seen in the background of one of the great families of eighteenth-century England, and of that century's world of sinecures and patronage" (81).

21. Other restatements of this explanation for his writing include the following:

To Lady Hesketh: I find writing, and especially poetry, my best remedy. Perhaps had I understood music, I had never written verse, but had lived upon fiddle-strings instead. . . . I have been emerging gradually from this pit. As soon as I became capable of action, I commenced carpenter, made cupboards, boxes, stools. I grew weary of this in about a twelvemonth, and addressed myself to the making of birdcages. To this employment succeeded that of gardening, which I intermingled with that of drawing, but finding that the latter occupation injured my eyes, I renounced it, and commenced poet. (16 January 1786; 2:455)

To William Unwin: Such a Talent in Verse as mine, is like a Child's Rattle, very entertaining to the Trifler that uses it, and very disagreeable to all beside. But it has served to rid me of some melancholy Moments, for I only take it up as a gentleman Performer does his Fiddle. (7 February 1779; 1:290)

To William Unwin: I never write but for my Amusement, and What I write is sure to Answer that End, if it Answers no other. If besides this Purpose, the more desirable one of Entertaining You be effected, I then receive double Fruit of my Labor, and consider this Produce of it as a Second Crop, the more valuable because less expected. (11 July 1780; 1:365)

To Joseph Hill: When I can find no other Occupation, I think, and when I think, I am very apt to do it in Rhime. (9 May 1781; 1:470)

To Lady Hesketh: My dear Cousin, Dejection of Spirits, which I suppose may have prevented many a man from becoming an Author, made me one. I find constant employment necessary, and therefore take care to be constantly employ'd. Manual occupations do not engage the mind sufficiently, as I know by experience, having tried many. But composition, [especiall]y of verse, absorbs it wholly. (12 October 1785; 2:382–83)

22. Free, 63.
23. In another letter to Newton a few months later, he reiterates his lack of interest in fame: "No man ever wrote such quantities of Verse as I have written this last year, with so much indifference about the Event, or rather with so little ambition of public praise" (16 August 1781; 1:508). Since both these letters were written to Newton, a stern Evangelical preacher, Cowper was probably trying to fend off a charge of vanity or worldliness; but I think also he was emphasizing his amateur status. In a letter to William Churchey, an aspiring poet who wrote him for advice, Cowper makes the same assertion regarding his nonprofessional reasons for publishing: "For my own part, I could no more amuse myself with writing verse, if I did not print it when written, than with the study of Tacticks for which I can never have any real occasion" (13 December 1786; 2:617).
24. Lodwick Hartley, *William Cowper: The Continuing Revaluation* (Chapel Hill: University of North Carolina Press, 1960), 33.
25. Ibid., 54.
26. For instance, "In spite of those assertions we find in the letters that writing is a mere source of amusement for him, a way of passing time without thinking destructive thoughts, Cowper is very much aware of the importance of what he is doing" (Bill Hutchings, *The Poetry of William Cowper*, [London: Croom Helm, 1983], 87). Also see pages 9 and 108.
27. It is worth noting that as a reader himself, Cowper admired in poetry an impression of ease, a sense that the poet was not working too hard. For instance, in a letter to William Unwin he ranks Dryden's poetry above Pope's, saying, "I admire Dryden most, who has succeeded by mere dint of Genius, and in spite of a laziness and a carelessness almost peculiar to himself," while Pope "was certainly a mechanical maker

of verses, and in every line he ever wrote we see indubitable marks of the most indefatigable Industry and Labour" (5 January 1782; 2:3).

28. William Cowper, *The Poetical Works of William Cowper*, edited by H.S. Milford, fourth edition (London: Oxford University Press, 1934), ll. 169–74; 21. Subsequent quotations from Cowper's poems will be cited parenthetically in the text, by line numbers and the page numbers from his collected works.

29. Hutchings, 135.

30. In writing to William Unwin about "John Gilpin," Cowper tries to excuse the lightness of his subject by referring to the heaviness of his heart: "If I trifle and merely trifle it is because I am reduced to it by necessity. A melancholy that nothing else so effectually disperses, engages me sometimes in the arduous task of being merry by force" (18 November 1782; 2:91). And yet it is clear that he often found his trifling unexcusable. In a letter written a few months later to Newton, to whom he showed his gloomiest and most self-reproachful side, Cowper says (sounding rather like Samuel Johnson), "My days are spent in vanity, and it is impossible for me to spend them otherwise. No man upon earth is more sensible of the unprofitableness of a life like mine, than I am, or groans more heavily under the burthen; but this too is vanity, because it is in vain; my groans will not bring the remedy, because there is no remedy for me" (20 April 1783; 2:127).

31. As Cowper explained the situation to Samuel Rose,

The whole subscription-money, exclusive of extras, will amount to £1144 — The unsubscribed copies being 200 will sell at the advanced price that he proposes for £500 more. These sums together make £1644. With this money he means to pay the expenses of this first edition — viz — £600. And with this money he means to pay me £1000 for my copy right. When he has so done £44 will remain in his pocket.

This to me has much the appearance of giving me nothing for my copy, or rather it has the appearance of being paid £44 for accepting it. (6 July 1791; 3:538)

Eventually, Johnson agreed, as Cowper told Lady Hesketh, "to pay all expences and to give me a £1000 next Midsummer, leaving the copy-right still in my hands . . ." (11 July 1791; 3:542).

32. Cowper was uncomfortable discussing with Newton his involvement with Homer. He did not even mention it to Newton until December of 1785, almost a year after he began the translation. In this letter, he stresses the therapeutic value of translating and praises Homer's purity of language and the "many great and valuable truths" found in Homer's epics (3 December 1785; 2:411). In subsequent letters to Newton, Cowper keeps trying to justify his involvement with Homer, when he mentions it at all — as King says, "Of all Cowper's correspondents, Newton was the one with whom he was most reluctant to discuss Homer" (191).

33. Ibid., 192.

34. Cowper wrote to many of these people asking them to subscribe to his translation; Bagehot has a point, albeit a malicious one, when he says, "it is pleasant to observe the healthy facility with which one of the shyest men in the world set himself to extract guineas from every one he had ever heard of" (139).

35. And in another paradox, although the Evangelicals saw works as useless to salvation, they also censured idleness as sinful itself and as the cause of many other sins.

36. Of course, in yet another paradox, the Augustan tradition saw some work as undermining one's upper-class status, and therefore to be avoided by the gentle classes.

37. The poems also differ in other ways, of course. "Retirement" is only one-sixth the length of *The Task*, and it is a good deal more cohesive than the longer poem. (To some extent the relationship of the two poems seems similar to that of "Tintern Abbey"

and *The Prelude*.) "Retirement" might be seen as the more typically Augustan poem, since it is written in heroic verse rather than the blank verse of *The Task*, contains several satirical character sketches, and is wittier (though still pious and serious in intent).

38. Dustin Griffin, who reads *The Task* as georgic, points out a paradox in the very structure of the poem: "Cowper's georgic poem of course celebrates the life of retirement and 'repose.' He is aware of the implicit paradox and, perhaps somewhat defensively, takes pains to assert that the retired life is in fact a life of activity . . ." ("Redefining Georgic: Cowper's *Task*," *EHL* 57 [1990]: 871).

39. Martin Priestman, *Cowper's* Task: *Structure and Influence* (Cambridge: Cambridge University Press, 1983), 146.

40. Considering the increasing connection at this period between productive, profit-earning work and masculinity (which I say more about in my conclusion), Cowper's opposition between "trifler" and "man" seems unsurprising, until one remembers that the trifler has become a man by leaving the world of work.

41. Hutchings also notices that this question is not too well answered: " 'The Winter walk at Noon' . . . berates those who waste their time in such activities as board-games, billiards, shopping and attending auctions—this from the man who told us in Book 4 how much he enjoyed staring into the fire" (193).

42. This is not to say that the Evangelical movement was not interested in serving society; its members were quite active in good works. But it saw the works as useless to salvation (though something the saved would naturally want to do), as Cowper's hymn "Not of Works" indicates:

> Still the boasting heart replies,
> What! the worthy and the wise,
> Friends to temperance and peace,
> Have not these a righteousness?
> Banish ev'ry vain pretence
> Built on human excellence;
> Perish ev'ry thing in man,
> But the grace that never can.

(ll. 17–24; 474)

43. P. M. S. Dawson, "Cowper's Equivocations," *Essays in Criticism* 33 (1983), 29–30.

44. Vincent Newey, *Cowper's Poetry: A Critical Study and Reassessment* (Totowa NJ: Barnes & Noble Books, 1982), 184.

45. I am not, of course, the first to make this claim. Nicholson says, "[Cowper] does not really want to be thought of as a stricken deer, but as one which, in spite of his handicaps, was yet able to do something worthwhile . . ." (99). Newey says, "Like Gray, Cowper cannot, for all his praise of retirement, be content simply to pursue 'the silent tenour of his doom' far from 'the madding crowd's ignoble strife', his mind trained on the promise of 'eternal peace', but must seek at last to justify his existence to himself in terms of wider usefulness" (89); and, "Employment, the responsible business of being useful, is always a matter of great concern, and difficulty, to Cowper" (183).

46. King, 178.

47. Found in Matthew 21:18–22 and Mark 11:12–14 and 20–25.

48. William Cowper, *Letters and Prose Writings*, 1:26. Subsequent quotations from this memoir, *Adelphi*, will be cited internally in the text.

49. In his "critical life" of Cowper, Maurice J. Quinlan reads Cowper's preoccupation with the barren fig tree as having to do with his sexual problem: "Why in the first place did his mind turn to that particular parable? We cannot be sure, but if he was

sexually impotent, and there is some basis for this theory, he may have associated his barrenness with the tree that bore no fruit" (*William Cowper: A Critical Life* [Minneapolis: University of Minnesota Press, 1953], 33). Since Quinlan's book was written, however, plausible arguments have been advanced refuting the old notion of Cowper as sexually deformed or impotent; see especially chapter 9, "The Defect," in Charles Ryskamp's *William Cowper of the Inner Temple, Esquire*.

50. James Boswell, *Life of Johnson*, 6 vols. (Oxford: Oxford University Press, 1987), 4, 223.

51. Richard Feingold also notices this conflict in Cowper's thought:

> How then, and through which public mode of action, does public virtue express itself, removed as it necessarily is from the seat of power which is the state?
>
> *The Task* supplies no answer to this question; the only virtuous life portrayed is the life of retirement, and this option, as it is developed in the poem, can hardly be understood as the stage for the exercise of public virtue. But public virtue, like that undefined entity, society, is a crucial aspect of Cowper's thought. . . . (*Nature and Society* [New Brunswick, NJ: Rutgers University Press, 1978], 147)

52. The charming prose piece "The History of My Three Hares" which Cowper wrote for *Gentleman's Magazine*, says, after describing the three hares and their ways in delightful detail, that the sportsman "little knows what amiable creatures he persecutes, of what gratitude they are capable, how cheerful they are in their spirits, what enjoyment they have of life, and that, impressed as they seem with a peculiar dread of man, it is only because man gives them peculiar cause for it" (*Cowper: Poetry and Prose*, edited by Brian Spiller [London: Rupert Hart-Davis, 1968], 388). "The Negro's Complaint," "The Morning Dream," "Sweet Meat Has Sour Sauce," and "Pity For Poor Africans," as well as some of "Charity," all strongly protest the slave trade.

53. Dawson makes an interesting point about this cucumber-poem association:

> In 1780 Samuel Johnson said of Gray's Odes: 'They are forced plants raised in a hot-bed; and they are poor plants; they are but cucumbers after all'. We cannot assume that Cowper knew of this remark, of course. But we should bear in mind that he had great admiration for Gray; that he often evinced an almost paranoid anxiety concerning the opinions of "king critic"; and that he seems to have had indirect access to the great man. (32)

54. Indeed, Hutchings says of this passage, "The poet here is . . . a useful gardener; and [the garden] is not an escapist nest, but a growing environment" (213).

55. Dawson brings up yet another point of discomfort in the cucumber georgic; after quoting the lines ending with "the fruit / Of too much labor, worthless when produc'd," he says: "The jocularity has uneasy undertones. If growing cucumbers is a trifling occupation, is the writing of verse (especially about cucumbers) any better? They have much in common: both involve hard and assiduous labor to produce, and both are consumed as luxuries by the idle" (33). This comment seems to echo the reproach I discussed earlier of Cowper's spaniel in "Beau's Reply"; Cowper could be seen as "killing time" not only by growing cucumbers, but by writing about their growing.

56. Priestman, 158.

57. Griffin, 876.

58. Feingold, 152–53.

59. Patricia Meyer Spacks, *The Poetry of Vision: Five Eighteenth-Century Poets* (Cambridge: Harvard University Press, 1967), 180.

60. Priestman, 62.

61. Griffin also notes Cowper's ignoring of labor's contributions to his life

Cowper's redefined idea of georgic almost conceals the economic base that makes possible the life of retired leisure/labor that he celebrates. Occasionally we glimpse the hand of "lubbard labour." But for the most part Cowper prefers to look at physical labor from afar. . . . Labor goes on all around him, and makes possible the gentleman-farmer's quiet life, produces and delivers the bread promptly (l.244–45), and supplies his many wants. The "industrious hands" that satisfy his "temp'rate wishes" (l.597–99) are not—for the most part—his own. He is freed for leisurely walks. (877)

62. Cowper similarly characterizes the teamster in Book 4. After describing him struggling painfully through a snow-storm, Cowper denies him the sensibility required to feel pain:

> Oh happy; and, in my account, denied
> That sensiblity of pain with which
> Refinement is endued, thrice happy thou!
> Thy frame, robust and hardy, feels indeed
> The piercing cold, but feels it unimpaired.
>
> ll. 357–61; 190)

63. Cowper wrote much the same thing to Hill, more than once: "I should be glad to devote the leisure hours of another twelve month to the same occupation [writing]. . . . But I cannot write when I would . . ." (14 March 1782; 2:35); and, "I shall be glad to take your Advice, and produce a volume yearly; but it depends upon circumstances not in my own power—Health; Spirits; and above all that undefinable disposition of mind that fits me for such an employment, which I do not always possess, and without which I can do nothing" (1 April 1782; 2:42).

64. Thomas, 257–58.

65. King, 183.

66. Cecil, 205.

67. King, 8.

68. This sense of God's acting for him can be seen in one of Cowper's letters to Mrs. Madan, his Evangelical relative: "The Little we are enabled sometimes to render to him [God], we first receive from Himself, the Desire and the Power are derived from Him . . ." (9 July 1768; 1:201).

69. It is interesting to note how many of Cowper's biographers refer to his projects as "tasks"; for instance,

♦ Despite his jesting, [Cowper] took the task seriously and for six years produced mortuary verses for All-Saints parish (Quinlan, 163).

♦ He estimated that the task [of editing Milton] would require at least two years . . . (Quinlan, 170).

♦ Cowper set himself a double task in planning to write an authentic version of Homer that was at the same time a fine blank verse poem (King, 194).

♦ He laid *Milton* aside, but found the new task [of annotating Homer] hardly less of a burden (Thomas, 377).

♦ The work of translating Homer had overstrained his strength, and now he had taken on the still more worrying task of editing Milton (Nicholson,161).

♦ But he "equipped himself better for this immense journey" when he revised the work—a task which was performed with so much diligence, that the first copy bore very little resemblance to the second all the way through (Southey, 2:70).

♦ But his engagement with Milton engrossed him altogether; and when he looked into the task of commenting, his spirits began to fail (Southey, 2:186).

♦ No wonder he found [annotating Homer] a more laborious task than the translation, and said that he should be heartily glad when it was over (Southey, 2:280).

♦ He had never been a hard student, and his evident incapacity for the task [of editing Milton]

troubled and vexed him. A man who had never been able to assume any real responsibility was not likely to feel comfortable under the weight of a task which very few men would be able to accomplish (Bagehot, 142).

70. Free, 103.
71. Griffin, 869.
72. King, 27.
73. In light of what I said earlier about Cowper's passivity, it is interesting to note how he describes his suicide attempts. As Quinlan points out, "In his descriptions of his several attempts at suicide he appears almost as a passive agent" (27). Rather than describing what he did, he describes things being done to him; for instance, "I was continually hurried away from such places as were most favourable to my design to others where it was almost impossible to execute it . . ." (*Letters* 1:20); "Twenty times I had the phial at my mouth and as often received an irresistible check, and even at the time it seemed to me that an invisible hand swayed the bottle downwards as often as I set it against my lips" (ibid., 1:21); and "I reached forth my hand towards the basin, when behold, the fingers of both my hands were so closely contracted, and so forcibly drawn together as if bound with a cord, that they became entirely useless" (ibid., 1:21–22).
74. Bagehot, 114.
75. Quinlan, 79.
76. King, 86.
77. Southey, 1:188.
78. Ibid. Similarly, Quinlan quotes Cowper's friend Samuel Greatheed, who said Cowper "supposed that his involuntary failure at the performance [of suicide] had incurred the irrevocable vengeance of the Almighty! To this, and never to any other deficiency of obedience has he been heard to ascribe his imaginary exclusion from mercy" (91).
79. Cowper, *Letters*, 4:468.
80. King, 209.
81. As Lord David Cecil describes the situation,

The task had been commanded by God; and now God had rendered him incapable of carrying it out. What could this portend? Was God once more forcing him to commit a sin in order to damn him for it? Convinced as he was of his damnation, this new proof of it sent a thrill of horror through him. Again and again in desperation he nerved himself to make another attempt to get it done. And with each successive failure suspense gnawed more cruelly at his heart. (267)

82. King, 277.

7. CONCLUSION

1. Leonore Davidoff and Catherine Hall, *Family Fortunes: Men and Women of the English Middle Class, 1780–1850* (Chicago: University Press, Chicago Press, 1987), 162–72. Davidoff and Hall also name James Thomson as an especially popular writer for these people (28).
2. Charles Lamb, who lived and wrote a bit later than Cowper, was another writer who resisted the middle-class ideal of masculine industriousness. In *A Double Singleness: Gender and the Writings of Charles and Mary Lamb*, Jane Aaron argues that "many of Charles's essays which deal with childhood can be seen as a subtle attack upon the new

insistence on a male role dedicated to industriousness, competitiveness, and self-control" ([Oxford: Clarendon Press, 1991], 55). She goes on to say,

> Unlike the majority of men of the middle rank, Charles consistently refused to internalize the new morality of time-thrift. From his first piece of published prose, a pastiche of Robert Burton's writings in praise of truths which only visit the empty, idle mind, to one of his last, an argument against the folly of 'rising with the lark', he mocks and opposes the doctrines of the popular tract-writers of his times, with their perpetual warnings that sloth and time-wasting were the instruments of Satan. Moreover, he connects his resistance to the new time-consciousness with an antagonism towards related changes in the concept of sexual difference. . . . Amongst the middle ranks of society, adoption of the new time ethic was primarily a male prerogative, and as such it was one of the features which marked the growing sexual segregation between men's public worlds of industry, commerce, and politics, and the private domestic sphere of women. (57)

3. Clifford Sisken, *The Work of Writing: Literature and Social Change in Britain, 1700–1830* (Baltimore: The Johns Hopkins University Press, 1998), 107.

4. Davidoff and Hall, 230.

5. Although many of Cowper's critics, as Davidoff and Hall note, complained of Cowper's effeminacy (164).

6. Andrew Elfenbein's interesting chapter on "The Domestication of Genius: Cowper and the Rise of the Suburban Man" in *Romantic Genius: The Prehistory of a Homosexual Role* suggests that this may be the case: "at home, they could follow Cowper's example, which suggested that the home could soothe the secret wounds produced by the public world's demands for conformity. Whether or not men actually thought that their public lives hurt them as Cowper says his life did, *The Task* taught them that the private sphere was the space of compensation" ([New York: Columbia University Press, 1999], 79). Elfenbein also argues that Cowper was "a formative writer for nineteenth-century manhood" (Elfenbein, 72).

7. Sisken,108.

8. Saree Makdisi, *Romantic Imperialism* (Cambridge: Cambridge University Press, 1998), 4–5.

Works Cited

Primary Sources

Alexander, Sir James Edward. *An Expedition of Discovery into the Interior of Africa.* 1838. New York: Johnson Reprint Co., 1967.

Astell, Mary. *A Serious Proposal to the Ladies, for the Advancement of their True and Greatest Interest.* 1694. New York: Source Book Press, 1970.

Atwood, Thomas. *The History of the Island of Dominica.* 1791. London: Frank Cass and Co. Ltd., 1971.

Austen, Jane. *Emma.* Oxford: Oxford University Press, 1991.

Barnard, Anne. *The Cape Journals of Lady Anne Barnard, 1797–1798.* Edited by A. M. Lewin Robinson, Margaret Lenta, and Dorothy Driver. Cape Town: Van Riebeeck Society, 1994.

Barrow, John. *An Account of Travels into the Interior of Southern Africa in the Years 1797 and 1798.* 1804. 2 vols. New York: Johnson Reprint Co., 1968.

Bellers, John. *Proposals for Raising a College of Industry.* In *John Bellers, 1654–1725: Quaker, Economist and Social Reformer.* Edited by A. Ruth Fry. 33–48. London: Cassell and Company, 1935.

Blumenbach, Johann Friedrich. *On the Natural Varieties of Mankind.* 1775. New York: Bergman Publishers, 1969.

Bosman, William. *A New and Accurate Description of the Coast of Guinea.* 1705. New York: Barnes & Noble, n.d.

Boswell, James. *Life of Johnson.* 6 vols. Oxford: Oxford University Press, 1987.

Braddon, Laurence. *An Humble Proposal for Relieving, Reforming and Employing the Poor. And Herein By Vertue of One New General Law, Instead of Near Forty Statutes, Relating to the Premises. We May Comfortably Maintain all th' Impotent Poor, Judiciously Employ all the Capable Poor. . . .* London: Thomas Warner, 1729.

———. *A Corporation Humbly Propos'd, For Relieving, Reforming, and Employing the Poor. Herein There Will Be More Private Gain to the Subscribers, and More Publick Good to Great Britain, than by All Unparliamentary Subscriptions Already Taken. In a Letter to A Justice of the Peace of Middlesex.* London: Tho. Warner, 1720.

———. *To Pay Old Debts without New Taxes by Charitably Relieving, Politically Reforming and Judiciously Employing the Poor.* London: Thomas Warner, 1723.

Brougham, Lord Henry. *An Inquiry into the Colonial Policy of the European Powers.* 1803. 2 vols. New York: Augustus M. Kelley, Publishers, 1970.

Brunton, Mary. *Discipline.* London: Richard Bentley, 1849.

Buffon, Comte de [Georges-Louis Leclerc]. "From *A Natural History, General and Particular.*" In *Race and the Enlightenment: A Reader.* Edited by Emmanuel Chukwudi Eze. Cambridge, Mass.: Blackwell Publishers, 1997.

276

Burchell, William J. *Travels in the Interior of Southern Africa*. 1822. Edited by J. Schera. 2 vols. London: Batchworth Press, n.d.

Burke, Edmund. "An Appeal From the New to the Old Whigs." In *The Works of the Right Honourable Edmund Burke*, 4:56–215. 12 vols. Boston: Little, Brown, and Co., 1884.

———. "Thoughts and Details on Scarcity." In *The Writings and Speeches of Edmund Burke*, vol. 9, 119–45. Edited by R. B. McDowell. Oxford: Clarendon Press, 1991.

Burney, Frances. *The Wanderer*. Edited by Margaret Anne Doody, Robert L. Mack, and Peter Sabor. Oxford: Oxford University Press, 1991.

Burton, Robert. *The Anatomy of Melancholy*. 1621. New York: Tudor Publishing Co., 1968.

Cambridge, Richard Owen. *An Account of the War in India, Between the English and French, on the Coast of Coromandel, from the Year 1750 to the Year 1760*. London: T. Jeffreys, 1761.

Campbell, John. *Travels in South Africa*. 1815. Cape Town: C. Struik Ltd., 1974.

Campbell, R. *The London Tradesman*. 1734. Devon: David and Charles Reprints, 1969.

Carter, Elizabeth, and Catherine Talbot. *A Series of Letters Between Mrs. Elizabeth Carter and Miss Catherine Talbot, from the Year 1741 to 1770*. 1809. 4 vols. New York: AMS Press, n.d.

Chapone, Hester. *Letters on the Improvement of the Mind*. London: John Sharpe, 1822.

Cheap Repository Tracts; Entertaining, Moral, and Religious. Boston: E. Lincoln, 1803.

Clarkson, Thomas. *An Essay on the Slavery and Commerce of the Human Species, Particularly the African*. 1786. Miami, Fla.: Mnemosyne Publishing Co., 1969.

Clayton, John. *Friendly Advice to the Poor; Written and Publish'd at the Request of the Late and Present Officers of the Town of Manchester*. Manchester: Jos. Harrop, 1755.

Cobbett, J. M. Preface in *A Legacy to Labourers*, iii–xxxiv. William Cobbett. London: Charles Griffin and Company, 1872.

Cobbett, William. *The Autobiography of William Cobbett: The Progress of a Plough-Boy to a Seat in Parliament*. Edited by William Reitzel. London: Faber and Faber Limited, 1947.

———. *A Legacy to Labourers*. Edited by J. M. Cobbett. London: Charles Griffin and Company, 1872.

———. "The Rights of the Poor, and the Punishment of Oppressors." *Cobbett's Monthly Sermons*, 73–96. London: C. Clement, 1821.

Collier, Mary. *The Woman's Labour*. 1739. *The Thresher's Labour and The Woman's Labour*. Los Angeles: Augustan Reprint Society, 1985.

Cowper, William. "The History of My Three Hares." *Cowper: Poetry and Prose*. Edited by Brian Spiller, 385–89. London: Rupert Hart-Davis, 1968.

———. *The Letters and Prose Writings of William Cowper*. Edited by James King and Charles Ryskamp. 4 vols. Oxford: Oxford University Press, 1979–84.

———. *The Poetical Works of William Cowper*. Edited by H.S. Milford. 4th edition. London: Oxford University Press, 1934.

Cultivator. Letter. *Gentleman's Magazine* 21 (1751): 206–7.

Cunningham, James. (Tentative attribution.) *An Essay on Trade and Commerce Containing Observations on Taxes, As They Are Supposed to Affect the Price of Labour in our Manufactories: Together with Some Interesting Reflections on the Importance of our Trade to America. To which Is Added the Out-lines, or Sketch, of a Scheme for the Maintenance and Employment of the Poor, the Prevention of Vagrancy, and Decrease of the Poor's Rates*. London: S. Hopper, 1770.

D.D. Letter. *The Gentleman's Magazine* 31 (1761): 592–93.

Dampier, William. *A New Voyage Round the World*. 1697. London: Argonaut Press, 1927.

"Debates in the Senate of Lilliput." *Gentleman's Magazine* 13 (1743): 563–82.

Defoe, Daniel. *Giving Alms No Charity*. In *The Shortest Way with Dissenters and Other Pamphlets*, 153–88. Oxford: Basil Blackwell, 1927.

Dow, Alexander. "A Dissertation on the Origin and Nature of Despotism in Hindostan." In *The History of Indostan*, vol 3. 1770. New Delhi: Today & Tomorrow's Printers & Publishers, 1973.

Duck, Stephen. *The Thresher's Labour*. 1736. *The Thresher's Labour and The Woman's Labour*. Los Angeles: Augustan Reprint Society, 1985.

Durand, J. P. L. *A Voyage to Senegal; Or, Historical, Philosophical, and Political Memoirs*. London: Printed for Richard Phillips by J. G. Barnard, 1806.

Eden, Sir Frederick Morton. *The State of the Poor: Or, An History of the Labouring Classes in England, From the Conquest to the Present Period*. 3 vols. 1797. London: Frank Cass & Co. Ltd., 1966.

Edgewood, Maria. *Idleness and Industry Exemplified; in the History of James Prescott and Lazy Lawrence*. Philadelphia: J. Johnson, 1804.

———. *Letters for Literary Ladies, to which is added, An Essay on the Noble Science of Self-Justification*. London: J. Johnson, 1795.

——— and Richard Lovell Edgeworth. *Practical Education*, 2 vols. London: J. Johnson, 1798.

Edwards, Bryan. *The History, Civil and Commercial, of the British Colonies in the West Indies*. 2 vols. Dublin: Luke White, 1793.

The Effects of Industry and Idleness Illustrated; In the Life, Adventures, and Various Fortunes of Two Fellow-Prentices of the City of London. London: C. Corbett, 1748.

Fielding, Henry. *An Enquiry into the Causes of the Late Increase in Robbers. An Enquiry into the Causes of the Late Increase in Robbers and Related Writings*. Edited by Malvin R. Zirker, 61–172. Oxford: Clarendon Press, 1988.

———. *A Proposal for Making an Effectual Provision for the Poor*. Fielding, 219–78.

Finch, Anne. *Selected Poems of Anne Finch, Countess of Winchilsea*. Edited by Katharine M. Rogers. New York: Frederick Ungar Publishing Co., 1979.

Fitzmaurice, Henry William Edmund Petty, 6th Marquis of Lansdowne, editor. *The Queeney Letters: Being Letters Addressed to Hester Maria Thrale by Doctor Johnson, Fanny Burney, and Mrs. Thrale-Piozzi*. London: Cassell & Company, 1934.

Fleetwood, William. *The Relative Duties of Parents and Children, Husbands and Wives, Masters and Servants*. 1705. Marriage, Sex, and the Family Series. New York: Garland Publishing, Inc., 1985.

Fletcher, John. *An Appeal to Matter of Fact and common Sense. Or a rational Demonstration of Man's corrupt and lost Estate*. Bristol: William Pine, 1772.

Fordyce, James. *The Character and Conduct of the Female Sex, and the Advantages to Be Derived from the Society of Virtuous Women*. London: T. Cadell, 1776.

Gay, John. *Poetry and Prose*. Edited by Vinton A. Dearing and Charles E. Beckwith. Vol 1. Oxford: Clarendon Press, 1974.

Gisborne, Thomas. *Enquiry into the Duties of the Female Sex*. 1797. New York: Garland Publishing, Inc., 1974.

"The Good Mother's Legacy." *Cheap Repository Tracts*, 329–46.

Gregoire, Henri. *An Enquiry Concerning the Intellectual and Moral Faculties and Literature of Negroes*. 1810. Translated by D. B. Warden. College Park, Md.: McGrath Publishing Co., 1967.

Gregory, John. *A Father's Legacy to His Daughters*. 1774. New York: Garland Publishing, Inc., 1974.

Guthrie, William. *A New Geographical, Historical, and Commercial Grammar; and Present State of the Several Kingdoms of the World*. London: Charles Dilly, 1785.

Hacke, William. *A Collection of Original Voyages*. 1699. Delmar, N.Y.: Scholars' Facsimiles and Reprints, 1993.

Hale, Sir Matthew. "The Good Steward at the Great Audit," in *The Counsels of a Father*. London: Taylor and Hessey, 1816.

Halifax, Marquess of. *Advice to a Daughter*. In *The Complete Works of George Saville, First Marquess of Halifax*. Edited by Walter Raleigh, 1–46. Oxford: Clarendon Press, 1912.

Hall, Charles. *The Effects of Civilization on the People in the European States*. 1805. London: Routledge/Thoemmes Press, 1994.

Hands, Elizabeth. *The Death of Amnon. A Poem, with an Appendix: containing Pastorals, and other Poetical Pieces*. Coventry: N. Rollason, 1789.

Hanway, Jonas. *Virtue in Humble Life*. 2 vols. London: n.p., 1785.

Hassell, John. *Memoirs of the Life of the Late George Morland, with Descriptive Observations on the Whole of His Works Hitherto Before the Public*. London: Albion Press, 1806.

Hawkins, Laetitia Matilda. *Letters on the Female Mind, Its Power and Pursuits*. London: Hookham and Carpenter, 1793.

Hays, Mary. *Appeal to the Men of Great Britain in Behalf of the Women*. 1798. New York: Garland Publishing, Inc., 1974.

Haywood, Eliza. *A Present for a Servant Maid*. 1743. Marriage, Sex, and the Family Series. New York: Garland Publishing, Inc., 1985.

Home, Henry. *Sketches of the History of Man. Considerably Enlarged by the Last Additions and Corrections of the Author*. 4 vols. Edinburgh: William Creech, 1788.

"Hubbub, The" *Cheap Repository Tracts*, 153–68.

Inchbald, Elizabeth. *Wives as They Were, and Maids as They Are*. 1797. In Vol. 2 of *The Plays of Elizabeth Inchbald*. Edited by Paula R. Backscheider. New York: Garland Publishing, Inc., 1980.

Johnson, Samuel. *Diaries, Prayers, and Annals*. New Haven: Yale University Press, 1958.

― ― ―. *The Idler and the Adventurer*. New Haven: Yale University Press, 1963.

― ― ―. *Lives of the English Poets*, vol. 2. London: Oxford University Press, 1949.

― ― ―. *Poems*. New Haven: Yale University Press, 1964.

― ― ―. *The Rambler*. 3 vols. New Haven: Yale University Press, 1969.

― ― ―. *Rasselas and Other Tales*. New Haven: Yale University Press, 1990.

― ― ―. *Sermons*. New Haven: Yale University Press, 1978.

Kames, Henry Home, Lord. *Sketches of the History of Man*. 1774. Edinburgh: William Creech, and Bell and Bradfute, 1813.

Kolb, Peter. *The Present State of the Cape of Good-Hope, Or, A particular Account of the Several*

Nations of the Hottentots. Translated by "Mr. Medley." 1731. 2 vols. New York: Johnson Reprint Corp., 1968.

Ladies Dispensatory or, Every Woman her own Physician, The. London: James Hodges, 1740.

Lamb, Mary. "On Needle-work." In Vol. 1 of *The Works of Charles and Mary Lamb*, 176–80. London: Methuen & Co., 1903.

Law, William. *A Serious Call to a Devout and Holy Life.* 1729. New York: Paulist Press, 1978.

Leapor, Mary. *Poems, Upon Several Occasions.* 2 vols. London: J. Roberts, 1748–51.

Leguat, Francois. *The Voyage of Francois Leguat of Bresse to Rodriguez, Mauritius, Java, and the Cape of Good Hope.* Edited by Captain Pasfield Oliver. 2nd edition. 2 vols. London: Printed for the Hakluyt Society, 1891.

Lennox, Charlotte. *The Lady's Museum.* London: J. Newbury, n.d.

Letter. *Gentleman's Magazine* 6 (1736): 24–27.

Le Vaillant, Francois. *Travels from the Cape of Good-Hope into the Interior Parts of Africa.* 1790. London: Johnson Reprint Corp., 1972.

Lillo, George. *The London Merchant.* Edited by William H. McBurney. Lincoln: University of Nebraska Press, 1965.

Long, Edward. *The History of Jamaica.* 3 vols. 1744. London: Frank Cass & Co., Ltd., 1970.

Macaulay, Catherine. *Letters on Education.* 1790. New York: Garland Publishing, Inc., 1974.

Mackintosh, William. *Travels in Europe, Asia, and Africa.* 2 vols. London: J. Murray, 1782.

Mandeville, Bernard de. *The Fable of the Bees: Or, Private Vices, Publick Benefits.* 2 vols. Oxford: Clarendon Press, 1924.

Maton, William George. *Observations Chiefly Relative to the Natural History, Picturesque Scenery, and Antiquities, of the Western Counties of England, Made in the Years 1794 and 1796.* 2 vols. Salisbury: J. Easton, 1797.

Matthews, John. *A Voyage to the River Sierra-Leone, on the Coast of Africa.* London: B. White and Son, 1788.

Meanwell, Tom. Letter. *Gentleman's Magazine* 4 (1734): 198–99.

Medius. Letter. *Gentleman's Magazine* 38 (1768): 156–57.

Mentzel, O. F. *A Geographical and Topographical Description of the Cape of Good Hope.* Translated by H. J. Mandelbrote. 1785. 2 vols. Cape Town: Van Riebeeck Society, 1925.

More, Hannah. "Black Giles the Poacher." *The Complete Works of Hannah More*, 1:251–58. 2 vols. New York: Harper & Brothers, 1843.

———. *Coelebs in Search of a Wife.* Hannah More, 2:304–437.

———. "A Cure for Melancholy: Showing the Way to Do Much Good with Little Money." Hannah More, 1:167–72.

———. "The History of Mr. Bragwell; Or, The Two Wealthy Farmers." Hannah More, 1:129–62.

———. "The Honest Miller of Gloustershire." Hannah More, 1:56–57.

———. "The Shepherd of Salisbury Plain." Hannah More, 1:190–200.

———. *Strictures on the Modern System of Female Education.* 1799. 2 vols. New York: Garland Publishing, Inc., 1974.

———. "The Two Shoemakers." Hannah More, 1:201–23.

— — —. "Village Politics. Addressed to All the Mechanics, Journeymen, and Labourers, in Great Britain." Hannah More, 1:58–63.

— — —. "The Way to Plenty, or the second part of Tom White." Hannah More, 1: 227–33.

More, Martha. *Mendip Annals: Or, A Narrative of the Charitable Labours of Hannah and Martha More in Their Neighbourhood*. Edited by Arthur Roberts. London: James Nisbet and Co., 1859.

Moseley, Benjamin. *A Treatise on Tropical Diseases; on Military Operations; on Military Operations; and on the Climate of the West-Indies*. 1787. London: T. Cadell, 1792.

"Of Publick Cricket-Matches." *Gentleman's Magazine* 13 (1743): 485–86.

Orme, Robert. *Historical Fragments of the Mogul Empire*. London: F. Wingrave, 1805.

— — —. *A History of the Military Transactions of the British Nation, in Indostan, from the Year MDCCXLV*. London: John Nourse, 1763.

Ovington, John. *A Voyage to Surat in the Year 1689*. 1696. Edited by H. G. Rawlinson. London: Oxford University Press, 1929.

Paley, William. "Reasons for Contentment, Addressed to the Labouring Part of the British Public." *The Works of William Paley, D.D.*, Vol. 7, 177–98. London: S. Hamilton, 1816.

Pennington, Lady Sarah. *A Mother's Advice to Her Absent Daughters*. 1817. New York: Garland Publishing, Inc., 1974.

Percival, Robert. *An Account of the Cape of Good Hope*. 1795. New York: Negro Universities Press, n.d.

Piozzi, Hesther Lynch Thrale. *Anecdotes of the Late Samuel Johnson, LL.D.* 1786. London: Oxford University Press, 1974.

— — —. *Autobiography, Letters and Literary Remains of Mrs. Piozzi (Thrale)*. Edited by A. Hayward, Esq. London: Longman, Green, Longman, and Roberts, 1861.

Place, Francis. *The Autobiography of Francis Place*. Edited by Mary Thale. Cambridge: Cambridge University Press, 1972.

A Present for Servants, From Their Ministers, Masters, or Other Friends. 1787. Marriage, Sex, and the Family Series. New York: Garland Publishing, Inc., 1985.

Pryce, *William. Mineralogia Cornubeiensis; A Treatise on Minerals, Mines, and Mining*. . . . London: James Phillips, 1778.

Radcliffe, Mary Ann. *The Female Advocate*. 1810. New York: Garland Publishing, Inc., 1974.

Ramazzini, Bernard. *A Treatise of the Diseases of Tradesmen, Shewing the Various Influence of Particular Trades Upon the State of Health; With the best Methods to avoid or correct it, and useful Hints proper to be minded in regulating the Cure of all Diseases incident to Tradesmen*. London: Andrew Bell, 1705.

Ramsey, James. *Objections to the Slave Trade, with Answers*. Miami, Fla.: Mnemosyne Publishing Co., 1969.

Raynal, the Abbe. *A Philosophical and Political History of the Settlements and Trade of the Europeans in the East and West Indies*. 14 books. Translated by J. O. Justamond. London: A. Strahan and T. Cadell, 1783.

Reeve, Clara. *Plans of Education*. 1792. New York: Garland Publishing, Inc., 1974.

"Remarks on the Poor Laws; with some Proposals for the Amendment of them." *Gentleman's Magazine* 67 (1790): 440–42.

Reynolds, Sir Joshua. *Portraits*. Edited by Frederick W. Hilles. New York: McGraw-Hill, 1952.

Richardson, Samuel. *The Apprentice's Vade Mecum*. 1734. Edited by Alan Dugald McKillop. Los Angeles: Augustan Reprint Society, 1975.

――――. *Pamela: Or Virtue Rewarded*. New York: Penguin Books, 1985.

Salmon, Thomas. *A New Geographical and Historical Grammar; Containing the True Astronomical and Geographical Knowledge of the Terraqueous Globe*. London: C. Bathurst et al., 1772.

Scott, Sarah. *A Description of Millenium Hall*. New York: Penguin Books, 1986.

Scrafton, Luke. *Reflections on the Government of Indostan*. London: G. Kearsley and T. Cadell, 1770.

Seaton, Thomas. *The Conduct of Servants in Great Families*. 1720. Marriage, Sex, and the Family Series. New York: Garland Publishing, Inc., 1985.

Smith, Adam. *An Inquiry into the Nature and Causes of the Wealth of Nations*. 2 vols. Oxford: Clarendon Press, 1976.

Smith, Samuel Stanhope. *An Essay on the Causes of the Variety of Complexion and Figure in the Human Species*. 1810. Cambridge, Mass.: Belknap Press, 1965.

"Some Thoughts for the New Year." *Cheap Repository Tracts*, 153–68.

"Sorrowful Sam." *Cheap Repository Tracts*, 239–58.

Sparrman, Andrew [Anders]. *A Voyage to the Cape of Good Hope . . . from the Year 1772, to 1776*. 1786. 2 vols. New York: Johnson Reprint Corp., 1971.

Stewart, John. *An Account of Jamaica, and Its Inhabitants*. London: Longman, Hurst, Rees, and Orme, 1808.

"Substance of a Proposal for the Employment of the Poor." *Gentleman's Magazine* 21 (1751): 559–60.

Taylor, Jeremy. *The Rule and Exercises of Holy Living*. 1650. London: Bell and Daldy, 1857.

Temple, William. *The Case As It Now Stands, between the Clothiers, Weavers, and Other Manufacturers, With Regard to the Late Riot, in the County of Wilts*. In *Labour Problems Before the Industrial Revolution: Four Pamphlets, 1727–1745*. 1739. New York: Arno Press, 1972.

――――. *A Vindication of Commerce and the Arts: Proving They Are the Source of the Greatness, Power, Riches and Populousness of a State*. 1758. Classic English Works on the History and Development of Economic Thought. New York: Johnson Reprint Corp., 1971.

Tennant, William. *Indian Recreations: Consisting Chiefly of Scrictures on the Domestic and Rural Economy of the Mahomedans and Hindoos*. 2nd edition. London: Longman, Hurst, Rees, and Orme, 1804.

Ten Rhyne, William. *An Account of the Cape of Good Hope and the Hottentots . . . , in A Collection of Voyages and Travels*. 1685. Edited by Awnsham and John Churchill. Vol. 4. London: Awnsham and Churchill, 1704.

Thomson, James. *The Castle of Indolence and Other Poems*. Edited by Alan Dugald McKillop. Lawrence: University of Kansas Press, 1961.

――――. *Letters and Documents*. Edited by Alan Duglad McKillop. Lawrence, Kansas: University of Kansas Press, 1958.

――――. *The Complete Poetical Works of James Thomson*. Edited by J. Logie Robertson. London: Oxford University Press, 1951.

Townsend, Joseph. *A Dissertation on the Poor Laws By a Well-Wisher to Mankind*. Berkeley: University of California Press, 1971.

Wakefield, Priscilla. *Reflections on the Present Condition of the Female Sex*. 1789. New York: Garland Publishing, Inc., 1974.

West, Jane. *Letters to a Young Lady, in Which the Duties and Character of Women Are Considered*. 1806. 3 vols. New York: Garland Publishing, Inc., 1974.

"Wild Robert." *Cheap Repository Tracts*, 425–28.

Wilkes, Wetenhall. *A Letter of Genteel and Moral Advice to a Young Lady*. Dublin: E. Jones, 1740.

Wilson, Thomas. *Distilled Spiritous Liquors the Bane of the Nation: Being Some Considerations Humbly Offer'd to the Legislature*. London: J. Roberts, 1736.

Wollstonecraft, Mary. *The Female Reader*. In Vol. 4 of *The Works of Mary Wollstonecraft*. Edited by Janet Todd and Marilyn Butler, 53–350. New York: New York University Press, 1989.

———. *Thoughts on the Education of Daughters*. In Vol 4 of *The Works of Mary Wollstonecraft*, 1–49.

———. *A Vindication of the Rights of Woman*. In Vol. 5 of *The Works of Mary Wollstonecraft*, 61–266.

Y.D. Letter. *Gentleman's Magazine* 35 (1765): 613–16.

Young, Arthur. *A Six Months Tour through the North of England*. 4 vols. 1771. Reprints of Economic Classics. New York: Augustus M. Kelley Publishers, 1967.

———. *A Six Weeks Tour, Through the Southern Counties, of England and Wales*. 2nd edition. London: W. Strahan, W. Nicoll, B. Collins, and J. Balfour, 1769.

Secondary Sources

Aaron, Jane. *A Double Singleness: Gender and the Writings of Charles and Mary Lamb*. Oxford: Clarendon Press, 1991.

Abelove, Henry. "Some Speculations on the History of Sexual Intercourse During the Long Eighteenth Century in England." *Genders* 6 (fall 1989): 125–30.

Adams, James Eli. *Dandies and Desert Saints: Styles of Victorian Masculinity*. Ithaca: Cornell University Press, 1995.

Alkon, Paul Kent. *Samuel Johnson and Moral Discipline*. N.p.: Northwestern University Press, 1967.

Andrew, Donna T. *Philanthropy and Police: London Charity in the Eighteenth Century*. Princeton: Princeton University Press, 1989.

Antal, Frederick. *Hogarth and His Place in European Art*. New York: Basic Books, 1962.

Armstrong, Nancy. *Desire and Domestic Fiction: A Political History of the Novel*. Oxford: Oxford University Press, 1987.

———, and Leonard Tennenhouse. *The Ideology of Conduct*. New York: Methuen, 1987.

Bagehot, Walter. "William Cowper." *Literary Studies*, 1:87–143. 3 vols. London: Longmans, Green, and Co., 1898.

Balderston, Katherine C. "Doctor Johnson and William Law." *PMLA* 75 (1960): 382–94.

Barker, Anthony. *The African Link: British Attitudes to the Negro in the Era of the Atlantic Slave Trade, 1550–1807*. London: Frank Cass and Co. Ltd., 1978.

Barrell, John. *The Birth of Pandora and the Division of Knowledge*. Philadelphia: University of Pennsylvania Press, 1992.

— — —. *The Dark Side of the Landscape: The Rural Poor in English Painting, 1730–1840*. Cambridge: Cambridge University Press, 1980.

— — —. *English Literature in History, 1730–80: An Equal, Wide Survey*. New York: St. Martin's Press, 1983.

Bate, W. Jackson. *The Achievement of Samuel Johnson*. Chicago: University of Chicago Press, 1955.

— — —. *Samuel Johnson*. New York: Harcourt, Brace, Jovanovich, 1979.

Bloomfield, Morton W. *The Seven Deadly Sins: An Introduction to the History of a Religious Concept, with Special Reference to Medieval English Literature*. Michigan: Michigan State College Press, 1952.

Browne, Alice. *The Eighteenth-Century Feminist Mind*. Detroit: Wayne State University Press, 1987.

Cecil, Lord David. *The Stricken Deer*. London: Constable & Co., 1944.

Chambers, Douglas. *The Reinvention of the World: English Writing, 1650–1750*. New York, St. Martin's Press, 1996.

Chatterjee, Amal. *Representations of India, 1740–1840: The Creation of India in the Colonial Imagination*. New York: St. Martin's Press, 1998.

Coetzee, J. M. *White Writing: On the Culture of Letters in South Africa*. New Haven: Yale University Press, 1988.

Colley, Linda. *Britons: Forging the Nation, 1707–1837*. New Haven: Yale University Press, 1992.

Craton, Michael. "Reluctant Creoles: The Planters' World in the British West Indies." In *Strangers Within the Realm: Cultural Margins of the First British Empire*. Edited by Bernard Bailyn and Philip D. Morgan. Chapel Hill: University of North Carolina Press, 1991.

Cunningham, Hugh. *Leisure in the Industrial Revolution*. New York: St. Martin's Press, 1980.

Curtin, Philip D. *The Image of Africa: British Ideas and Action, 1780–1850*. Madison: University of Wisconsin Press: 1964.

Davidoff, Leonore, and Catherine Hall. *Family Fortunes: Men and Women of the English Middle Class, 1780–1850*. Chicago: University of Chicago Press, 1987.

Dawson, P. M. S. "Cowper's Equivocations." *Essays in Criticism* 33 (1983): 19–35.

Doody, Margaret Anne. *Frances Burney: The Life in the Works*. New Brunswick, N.J.: Rutgers University Press, 1988.

— — —. "Whig Dreams." *London Review of Books* (27 February 1992): 9–11.

Elfenbein, Andrew. *Romantic Genius: The Prehistory of a Homosexual Role*. New York: Columbia University Press, 1999.

Fausto-Sterling, Anne. "Gender, Race, and Nation: The Comparative Anatomy of 'Hottentot' Women in Europe, 1815–1817." In *Deviant Bodies: Critical Perspectives on Difference in Science and Popular Culture*. Edited by Jennifer Terry and Jacqueline Urla. Bloomington: Indiana University Press, 1995.

Feingold, Richard. *Nature and Society*. New Brunswick, N.J.: Rutgers University Press, 1978.

Ferguson, Moira. Introduction in *The Thresher's Labour and The Woman's Labour*, iii–xii. Los Angeles: Augustan Reprint Society, 1985.

— — —. "Resistance and Power in the Life and Writings of Ann Yearsley." *The Eighteenth Century: Theory and Interpretation* 27 (1986): 247–68.

Flynn, Carol Houlihan. *The Body in Swift and Defoe*. New York: Cambridge University Press, 1990.

Free, William Norris. *William Cowper*. New York: Twayne Publishers, Inc., 1970.

Furniss, Edgar S. *The Position of the Laborer in a System of Nationalism*. New York: Kelley & Millman, Inc., 1957.

Fussell, Paul. *Samuel Johnson and the Life of Writing*. New York: Harcourt Brace Jovanovich, 1971.

Gerrard, Christine. "*The Castle of Indolence* and the Opposition to Walpole." *Review of English Studies* 41 (1990): 45–64.

Golden, Morris. "The Imagining Self in the Eighteenth Century." *Eighteenth-Century Studies* 3 (1969): 4–27.

Grant, Douglas. *James Thomson: Poet of 'The Seasons'*. London: The Cresset Press, 1951.

Greene, Donald. "From Accidie to Neurosis: The Castle of Indolence Revisited." In *English Literature in the Age of Disguise*. Edited by Maximillian E. Novak. Berkeley: University of California Press, 1977.

Griffin, Dustin. "Redefining Georgic: Cowper's *Task*." *ELH* 57 (1990): 865–79.

Grundy, Isobel. *Samuel Johnson and the Scale of Greatness*. Leicester: Leicester University Press, 1986.

Hartley, Lodwick. *William Cowper: The Continuing Revaluation*. Chapel Hill: University of North Carolina Press, 1960.

Hay, Douglas. "Poaching and the Game Laws on Cannock Chase." *Albion's Fatal Tree: Crime and Society in Eighteenth-Century England*. Edited by Douglas Hay et al. New York: Pantheon, 1975.

Hill, Bridget. *Eighteenth-Century Women: An Anthology*. London: George Allen & Unwin, 1984.

Hutchings, Bill. *The Poetry of William Cowper*. London: Croom Helm, 1983.

Huxley, Aldous. "Accidie." In *On the Margin*, 25–31. New York: George H. Doran Co., 1923.

Irwin, George. *Samuel Johnson: A Personality in Conflict*. New Zealand: Auckland University Press, 1971.

Jones, M. G. *The Charity School Movement*. London: Frank Cass and Co. Ltd., 1964.

Jones, Vivien, editor. *Women in the Eighteenth Century: Constructions of Femininity*. London: Routledge, 1990.

Kernan, Alvin. *Samuel Johnson and the Impact of Print*. Princeton: Princeton University Press, 1987.

King, James. *William Cowper*. Durham, N.C.: Duke University Press, 1986.

Kowaleski-Wallace, Elizabeth. *Their Fathers' Daughters: Hannah More, Maria Edgeworth, and Patriarchal Complicity*. New York: Oxford University Press, 1991.

Landry, Donna. *The Muses of Resistance: Laboring-Class Women's Poetry in Britain, 1739–1796*. New York: Cambridge University Press, 1990.

Langford, Paul. *A Polite and Commercial People: England, 1727–1783*. New York: Oxford University Press, 1989.

Laqueur, Thomas Walter. *Religion and Respectability: Sunday Schools and Working Class Culture, 1780–1850*. New Haven: Yale University Press, 1976.

Linebaugh, Peter. *The London Hanged: Crime and Civil Society in the Eighteenth Century*. New York: Cambridge University Press, 1992.

— — —. "The Tyburn Riot Against the Surgeons." Hay et al., 65–117.

Litvak, Joseph. "Reading Characters: Self, Society, and the Text in *Emma*." *PMLA* 100 (1985): 763–73.

Lyman, Stanford M. *The Seven Deadly Sins: Society and Evil*. New York: St. Martin's Press, 1978.

Mack, Maynard. *Alexander Pope: A Life*. New York: W. W. Norton & Co., 1985.

Mahl, Mary R., and Helene Koon, editors. *The Female Spectator: English Women Writers Before 1800*. Bloomington: Indiana University Press, 1977.

Makdisi, Saree. *Romantic Imperialism*. Cambridge: Cambridge University Press, 1998.

Malcolmson, Robert W. *Life and Labour in England, 1700–1780*. New York: St. Martin's Press, 1981.

— — —. *Popular Recreations in English Society, 1700–1850*. Cambridge: Cambridge University Press, 1973.

Mansell, Darrel. *The Novels of Jane Austen: An Interpretation*. London: Macmillan, 1974.

Marshall, P. J., and Glyndwr Williams. *The Great Map of Mankind: British Perceptions of the World in the Age of Enlightenment*. London: J. M. Dent & Sons Ltd., 1982.

Mathias, Peter. *The Transformation of England: Essays in the Economic and Social History of England in the Eighteenth Century*. New York: Columbia University Press, 1979.

McBurney, William Harlin. Introduction in Lillo, 1–xxvi.

McClintock, Anne. *Imperial Leather: Race, Gender and Sexuality in the Colonial Contest*. New York: Routledge, 1995.

McClure, Ruth K. *Coram's Children: The London Foundling Hospital in the Eighteenth Century*. New Haven: Yale University Press, 1981.

McKendrick, Neil. "Josiah Wedgwood and Factory Discipline." *The Historical Journal* 4 (1961): 30–55.

Mellor, Anne. *Mothers of the Nation: Women's Political Writing in England, 1780–1830*. Bloomington: Indiana University Press, 2000.

Merians, Linda. *Envisioning the Worst: Representations of "Hottentots" in Early-Modern England*. Newark: University of Delaware Press, 2001.

— — —. "What They Are, Who We Are: Representations of the 'Hottentot' in Eighteenth-Century Britain." *Eighteenth-Century Life* 17.3 (1993): 14–39.

Mingay, G. E., editor. *Arthur Young and His Times*. London: MacMillan Press, Ltd., 1975.

Newey, Vincent. *Cowper's Poetry: A Critical Study and Reassessment*. Totawa, N.J.: Barnes & Noble Books, 1982.

Nicholson, Norman. *William Cowper*. London: John Lehman, 1951.

Nicolas, Sir Harris. "Memoir of Thomson." In *The Poetical Works of James Thomson*. London: William Pickering, 1847.

Paulson, Ronald. *Hogarth: High Art and Low, 1732–1750*. New Brunswick: Rutgers University Press, 1992.

Perry, Ruth. *Women, Letters, and the Novel*. New York: AMS Press, 1980.

Pierce, Charles E., Jr. *The Religious Life of Samuel Johnson*. Hamden, Conn.: Archon Books, 1983.

Poovey, Mary. *The Proper Lady and the Woman Writer*. Chicago: University of Chicago Press, 1984.

Popkin, Richard H. "The Philosophical Basis of Eighteenth-Century Racism." *Studies in Eighteenth-Century Culture*, vol. 3, 245–262. Cleveland: Press of Case Western Reserve University, 1973.

Pratt, Mary Louise. *Imperial Eyes: Travel Writing and Transculturation*. London: Routledge, 1992.

Priestman, Martin. *Cowper's Task: Structure and Influence*. Cambridge: Cambridge University Press, 1983.

Pynchon, Thomas. "Nearer, My Couch, to Thee." *New York Times Book Review*. 6 June, 1993: 3 + 57.

Quinlan, Maurice J. *William Cowper: A Critical Life*. Minneapolis: University of Minnesota Press, 1953.

Roberts, Arthur. Introduction in Martha More, 1–12.

Rogers, Katharine M. *Feminism in Eighteenth-Century England*. Chicago: University of Illinois Press, 1982.

Rule, John. *The Experience of Labour in Eighteenth-Century English Industry*. New York: St. Martin's Press, 1981.

― ― ―. *The Labouring Classes in Early Industrial England, 1750–1850*. London: Longman, 1986.

― ― ―. *The Vital Century: England's Developing Economy, 1714–1815*. London: Longman Group, 1992.

Rule, John, and Roger Wells. *Crime, Protest, and Popular Politics in Southern England, 1740-1850*. London: Hambledon Press, 1997.

Ryskamp, Charles. *William Cowper of the Inner Temple, Esq*. Cambridge: Cambridge University Press, 1959.

Sachs, Arieh. *Passionate Intelligence*. Baltimore: Johns Hopkins University Press, 1967.

Sambrook, James. *James Thomson, 1700–1748: A Life*. Oxford: Clarendon Press, 1991.

Sherman, Stuart. *Telling Time: Clocks, Diaries, and the English Diurnal Form, 1660–1785*. Chicago: Chicago University Press, 1997.

Shesgreen, Sean. "Hogarth's *Industry and Idleness*: A Reading." *Eighteenth-Century Studies* 9 (1976): 569–98.

Siskin, Clifford. *The Work of Writing: Literature and Social Change in Britain, 1700–1830*. Baltimore: Johns Hopkins University Press, 1998.

Sitter, John. *Literary Loneliness in Mid-Eighteenth-Century England*. Ithaca: Cornell University Press, 1982.

Smith, Mark M. *Mastered by the Clock: Time, Slavery, and Freedom in the American South*. Chapel Hill: University of North Carolina Press, 1997.

Southey, Robert. *The Life of William Cowper, Esq*. 2 vols. Boston: Otis, Broaders, and Co., 1839.

Spacks, Patricia Meyer. *Boredom: The Literary History of a State of Mind*. Chicago: University of Chicago Press, 1995.

― ― ―. *The Poetry of Vision: Five Eighteenth-Century Poets*. Cambridge: Harvard University Press, 1967.

Spender, Dale. *Mothers of the Novel*. London: Pandora, 1986.

Stallybrass, Peter, and Allon White. *The Politics and Poetics of Transgression*. Ithaca: Cornell University Press, 1986.

Staves, Susan. *Married Women's Separate Property in England, 1660–1833*. Cambridge: Harvard University Press, 1990.

Steinman, Lisa M. *Masters of Repetition: Poetry, Culture, and Work in Thomson, Wordsworth, Shelley, and Emerson*. New York: St. Martin's Press, 1998.

Tanner, Tony. *Jane Austen*. Cambridge: Harvard University Press, 1987.

Teltscher, Kate. *India Inscribed: European and British Writing on India, 1600–1800*. Delhi: Oxford University Press, 1995.

Thomas, Gilbert. *William Cowper and the Eighteenth Century*. London: Ivor Nicholson and Watson, 1935.

Thompson, E. P. *The Making of the British Working Class*. New York: Vintage Books, 1966.

———. "Time, Work-Discipline, and Industrial Capitalism." In *Customs in Common: Studies in Traditional Popular Culture*, 352–403. New York: The New Press, 1991.

Tobin, Mary-Elisabeth Fowkes. "Aiding Impoverished Gentlewomen: Power and Class in *Emma*." *Criticism* 30 (1988): 413–30.

Voitle, Robert. *Samuel Johnson the Moralist*. Cambridge, Mass.: Harvard University Press, 1961.

Waldron, Mary. "Ann Yearsley and the Clifton Records." *The Age of Johnson: A Scholarly Annual* 3 (1990): 301–29.

Wallace, David. "Bourgeois Tragedy or Sentimental Melodrama? The Significance of George Lillo's *The London Merchant*." *Eighteenth-Century Studies* 25 (1991–92): 123–43.

Warner, Wellman J. *The Wesleyan Movement in the Industrial Revolution*. New York: Russell & Russell, 1930.

Watkins, W. B. C. *Perilous Balance*. Princeton: Princeton University Press, 1939.

Weber, Max. *The Protestant Ethic and the Spirit of Capitalism*. Translated by Talcott Parsons. New York: Charles Scribner's Sons, 1958.

Wechselblatt, Martin. *Bad Behavior: Samuel Johnson and Modern Cultural Authority*. Lewisburg: Bucknell University Press, 1998.

Wenzel, Siegfried. *The Sin of Sloth: Acedia in Medieval Thought and Literature*. Chapel Hill: University of North Carolina Press, 1967.

Wilson, Kathleen. *The Sense of the People: Politics, Culture, and Imperialism in England, 1715–1785*. New York: Cambridge University Press, 1995.

Wiltshire, John. *Samuel Johnson and the Medical World: The Doctor and the Patient*. Cambridge: Cambridge University Press, 1991.

Zionkowski, Linda. "Strategies of Containment: Stephen Duck, Ann Yearsley, and the Problem of Polite Culture." *Eighteenth-Century Life* 13 (1989): 91–108.

Zirker, Malvin R. General introduction in Fielding, xvii–cxiv.

Zonitch, Barbara. *Familiar Violence: Gender and Social Upheaval in the Novels of Frances Burney*. Newark: University of Delaware Press, 1997.

Index

Numbers in italics refer to illustration pages